WIMPY

By
Patrick S. Halley

ISBN: 1-4196-9660-2
ISBN-13: 9781419696602
Library of Congress Control Number: 2008903822

Visit www.booksurge.com to order additional copies.

Printed by Kelly Press, Inc.

Patrick S. Halley is the author of On the Road with Hillary (Viking, 2002), the story of his nine years doing advance for Hillary Rodham Clinton. He was Executive Director of the Massachusetts Democratic Party and worked as an advance man or state director in six presidential campaigns. Prior to that, he had a career in law enforcement, serving as chief of operations for both the Attorney General of Massachusetts and the Middlesex District Attorney. He is the son of a proud union man, and lives in the Boston area.

ACKNOWLEDGEMENTS

A work of this magnitude would not be possible without the contribution of many people who shared the vision of recounting the life story of this remarkable man.

First and foremost, I'd like to thank President Tom Buffenbarger and the IAM Executive Council for the opportunity to undertake this project.

Former International President George Kourpias provided invaluable insight into Wimpy and the inner workings of the IAM. He sat through many interviews and his encyclopedic recall and thoughtful analysis are the backbone of the narrative.

Elizabeth Benedict edited the first draft of the manuscript and did a splendid job of bringing out the essence of our subject.

Dr. Dorothy Fennell of Cornell University got things started with her Winpisinger Oral History Project, and her research and interviews with Wimpy's contemporaries were invaluable. The staffs at the Georgia State University Archives and at the William W. Winpisinger Education and Technology Center were most helpful.

IAM Communications Director Rick Sloan and his staff, particularly Bill Upton and Donna Georgallas, were exceedingly helpful with editing, securing access, and providing timely and effective support.

Last, but certainly not least, I wish to thank the many people who shared their personal memories of Wimpy, especially his children, Ken, Vickie, Mike, Bill, and Linda, each of whom are rightfully proud of their father, who no doubt, was very proud of them.

LIBERTY

ONE

MIDNIGHT MEETING

The clock, an old Simplex wall model with black arms that advanced in sudden sharp movements, edged toward midnight. It had been a hot, humid day in Washington, and the weight of the sticky night air at the open window made beads of sweat form on the brows of the department heads gathered at the large oak conference table, facing other members of the senior staff of the union.

It was July 1, 1977. Jimmy Carter was President of the United States, and William Winpisinger had just become President of the million-member IAM - the International Association of Machinists and Aerospace Workers, one of America's largest industrial unions. Gathered around the table were about twenty-five people, most of them men, who handled the organization's day-to-day business. They had been summoned to the unusual meeting at this ungodly hour two days earlier in a memorandum from Administrative Assistant George Kourpias. At first, some regarded the memo as a joke and suggested they kill the hours between six o'clock and midnight at a local bar. Kourpias assured them that would be a very bad idea, and actually hosted a booze free cookout for some of them at his Maryland home.

Now, as midnight approached, the staff was gathered to hear the words of their new International President, fifty-two-year-old William W. Winpisinger. Wimpy, as he was known to just about everyone, had enjoyed a meteoric rise through the ranks, having begun his IAM career as a high school drop-out auto mechanic on Cleveland's West Side. The lack of a formal education never stood in his way. His drive, focus, and charisma impressed everyone, his obvious talent caught the eye of the local union leadership, and his appetite for reading widely in many subjects made up for what he hadn't learned in school. He was one of the youngest people ever appointed to the Grand Lodge staff, and had earned his spurs organizing, bargaining, and troubleshooting in virtually every corner of the sprawling union.

As the clock struck twelve, the door to the auditorium swung open and the tall, stocky, bespectacled president entered, flanked by Kourpias and Plato Papps, the union's Chief Legal Counsel.

The staff came to attention, eager to learn why they were gathered in the dead of night. Wimpy, a spellbinding speaker with a melodic voice and a strong Cleveland accent, marched to the head of the conference table, nodded to his secretary Maria Cordone, stole a quick glance at his notes, and looked out at his audience.

"I don't mean to be poetic, but you might liken this to a new dawn," he began.[1] "Forget the old way of doing things. That was for yesterday. We're going to put this union on the map, and we start now. Right here and right now."

Louis Poulton and Michael Forscey, from the legal department, scribbled on long yellow pads. Dean Ruth and Bob Kalaski of The Machinist, the union's award winning weekly newspaper, scribbled in reporter's notebooks. George Nelson and Jerry Thompson of the legislative department leaned forward to get a better view.

"I want you to make decisions and make things happen. Don't be afraid of making a mistake; we can always correct mistakes. The biggest mistake, the one I find totally unacceptable, is to stand still."

Grand Lodge Representatives George Poulin and Jim Pinto nodded. Research Director Reginald Newell managed a slight smile.

These words, while not totally unexpected, were a sharp departure from the way the Machinists usually did business. The IAM had begun as a railroad union, run by railroad men who did everything by the clock—and the clock was connected to a bell. Be at your desk by the 8:00 AM bell. Take your lunch and coffee breaks when the bell rings. Pack up and head home at the 4:00 PM bell. The outgoing International President, Red Smith, had been a micro-manager, a clock and bell man, who felt his job was to stand guard at the union headquarters in Washington, DC. He rarely traveled and always avoided the news media. He didn't take to the concepts of the union needing "a presence," "an image," or a way to leverage its power and influence. Wimpy was going to change that. Immediately.

No minutes of this midnight meeting survive, and no one who was there that night had a clear memory of all that Wimpy said. He would do so much for the union in the next twelve years that it hardly matters what plans he announced when. He had big ideas, and he got things done. The record shows that during his three terms as President, Wimpy made sure the IAM and its concerns were noticed well beyond the confines of union halls and the weekly issue of The Machinist.

Wimpy would begin his term buying a jet airplane and making regular calls on the far-flung outposts of the union, from Florida to California and western Canada. He would establish a face to face relationship with the membership and make himself widely available to the news media. Acutely aware of the value of branding and name recognition, he would institute an Indy race car program, with the IAM car speeding around race tracks at nearly two hundred miles an hour, putting the union's name in front of millions of sports fans.

With his burgeoning political interests, his outspoken views, and his easy access to anger at injustice, Wimpy would become a voluble, controversial, and quotable media darling. In ways he could not have predicted that night, he became a powerful voice rising in protest against tax cuts for the rich, the outsourcing of jobs, and the union-busting practices of Ronald Reagan and George H.W. Bush. He would be profiled on television's top rated show, 60 Minutes, and by Newsweek, Fortune Magazine, and The New York Times. His face would become familiar to millions of American television viewers from multiple appearances on Meet the Press and Face the Nation, and he would be quoted as the most progressive voice of the labor movement in scores of newspapers and magazines. He would start by speaking the unspeakable, calling rather colorfully for the retirement of the revered but aged AFL-CIO President, George Meany: "The best thing that could happen to the American Labor Movement would be for George Meany to drop dead."

A union that had by tradition and inclination kept largely to itself would begin to aggressively live up to the second part of its motto, "Justice on the job, service to the community," by forming alliances with community groups, churches, and the liberal activist community.

During his first year in office, Wimpy would make a name for himself by protesting Jimmy Carter's volatile presidency, which was marked by rampant inflation, a major energy crisis, staggering interest rates, and crushing job losses. The losses would shrink union rolls and lead to Wimpy's "Anybody But Carter" campaign, which nudged Senator Kennedy into a race against his fellow Democratic incumbent.

In the 1980s, Wimpy and the Machinists Union would face unimaginable challenges in the form of industry deregulation, an erosion of public support for organized labor, automation that replaced millions of factory workers and the onset of a global economy that shipped high paying IAM jobs to low wage countries around the world. But through it all, Winpisinger would still manage to make incredible strides, appointing women and minorities to positions of power and influence in the labor movement, establishing a world-class training center, strengthening and protecting his union and positioning it to survive and thrive for decades to come.

But at the midnight meeting, Wimpy couldn't see into the future any more than his staff could. What exactly did he promise that night? What exactly did he foresee? People may never know. But Bob Kalaski, who would become Wimpy's Communications Director, clearly remembered looking around and noticing that his colleagues hung on Wimpy's every word. People always did. He was a powerful speaker with an engaging mind—and a soft heart beneath his gruff exterior.

"Two things and then I'll let you go," Kalaski remembered him saying. "I'm going to be gone a lot. When I'm gone and there's nobody in leadership around when something happens and you confront a problem, you think of the most liberal thing you can do and do it. If you screw up, we'll come back and redress it later. But at least we'll be off and running for ninety percent of it."[2]

Wimpy paused and looked at the audience, his trademark gleam in his eye, a smile spreading across his face.

"And finally, the first thing I'm going to do tomorrow is instruct the maintenance department to disconnect those goddamned bells."

TWO

CLEVELAND CHILDHOOD

It was called the "Roaring Twenties," and Cleveland roared about as loudly as anyplace.

Its location on the southern shore of Lake Erie along the Cuyahoga River and the man-made Ohio and Erie Canal allowed ore from Minnesota's Iron Range to travel up the canal and coal, cotton, corn, and a vast array of other commodities to arrive from the south by rail, providing raw material for one of the country's largest manufacturing centers. By the mid-1920's, it had become the nation's fifth largest city.

Smokestacks dotted the skyline like church steeples, belching the thick, dark smoke that bespoke prosperity in that gilded age. Immigrants flocked there by the thousands seeking factory jobs and establishing neighborhoods and ethnic enclaves teeming with Czechoslovaks, Poles, Italians, Irish, Germans, Hungarians and Slavs. It was a wide-open town with flourishing gambling halls, speak-easys, houses of prostitution, and a fabulously corrupt police department. The Republicans held their 1924 National Convention in Cleveland and sent Silent Calvin Coolidge on his way to the White House.

It was there, amidst the hustle, hope, and heartache of this quintessential American city that Wayne William Winpisinger was born on Wednesday December 10, 1924. He was born at home, a common occurrence in those days, in his parents' rented apartment in a two-family house on the city's west side, less than a mile from the shore of Lake Erie.

His father, Joseph Winpisinger, known as "Joe Winnie," was a printer at the city's largest newspaper, the Cleveland Plain Dealer, and a proud union man. He was Catholic, born at the turn of the century in the small Ohio town of Leetonia, eighty miles southeast of Cleveland, near the Pennsylvania border. His father, Wimpy's grandfather, had emigrated from Austria and married an Ohio woman. Joseph's aunt, who remained in Europe after her three brothers moved to the United States, kept the original spelling of the family name, "Wimpissinger." Family members described Joe Winnie as a quiet man who worked hard, kept to himself, and wasn't particularly devout.

He married Edith Knodel in 1922, when both were twenty years old. Edith was born in 1902 in New Philadelphia, Ohio, about ninety miles south of Cleveland. She endured a hardscrabble upbringing, largely on her own, in which she moved often. Both her parents had been born in Ohio, but by 1910, at age eight, she was living with her older sister, Carrie Reitz, and her husband, Peter, on Cleveland's West Side. Peter Reitz, then thirty-three years old, and Carrie, age twenty-eight, had a daughter six years younger than Edith. Peter drove a meat wagon for a living.

By the time she was eighteen, Edith had taken a job working in a knitting mill and had moved in with her another of her sisters, Ethel, and her husband, William Sander, a street car inspector. Four years later, she married Joseph Winpisinger, and the young couple made their home on Cleveland's thriving West Side. Young William, born in 1924, would soon be joined by two brothers, Joseph (known as Bud) born in 1926, and Raymond, born in 1927. In kindergarten, his teacher would be the first in a long line of authority figures to brush up against his brash, independent streak. She cited him for being unruly and "sitting or standing on his own whim" rather than upon her command.

At the start of the new decade, the Winpisinger family rented a comfortable wood frame house for fifty dollars a month on Sedalia Avenue, a tree-lined street just under three miles from the newly constructed Cleveland Municipal Airport. It was typical of the houses in the West Park neighborhood, where there was a healthy sampling of the area's large foreign born population, people from Ireland, Germany, Hungary, England, and Canada.

William entered the first grade at the McKinley School in 1931, where his teacher rated him satisfactory in all aspects save "industry," noting that he did not fully apply himself to his work. Still, he got A's and B's. When he was not in school, he enjoyed the sports and spectacles the city offered.

The country's first national air races, featuring female flying sensation Amelia Earhart, were held at the airport near his house in 1929. The airport itself was a sensation. More than 100,000 people attended its grand opening in 1924. Before long, it would boast the first airport lighting system for nighttime landings and the country's first radio-equipped control tower. Downtown, on the shores of Lake Erie, was the sparkling new 78,000 seat Municipal Stadium that opened with the internationally broadcasted Max Schmeling vs. Young Stribling heavyweight boxing match on July 3, 1931. The German Schmeling defeated America's favorite son, Young Stribling, in a grueling fifteen round decision and retained the world heavyweight crown. The Cleveland Indians, the baseball team William would follow throughout his life, began playing their night and weekend games at the stadium, and in 1935 Major League Baseball held its All-Star Game there.

Clevelanders were also kept riveted by tales of crime and corruption played out on the front pages of the newspapers. Scandals in the police department led Mayor Harold Burton to hire famed crime fighter Eliot Ness, who reprised his Chicago "Untouchables" in Cleveland and cracked down on the city's bordellos, illegal watering holes, and booming gambling parlors. Ness was put to the test when decapitated bodies turned up on the city's South East side in what would become known as the "Torso Murders." Twelve dismembered bodies were recovered before Ness, with funding from an anonymous group known as the "Secret Six," burned the Kingsbury Run Shantytown area to the ground, which brought an end to the killings without ever catching the perpetrator.

The biggest thrill for the young Winpisinger boys may have been the Great Lakes Exposition, which opened in June 1936 and attracted more than seven million visitors in its two-year run. The exposition featured a Court of Presidents, a Hall of Progress, an Automotive Building, and a gigantic midway with rides, games, and sideshows.

But life in Cleveland was not all fun and games. The stock market crash of 1929, when William was in the second grade, cost nearly a third of the city's workers their jobs.

The Winpisingers, while not rich, managed to survive the Depression thanks largely to the job protection Joe Winnie enjoyed under the union's collective bargaining agreement with The Plain Dealer.

"All during the Depression, I ate while other kids didn't because my old man was a union printer," William said in a 1978 newspaper interview.[1]

He would later recall the effect that period had on his world view:

> ...the kind of thing that always disturbed me was seeing a picture on the front page of the newspaper of bulldozers down in Georgia plowing into the ground an enormous big pile of potatoes which, the commentary said, was being done because there was no market for them. The market price was so depressed that they couldn't sell them at a profit. Yet all around me there were people hungry, in some cases on the ragged edge of starvation. I asked myself why couldn't they give those potatoes away instead of plowing them under? They could take care of an identified, real need and come out just

as well as if they plowed them under. Well, I rapidly
found out that if you question things like that, you're
automatically a socialist.[2]

In 1936, the Winpisingers moved to another rented house
in the neighborhood from which William, now called "Bill," had
a short walk to junior high school. He continued to rack up
good grades and perfect attendance, earned a merit ribbon,
joined the math club, and played football and baseball. His
rambunctious side came out at this time and it conflicted
with his mother's iron-willed personality. Bill landed his first
job: delivering free newspapers door to door in his West
Side neighborhood. Unlike subscription newspapers such as
The Plain Dealer, free papers were supported entirely by the
advertisements in them, and the paperboys were paid by the
company based on the number they delivered. After a few
weeks of lugging the bulky flyers, Bill discovered that since
his "customers" weren't paying for the papers, no one would
complain if they weren't delivered. He skipped a house here
and there to see what would happen. When several weeks
went by with no complaints from his bosses, he lobbied to
expand his territory. Soon, he had one of the biggest routes
in the city, and he was able to pull off his deliveries with time
left over for baseball and football because a significant portion
of his papers were dumped in a sewer pipe near his home.
Edith Winpisinger became skeptical about her son's prosperity
and his constant availability for pick-up baseball games. One
day, she watched him stuff newspapers into a pair of shoulder
sacks bulging so tightly he could barely lift them. She followed
at a distance and soon saw him dumping papers down a large
sewer conduit. His mother approached and gave him a sharp
smack, explaining that this was the same as stealing money
from his employers. Caught red-handed, Bill was shocked and
ashamed. Edith all but dragged him home by the ear and called

his boss at the newspaper. They worked out a plan: he would work for one month without pay to make up for the papers he had destroyed. Then he would be unceremoniously drummed out of the corps of newspaper boys. Bill Winpisinger, future giant of the labor movement, learned the value of integrity on the job at an early age when his mother got him fired from his first job.

By the time he entered John Marshall High School in 1938, both his leadership skills and rebellious streak were in full bloom. He was elected President of his freshman class, but was not nearly as popular with the teachers as he was with the students. Many thought he was immature, lazy, and too talkative. But, he maintained a B average in his freshman year, scored high on intelligence tests and kept playing baseball.

At seventeen, with Europe at war and the US soon to be drawn into World War Two, Bill had started hanging out with a wild crowd, including two fast-talking West-enders, Clyde Foster and his cousin, Ollie Holley. Clyde was a distant relative of famed American composer Stephen Foster. Their tenuous attachment to fame notwithstanding, Edith had no use for Clyde or Ollie, and they were not welcome at the Winpisinger home.

It was his two sidekicks who gave Bill a new name that would stick with him for the rest of his life. "Wimpy" was an interesting choice. While obviously a diminutive of "Winpisinger," like his father's "Joe Winnie," it was also the name of a famous newspaper cartoon character of the day. Cartoonist Elzie Crisler Segar had created "J. Wellington Wimpy," in 1931 as a corpulent, educated, and intelligent foil to his main character, "Popeye." Wimpy became widely known in American culture when he appeared in the first scene of an animated 1938 cartoon We Aim to Please and uttered the line, "I'd gladly pay you Tuesday for a hamburger today."[3]

Like his namesake, Bill Winpisinger was exceedingly bright, well educated (at least to that point), courteous, and manipulative. But while the cartoon Wimpy was fat and lazy, the flesh and blood Wimpy was a strapping young man nearly six feet tall with the muscular build of an athlete. Wimpy, Clyde, Ollie, and the rest of their gang would congregate at Kingham's Corner as the sun went down, smoking cigarettes, sipping beer from quart bottles, and trying to look tough. The Andrews Sister's "Beer Barrel Polka" blared on the car radio. There'd be an occasional drag race down Rocky River Drive when someone from another neighborhood showed up with a hotrod, but the group usually managed to keep it tame enough to avoid involving the police.

Wimpy's newfound friends did not inspire him academically. By the second semester of his junior year, his "bad boy" persona was in full bloom and his grades in a rapid descent. He became even more disruptive in class and on several occasions was caught smoking, a serious breach of the rules. By the end of his junior year, when it became clear that he would not go to college, the principal at John Marshall High School said he would not be welcomed back for his senior year. Wimpy transferred to West Technical High School, where young men were taught job skills. Students split their time between the classroom and the workplace. It was not a great move for Wimpy.

Away from his many friends at John Marshall but still hanging around with the Clyde and Ollie and the rest of the gang from Kingham's Corner, Wimpy became terribly restless and developed a sense that his world wasn't moving fast enough. His attendance was sporadic at best and he paid little or no attention to class work. In January 1942, one semester shy of completing high school, he dropped out.

"I got smarter than the teachers so I packed it in," he said several years later.[4]

To the anguish of his parents and teachers, Wimpy had gone from Freshman Class President to high school dropout. War raged in Europe and the Pacific, and Wimpy couldn't wait to grab this frightening new world by the horns.

THREE

NAVY SERVICE IN WORLD WAR II

Faster. He wanted his world to move faster. Wimpy dropped out of high school at age eighteen, leaving him plenty of time to pursue his overriding interest: becoming a big league ballplayer. He was a catcher for Fisher Foods, one of the adult league teams in Cleveland, and a good one. He had a rifle arm and a short, powerful swing. His coaches and teammates recognized his athletic talents, and occasionally big league scouts came sniffing around to get a look at the lanky receiver from the West Side.

The Japanese raid on Pearl Harbor the previous December had dragged America into the war. In his January 6, 1942, State of the Union Address, President Franklin Delano Roosevelt asked Congress for an unprecedented $56 billion to wage war. He said, "This means taxes and bonds, bonds and taxes."[1]

For Wimpy, it would mean his transition from adolescence to adulthood would not be spent on a baseball diamond working his way up to the big leagues; instead, he'd be abroad, in the military, defending his country.

Clevelanders were gearing up to help the war effort and rationing was instituted for sugar, meat, clothing, and gasoline. The national Office of Civilian Defense, under the direction of Fiorella LaGuardia, the colorful former Mayor of New York City, oversaw the rationing, along with blackout drills, scrap drives, and the reinstitution of a Victory Garden program encouraging Americans to grow extra food.

The city's newspapers were full of accounts of Japanese aggression in the Pacific. On January 11, they invaded Dutch

Borneo, Timor, and Celebes. A month later, Singapore was captured, and by March 10, Rangoon fell.

Wimpy knew he had to find a job while he waited to see if his baseball dreams would pan out. His father tried to talk him into following him into the printing trade, as his younger brother Raymond would later do, but he was having none of it. Trudging off to the *Plain Dealer* printing plant every day with his lunch in a metal pail, even if it was for a good paying union apprenticeship, was not his idea of how to get ahead in the world.

His first full time job at a tool company came to an abrupt end when he got into an altercation with a company foreman and was fired. Wimpy would soon learn that his quick temper and sharp tongue were not a good fit on the floor of a factory.

The war continued to escalate in the Pacific. Lashio fell on April 28, and on May 6, after a fierce six month battle, the Philippines surrendered to the Japanese. Cleveland was participating in nightly blackout drills. At nine o'clock, the Yellow signal was sounded and residents knew to extinguish all lights. Volunteer spotters took to the streets. Fifteen minutes later, the Blue signal officially started the blackout. If enemy aircraft were spotted within ten miles, the Red warning was given, which stopped traffic and started air raid sirens and search lights.

Wimpy managed to land a position at a plating company, but soon developed a serious case of dermatitis and quit. Finally, he signed on as an etcher at National Tool Company where he managed his longest employment stint, three months, before being unceremoniously terminated when he was found at his boss's desk, feet up, eating his lunch. Despite his short and undistinguished spell in the private sector, Wimpy formed impressions that would influence him for the rest of his life. He witnessed firsthand the power of management over workers, and bristled at the rote discipline and quiet acquiescence required of hourly wage earners. One experience he would cite in later years involved the case of a co-worker at the factory, fired for what Wimpy described as trumped up charges. He was a decent sort in Wimpy's book, and had a large family to support. One day, he ran afoul of the shop foreman and was terminated almost immediately. Wimpy took serious exception to what he deemed a rank injustice and worried about how his friend would find another job in such a tough economy. Several fellow employees advised him to keep his mouth shut lest he too be shown the door. Wimpy couldn't believe the company could act so imperiously and get away with it.

By May 1942, Wimpy was unemployed again, back hanging out with the crowd at the corner and playing baseball almost every day. Throughout his life, Wimpy retained a passion for baseball, particularly his hometown Cleveland Indians.

It was the Indians who had finally managed to bring Joe DiMaggio's storied fifty-six game hitting streak to an end the previous summer, holding the Yankee Clipper hitless at Municipal Stadium on July 17, 1941. The Yankees went on to win the World Series that year, so it was no small matter when in the spring of 1942, one of their farm teams offered Wimpy what he so badly wanted: a tryout to play professional baseball. Much to Wimpy's chagrin, he learned that, while his talent was formidable against the players in the local league, he didn't have the skills to compete in professional baseball.

The war effort was in full swing, and Clevelanders were beginning to feel the pinch. Gasoline rationing was in effect, and drivers were limited to five gallons per week. The war dominated discussion. The Battle of Midway occurred in June, and the Battle of Guadalcanal was fought in August. One by one, the members of Wimpy's Kingham's Corner group drifted off to join the service.

Wimpy, just shy of his nineteenth birthday, his hopes of a baseball career dashed, answered the call and signed on to join the Naval Reserve. He signed his enlistment papers October 14, 1942, and was inducted two days later. A photograph that ran in both the *Cleveland Press* and the *Cleveland News* on October 16 shows a tall, lanky William W. Winpisinger with a mop of brown hair and a wry smile in a sea of faces under the caption: "175 more recruits for the Navy."[2] They were sent by train to the Great Lakes Naval Training Center just north of Chicago on the shore of Lake Michigan. Great Lakes was the starting point for nearly a million sailors during the war years, just over a third of all naval personnel. By the time Wimpy arrived in October 1942, there were more than 75,000 men on the base.

All arriving personnel were administered a battery of tests to establish their physical conditioning and mental aptitudes. Wimpy was in prime physical condition from his baseball training and scored exceedingly well in the intelligence test as he had in high school. The Navy, desperate to find enough junior officers to man their new and rapidly expanding inventory of warships, had just instituted a program known as "Navy V-12." The program enrolled young naval personnel in courses at 131 colleges and universities across the country, allowing them to earn college credit and become eligible to enroll in midshipman schools or Marine Officer Candidate School and gain the chance to be commissioned as Navy ensigns or Marine Corps second lieutenants. 120,000 men were accepted and about half completed it successfully, including Warren Christopher, who would become Secretary of State; William Webster, future Director of the FBI; Senator Daniel Patrick Moynihan; and actors Jack Lemmon and Johnny Carson.

When the screeners reviewed Wimpy's intelligence scores, he was admitted to the program and shipped off to the School of Basic Medical Science at the University of Missouri. The Navy thought they had a potential officer in Wimpy, and possibly a doctor. After a brief stint there, Wimpy was transferred to the Navy V-12 Training School in Portsmouth, Virginia. A medical career was not in the offing, but he was still on track to gain a commission. Official records are mute as to the reason, but Wimpy was terminated from the program within a matter of weeks. The young man who had chaffed at every form of authority he had encountered would instead be trained to become a diesel mechanic.

He was sent to the Amphibious Training Base in Little Creek, Virginia, the largest facility of its sort in the world. More than 100,000 troops would pass through the base between May 1943 and January 1944 as the Navy geared up for invasions in North Africa, Italy, and France.

After completing his courses at Little Creek, Wimpy was sent to another base in Arzew, Algeria, to finish his training. From there, he got his first ship-board assignment as a motor mechanics mate aboard the USS LST 310.

The Navy's LST (Landing Ship, Tank) fleet was a new tool in its arsenal. The slow behemoth vessels were built to haul 20 Sherman Tanks or 30 heavy trucks on their 230 foot decks and deposit them on enemy shores. The ships were staffed by a crew of 110 sailors and 10 officers, and could transport up to 400 battle ready troops on short trips.

Crews of the LST's, while every bit as proud of their vessels as the crews of battleships and destroyers, joked that the initials stood for "Long, Slow, Target."

LST 310 docked in Bizerte, Algeria, in early June 1943, where it took on fresh water, supplies, and a newly trained motor mechanics mate named Winpisinger.

Wimpy would get his first taste of battle in Operation Husky, the Allied invasion of Sicily beginning on July 10, 1943.

Kenneth Smith, one of his shipmates, would later recall the battle:

We came up to the three-mile limit and immediately discharged our small boats, lowering them from the davits. After a while, the lights on shore began to flash around. We could see the big ships anchored out a ways firing at the beach. By now, it was getting light and a couple of enemy planes flew over. We were the first LST to unload to an LCT. While we were unloading, enemy planes would fly over a big hill and bomb the shore equipment and beat it back over the hill again. They did quite a bit of damage. After we unloaded, the enemy shore battery started to concentrate on us. Their shells began getting closer and closer. The warship Brooklyn took one shot and put that battery out of commission. The next shell, we figured, would have had our number on it.[3]

The LST 310 was commanded by twenty-six-year-old Naval Reserve Lieutenant Wilfred P. "Buddie" Lawless, of Charlotte, North Carolina. The ship was largely staffed with southerners, and some called it "Rebel's Folly." Despite his relative youthfulness, Lieutenant Lawless earned a reputation for being fearless in battle and enjoyed the undivided loyalty of his crew. He was famous for putting his ship as far ashore as possible during landing operations, allowing men and materials to go straight into battle without having to navigate treacherous waters on hostile beaches.

The troops the 310 was carrying for the Sicilian Invasion were attached to General George S. Patton's Seventh Army. Charles Harris, one of Wimpy's shipmates, recalls seeing General Patton on the day of the battle:

All at once this jeep came flying up and who stepped out but General Patton, pearl handled pistols on his side. He stepped over to another ship alongside which had not yet unloaded and Patton yelled, "Why the hell hasn't this ship been unloaded? Get it unloaded right now or some son of a bitch is going to blow the hell out of you just like that ship over there." The general pointed over to a ship burning nearby. Needless to say, they started immediately to unload.[4]

After the initial assault, the LST 310 made seven round trips from its base in Bizerte to bring troops and supplies to Sicily, making landings in Palermo, Syracuse, Gela, and Licata.

In September, the 310 took part in the landings at Salerno, a mere six days after Italy surrendered. Salerno was the gateway to the strategically important city of Naples and its expansive harbor. The Germans were determined to repel any landings and Field Marshal Albert von Kesselring defended it for several days with a force of 600 tanks.

It was in this action, on its way to Salerno, that the 310 came under attack for the first time. Ken Smith recalled:

The bow watch reported smoke on the horizon. About 17:00 we were attacked by one lone plane that dove in low and dropped a couple of bombs but did no damage. Around dark we passed the spot where smoke was reported earlier in the day. There was a lot of wreckage on the water and some was still burning. A ship from the convoy in the first wave must have been hit. From the time that first plane attacked us, the crew remained at General Quarters for forty hours.

Late in the evening we were thirty odd miles from land. The convoy to the starboard was under heavy attack. A half hour later we were attacked. They dropped flares and bombs on the sides and

*stern of us but none very close. The planes would
dive in close and drop their bombs but they only got
one escort ship. They dropped flares directly over us
and they really lit up. Four bombs hit real close.*[5]

When the 310 made it to Salerno, things weren't much
better. The ship came under heavy bombardment as they
attempted to make their landing. Ken Smith reported:

*It must have been about the time the small boats hit
the beach or thereabouts when we started to hear
enemy shore batteries going off and occasionally a
shell would explode close to our ship. We were sitting
near the starboard side of the ship when three shells
exploded about 30 yards away. We all hit the deck,
then beat it for cover. We had to lie there and let
them shell us; there wasn't anything we could do
about it. The equipment we had aboard had to be
landed on the beach, so we had to stay there. They
had our ship in their gun sights, but their aim was
too high or too low.*[6]

By the time they made it to the beach, the battle was
raging in full force. Charlie Harris remembered a particularly
harrowing encounter with a German plane:

*The Captain put us up on the beach high and dry.
At one point, I looked forward from the bridge and
saw a German plane coming straight at us. I alerted
our bow guns but they could not get their guns in
position fast enough. By this time the plane was
overhead and I saw him release his bombs. Our stern
guns began firing. The German bombs dropped in
the water. Our ship shook and trembled. The nearby*

cruiser Birmingham opened up. The last thing I saw
was the plane was still flying. Why we never knocked
it down I'll never know. We had trouble pulling off the
beach with our stern anchor, but we got the help of a
seagoing tug, retracted and anchored. We were about
to leave when orders came through not to leave
because we might have to take the troops back off
the beach. The troops could not get moving. So, we
spent that night off the beach of Salerno. About noon
we set Condition II with half our guns continuing to
be manned and sailed for Tripoli, Libya.[7]

The 310 spent the next five months in the Mediterranean, ferrying supplies to Lieutenant General Mark Clark's Fifth Army as it battled the Wehrmacht troops of Field Marshal Albert Kesselring on the long, hard slog up the peninsular to conquer Rome.

The crew was given liberty in Tripoli on September 26, and most took the opportunity to prowl through what was left of that Libyan city after the bombing raids. The British had taken complete control of the town and wouldn't let the Americans get a drink. A few sailors went out of bounds into the native quarters and managed to buy some anisette, but most returned to the 310 sober and grumbling about their stingy British counterparts.

Not every trip the 310 made was a fraught with danger as the invasions had been. Just before Christmas, 1943, the ship was tasked with carrying a rather unusual cargo from Bizerte to Naples: eight beautiful French nurses and several huge casks of wine. The sailors, who hadn't laid eyes on a female in months, thought Christmas had come early. Unfortunately, none of the nurses had a command of English and the sailors weren't able to dredge up enough French to establish meaningful conversation.

On the last day of 1943, the 310 was on its way back to its base in Bizerte from Naples when it got caught in a horrific storm and nearly broke apart. Crew member Ric Marollo remembered:

> We were on our way back from Naples on December 31st when we ran into trouble. We pulled into the Palermo area in an eighty mile per hour gale. We lost anchor and nearly broached. The skipper was advised to head toward Bizerte.[8]

Wimpy recalled his experiences that harrowing night vividly:

> I was in the main engine room and had the earphones on. It was the middle of the night and I heard the banter between the bridge and the auxiliary engine room. The bridge was screaming to empty the big ballast tank just forward of the engine room. The young man in the auxiliary engine room said, "I'm trying." The bridge kept yelling the order and the man kept saying "I'm trying, I'm trying." So I decided to take a look. I ran up the ladder and down another, got in the auxiliary engine room and asked the machinist mate what he was doing. He showed me. He had a 1500-gallon a minute pump hooked up to the tank and the pump was running and discharging water. So, I ran over to the starboard side and fired up its twin. Now we were discharging 3000 gallons a minute. I stood there about five minutes and watched the gauge and started to laugh. The other fellow asked me what I was laughing about and I said it's obvious what is happening. I told him as fast as we were pumping the ocean out of the tank it was running

back in. We had a hole in the tank. Well, when we got
to port we put a cofferdam under the old tub and
found out she was cracked across the hull where the
tank was filling up with sea water as fast as we were
pumping out the tanks.[9]

After spending a month repairing the damage to the ship
from the New Year's Eve storm, the LST 310 set sail from
Oran on February 1, 1944, to take part in Operation Overlord,
the invasion of Europe, the largest military maneuver in
history.

The journey took nearly a month and a half for the slow
moving LST, and they were constantly wary of German planes
and submarines that might attack their growing convoy. Two
days out, they were called to General Quarters when an escort
ship made contact with a German submarine off the Bay of
Biscay. After a tense few hours, they received word that they
could stand down. Their air escort had sunk three German
subs.

The LST 310 reached what was to become its new base at
Plymouth Harbor on March 12, 1943.

The massive buildup of war material that would be used
in the D-Day attack had already started to assemble, and the
whole English countryside was bristling with trucks, tanks, and
troops.

Even healed of its wounds from the Italy invasions and the
Mediterranean storm, the LST 310 was still not a pretty sight.
It had been banged and bruised and put back together with
roughshod at-sea methods. Some took to calling it the "Ugly
Duckling" of the fleet.

Crew members were sent to "gas school" to learn how to
use gas masks and other equipment in the event the Germans
resorted to that deadly tactic.

For the next two months, the ship made its way to various ports in the area ferrying materials. They made calls in Cardiff, Swansea, Penarth, Londonderry, and Belfast, always returning within a day or two to their base at Portland–Weymouth Harbor.

At Londonderry, the LST 310 took on twenty-one additional gunners. In a comical aside only the Navy could provide, all twenty-one gunners were named "Smith." When they distributed personnel to the various ships that would participate in the invasion, the Navy was so busy that they used alphabet to decide who went where. So, for the duration of the Normandy invasion, it was the "Smith Boys" who manned the 310's guns.

On May 25, the LST 310 tied up alongside the repair ship USS Melville to receive a final tune-up for the move on Normandy.

The invasion of Europe would mark the beginning of the final phase of World War II. The LST 310 was slated to be in the initial wave of the assault. They sailed out of Portsmouth-Weymouth Harbor on June 4 into choppy seas, but were called back when the bad weather forced General Eisenhower, the Supreme Allied Commander, to delay the start of the battle by a day.

The 310 would carry the 111th Field Artillery Battalion of the US First Division to Omaha Beach, the bloodiest of all possible destinations, on that fateful day. Its cargo would include thirteen DUKWS, the converted Army two-and-a-half-ton trucks that had been designed to float (although slowly and awkwardly) by use of sealed empty tanks for buoyancy, and then operate as a truck when they reached dry land. They were to offload the "Ducks" several miles from the beach, then proceed in to shore to drop the rest of their cargo. The 310's objective was "Easy Green" Beach at H plus 110 minutes. There was nothing easy about Easy Green. It was smack in the middle of Omaha's eight designated landing areas, and the Germans had set up a fierce defense.

In his riveting and informative account of D-Day, author Stephen E. Ambrose described the scene:

> *If the Germans were going to stop the invasion anywhere, it would be at Omaha Beach. It was an obvious landing site, the only sand beach between the mouth of the Douve to the west and Arromanches to the east, a distance of almost forty kilometers. On both ends of Omaha the cliffs were more or less perpendicular.*
>
> *...A man could climb the bluff, but a vehicle could not. The grass covered slopes appeared to be featureless when viewed from any distance, but in fact they contained many small folds or irregularities that proved to be a critical physical feature of the battlefield.*
>
> *...No tactician could have devised a better defensive situation. A narrow, enclosed battlefield, with no possibility of outflanking it; many natural obstacles for the attacker to overcome; an ideal place to build fixed fortifications and a trench system on the slope of the bluff and on the high ground looking down on a wide, open killing field for any infantry trying to cross no-man's land.*
>
> *The Allied planners hated the idea of assaulting Omaha Beach, but it had to be done.*[10]

The *New York Times* described the scene as the Allied Armada made its way across the English Channel:

> *From the coast of England to the French beaches of the Channel the relatively calm water was churned*

up by wave after wave of ships, some large enough
to cast their eerie shadows in the early morning glow
and others darting through like so many water-bugs.
As they neared the shore great bombing salvos roared
from gun emplacements on the land. As the ships
moved relentlessly forward, the larger ones firing as
they plowed ahead, tremendous geysers mushroomed
from the sea. It looked as if the Channel were dotted
with a strange assortment of fountains.

While the early waves of landing craft disgorged
their passengers on the beaches and equipment rolled
forth from others, shells from German guns concealed
in ridges and embankments became intense, but
there was no slackening in the stream of men and
materials. It seemed that no power on earth could
impede the momentum of this unending flow.[11]

The LST 310 reached its assigned area off Omaha Beach
before the start of the invasion and, per orders, began to
offload the DUKWS. Tragedy ensued. In the words of Wimpy's
shipmate, Gerry Smith:

We were carrying 13 or 14 DUKWS on our tank
deck. These were amphibious trucks. They were to be
launched several miles from the beach and they were
duly launched. But as soon as they came in contact
with the water, they immediately started to founder.
These DUKWS were sinking all around us. The men
on them were fighting for their lives, drowning in
the icy waters of the English Channel. They were all
loaded with full packs and as they hit the water they
were helplessly rotating on their life belts, feet up
in the air and heads down in the water. They could

not swim. You can understand how difficult it was to
overcome the situation. I can never forget the sound
of those drowning men as they kept calling for help
in the darkness that morning, and the futility of it all
that we were not able to help them. Most of these
men were never to be seen again. There were some
rescued but many of them died.[12]

Despite the tragedy with the DUKWS, the 310 made its way to shore and, true to form, Captain Lawless drove the ship farther up the beach than any other landing craft. Pictures from Omaha Beach that day show the 310 with its doors open and ramp down well up onto dry land as the battle raged.

After D-Day, the 310, as it had done in North Africa and Sicily, began shuttling back and forth delivering more and more men and materials. The crossings after the initial battle were far less dangerous and became regular if not routine.

Having served admirably in the face of some of the fiercest fighting of the Second World War, Wimpy, as he would do repeatedly throughout life, began champing at the bit and challenging authority at every turn.

In his own words: "I suppose the military made some contribution to my views. I learned in a hurry what happens in an absolutely autocratic environment, and I didn't particularly like it."[13]

Wimpy got into a confrontation with the commanding officer of the engine room of the 310 and was told he would be given the first possible transfer off the ship, provided that it didn't allow him to return to the United States.

He was eventually transferred to the staff of LST Flotilla Twelve, then sent aboard the USS Melville, the repair ship that had prepared the LST 310 for battle at Normandy.

The Melville was an older ship, having entered service in 1915, rated initially as a destroyer-tender #2, then later as an AD-2.

Wimpy seemed to have adjusted well to life aboard the larger Melville and worked hard to improve his skills as a mechanic. When the Germans surrendered in July 1945, he was aboard as the ship sailed to New York, where it was to be refit and sent to support the ongoing battles in the Pacific. While the ship was in port being refitted, the Japanese surrendered and the deployment was scrapped.

Wimpy made it back to Ohio in time for Christmas, 1945, and was formally discharged from the Navy on December 27, 1945, having served three years, two months, and fourteen days. His final rating was as Motor Machinists Mate First Class, and he received four medals: the African-European Middle Eastern Medal, with four stars, the American Area Medal, the Victory Medal, and somewhat surprisingly, the Good Conduct Medal.

He was given a grand total of $164.71 in severance pay and thanked for his service to a grateful nation.

FOUR

BACK FROM THE WAR

The question after the First World War, posed in song, had been "How you gonna keep 'em down on the farm once they've seen Paree?" Most people wondered the same about the returning veterans from World War Two, but for Wimpy and thousands of other young Clevelanders who had fought for their country, there was never any doubt that they'd return to their city by the lake and light it up with the energy that had made it such an exciting place before the war.

Wimpy missed the three-hour-long victory parade down Euclid Avenue in September 1945, because he was still aboard the Melville. By the time he was mustered out in late December, at age twenty-two, many of his cohorts had already made it back to town and were trying to get on with their lives. The old gang from Kingham's Corner got together now and then, but things just weren't the same. Wimpy resumed paling around with Clyde Foster and Ollie Holley, much to his mother's chagrin, but it was Clyde's younger sister Pearl, now nineteen and exceedingly comely, who captured his attention. Pearl, the fourth of six children of Clyde Foster, Senior, and Mildred Foster, was born on January 15, 1927. She lived with her family in North Olmstead, a suburb west of Cleveland. Her father worked as a carpenter. The Fosters had not been as fortunate as the Winpisinger's during the Great Depression. Clyde Foster was often out of work for long stretches of time, and the family barely got through the tough times.

Wimpy's father tried again to no avail to convince him to become an apprentice printer. Instead, Wimpy applied to both the New York Central and Nickel Plate Railroads for a position as a machinist. But the railroads, like many industries, were scaling back operations from their wartime peak and there were no jobs. Not sure what else to do, Wimpy used his Navy skills to become a tune-up mechanic at a local Sohio gas station. Sohio was a chain of gas stations spun off from John D. Rockefeller's Standard Oil Company in 1911, to avoid federal action against the tycoon's monopoly. Wimpy had no way of knowing it at the time, but the job would link him to two evils he would fight throughout his career: energy price fixing and "company" unions, which exist primarily to benefit owners instead of the workers.

Years later, Wimpy recalled his days at Sohio with great disdain:

> I joined the union immediately and found out it was a company union. And I found out when I got fired that it really was a company union...I was a big, raw-boned kid in those days, fresh off a war, in pretty decent shape; and I wound up with the district manager all balled up against the wall..which eliminated any grievance procedure.[1]

The next day, Wimpy began looking in earnest for a real job. Meanwhile, he worked as a "nomad mechanic," taking day jobs wherever he could at Pontiac, Oldsmobile, and Buick dealerships. He became adept a repairing transmissions, a specialty that meant he was called often by the foremen at the dealerships when a customer came limping in with a faulty drive train.

He paused long enough between transmission jobs to venture a couple hundred miles south of Cleveland where he slipped over the Ohio border into Campbell County, Kentucky, and on Tuesday, July 16, 1946, took Pearl Evangeline Foster as his wife in a civil ceremony performed by a Justice of the Peace and witnessed by Ollie's sister, Anne Holley, a lifelong friend of

Pearl's and Charles Hughes, a friend of Wimpy's. Wimpy was twenty-two and Pearl was nineteen.

Wimpy wasn't the only returning veteran to look for work as a mechanic in Cleveland. Phil Zannella, a brash, barrel-chested, tough talking former army soldier from Cranston, Rhode Island, had become smitten, sight unseen, with a Cleveland woman who had been his pen pal during his service in the Pacific. On a train from the West Coast to Rhode Island after his discharge, Zannella decided, on a whim, to hop off in Cleveland to see if he could locate Ruth Polomsky. She was a long distance telephone operator whose warm, witty, and intelligent letters had kept him company in the sweltering South Pacific. Zannella marched from the train station to the telephone company office in downtown Cleveland, found the girl of his dreams, and never got back on the train to Rhode Island.

Phil Zannella would become Wimpy's mentor in the labor movement and perhaps his closest friend. He was the son of Italian immigrants. His father, Charles Zannella, had arrived through Ellis Island, moved to Providence, and married a woman who had come from Italy when she was four years old. Despite Charles' industriousness, the family lived in abject poverty. For two years they lived in a boxcar to save enough money to buy a small house. Charles eventually made it out of poverty and even became an investor, along with many fellow immigrants, in a small community-based bank that lent money in the Italian neighborhoods. Phil, born on December 4, 1918, was the first of five Zannella children. Like Wimpy, he was a smart, rebellious, and resourceful kid who quit high school.

Phil left high school after only one year and went to an automotive technical school in New York. He loved working on cars and trucks but hated the structure of school and soon dropped out of that as well. By March 1941, the storm clouds of war were gathering and Phil saw an opportunity. He spoke with an Army recruiter who told him they were in need of soldiers to staff their engineering units. Phil could advance his knowledge of diesel engine repair at the government's expense. He enlisted voluntarily, nine months before Pearl Harbor, on March 18, 1941. At twenty-three, he was a bit older than the average enlistee. He stood five foot six inches tall and weighed a solid 193 pounds. The Army listed eight proficiencies on his enlistment papers: gunsmith (armorer); diesel mechanic; camera repairman; instrument repairman, non-electrical; instrument maker; utility repairman; equipment maintenance man; and motion picture equipment. Phil was eventually sent to the South Pacific and assigned to an engineering unit similar to the Seabees, which would build airstrips and fortifications for sailors and Marines. His unit saw action throughout the region; before the war was over, like Wimpy, he had participated in many invasions.

Tom Buffenbarger, who would serve as International President of the International Association of Machinists and Aerospace Workers, described Zannella's re-entry into post war society:

> It was the armed forces that really put the diesel engine, which was new technology at that time, to big-time use. So the need for mechanics was there. After the war, Ohio's industry, the heavy equipment, the bulldozers, the power shovels, Ohio was the center of all that manufacturing: Cyrus and Erie and all the big companies were located along Lake Erie. They needed diesel mechanics for that equipment, and Phil was Johnny-on-the-spot because a diesel mechanic made far more than automotive gasoline mechanics.[2]

Phil signed on as a diesel mechanic at the McClurg Ford dealership on Cleveland's East Side. It was a union shop, and Phil was initiated into the International Association of Machinists and Aerospace Workers. The union had been founded fifty-eight years before, in a railroad pit in Atlanta. Phil became a member of Local Lodge 1363, a large local representing Cleveland area auto and truck mechanics.

Wimpy and Pearl set up residence in a second floor rented apartment in Cleveland's West End. In mid-1946, the city was brimming with returning veterans eager to find jobs, start families, and reestablish their social lives. The massive layoffs brought on by the war's end were still in the future. Unemployment was under four percent. Per capita income was $1,223, and a postage stamp cost three cents. Television was fast replacing radio as the major source of home entertainment, and the Du Mont Network debuted a show called *Faraway Hill*, television's first ongoing drama series. Moviegoers were treated to Frank Capra's *It's a Wonderful Life*, and the radio crackled with upbeat tunes like "There's No Business Like Show Business," "Chiquita Banana," and "Zip-a-Dee-Do-Dah." Wimpy's Indians finished the season a disappointing sixth in the American League with a record of 68-86, but they still managed to draw 1,057,289 baseball hungry fans.

Far beyond Cleveland, the post-war world was changing rapidly. The first meeting of the United Nations General Assembly took place in San Francisco. British Prime Minister Winston Churchill delivered a speech deep with foreboding when he received an honorary degree at Westminster College in Fulton, Missouri. In what became widely known as the "Iron Curtain Speech," Churchill warned of a new world altering dynamic in Europe:

> *From Stettin in the Baltic to Trieste in the Adriatic*
> *an Iron Curtain has descended across the Continent.*
> *Behind that lie all the capitals of the ancient states of*

> *Central and Eastern Europe. Warsaw, Berlin, Prague,*
> *Vienna, Budapest, Belgrade, Bucharest and Sofia;*
> *all these famous cities and the populations around*
> *them lie in what I must call the Soviet Sphere, and*
> *all are subject, in one form or another, not only to*
> *Soviet influence but to a very high and in some cases*
> *increasing measure of control from Moscow.*[3]

As 1947 dawned, life was beginning to take on a more normal rhythm, but there was a steady increase in unemployment as factories scaled back from their wartime production levels. Wimpy continued to work whenever he could fixing transmissions while looking for steady employment, a need that grew more pressing when Wimpy and Pearl welcomed their first child into the world, a boy they named Kenneth, on March 25, 1947.

Elsewhere in the country, baseball's color barrier was broken in April, when Jackie Robinson suited up for the Brooklyn Dodgers. Robinson became the first African-American to play in the Major Leagues. President Truman put forth the Marshall Plan to rebuild war ravaged Europe. A growing suspicion of anything even remotely smacking of Communism led Congress to establish a House Un-American Activities Committee, which began a so called "Black-List" of Hollywood writers, producers, and performers. Halfway through 1947, eighteen months after his discharge from the Navy, Wimpy finally landed a real job. He became a full time mechanic at Lake Buick, a family owned dealership on Lavern Avenue, located only a couple of blocks from where he had grown up.

On July 15, 1947, twenty-three-year-old William Wayne Winpisinger paid an initiation fee of three dollars and fifty cents and was obligated to Local Lodge 1363 of the International

Association of Machinists and Aerospace Workers. Two young veterans, Phil Zannella and William Winpisinger, would soon have a profound impact on their union, the American Labor Movement, and the political history of the United States.

FIVE

CLEVELAND: LABOR'S CRADLE

Cleveland has a long history of bare knuckles organized labor activity. Prior to 1825, the city's workers were farmers, proprietors of small shops, and a small group of professionals. All that changed with the construction of the Ohio and Erie Canal and the beginning of large scale manufacturing at the outset of the Industrial Revolution. Big factories required many unskilled laborers willing to work long hours for minimal pay. They began to flood into the city, mostly from Europe, for jobs that paid an average of three dollars a week for sixty hours of toil.

Conditions in the factories could be brutal—cold in the winter, swelteringly hot in the summer, with noise levels, dangerous chemicals, and claptrap machinery that posed constant threats to the workers' safety. Management dealt with injury, sickness, or the slightest insubordination by firing the worker and black listing them with other employers.

The printers took the first stab at organizing. The Cleveland Typographical Association was formed in 1834 by journeymen printers who affiliated with a similar group in Columbus, Ohio, and with the New York Trades Union. Two years later, carpenters banded together to wrest a ten-hour work day from the city's major builders. This nascent labor movement came to a screeching halt three years later when New York banks balked at the speculation taking place by wealthy investors buying stock in far flung companies and stopped all payments, setting off what became known as the Panic of 1837, which led to a five-year depression.

Cleveland's mechanics first organized in 1848, forming the short-lived Association of United Mechanics, a group that was largely educational and left no record of strikes or collective bargaining. The 1850's saw the city's first strike activity, with work stoppages staged by the printers, painters, and waiters. These strikes were small and largely ineffective. Another economic crisis in 1857 put a damper on further organizing activity, but once the economy rebounded, the printers organized again and hosted the National Typographical Union Convention. They received a charter from the national group in 1868, and finally, after four failed attempts, managed to stay organized.

Large, violent strikes began to occur as the Coopers, the men who made the wooden barrels for Rockefeller's oil company, struck in 1867, 1869, and 1871, with the last strike setting off widespread violence. Railroad shopmen struck in 1868, and in 1871, the Cleveland affiliate of the Telegrapher's Protective League participated in a nationwide strike against Western Union. By the middle of the 1870's, more and more working people began to see the value of collective action as a means of protesting unfair working conditions and low pay. Cleveland hosted the National Industrial Congress in its week-long convention in 1873, and formed the Industrial Council of Cuyahoga County, representing ten local unions. The Industrial Council affiliated with the Knights of Labor, a federation of labor organizations begun in New York in 1869 that grouped workers by industry without regard for their specific skills. This "industrial" organizing was new to the labor movement, which until then had organized strictly along "craft" lines.

The Knights of Labor, whose motto was "An injury to one is the concern of all," was the first large-scale national union. It spearheaded the call for equal pay for equal work by men or women, an eight hour work day, the end of child labor under age fourteen, and the use of arbitration to settle disputes rather than strikes. The Knights drew heavily on Freemasonry for their organizational structure and rituals and aligned closely with the populist Greenback Party. The egalitarian nature and socially progressive agenda of the Knights attracted a great number of Marxists and socialists, many of whom managed to secure positions of leadership within the group.

Labor strife in Cleveland kicked into high gear in 1877, when the ever scrappy Coopers Union, whose leadership contained many socialists from Eastern Europe, decided to strike against the low pay and hostile working environment at John D. Rockefeller's Standard Oil Company. Union leaders called for a city-wide general strike and bricklayers, masons, sewer workers, and members of several smaller unions joined the picket lines. Newspapers in Cleveland and throughout the country, predisposed to side with the upper class capitalists who ran the city, were alarmed by the socialist bent of the labor organizations and began to call for the suppression of trade unions in their pages. Cleveland police, the street level troops of management's interests, appeared menacingly at the Standard Oil picket lines. While workers on the lines knew better than to confront the cops, their wives harbored no such reservations. When the police resorted to bullying and verbal abuse of the men walking the line, their wives, who had been watching silently, attacked the men in blue. The cops responded by using their clubs on the women, causing the biggest riot the city had ever seen.

The growing militancy of the working class scared the Cleveland gentry into forming two paramilitary organizations, the Cleveland Gatling Gun Battery and the First City Troop of Light Cavalry, and into building an armory to defend themselves against the angry masses. Meanwhile, there was growing tension within the labor movement between the Knights of Labor and a craft union association known as the Federation of Organized Trades and Labor Unions, formed in 1881 in Terre Haute, Indiana, by a group that included Samuel Gompers. The federation called for a "New Unionism," aimed at focusing labor unions on the specific economic interests of their members, such as wages and work hours, rather than the broader social and political agenda advocated by the Knights, such as equality in pay for men and women, government fiscal policy and the exclusion of prison laborers. Gompers's new group restricted its membership to skilled craft unions and specifically excluded political organizations and unskilled workers.

The two organizations feuded bitterly. The Knights raided Federation unions for members, and the Federation did all it could to disparage the Knight's legislative proposals and organizing efforts. Animosity between the two groups came to a head in Chicago, where they were locked in a heated battle for control of the city's cigar makers unions. On May 4, 1886, during what started as a peaceful labor march, a bomb was set off. One police officer was killed immediately and seven others, seriously wounded, would soon die. Police opened fire on the assembled union members, killing eleven of them in what would become known as the Haymarket Riot.

Leaders of both groups knew that their feud had to end before they were each destroyed by public outrage at the killings in Chicago. Two weeks later, officials of the two organizations met in Philadelphia to attempt a compromise. After several hours of heated discussion, they drafted a peace agreement known as the Philadelphia Proposal. The Knights, who now numbered more than 702,000, faced other challenges as well. They were in danger of losing members because of a failing strike of 200,000 rail workers and their ongoing battle with the Federation. Their General Assembly met in Cleveland a week after the Philadelphia meeting. Terrance V. Powderly, the Knight's Grand Master Workman, brought the Philadelphia proposal to the Cleveland convention, but in the wake of the Knight's failing railroad strike, the meeting was so contentious he was never able to bring it up for a vote. Instead, almost all of the craft unions that were members of the Knights of Labor bolted to Gompers's Federation, which soon changed its name to The American Federation of Labor. The Knights of Labor crumbled quickly. By 1895, their once robust national membership had dwindled to less than 17,000 men and women.

These tumultuous events had a profound impact on the direction and future of organized labor in America. Railroads, the lifeblood of American capitalism in the 1880's, employed more people than any other industry except agriculture. They were the primary provider of transportation, and the main means of moving goods from city to city. The Knights, representing hundreds of thousands of railway workers, had struck the Union Pacific Railway, the Wabash Railroad, and the Missouri Pacific Railroad to improve working conditions or to stave off pay cuts. Their strike against the Missouri Pacific, which they lost, proved to be their undoing. With their demise at the Cleveland convention, there was a major void in safeguarding the rights of the many skilled craftsmen it took to run a railroad.

Organizing railroad workers was a dangerous undertaking because of what happened in 1877, when a strike in Martinsburg, West Virginia, against the Baltimore and Ohio railroad, instigated by the company's demand for a ten percent wage reduction, spread throughout the country and became deadly. When the B&O hired replacement workers, the strikers at Martinsburg beat them and burned the company's rail cars. The Governor of West Virginia called out the state militia, but mobs of strikers and their supporters overwhelmed them, forcing their retreat. Word of the angry confrontation spread quickly from city to city and other rail workers walked off the job. Railroad lines ground to a halt in Baltimore, Pittsburgh, and Reading, Pennsylvania. When the Maryland State Militia refused orders to fire on striking workers in Baltimore, President Rutherford B. Hayes sent in 250 federal troops armed with Springfield rifles and three Gatling guns. Hayes had been in office less than four months after a hotly contested election in which he lost the popular vote by a large margin and had been seated by a special body comprised of congressional representatives, the Supreme Court, and special commissioners, one of whom owned one of the railroads being struck. The angry Baltimore mob confronted the troops, who opened fire, killing eleven people and wounding forty. Rather than quell the violence, the appearance of the federal troops only served to incite strikers in other cities. Over the next month and a half, the strike extended to Chicago (where twenty strikers were shot dead), St. Louis, and Denver. In Pittsburgh, forty strikers were killed by federal troops, twenty more in West Virginia, and twenty-three in Reading. Federal troops finally restored order forty-five days after the strike had begun, but in the mean time thousands of railroad cars and buildings had been destroyed, hundreds of lives lost, and millions of dollars of damage done.

Nine years later, in 1886, the Knights of Labor's strike against the Great Southwest Railroad conjured up fears that the bloodshed of 1877 might be repeated. Great Southwest was owned by Jay Gould, famous for supposedly having bragged: "I can hire one half of the working class to kill the other half." Despite his bombast, he was one of the most influential men in America, and all the political, economic, and editorial power possible was mustered to break the strike before it could spread and become violent. The Knights were defeated, and as 1888 dawned, anything that remotely resembled an attempt to organize a railroad union was dealt with harshly.

In Atlanta, thirty-nine-year-old Thomas W. Talbot was working in the machine shop of the Eastern Tennessee, Virginia, and Georgia Railroad. It was one of the holdings of the Richmond and West Point Terminal Railway and Warehouse Company. The conglomerate controlled 4,500 miles of railroad, including the Georgia Pacific, the Atlanta and Charlotte Line, the Northeastern of Georgia and the Central of Georgia, in addition to the railroad on which Talbot worked.

Several years earlier, Talbot had been an organizer for the Knights of Labor in their heyday and had organized eleven assemblies for them in that capacity, gaining the title of master workman and state organizer for South Carolina. His first attempt at organizing while working for the Wilmington, Columbia, and Augusta Railroad in Florence, South Carolina, had failed, but he kept at it and eventually became adept at the art of union building under the most difficult conditions.

Now older and working for the conglomerate in Georgia, he was informed that the company was going to reduce wages for all employees by ten percent. That piqued the anger of the veteran organizer and he vowed to seek justice. He began to quietly nose around with his fellow workers. By Saturday night, May 5, 1888, Talbot was ready to act. Robert G. Rodden described the scene in his book *The Fighting Machinists*:

> *Carefully, slowly, he felt out others in the machine shop. He went visiting at night, talking to groups of two or three gathered at the homes of fellow workers. Undoubtedly, word was passed back and forth over lunch boxes and was whispered around lathes and milling machines. As a result of such ground work, Talbot and eighteen other machinists met secretly on the evening of May 5, 1888. They came singly or by two's or three's to an engine pit where they were sheltered by surrounding locomotives from snooping stooges or spies.[1]*

Talbot called his new group the Order of United Machinists and Mechanical Engineers of America, and printed and distributed a circular on September 10, 1888, inviting machinists of "honorable, industrious and sober habits" to join forces with them.

In his book about the first fifty years of the International Association of Machinists, author Mark Perlman describes the nascent organization:

> *Talbot and his associates borrowed the formal organizational aspects of their new union from the Knights. The union was presided over by a grand master machinist (instead of a grand master workman); the second officer was called the grand foreman (instead of a worthy foreman). The officialdom consisted of a grand guard, a grand sentinel, and so on. Local units were termed local lodges; the parent or roof organization the grand lodge. The founders devised a secret ritual and invented secret passwords. No regalia was adopted, however, because although the Order of United Machinists and Mechanical Engineers was "strictly a secret society, [it was] in nowise [to conflict] with one's Religious or Political opinion." Though the Knights' ritual was originally derived from the Masons and was thus repugnant to Catholics, by the 1880's it had lost its anti-Catholic connotations. Several of the nineteen founders of the Machinists Union were Irish Catholics. The Mason-like character of the ritual did not seem to be a problem to them, transmuted as it had been by its association with the Knights.*[2]

Talbot's reference to a "strictly secret society" and the use of the term "lodge" to describe local units was a throwback to a system used by skilled craftsmen in Europe for centuries. Absent the yardsticks of presumed competence used today, such as an engineering degree or a government issued license, tradesmen needed a system to identify those who possessed the skills to do their jobs. And since many jobs involved itinerant craftsmen showing up at the site of a major project, the construction of a cathedral or a waterworks, it was vitally important that the man's skill level be easily defined. This was accomplished by a system of secret code words, handshakes or signs that became known to the craftsman only after he had completed sufficient apprenticeship to be a master of his trade.

Labor historian Bob James described the phenomenon:

> From the time the Gothic cathedrals were under construction, stonemasons, and other artisans in guilds controlled entry into their trade or "misterie." Thus they controlled who worked, and what they were paid and under what conditions, with secret handshakes, passwords and secret signs of recognition. Apprentices were taught the skills "in lodge" and qualification was marked by their being "made," or admitted, at the higher degrees of Craftsman and Master Mason, for example.[3]

Tom Talbot's fledgling group grew quickly. By the time he and the union's secretary, William Dawley, distributed their circular in September 1888, they boasted lodges already organized in Georgia, North Carolina, South Carolina, and Alabama. Correspondents were urged to form lodges consisting of eight or more machinists in their locales and to send seven dollars to Talbot in order to receive "all printed blanks, rituals, constitution, etc. necessary for operating a lodge."[4]

Each member of the organization contributed at least fifty cents per month, and if he became disabled, the Order would pay out a benefit of five dollars per week. Talbot also pledged to publish a monthly journal to help members locate work and provide a forum for any member to publish their thoughts, "no matter how limited he may be in education or journalistic qualification."[5]

A year after that first secretive meeting in the Atlanta railroad pit, the order had made tremendous progress. They held their first convention May 6, 1889, in the Georgia State House, in the Senate Chamber. They were addressed by Hoke Smith, publisher of the *Atlanta Journal*, who would eventually become Governor of Georgia and a United States Senator. After a lengthy discussion and two votes, the group changed its name to the National Association of Machinists.

Tom Talbot served only two years as Grand Master Machinist of the NAM, at its headquarters in Atlanta. He was unanimously re-elected at the union's next convention in Louisville, Kentucky, but resigned within months, citing "matters of a personal nature." He left Atlanta and moved his family back to Florence, South Carolina, where he was shot dead a year later in a street fight brought about by a perceived slight to his young daughter. Talbot's successor at the NAM, James J. Creamer, also served only two years. He was replaced by John O'Day, a machinist from Indianapolis. O'Day's term lasted less than a year, cut short when his hand-picked treasurer, J.J. Lamb, withdrew the union's entire $5,300 nest egg from the bank and vanished. With the NAM bankrupt and facing extinction, James O'Connell, a member of the NAM Executive Board from Pennsylvania, stepped in and provided stability and leadership over the next eighteen years.

Railroads served as the veins of the organization. Organizers would ride the rails, stopping at railheads and terminuses to recruit new members. These early organizers, almost all of them volunteers, were known as "Boomers," a term that eventually came to mean any itinerant craftsman who traveled to find work. They were also called Ho-Bo's, or hobos, because of their penchant for copping a free ride by "hitting a boxcar." In the early days of the union, the term hobo was a badge of honor. It was only years later when "undesirables" who "indulged too freely in the ever tempting cup," and abused their "pie cards," that the term took on a negative connotation.

"Pie Cards," formally known as "Traveling Cards," enabled members to receive financial aid as they were going from one locale to another to find work or to organize.

Peter "P.J." Conlon, perhaps the most famous of all the Boomers, recounted the early days when he took to the road with Pie Cards for four months in 1896 and managed to reorganize twenty-two lodges and establish twelve new ones:

> *President O'Connell wrote me many letters urging me to quit my job and take to the road as an organizer. He offered me the princely sum of $100 a month, this sum to include my salary, railroad fare and hotel expenses...In short, my commission was to beg, borrow, and do anything but steal in order to get over the road [range from one end of the rail system to the other]...I would have to occasionally patronize a side-door Pullman [hop a ride in a boxcar]. However, whatever method employed to get over the road in those days it was no crime. When a boomer took a notion to leave town, he left; if he could not go one way he went another, the big idea was, to be on his way...Many times I was criticized for not being dressed up and dolled up, which everybody knew was impossible on the salary and expenses I was receiving. As a matter of fact I was supposed to be an official tramp.*[7]

Conlon and his cohorts organized not only the machinists working on the railroads but also those working in manufacturing machine shops along their route. This led to a rapid expansion of membership and extended the Association's scope well beyond that of other unions representing only railroad workers. Cleveland Local Lodge 83 of the National Association of Machinists was chartered in January 1890, representing machinists in several local shops. Organizing continued at a rapid pace, including new lodges in Mexico and Canada, where the first local was established at Stratford, Ontario. When the union held its convention in Pittsburgh in 1891, in accordance with this new territorial reach, it changed its name, appropriately, to the International Association of Machinists.

By the time the union met in convention in Kansas City, Missouri, in 1897, it boasted a membership of 15,000 and a treasury of $15,000. After removing a "whites only" clause from their constitution (by moving it to the secret ritual), the union received an American Federation of Labor charter.

One of the battles that raged within the union for years was the tension between the issues of Socialism and industrial unionism versus craft unionism. Eugene Debs, the famed Socialist, formed a competing union called the American Railway Union in Chicago in 1893, and tried to organize all of the railroad's workers into "One Big Union." The effort was attractive to many workers, including some who were members of the craft oriented IAM, but came to a screeching halt with the imprisonment of Debbs in 1894, for conspiring to interfere with the US Mail during a strike against the Pullman rail car company.

In 1896, the IAM hired its first full-time business agents and assigned them to Chicago, New York, Cleveland, and Lynn, Massachusetts. It was still strictly a craft union, but had liberalized membership requirements to admit specialists, journeymen and women.

The IAM struck the Brown Hoisting Works in Cleveland that year, demanding a nine hour work day for ten hours pay, and time and a half for overtime. The company eventually bargained to award time and a half for work in excess of ten hours per day, and granted what they called a "Saturday half holiday."

By the end of the first decade of the twentieth century, automobiles and trucks began to replace trains as the main means of moving people, which created a new trade: the automobile mechanic. Many first generation mechanics had learned their trade on the railroads, and the IAM was eager to represent them in their new positions. The first Automotive Lodge was chartered in New York City in 1912, adding an ever growing army of auto and truck mechanics to the union's ranks.

SIX

THE FIGHTING MACHINISTS

By 1915, the IAM was at the forefront of the movement for an eight hour work day. World War One had caused machine shops, particularly those in the armaments industry, to ramp up production. P.J. Conlon, the old boomer, by then a Vice President of the IAM, led workers in New England in successful strikes to secure the eight hour day. When Conlon and the union took the fight to Cincinnati, the National Metal Trades Association, a group representing the owners of companies and hence the IAM's nemesis, tried every trick in the book to put a stop to the eight-hour movement. Conlon called a meeting of all union machinists at Turner Hall, one of the largest meeting places in Cincinnati on September 24. More than 1,800 machinists filled the hall to overflowing and hundreds had to be turned away. Six days later, a meeting at the same facility for non-union machinists drew an even larger crowd "packing the hall to suffocation."[1] Conlon and his organizers in Cincinnati began obligating new members as fast as they could process the paperwork, with Conlon reporting that he had personally initiated more than 1,200 members in the course of two weeks.

The Metal Trades Association sent threatening typewritten letters to the machinists and began a steady anti-union drumbeat in the newspapers. When that tactic didn't work, they ginned up their own "newspaper," the *Cincinnati Republican*, and accused Conlon plotting to blow up the Lodge and Shipley Machine Tool Company in league with the Cincinnati's Australian Counsel and a mysterious "Doctor Ludwig." The paper also called for Conlon to be killed.

By the first week in October, a general strike blanketed the city, and shop after shop ground to a halt as machinists hit the bricks demanding an eight hour work day. On October 6, nearly 800 machinists marched down Walnut Street to the Machinists Headquarters with their tool boxes perched on their shoulders and placards affixed to their caps calling for an eight hour day. Soon, nearly 2,000 machinists were on strike at more than thirty firms.

In his December report to the membership, Conlon detailed tactics used to try to break the strike:

> *Thousands of typewritten letters have been sent to the strikers imploring them to come back. Thousands of dollars have been spent by petty foremen in beer fests and entertainments to the strikers to win them over. Policemen have been very officious in an endeavor to break up the picket lines. Plain clothes men have escorted strikebreakers from their homes to the shops and even a judge of a juvenile court has sentenced his prisoners to work in scab machine shops...When companies asked for police protection the mayor appointed fifty strikers as special policemen. This did not suit the shop owners, who applied to the sheriff and had fifty deputy sheriffs sworn in, so the plants were being amply protected by deputy sheriffs and policemen.[2]*

In Cleveland, IAM organizers, business agents, and members adopted the slogan: "A Cent a Minute, Eight Hours a Day," and some 5,500 members of District 54 joined in a general strike, which eventually led the area's employers to capitulate to their demands.

Using the crusade for an eight hour day as a rallying point, the IAM, under the leadership of William H. Johnston, grew from 71,000 members in September 1915, to 113,000 members in June 1916. Membership continued to climb exponentially during World War I, peaking at 331,400 in 1919. But the rapid growth came at a cost. The big city machine shop members began to outnumber the railroad members who had started the union. A civil war of sorts broke out between two factions dubbed the "Masons," and the "Catholics." The Masons, largely from the South and smaller rural machine shops, supported IAM President Johnston, and the Catholics, who for the most part worked in big cities, job shops, and as construction and erection machinists, supported J. F. Anderson, one of his sharpest critics. Friction between the two groups led to a divisive election in which Anderson defeated Johnston's ally Pete Conlon for the position of American Vice President of the IAM. Johnston managed to maintain his position as President, but the split within the ranks of the membership—between railroaders and job shop machinist—would echo through the next four decades.

The overthrow of Russian Tsar Nicholas II by Bolshevik revolutionaries in 1917 emboldened many within the Labor Movement who longed for the destruction of the capitalist system. The International Workers of the World, or "Wobblies" as they were called, were founded in 1905 by a group that included Mary "Mother" Jones and Eugene Debbs, who had failed at his earlier attempt to form an industrial railroad union. The Wobblies advocated the formation of "One Big Union," and the violent overthrow, if necessary, of capitalism.

These developments led to a widespread anti-Bolshevik hysteria that swept the country in 1919, and became known as the "Red Scare." In Cleveland on May Day of that year, thirty-two labor and Socialists groups held a parade to protest the recent jailing of Wobblies founder Debbs. As they marched to Public Square, local veterans confronted the socialists on

Superior Avenue and condemned their using the American flag. A riot ensued. Two people were killed, forty injured, and 116 were arrested. The angry mob also destroyed Socialist party headquarters on Prospect Avenue.

The economic slump in the wake of the end of World War I led to a decline in IAM membership as the nation's manufacturers reverted to peace time production. The number of members dropped from 300,000 to 69,000 by 1928. By the summer of 1929, it had started to rebound slightly and stood at 73,000. The stock market crash of October 29, 1929, dealt a severe blow to the IAM. By late spring, 1933, the union's ranks had fallen to 56,000, with 23,200 on unemployment stamps.

By 1934, President Franklin Delano Roosevelt's New Deal, and particularly the National Industrial Recovery Act (NRA), finally began to bring about a rebound in the American economy. Among other things, the NRA guaranteed workers the right to collective bargaining and encouraged employers to come to mutual agreements with workers on maximum hours of work, minimum wages and other conditions of employment. The NRA established a code for the automotive repair industry, ensuring the right to collective bargaining and outlawing company unions. In Cleveland, Automotive Lodge 1363, which had been chartered in 1919, saw its membership swell from fifty members in 1934, to more than 1,000 members in 1935.

The economic progress realized under the NRA was imperiled when the US Supreme Court struck it down as unconstitutional in May 1935. However, Congress acted swiftly and passed a new broader statute that established collective bargaining as governmental policy. At the same time, the National Labor Relations Act, more commonly referred to as the Wagner Act, set forth prohibitions against unfair labor practices, such as interference in union elections, discrimination against workers who joined a union, financial support for a company union or acting against a whistle blower.

Employers were stunned and upset by the new labor-friendly policy of the US government, while labor unions for the most part rejoiced. Some of the AFL craft unions, including the IAM, were reluctant at first to throw open their membership rolls to less skilled workers, still mindful of the debacles the concept of "One Big Union" had caused the American Railway Union and the International Workers of the World.

One labor leader who recognized the new opportunity immediately was John L. Lewis, President of the United Mine Workers. Tall, powerfully built, with a jowly face and improbably bushy eyebrows, at fifty-five, Lewis was an incredibly powerful orator. He began agitating for the AFL to organize mass production workers. His efforts were rebuffed at the 1934 AFL convention, when the Federation met again in Atlantic City in 1935, Lewis was loaded for bear.

The Executive Committee of the AFL, which included IAM President A.O. Wharton, opposed Lewis' efforts to expand organizing by a margin of twelve to two. When Lewis brought a minority report to the floor of the convention, the Carpenters, Teamsters, and Machinists all rose to speak against it.

Robert H. Ziegler, in his biography, *John L. Lewis, Labor Leader,* set the scene:

> *With his bushy eyebrows, his perfectly cut three piece suit, and his booming voice, he stood out vividly from the dry-as-dust functionaries who normally occupied the floor at AFL gatherings. In prose salted with biblical, Shakespearean, and classical allusions, Lewis gained a ready audience among the scores of newspapermen covering the proceedings. Here indeed was quotable copy. Nor did Lewis always observe the federation's polite protocols, for his pointed barbs and scathing asides named names, leaving dignified fellow chieftains squirming in their*

chairs. Master of the high sounding phrase and the
proverbial meat cleaver, Lewis in full voice turned a
dreary convention into exciting theater.[3]

Lewis proclaimed that the labor movement "is organized upon a principal that the strong shall help the weak," and implored the delegates to adopt the minority report, claiming that should they fail to do so, "despair will prevail where hope now exists." He called on them to "heed this cry from Macedonia that comes from the hearts of men." The delegates, casting weighted votes according to the wishes of their leadership, rejected Lewis' proposal by a vote of 18,024 to 10,933.

Describing the scene that followed in their book *John L. Lewis, a biography*, authors Melvyn Dubofsky and Warren Van Tine related:

> *When a delegate for the rubber workers raised the question of jurisdiction for his union, Hutcheson of the carpenters interjected for a point of order. It was a moment that Lewis had been waiting for, an event he would have manufactured if necessary. "This thing of raising points of order all the time on minor delegates," Lewis challenged the burly, oversized carpenter's leader, "is rather small potatoes." More heated words passed between the two labor barons, with Hutcheson finally calling Lewis a "bastard." At that, Lewis jumped to his feet, leaped over a row of chairs toward Hutcheson, jabbed out his right fist, and sent the carpenters' president sprawling against a table. Moments later the fight was over, a blood streaked Hutcheson left the convention floor guided by friends.[4]*

Lewis' mineworkers and eleven other unions immediately bolted from the AFL and established a new federation, known as the Congress of Industrial Organizations, to organize mass production workers on an industry-wide basis.

Arthur Wharton, the IAM President, "had a fundamental distrust of 'easy' gains in membership—maintaining that swollen ranks were likely to encourage irresponsible leadership. Instead, he favored locally planned organizing programs growing out of local demands, rather than situations in which the union engineered membership demands from the top."[5]

Nonetheless, when the AFL Executive Committee settled a jurisdictional dispute between the machinists and the carpenters in the aircraft industry at a meeting in Los Angeles in 1934, the stage was set for the first industry-wide organizing campaign in IAM history.

Aircraft production in the 1920's, when the airframes were made of wood and the engines of metal, required both carpentry and machining skills. The carpenters established a local at the Douglas Aircraft Company with nearly 1,000 members. But by the mid-1930's, airplane manufacture became less about woodworking and more about metalworking. When the IAM committed to ramp up its' organizing in the industry and to include both aircraft mechanics and aircraft factory workers, the carpenters agreed to step aside giving the Machinists the best shot at organizing the industry. Aeronautical Mechanics Lodge 751, in Seattle, Washington, home of Boeing, the nation's largest aircraft manufacturer, was chartered in September 1935.

The United Auto Workers sensed and opportunity when the carpenters left the fray and tried to organize workers at the Lockheed and Douglas companies. They were determined to challenge the IAM for the right to represent workers in the West Coast aircraft industry. However, with the rapid expansion of aircraft production at the onset of World War

II, IAM organizers were able to beat back the UAW challenge and remain dominant in the aircraft industry.

IAM membership began to rise again. The first six months of 1937 brought 152 new lodges and more than 42,000 members. Despite this new foray into industrial organizing, the relationship between the IAM and the CIO remained icy. IAM staff members were quoted as calling CIO organizers "traitors," "Communists," or "dual unionists," and often described them as "power-hungry," "misguided," or "recalcitrant."[6]

The IAM's steadfast opposition to Communists in its ranks dated to the 1920's when it barred them from membership. But new tensions arose during the run-up to World War II, as the IAM's expansive organizing efforts attracted new members of every political philosophy, including Wobblies, socialists, and even members of the Communists. When the radicals tried to take over several local lodges, IAM leadership reacted swiftly and aggressively to expel them.

President Roosevelt signed legislation in 1936 to bring airline workers under the provisions of the Railway Labor Act, providing them with the same collective bargaining rights and protections. The IAM pounced on the opportunity and began aggressively organizing workers on the country's twenty six airlines. By 1939, the IAM had negotiated industry-wide agreements with carriers in both the United States and Canada, making it the predominant airline union.

After the attack on Pearl Harbor, with the United States and Canada drawn into the war, the IAM had members working in all the strategic centers of production and transportation. In December 1941, IAM President Harvey Brown sent President Roosevelt a telegram expressing the union's commitment to the war effort:

> The International Association of Machinists has over a half century of experience. Its members are

employed in navy yards, arsenals, munitions plants, shipyards, on railroads, in plants manufacturing airplanes, machine tools, power machinery, tools, dies and scientific instruments and machinery of all description. The Executive Council and members of our Field Staff, all of whom are practical mechanics with training and experience handling problems within our industry, unanimously announce to you, our leader, that our services and the facilities of the International Association of Machinists are yours to command.[7]

Across the continent, production facilities buzzed day and night with activity. Between 1942 and 1943, 27,000,000 tons of merchant ships and 3,700,000 tons of new fighting ships for the Navy were produced. Airplanes were manufactured at plants represented by the IAM at a rate of nearly 10,000 per month.

Despite the nearly 76,000 IAM members who were away serving in the military, membership soared from 284,500 before Pearl Harbor to 661,800 by D-Day in 1944.

When the war ended and William Winpisinger, Phil Zannella, and the rest of the boys returned home, the American Labor Movement was an economic and social force to be reckoned with. The IAM had grown from a small railroad union to a sprawling industrial union, and Cleveland, Wimpy's hometown, was the epicenter of much of the manufacturing and labor organizing activity in the country.

SEVEN

A TRADE UNIONIST GETS HIS START

It didn't take long for returning veterans to become active in the labor movement. Wimpy, Phil Zannella and hundreds like them were tough, scrappy and battle tested. Their resolve would soon be tested in one of the epic political fights of all time.

Within a couple of months of going to work at Lake Buick, Wimpy became the shop steward, displaying the gift of gab, leadership and willingness to confront authority that had marked his high school and military careers. He managed to beef so often that his predecessor finally, in frustration, suggested that if Wimpy knew so damn much maybe *he* should be shop steward. Wimpy happily complied. "I guess I was gifted with a big mouth," he would recall later.[1]

As steward, he would often travel downtown to Euclid Avenue to represent his members at meetings of Local Lodge 1363, where Business Agent Bob Trimbel would report in meeting after meeting that the local was in dire financial straits, near bankruptcy. Trimble convinced the pragmatic and fiscally astute Phil Zannella to help him rebuild the local's coffers. Before long, Zannella gave up his lucrative position as a diesel mechanic at McClurg Ford and signed on as a business agent for the struggling local.

Local 1363 was housed in the basement of the District 54 headquarters, presided over by District President Matt DeMore, a legendary figure in the IAM.

DeMore, the son of Italian immigrants, was born on Cleveland's East Side on April 5, 1903. By age nine, he was hawking newspapers in his family's Little Italy neighborhood.

By age eleven, he had secured a job as a clerk at a local hardware store to help support his widowed mother, three brothers, and two sisters. He quit high school at sixteen and left Cleveland to become a blacksmith's helper on the Michigan Central Railroad in Detroit, and returned a year later to a job as a motorman for the Cleveland Railway Company. By 1920, he was working as a maintenance mechanic at the local General Electric vacuum cleaner plant. When the IAM began industrial organizing in 1935, the thirty-two-year-old DeMore leapt at the opportunity, helped organize his fellow workers into Local Lodge 439, and fought off attempts to raid his membership by the Communist-influenced United Electrical, Radio and Machine Workers of America. He was the shop's first IAM steward and was elected local lodge President by his members the following year.

Two years later, in 1938, the energetic DeMore, who was described as "solidly muscular and compact," and possessed of a booming voice, headed a slate of reform candidates pledged to streamlining operations of District 54, and was elected its President. The district consisted of ten locals in Cleveland and the surrounding area, and had a total membership of 4,500 when DeMore took control. Through his dogged determination and superior organizing skills, the district would soon grow to include more than 6,000 members.

Local Lodge 1363 meetings were held upstairs in the District Headquarters' main meeting room. The hall had light wood paneling, a tin ceiling, and three big windows that were cracked open to let in fresh air when members lit up their cigarettes and cigars. There was seating for about three hundred, with a raised podium at the front of the hall. Members would rush in to get good seats, the ones not obstructed by the poles that dotted the room.

Most lodge meetings focused on the ins and outs of collective bargaining agreements the union had negotiated, but when discussion turned to the "Good and Welfare" portion of the agenda, Wimpy would chime in with a running commentary on how he viewed the social issues of the day.

Phil Zannella, a life-long conservative who helped run the local's meetings, rarely agreed with Wimpy. But he was taken by his eloquence and saw the reaction he inspired whenever he spoke.

One evening in early 1948, the recording secretary of Lodge 1363 abruptly and unexpectedly tendered his resignation. Wimpy, seated in the middle of the crowded room, was surprised to see Zannella signaling him from the front of the room, indicating that he should get himself nominated. Stunned but compliant, Wimpy leaned over and whispered to a buddy seated next to him, "Nominate me for Secretary." In the blink of an eye, nominations were closed, Zannella called for the vote, and William W. Winpisinger became Recording Secretary of Local Lodge 1363. "I didn't even know what the hell I was doing that night, getting elected," he recalled.[2]

The pairing of Zannella and Winpisinger was an odd couple indeed. While they had a lot in common as fellow high school dropouts, World War Two veterans, automobile mechanics and fervent trade unionists, but their social views and sense of loyalty to hierarchical structure couldn't have been further apart.

Tom Buffenbarger would relate:

> Here is Wimpy, the world's not moving fast enough for him. And here's Phil, who believes in democracy, but controlled democracy and stair stepping, carefully plotting out the pros and cons. Wimpy was the bull in the china shop.[3]

This dynamic duo and the very political Matt DeMore, who ran for Congress unsuccessfully in 1946, (losing a close race to incumbent Frances P. Bolton), would soon face an enormous political challenge. President Harry S. Truman, the Democratic standard bearer, was in a fight for his political life—a fight few thought he could win. But those predicting his imminent demise—virtually every political pundit in the country—failed to recognize that Truman, the old poker player from Missouri, had an ace up his sleeve: the backing of the IAM Fighting Machinists. In what proved to be one of the closest and most bitterly contested Presidential races in history, it was the political muscle of organized labor, especially of the Ohio Machinists, that made the difference.

The years immediately after World War II presented a great challenge to the American economy. More than thirteen million men and women discharged from the armed forces were trying to get back into the workforce. By 1947, more than 700,000 remained unemployed. Demand for housing, cars, and consumer goods was at an all time high. War-time price controls had been removed and rampant inflation took over. Pork chops which had sold for forty-eight cents per pound under the controlled system, now sold for seventy-five cents a pound, a fifty-six percent increase. Steak went from sixty-five cents per pound to $1.25, and bacon from sixty-four cents to eighty-nine cents per pound.

Although wages were up eleven percent, the increase was more than offset by the price of food, housing, and energy. Interest rates were up nineteen percent.

Not everyone was suffering. Corporate profits were up ninety-nine percent, and even small business profits had soared fifty-three percent over their war-time levels.

Labor, naturally, tried to advocate on behalf of the working class, and its representatives met fierce, often brutal, opposition. When members of Lodge 1337 in Cleveland asked the Pipe Manufacturing Company to re-open their agreement to allow for a wage increase, management was silent. Frustrated by the pressure of higher prices and an uncooperative employer, members voted to strike. The US Conciliation Service, the government entity that oversaw collective bargaining agreements, intervened immediately and postponed the strike. Soon after, on February 13, 1947, Lodge 1337 leadership asked permission for forty-nine members to take two hours off for union business. The company did not object, and the members held their meeting. When they returned, they found the plant gates locked and a notice posted dismissing all forty-nine employees.

Three days of negotiations by Matt DeMore and the leadership of the lodge resulted in an offer from the company to rehire all the workers except the four members of the Shop Committee. When the company refused to budge, the union struck the plant and set up picket lines. Three months later, in May 1947, the company got tough and unleashed the Cleveland Police. Cops on horseback wielded clubs and fired tear gas at picketing IAM members, seriously injuring eight of them, including DeMore, who was walking the line when the police attacked. His head spilt open, he was taken to the hospital.

The political turmoil that led to the Cleveland strike and many others like it had begun with the 1946 Congressional Elections, when Republicans captured both the House and the Senate for the first time since 1930. The class of radical conservatives that took control was bent on destroying the New Deal and rolling back labor's impressive gains, which had included passage of the Wagner Act. Two figures who won political office that year would go on to be among the most controversial men of the twentieth century: Wisconsin Senator Joseph McCarthy, whose anti-Communist witch hunts divided the country, ground the government to a halt, and destroyed the lives of many innocent people, and California Congressman Richard M. Nixon, whose paranoid personality would cause a constitutional crisis and ultimately lead to his resignation in disgrace from the Presidency.

High on the agenda of this rapacious group of social conservatives was reigning in the power of organized labor. Gone were labor's friends at the helm of congressional committees overseeing labor-management relations. They had been replaced by radical Republicans determined to destroy the unions. Congressman Fred Hartley of New Jersey and Senator Robert Taft of Ohio took over those committees and soon introduced a comprehensive anti-union bill that the IAM's weekly newspaper, *The Machinist,* called "The most monstrous anti-labor measure ever proposed."[4]

The labor movement charged that the Taft-Hartley bill, which among many things would outlaw industry-wide bargaining and remove the authority of International Unions over their own locals, had been written by lobbyists for the most flagrant violators of the Wagner Act, including some of the largest employers of the time, such as Allis-Chalmers, Fruerhauf, J.I. Case, and Inland Steel.

Taft-Hartley would be a terrible blow to the labor movement. Among the bill's many pernicious elements were passages that would revive injunctions, ban hiring practices that helped stabilize employment in many industries, limit a union's ability to prevent infiltration by undesirable elements, and prohibit secondary boycotts. The first draft of the law, later amended, contained insinuations about the presence of Communists in the labor movement and required union officers, but not employers, to take a loyalty oath. The most pernicious section of the legislation was called Section 14-B. It allowed non-union workers to be employed in union shops, where they would enjoy the benefits of collective bargaining agreements without paying their fair share of the dues.

The Machinist claimed that the bill would give "... employers powers which an earlier Congress recognized as vicious and took away from employers because they were used to destroy the right to organize."[5] Despite heavy lobbying efforts by labor, the bill cleared Congress on May 13, 1947, with a Senate vote of sixty-eight to twenty-one in favor, which included the support of twenty-one Democratic Senators.

Taft-Hartley posed an enormous political challenge to Truman. It had passed the Senate with a veto-proof majority—the President would have to turn around forty-five votes to sustain a veto—and his poll numbers were slipping dramatically. Franklin D. Roosevelt was a tough act to follow, and Truman bore the brunt of some nasty jokes: "To err is Truman," "What would Truman do if he were alive?" and "Don't shoot our piano player, he's doing the best he can."

IAM International President Harvey Brown sent President Truman a letter on June 4, 1947, urging in the strongest possible terms that he veto the measure:

> At present our economy is threatened because of enormous profits on one side and, because of skyrocketing prices, and declining purchasing power on the other. Labor has been striving to restore the balance between wages and prices which was lost after the government abandoned its wartime economic controls. To weaken Labor's efforts at the bargaining table at this time is to invite depression... By permitting minority groups in any plant, as well as the employer himself to petition for a representation election at any time, including the period when a plant is on strike and at the same time depriving strikers the right to vote in such an election, our strike weapon would be blunted. Withholding their labor is the only last resort labor has for improving its lot. This is an invitation for the return of company unions.

Truman was torn. His veto of a measure that had passed with such a significant plurality would be politically unpopular. On the other hand, he recognized the inherent unfairness of the bill to the working people of America.

Throughout his Presidency, Truman kept two signs on his desk in the oval office. The more famous proclaimed "The buck stops here." The other, which quoted Mark Twain, would guide his actions in this matter: "Always do right. This will gratify some people and astonish the rest."

On June 20, 1947, President Harry S. Truman stood tall for labor and vetoed the Taft-Hartley bill. *The Machinist* called his veto message "One of the most blistering veto messages a President has ever sent to Congress."[6] In it, the President said:

> *Taken as a whole, this bill would reverse the basic direction of our national labor policy, inject the government into private economic affairs on an unprecedented scale, and conflict with important principles of our democratic society. Its provisions would cause more strikes, not fewer. It would contribute neither to industrial peace nor to economic stability and progress. It would be a dangerous stride in the direction of a totally managed economy. It contains seeds of discord which would plague this nation for years to come.*

The House, reacting angrily to the President's comeuppance, overrode his veto less than an hour after the stinging rebuke was delivered to Capitol Hill.

That evening, both the President and Senator Taft took to the radio airwaves to defend their positions. Truman spoke forcefully of the rights of workers to organize and conduct collective bargaining and Taft derided and disparaged those rights. Three days later the Senate joined the House and overrode the President's veto with seventy-two votes (twenty-four of them Democratic). The Machinists and the rest of the labor movement were furious with the congress, particularly the 126 Democratic members who had joined the Republicans and voted against working people.

In *The Fighting Machinists*, Robert G. Rodden wrote:

> *This assault on labor's right to organize and bargain set off a surge of political awareness in union halls everywhere. Before Taft-Hartley political issues tended to be rather low key in the IAM. The Grand Lodge Convention endorsed Robert LaFollette in 1924 and the Executive Council urged support for each of Roosevelt's re-election bids. But from the very earliest days machinists tried to avoid the divisiveness of political dissension in conducting local lodge affairs. Under the Grand Lodge Constitution, members could discuss "subjects of political economy under the heading 'Good and Welfare' providing such discussion does not occupy more than twenty minutes...and does not include matters sectarian in religion or partisan politics.*[7]

That was about to change. International President Harvey Brown was determined to unleash the political might of his 600,000 member union to protect the rights of working people.

He began by directing all local and district lodges to establish political programs to educate their members and their families. He suggested they start by organizing voter registration drives and by becoming familiar with their political representatives, particularly on how they had voted on Taft-Hartley.

Matt DeMore responded by hosting a massive anti-Taft-Hartley rally in Cleveland, the heart of Senator Taft's home state. DeMore, Zannella, Wimpy, and the rest of the District 54 organizers did everything they could to drum up a crowd for a September 20 rally at Geauga Lake Park, including giving away fantastic prizes, among them a brand-new Willys station wagon. When General Secretary Treasurer Eric Peterson strode to the microphone that afternoon, he was greeted by more than 20,000 enthusiastic IAM members and their families.

Taft, who was toying with a Presidential run, must have noticed so many angry constituents gathered in his backyard. Meanwhile, Harvey Brown was not about to take a potential Taft candidacy and the defection of so many Democratic members of Congress lightly. On Monday evening, November 24, 1947, he convened the first meeting of the Machinists Non-Partisan Political League (MNPL).

He said of the effort, "Our objective is to help elect to public office men and women who will use their voice and their vote for the greatest good of the greatest number."

Their initial goal was to raise one million dollars (an incredible sum in those days) to oust pro-employer members of the Congress who had foisted Taft-Hartley upon them and to support the re-election of the Democratic President who had gone to bat for them.

As the 1948 election approached, President Truman found that he had even bigger political problems than Taft-Hartley. The Cold War was ramping up, the Middle East was reeling out of control, and he still faced the evils of rampant inflation, a tight job market, and the urgent need to create more housing for returning servicemen. His numbers continued to plummet in the polls and both extreme wings of his party—liberals led by former Vice President Harry A. Wallace and conservative

Southerners led by South Carolina Governor J. Strom Thurmond—began to make noises about bolting to form their own parties.

By the time the party met in convention at Philadelphia's Municipal Auditorium July 12-14, the Republican Party had already nominated New York Governor Thomas E. Dewey as their standard bearer. Dewey had prevailed on the third ballot, beating back challenges from former Minnesota Governor Harold Stassen, California Governor (and later Supreme Court Chief Justice) Earl Warren, and the man Labor considered the devil incarnate: Ohio Senator Robert Taft.

Dewey was a seasoned political campaigner who had been the party's nominee in 1944 for an unsuccessful race against the Roosevelt-Truman ticket. Then he had run against a popular war-time President and lost. This time it looked like his luck was about to change. *The New York Post* went so far as to say, "The (Democratic) Party might as well immediately concede the election to Dewey and save the wear and tear of campaigning." The electoral coalition of liberals, industrial state "lunch pail Democrats" and conservative Southern Democrats that FDR had so skillfully assembled and maintained through four elections was fraying badly. One sign in the convention hall summed up the feeling of many of the delegates: "I'M JUST MILD ABOUT HARRY."

The liberal wing, calling themselves "the Progressives," detested Truman's foreign policy and advocated a more conciliatory stance toward Moscow. They longed for a return to what they perceived as the more enlightened leadership of Roosevelt and rallied around the liberal Vice President from his third term, Henry A. Wallace of Iowa. Wallace had been bumped from the Democratic ticket in 1944 for what party leaders viewed as his unorthodox and ultra-liberal views (such as advocating full voting rights for blacks and universal health-care) and replaced by Truman. Roosevelt had appointed Wallace Secretary of Commerce as something of a consolation prize, but Truman fired him in September 1946 for what he considered a lack of support for his foreign policy. Wallace then became the editor of *The New Republic*, where he predicted that the Truman Doctrine would usher in a "Century of Fear."

Truman's problems with the right wing of his party were even more severe and rooted in his support for integration. The issue was being hotly debated—in the guise of "State's Rights" —and Truman was about to issue Executive Order 9981, "Calling on the armed forces to provide equal treatment and opportunities for black servicemen."

Conservative Southern delegates tried to defeat a plank making a strong statement in favor of civil rights, arguing that the matter should be left up to the states. Truman knew that if he was to gain the support of a growing number of African-Americans in critical urban states such a plank would be vital to his candidacy. A long, bitter, often emotional debate ensued.

Minneapolis Mayor Hubert H. Humphrey, a candidate for the Senate, rose to deliver one of the most famous speeches of his career, supporting civil rights and exhorting delegates to embrace the plank:

> To those who say we are rushing this issue of civil rights, I say this: we are 172 years late!
>
> To those who say, to those who say this civil rights program is an infringement on state's rights, I say this: the time has arrived in America for the Democratic Party to get out of the shadow of state's rights and walk forthrightly into the bright sunshine of human rights.

Humphrey's rousing speech led to the walk-out of thirty-five delegates from Mississippi and Alabama. With the recalcitrant delegates gone, Truman's operatives twisted enough arms to push through the statement and secure him the nomination, but at a tremendous cost. In the first televised Democratic National Convention in history, the President didn't get to deliver his acceptance speech until two o'clock in the morning. Within days after the Democratic Convention rejected the state's rights argument and re-nominated Truman for President and Kentucky Senator Alben W. Barkley for Vice President, the two wings of the party bolted. Wallace teamed with Idaho Senator Glen Taylor to form the Progressive Party, and the Southern Democrats left to form the State's Rights Democratic Party, commonly called the "Dixiecrats." The Dixiecrats, running under the slogan "Segregation Forever" nominated South Carolina Governor Jesse (Strom) Thurmond for President and Mississippi Governor Fielding L. Wright for Vice President.

By the time Harvey Brown gaveled the twenty-second IAM Grand Lodge Convention to order in Grand Rapids, Michigan, on Monday, September 15, 1948, the Truman campaign was in free-fall. *Fortune* went so far as to say "The prospects of Republican victory are now so overwhelming that an era of what will amount to one party may well impend." Truman had lost a considerable portion of the Democratic coalition and his chances to retain the White House looked bleak.

Brown stared out at the 900 delegates seated in the Civic Auditorium, the largest convention in the IAM's sixty year history, cleared his throat, and, grasping the sides of the podium tried to breathe life into Truman's candidacy.

"If we mean what we say when speaking of the Tafts and Hartleys in the legislative branch of government, we will be lacking in sincerity, and can be charged with inconsistency if we fail to pay tribute and to pledge support to that distinguished gentleman in the White House who vetoed the Taft-Hartley bill and who in his message to Congress issued a scathing denunciation of that bill and called upon Congress to support his veto."

Brown's move to secure a convention endorsement for Truman was no small gamble. The candidate he wanted to support was viewed as unelectable by most political observers. The Machinists had endorsed only one other Presidential candidate at a convention, in 1924, when they had thrown their support to "Fighting Bob" LaFollette, the Progressive Independent Party candidate who would ultimately carry only his home state of Wisconsin.

Brown also faced some of the same dynamics Truman had encountered at the Democratic Convention in Philadelphia. Southern railroaders who had founded the IAM in 1888 were still a mainstay of the membership. The issue of changing the ritual to delete any mention of race or color as a criteria for IAM membership, hotly debated at the last two conventions, would finally pass this convention in the form of a voice vote to ratify the Executive Council's "Official Circular 487" issued in the fall of 1947.

Brown also had to contend with the liberal wing of the convention that moved to endorse Wallace, and proposed leaving the Democratic Party to form a Labor Party. Both motions were dismissed as wrong and divisive.

After a long week of debating, pleading, and cajoling, Brown finally secured the convention's endorsement for Truman on Thursday, September 23.

He and General Secretary Treasurer Eric Peterson immediately fired off a telegram to the President, who was on a train en route to Los Angeles:

> We are pleased to inform you that the 22nd Grand Lodge Convention of the International Association of Machinists, representing more than 600,000 Americans employed in every state and county in our country, has endorsed your candidacy for reelection.

> *We do so in appreciation of your past and present opposition to the vicious Taft-Hartley Act and for your efforts on behalf of the average citizens of this country.*

It was some of the best news President Truman had had in months. He wrote back to Brown:

> *I am deeply grateful for your letter of September 23rd...Please assure those associated with you that I appreciate more than I can say the pledge of confidence in my leadership embodied in your resolution. We must go forward with progress while our opponents continue to serve special privilege. The resolution which your organization adopted gives me new strength and courage in these difficult days to carry on the fight in the weeks ahead.*

Brown and the Executive Council were proud of their decision and anxious to get to work on the campaign. In his closing remarks to the convention, the last one he would ever attend as an officer or delegate of the IAM, President Brown said, "If we do not prove equal to the occasion on November 2nd, then when the next congress convenes, I am fearful that they are going to do more damage. They are going to do more to intimidate our people. They are going to do more to make it more difficult for the organized labor movement to function."

In addition to the convention endorsement for the President, the newly formed MNPL issued endorsements in seventeen Senate races and 212 House races across the country. Demonstrating that support for labor issues, not party identification was the criteria for earning IAM support, the MNPL included fifteen Republican Congressmen who had voted to sustain Truman's veto of Taft-Hartley among those they endorsed.

They deemed nine of the Senate races "crucial," those in Idaho, West Virginia, Wyoming, Illinois, Minnesota, Tennessee, Colorado, New Mexico, and Montana, calling upon members to work particularly hard in those contests.

The membership of the IAM, always a combative and industrious lot, took to the campaign trail like ducks to water. A sizeable number of the members, approximately 76,000, were newly returned from the armed forces and were quite adept at organizing and giving or following orders. Members formed planning committees, designed voter registration and get-out-the-vote programs and raised bundles of cash for the MNPL to plow into the targeted races.

International President Brown was appointed to the Truman-Barkley Labor Committee, and began meeting with the President regularly at the White House to discuss campaign strategy. IAM members whose families owned cars were urged to get them tuned up and ready to be pressed into service on Election Day. Local lodges across the country formed babysitting networks so that member's wives would be free to work at the polls. *The Machinist* began to trumpet an upbeat message, distinctly at odds with that of the mainstream media: "Labor is Mobilizing Support for Truman," October 7, 1948; "Truman Campaign Gathering Strength," October 14, 1948; "Truman Closing Gap, Every Vote Counts," October 21, 1948. Mainstream papers, meanwhile, saw the contest differently: "Gallup Poll Forecasts Victory by Dewey," "A Fond Farewell to Harry Truman," "Dewey Sweep Forecast."

The Fighting Machinists pressed on. Members in the Twin Cities held a rally that attracted 300 people at the American House in Minneapolis. The local branch of the MNPL printed handbills and donated funds to help local liberal organizations. When President Truman's campaign came through Minnesota, the IAM went all out on crowd building. The chair of the local MNPL was invited to join the President on the platform of his rally at the St. Paul Auditorium. In mid-October, District 4, representing numerous southern railroading lodges held their convention in Chattanooga, Tennessee, where at the urging of General Vice President Earl Melton, they ratified the Grand Lodge's endorsement of Truman, urging their members to roll up their sleeves and get behind the effort. *The Machinist,* reporting on the convention in the October 21 issue, headlined their coverage: "No Dixiecrats Here!"

The Machinists political efforts on behalf of the President and their endorsed candidates rolled on, with crowd building efforts at every Truman stop throughout the Northeast, the industrial Mid-West, the Northern Great Plains, and even in the South. As Election Day approached, the Connecticut Council of Machinists developed maps for a door to door get-out-the vote drive, arranged for members to appear on local radio broadcasts, and lined up cars and babysitters. Because of their special relationship with Guide Dogs of America, they also arranged a program to assist the blind in voting. Trucks and Model T automobiles traveled the streets across the country with MNPL signs asking voters to support "Labor's Friends."

On October 21, the final *Machinist* issue before the election carried an MNPL memorandum outlining, state by state, the laws that allowed union members the right to take time off from work to vote. General Vice President Al Hayes took to the radio airwaves in New York, the country's media capital, urging working men and women across the country to get out and vote. By the time dawn broke on Tuesday, November 2, 1948, the once fledgling political operation of the IAM was a well-oiled machine. The 600,000 members of the Fighting Machinists took to the streets and delivered the votes for Harry S. Truman and the candidates they had endorsed in Congressional elections. In Illinois, Massachusetts, and Wisconsin, IAM members went door to door in their neighborhoods, shepherding friends, family members, and every last breathing soul to the polling booths.

Members in the big Cleveland locals, including Lodge 1363, with Phil Zannella and Wimpy calling the shots, hit the bricks, spreading the Democratic message in their veteran's posts, church groups, and bowling leagues.

Brother Guy Sample, a member of Local Lodge 548 in Moline, Illinois, had broken both of his legs in an accident and was distraught that he might not be able to vote. Fellow lodge members Mike Miller and James Passin borrowed a wheelchair and a pickup truck and delivered Sample to his precinct.

The first few returns to come in showed Truman winning. These were largely discounted, in these days before exit polling, as unrepresentative of the ultimate outcome. After all, the pundits had all agreed that Dewey would be the next President, and who were the voters to disagree with the pundits? President Truman, holed up at a hotel in Excelsior, Missouri, seemed oddly sanguine. Radio commentators were persistent in dismissing the Truman leads in key states and assured listeners that when the dust settled there would be a new President. Dewey carried New York as expected. Tom Evans, one of Truman's political advisors, called the President in something of a panic.

"Mr. President," he said, "Dewey has taken New York. We've got to win Ohio, Illinois, or California."

"Tom, don't call me anymore, I'm going to bed."

"What do you mean?" croaked Evans.

"Just that. I'm going to carry all three states, so don't call me anymore. I'll be over at eight in the morning."

Truman's confidence proved well placed, but just barely. In the end, the race came down to the returns from Ohio, a state the New York Times called "The mother of Republican Presidents." Ohio, where the Machinists who had felt the lash of police whips the previous year waged a scorched earth campaign to deny the state's electors to Bob Taft's party. Ohio, where District 54 President Matt DeMore, who would eventually become General Secretary Treasurer of the IAM, had raised a crowd of more than 20,000 people to protest Taft-Hartley.

The Thursday November 4 edition of the *New York Times* wrapped up its election coverage:

> *The state of Ohio, 'mother of Republican Presidents,' furnished the electoral bloc early yesterday forenoon which assured to President Harry S. Truman a four year term in his own right as Chief Executive of the United States. Until this late accounting of votes cast in Tuesday's general election put Ohio firmly in Mr. Truman's column, after it had fluctuated throughout the night, he was certain of but 254 electoral votes, which were twelve less than the 266 required.*[8]

Truman won Ohio by less than two tenths of one percent of the nearly 3,000,000 votes cast. The final tally showed 1,452,791 for Truman to 1,445,684 for Dewey, a razor-thin 7,107 vote margin. It was a magnificent victory for the Fighting Machinists. Tipping the balance in Ohio and returning labor's friend Harry S. Truman to the White House was significant, but the union made other contributions as well.

Machinists had helped make the difference for Truman in other states where they had significant membership: Illinois, Iowa, Minnesota, Missouri, West Virginia, and Wisconsin in the Midwest; Massachusetts and Rhode Island in the Northeast; California and Washington in the West; Kentucky, Tennessee, and Texas in the South; and Georgia, where the union had been founded sixty years earlier.

Truman's final popular vote total was 24,105,817 to Dewey's 21,970,065, meaning the all-out support of the 15,000,000 union members and their families had provided the critical difference.

The MNPL's record in its first election was nothing less than astonishing: victories in 160 of the 212 House races where they made an endorsement (seventy-five percent), and a remarkable fourteen for seventeen (eighty-two percent) in Senate races, including going nine for nine in the races they had termed "crucial."

More than fifty members of the House or Senate who had turned their backs on labor to override the President's veto of Taft-Hartley were shown the door. Both the House and the Senate returned to Democratic hands, with the party picking up nine seats in the Senate and seventy-three seats in the House. It was a smashing victory for working men and women across the country, and it established the MNPL as a major political force.

The pivotal role the Machinists had played in the election was recognized and acknowledged at 1600 Pennsylvania Avenue. When the Executive Council reacted with outrage to news that $12,000,000 had been spent to lobby the 80th Congress and called for an investigation, President Truman immediately wired his personal support and encouragement.

General Vice President Al Hayes, on tap to be the next International President, was invited to serve as Co-Chair of the Labor Committee for the Inaugural. For the first time in history, labor would be invited to participate in the Inaugural Parade, and the IAM would have one of labor's five floats. The others would be sponsored by the AFL, the Railroad Clerks Union, who had chaired the Truman-Barkley Labor Committee, the CIO, and the Musician's Union, who played "I'm Just Wild about Harry" over and over again, to the delight of the crowd.

On Thursday, January 20, 1949, more than one million people crowded the parade route under brilliant sunshine and bright blue skies as a jeep pulling the IAM float began its way down Pennsylvania Avenue toward the White House. Ten members of Local Lodge 174 at the Washington Naval Yard manned the float, which had been built by the Alan Metreger Company ("the nation's foremost float builder, and a union shop"), accompanied by the comely Gina Bolton, a model wearing a tight skirt, a worker's blue blouse and an IAM cap, and sporting an enormous bow-tie, almost comical in dimension, that said "Good Luck" on one bow and "Harry Truman" on the other. The float consisted of two meshed gears, with the pinion bearing the IAM logo, connected to a massive gear box in the shape of the United States, with the message "Freedom Still Makes this Nation Great" emblazoned on the side. A hand coming out of the gearbox is miking a jo-block labeled "World's Highest Standards."

As the float rumbled along the parade route to resounding cheers, not a single political pundit could be seen. Eventually it made the turn past the Treasury building and as it approached the White House, the machinists on board snapped to attention.

The IAM float passed the reviewing stand, a proud symbol of the hard work of hundreds of thousands of brothers and sisters nationwide who had saved the Truman presidency.

EIGHT

DAWN OF THE AL HAYES ERA

Harry S. Truman wasn't the only President to take the oath of office in 1949. 360 miles away on Euclid Avenue in downtown Cleveland, after an epic strike lasting six months and eighteen days, twenty-five-year-old William W. Winpisinger was sworn in as President of Local Lodge 1363 of the International Association of Machinists.

Throughout the country, IAM members were flush with a sense of victory from their efforts on behalf of President Truman and their chosen House and Senate candidates. While 1948 had proven to be a tremendously successful year for the IAM, 1949 would turn out to be a watershed year. Events in the world and within the union would set in motion a chain of events that would shape history for the next half century and lead to Wimpy's eventual elevation to the union's highest post.

Post-war life was good for Wimpy. He had married Pearl, welcomed their infant son, Kenneth, and found a full time job in 1947. The following year, he could point to his election as Recording Secretary of Lodge 1363, the successful Truman campaign, and a World Series victory for his beloved Cleveland Indians.

The team included future hall of fame pitchers Bob Feller, Bob Lemon, and forty-two-year-old Satchel Paige, who became the first black pitcher to appear in a World Series Game. Wimpy's euphoria over the victory had hardly subsided when he had reason to rejoice again: his second child, a boy he and Pearl named William Richard Winpisinger, was born in November.

The confetti had barely been swept from the capital's streets after Truman's inaugural parade before seismic shifts began within the IAM. International President Harvey Brown, who had led the union through some of the most significant and rapid changes in its history, celebrated his sixty-fifth birthday and became the first President to fall under a mandatory retirement requirement established at the 1945 convention. Brown, described as a "stubborn, pugnacious man," had led the union for ten years. And while he had significant triumphs he could point to, such as the move into industrial organization, the establishment of the MNPL, and Truman's improbable victory, he also left a lot of hard feelings with other unions and within the IAM.

Robert Rodden, the IAM staff historian, was uncharacteristically frank:

> A plain, blunt, old-fashioned machinist, unencumbered by finesse, tact or other arts of diplomacy, Brown usually reacted like an enraged bull when opposed. To those who bored or irritated him he displayed the charm and grace of an untipped waiter. During his ten years as IP, Brown was constantly in conflict with other unions and, often, his own membership.[1]

Mark Perlman, who wrote a history of the union as part of a Harvard University labor-management study project, was a bit more charitable:

> In most respects the turbulence of the Brown administration was the result of external pressures, although... President Brown's intransigence of manner often turned mere disagreements into major crises.[2]

On his retirement, Brown was replaced by forty-nine-year-old Albert J. Hayes, the first IAM International President to be born in the twentieth century. Hayes had grown up in

Milwaukee as one of ten children of a German immigrant family. Bilingual since childhood, he changed the original German spelling of his name from "Haese," to the Americanized "Hayes."

Hayes assumed his first union position at the tender age of seventeen, when his fellow apprentice boys on the Milwaukee Railroad chose him to represent their shop committee.

George Kourpias, who would be called to work at headquarters by Hayes and later would become International President himself, recalls him as "a statesman," with a "Milwaukee accent," "a no-nonsense guy who ran a strict operation at headquarters," and "very intelligent." "When he talked, you knew that he demanded respect."[3] He was described by other contemporaries as a bright student and a gifted athlete who maintained a competitive spirit throughout his life. As International President, he inherited a membership of 518,456, down twenty-two percent from its war-time peak in 1944. While Hayes represented a quantum leap forward in equanimity and finesse from his predecessor, the man he brought in to be his chief of staff, or Resident Vice President, was more out of the Harvey Brown mold.

Forty-nine-year-old Elmer Walker was described as "six foot three, and 235 pounds of solid bones and muscle." He had joined the IAM at age eighteen through Local Lodge 121 in rough and tumble East St. Louis, and later would recall that his rise through the union ranks was due to his "two big fists, and a willingness to use them." Rodden described him:

> ...Walker was a rumbling lumbering mass of crude energy. He was built like a bull and at times literally snorted and pawed the ground like one. At a time when few machinists would utter even such mild expletives as "hell," or "damn," in front of "ladies," his speech was liberally laced with obscenities and

profanity. To Walker, this was "shop language." And
if it offended anyone, male or female, that was just
too bad.[4]

Hayes brought Walker to the union's Washington, DC, headquarters from Cleveland, where he had been General Vice President for the Great Lakes Region since 1945. Newly elected General Vice President Ernest R. White, a forty-six-year-old former railroader from San Rafael, California, who made his reputation organizing in the aircraft industry, was dispatched to the Cleveland office on the fourth floor of the National City Bank Building on Euclid Avenue to replace the volatile Walker. White was as much a departure from Walker as Hayes was from Brown. He was born in upstate New York, but moved to San Francisco as a young man. He did his apprenticeship in the Tiburon shops of the Southern Pacific Railroad, and studied nights at the Samuel Gompers Trade School, where he learned math, drafting, and metallurgy. He obligated to Local Lodge 238 in San Rafael in 1933, and was soon elected Financial Secretary of the lodge and a delegate to the Central Labor Union. By 1938, he was President of that group and was chosen to be executive secretary of the Marin County central labor body.

He began his IAM career as a Grand Lodge Representative in 1942, in San Rafael, processing Labor Board cases and organizing new members. That was a period of rapid growth for the union in California as they organized the burgeoning aircraft industry. Ernie White led successful drives at Douglas Aircraft and Lockheed Aircraft, bringing in thousands of new members. He was appointed Administrative Assistant to the highly successful and extraordinarily controversial General Vice President Roy M. Brown (no relation to former IP Harvey Brown). As Brown's top lieutenant, he helped assemble a team of bright, young, aggressive Grand Lodge Representatives who put loyalty to Brown above all else. At the 1948 Grand Lodge

Convention in Grand Rapids, Michigan, they attempted a behind the scenes coup to derail Hayes' election as International President and install Brown, but were unsuccessful. Brown used his influence the following year to put White's name in nomination for General Vice President, and he was elected on the same slate as Hayes.

George Kourpias recalled Ernie White as a slight, gentle man with thinning red hair who sometimes wore a pencil moustache, and was well-liked by the staff and the members he represented.

When Hayes brought the two-fisted Walker to Washington to watch his back, he also brought in one of Walker's protégés, Howard Tausch, to serve as Coordinator of the new IAM Automotive Department. The Grand Rapids convention, recognizing that the IAM now represented some 100,000 auto mechanics nationwide, decided it was time that automotive workers had their own unit within the union. The forty-seven-year-old Tausch had been born and raised on Cleveland's East Side, and had joined Local Lodge 1363 as an automobile mechanic in 1938. He was active in lodge affairs and had served as recording secretary, treasurer, and business representative before being appointed a Grand Lodge Representative in 1941. During the eight years he worked under Walker in Cleveland, Tausch helped organize the auto mechanics coordinating committee in the Great Lakes Region, and served as its chairman from 1942 to 1946. George Kourpias remembered Tausch as even tempered, pleasant, and soft spoken.[5]

In the spring of 1949, as musical chairs were being played in Washington and at the Great Lakes Region office in downtown Cleveland, change was coming to the Local Lodge 1363 hall as well.

Members voted to strike beginning May first for a dealership association agreement to replace the dozens of individual contracts the local had with automobile dealerships and independent garages. The dealer's association sensed an opportunity to break the union and rid themselves of their IAM contracts. They stood firm and refused to negotiate. More than one thousand members of Local 1363 set up picket lines outside dealerships across the city. The strike dragged on for weeks. New car sales flagged and repair work began to back up. The dealers wouldn't budge. Weeks turned into months. Matt DeMore, Bob Trimbel, Phil Zannella, and Wimpy made the rounds day after day, rallying the troops and shoring up the picket lines.

The financial burden on the striking members was extraordinary. The entire summer passed, and the strike entered its sixth month without any progress. Cars started to pile up on the dealer's lots as their inventory of unsold 1949 models were joined by newly arrived 1950 models in the early fall.

After six months and eighteen days, the dealers realized they were no match for the determined members of Local Lodge 1363. They capitulated and signed an association agreement that would unify collective bargaining agreements with the IAM on November 18, 1949.

Wimpy, who had been recording secretary of the local throughout the strike, formed a slate: he would run for President, and Phil Zannella would run for secretary treasurer and business agent. Both had developed deep ties with the members through the course of the battle, walking picket lines and trying time after time to negotiate an acceptable agreement. As 1949 wound to a close, the Winpisinger-Zannella slate was elected. All the pieces were in place for what would eventually prove to be Wimpy's march to the presidency of the IAM.

1949 brought new fears about "the Communist menace," when the Soviets exploded their first nuclear bomb in Kazakhstan and Mao Zedong's Communist army defeated the forces of Chiang Kai-shek (with considerable help from

Moscow) to establish the People's Republic of China.The United States and its allies countered by forming the North Atlantic Treaty Organization to help beat back the growing threat of what many feared would be Communist domination.

While still President of the IAM, Harvey Brown sounded positively eloquent and statesmanlike as he threw the union's support behind the Atlantic pact before the Senate Foreign Relations Committee. He called NATO "an essential part of our campaign for peace, our battle against war." Furthermore:

> Let us be frank about it. The Soviet dictatorship has obstructed all attempts at bringing peace to a shattered world...It is clear that in the case of a new aggressor- as in the case of Nazi Germany—control of the European continent, once achieved, would merely serve as the first step in the grand strategy of an attack on Great Britain and then the United States and the whole Western Hemisphere...no price is too high to avoid an atomic war which will wreak even greater havoc and destruction.[6]

The growing threat of Communist expansion and the possibility of another war, this time involving nuclear weapons, alarmed the American people. In an August editorial against a Communist front organization called the Civil Rights Congress, The Machinist recalled the referendum vote of IAM membership to bar Communists and their supporters from membership and referred to "this moment of near-hysteria about Communists."[7]

By mid-September 1949, the Senate had passed the NATO legislation, and all that remained to be done was to work out slight differences with the version the house had passed earlier.

On Friday, September 23, there was a special cabinet meeting at the White House. Just before 11:00 AM, a secretary rounded up members of the White House press corps and herded them into the office of Charles Ross, the President's Press Secretary. All were stunned by the news Ross delivered, a statement from President Truman confirming that Russia had the nuclear bomb. It said in part:

> I believe the American people to the fullest extent consistent with the national security are entitled to be informed of all developments in the field of atomic energy. That is my reason for making public the following information. We have evidence that within recent weeks an atomic explosion occurred in the U.S.S.R. ...[8]

The Cold War, given its name by journalist Walter Lippmann in a series of newspaper articles two years earlier, was heating up. The 1949 annual report of the American Civil Liberties Union, quoted in *The Machinist* less than a week after Truman's startling announcement, described a country "beset by fear of war, Communist expansion and espionage."[9] The ACLU warned that maintenance of civil liberties and hard won government support for collective bargaining was at serious risk as the Cold War escalated.

Exactly one week after hearing of the Soviet bomb, on October 1, 1949, Mao Zedong, leader of the Communist Red Army, declared victory and announced the formation of The People's Republic of China.

As 1949 drew to a close, the labor movement began to take decisive action to rid its ranks of Communists. The CIO, in which leftist unions had long played a prominent role, was now headed by Phil Murray, a conservative former coal miner who had been a disciple of John L. Lewis. The CIO met in Cleveland that fall and voted to ban membership by Communists and Fascists. The vast majority of the delegates to what became known as the CIO Purge Convention voted to give their executive board the power to expel the officers of any union who were Communist sympathizers and to revoke the charter of their unions. First to go was the United Electrical Workers, who had fought Matt DeMore at General Electric. They were expelled on November 1st, as was the Farm Equipment Workers union.

The IAM ended the decade with a convincing victory over the Teamsters who attempted a raid at Boeing. Members of District 751 in Seattle beat back Teamster Vice President Dave Beck, who had provided scab labor during an IAM strike against the company, by a vote of 8,107 to 4,127.

President Al Hayes, relishing the win, took a major shot at Beck: "Beck is a poor loser," Hayes said. "He isn't used to democratic procedure in which the will of the majority prevails."[10]

While the victory in Seattle was a sweet way to bring the tumultuous decade of the 1940's to a close, it proved to be a mere prelude of battles yet to come.

NINE

WIMPY FINDS A MENTOR

Wimpy started the 1950's fixing transmissions at Lake Buick, but before the decade was out, he would be using his skills to help build one of the most powerful unions in America. Day after day, people would bring their Synchro-Mesh transmissions in for repair at Lake's Lorain Avenue dealership and Wimpy and his fellow mechanics would dutifully patch them up and get them back on the road. Wimpy was a flat rate mechanic, meaning that each job was assigned a number of hours by management, say, ten hours to replace a transmission, and if he was able to get the job done in eight hours, he still got paid for ten. This arrangement suited the energetic young mechanic. He was motivated to get his work done quickly, get paid for a full day, and have time left over to attend to his duties as President of the local.

Phil Zannella, his Secretary Treasurer, had already given up his wrenches, quitting a lucrative job at McClurg Ford to become a full time business representative, tending to the needs of the local full-time. Wimpy would head downtown at the end of his workday to meet Phil and go over the business of their 1,300 member local. Despite growing membership, Local Lodge 1363 hadn't recovered fully from the strike of 1949. For months, they didn't have the funds to meet the payroll for Phil, Bob Trimbel, or their office secretary. Wimpy and Phil fought like cats and dogs over each nickel in a pattern that would characterize their fifty-year-long friendship. Phil, the pragmatic, entrepreneurial one, wanted the money safely in hand and accounted for before even the most modest expenditure. Wimpy, bold, brash, and visionary, couldn't have cared less about the details of cash flow. His philosophy was that the local needed to spend money to make money, and that somehow it would all work out in the end.

Tom Buffenbarger would later describe the duo as "Mutt and Jeff," with Wimpy pushing for an extravagant proposal and Phil always objecting:

> Phil would tell him "You're nuts. We're going to get there, but we're going to do it in a controlled way." And that is part of the wonderful thing about their relationship. It was Mutt and Jeff. It was black and white. It was pro and con. As a matter of fact, that's a good way to describe it. Wimpy would be pro something. Phil would say "Well, let's figure out how to con them into going that way."[1]

While Wimpy and Phil worked to build the local, anti-Communist hysteria in the country continued to mount. On February 9, 1950, Wisconsin Senator Joseph McCarthy, who had defeated Machinists favorite Robert M. LaFollette, Jr. to win his Senate seat, gave a speech before the Republican Women's Club of Wheeling, West Virginia, claiming Communist infiltration of the US State Department. He said infamously, "I have here in my hand a list of 205 people that were known to the Secretary of State as being members of the Communist Party, and who, nevertheless, are still working and shaping the policy of the State Department." McCarthy's charges, vehemently denied by Secretary of State Dean Acheson, set off a furor and ushered in a reign of terror that would become known as "McCarthyism." The renegade lawmaker charged more and more people with Communist complicity and used his position as Chairman of the Senate Permanent Subcommittee on Investigations to hold widely publicized hearings.

Infiltration by Communists was a major concern for the IAM in Cleveland. They had absorbed a great deal of the membership of the United Electrical Workers Union when it was kicked out of the CIO at the Cleveland Purge Convention the preceding year. CIO President Phil Murray had called the UE "the Communist Party masquerading as a labor union" at the time of their expulsion. While the IAM explicitly barred Communists from membership, telling the difference between hard line UE activists and card carrying Communists was never easy.

Fear of Communist expansion abroad was fanned on June 25, 1950, when 135,000 North Korean Army troops, armed with Soviet tanks and aircraft, streamed across the 38th Parallel and attacked the Republic of South Korea. President Truman was so alarmed by the attack that he thought at first it might be the start of a third World War. American troops first took action in defensive combat when the Army's 24th Infantry Division engaged enemy forces at Osan on July 5th. US involvement in the fighting escalated significantly on September 15, when US Marines launched an amphibious assault at Inchon. The country was back at war, a war that became known as the "Korean Conflict."

Wimpy's relatively sedate personal life was rocked in 1950 with the sudden death of his father. Things had been going well for Wimpy since the war, and he now had a job, the presidency of his union local, and a wife and two kids, with a third on the way. His parents had moved to a nice single family home on Laverne Avenue in West Park, only a couple of blocks from where he had spent his early childhood, when his father was suddenly diagnosed with lung cancer. Joe Winpisinger was forty-eight years old and still working as a printer at the Cleveland *Plain Dealer*. Shortly after receiving the news, a very depressed Joe Winpisinger took his own life rather than subject himself and his family to a long, painful demise. Family, friends, and co-workers were shocked and saddened. Associates at the *Plain*

Dealer were so moved by his death that the paper devoted their lead editorial to him on Friday September 29, 1950, under the headline "Master Craftsman":

> *A community pays tribute to men and women whose lives reflected unusual accomplishments in arts, sciences, industry, or civic leadership. No less a contribution to the general welfare does a master craftsman make, although his name is unknown beyond the limits of his craft. And such a craftsman was Joe Winpisinger, who worked at the printer's trade for some 30 years.*
>
> *We bow in tribute to Joe Winnie, as he was known to his Plain Dealer associates, in memory of two things particularly. He not only was one of the most competent men ever to be employed in the composing room, but had rare qualities of good nature. So happy was his disposition, that he took the rough edge off the rest of us in the nervous press of daily work. Death at 48 saddens all who knew him.[2]*

The Winpisinger's burden of grief over Joe's death was lightened somewhat three months later when Pearl gave birth to their third son, Michael, the day after Christmas.

The financial situation of Local Lodge 1363 began to improve gradually under Phil Zannella's watchful eye, as membership increased monthly. Phil got along famously with Matt DeMore, the District President and fellow Italian-American. DeMore was becoming a powerhouse within the union, and had been elected to its influential Law Committee in 1941. The Law Committee served as the main filter between the membership and the Grand Lodge Convention, the union's highest authority.

Local Lodges or the IAM leadership would submit all proposed constitutional changes to the five member committee, which would screen and refine them before bringing them to convention delegates for a vote. DeMore also distinguished himself by being a top notch organizer and an astute political operative. The buttoned down DeMore did not share the same warm relationship with Wimpy. They lacked the cultural bond, and the ever vocal young President of Local 1363 was never one to bow down to authority. DeMore and Zannella, while every bit as committed as Wimpy to improving things for their members, believed in a calm, orderly approach to business. DeMore was sometimes less than thrilled with the whirlwind methods, brash pronouncement, and lavish promises, which were becoming Wimpy's trademark.

While Wimpy may have had his differences with Matt DeMore, he found a kindred spirit a little farther down Euclid Avenue in the offices of the Regional Vice President, Ernie White.

Forty-six-year-old Ernest Rutledge White was cut from a different cloth than the Midwestern labor leaders. He had been born in Westfield, New York, but his family moved west when he was a small child and he grew up in San Francisco, a booming town in a booming state. And while he had gotten his start on the railroads, most of his union activity had come in the new and expanding aircraft industry. Matt DeMore, Phil Zannella, and Wimpy were all high school dropouts. White had a more formal education and an urbane manner. He was soft spoken but eloquent and a sharp dresser.

Wimpy would later recall: "He was bright, a student of almost everything, and he knew where the union came from and why."[3]

Wimpy also struck up a friendship with the man White brought in to be Grand Lodge Representative in charge of the regional office, Robert R. "Pop" Simpson.

When White and Simpson realized they needed to put on additional staff to handle the growing membership in their region and to deal with a specific problem in one of the Cleveland locals, they didn't have to look far. Wimpy had been hanging around the regional office discussing politics and social issues whenever he got the chance. White and Simpson were far more socially liberal than DeMore and Zannella. While Wimpy was loyal to his fellow District 54 members, he enjoyed the intellectual bond he developed with White and Simpson.

Wimpy learned that there was going to be an opening at the Regional Office and began to angle to get appointed to it. He faced two major hurdles. At twenty-seven years old, he was much younger than the typical appointee to the Grand Lodge staff; and Matt DeMore, who would have to offer his name to Ernie White, could barely stand him.

Wimpy huddled with Phil Zannella, and the two worked up a plan. They would refer to it in later years as their "Master Plan." Phil would do everything he could to help Wimpy work his way up through the union's ranks while remaining attached to their base in Cleveland. Wimpy, in turn, would rise as far as his ability could take him and would make Phil his consigliore, a true partner in everything he did.

Phil went to work on DeMore on Wimpy's behalf. Phil's relationship with Matt DeMore was much like the one he had with Wimpy: they fought ferociously, but at the end of the day they were as close as brothers. When Phil first floated the idea of recommending Wimpy to Ernie White for a plum job, Matt told him he was crazy. Those jobs went to men who had put in their years, kept their mouth shut and toed the line. Wimpy was zero for three under those requirements. Phil was undaunted. He turned on the charm and suddenly stopped arguing with everything Matt said. He flattered Matt shamelessly. When Matt wanted coffee, he got coffee, *and* a few choice Italian pastries. When a couple of weeks of brown nosing got him nowhere, he changed tactics. The grumpy old Phil reappeared, in spades. Nothing Matt DeMore said or did passed without Phil complaining. Things got very tense around the District 54 offices.

Finally, Matt couldn't take it anymore. He knew that Wimpy was a bright, hard working, and ambitious young man who cared deeply for the union and its members, but he could also be insufferable. He also realized that if he kept Wimpy where he was, as President of one of the largest locals in his district, not only would Wimpy be upset with him, he'd have to listen to Phil's grumbling every day. He couldn't afford to have both of these dynamic young trade unionists mad at him for eternity. He picked up the phone and called Ernie White.

TEN

ROOKIE SPECIAL REPRESENTATIVE

Wimpy's rise to a position on the Grand Lodge staff had been nothing short of meteoric. In just over three years since he had obligated to Local Lodge 1363, Wimpy had been a shop steward, recording secretary, and President of the local. He had been part of the successful 1948 election effort, the 1949 strike, and the resurgence of the lodge's membership and finances. He had formed a powerful alliance with the dynamic Phil Zannella, and had even earned the grudging respect of the influential Matt DeMore. Now he would lay down his mechanic's tools and take a position on the staff of Ernie White, a man he admired greatly not only for his dedication to the union, but also for his commitment to social progress.

White had been looking to add someone to his staff to assist in organizing and to handle a dicey situation with Local Lodge 1253, at Warner and Swasey, which manufactured lathes and machine tools and was famous worldwide for its telescopes and precision instruments. Leadership of the local had been taken over by men who refused to sign the loyalty affidavits required under the Taft-Hartley Law and who were suspected of being members of the Communist Party. The Grand Lodge took the lodge under trusteeship, meaning it assumed supervision, direction and control. White needed someone to run the local until new elections could be held.

Anti-Communist hysteria was running so high at the time that the Ohio General Assembly formed the Ohio Un-American Activities Committee, modeled on its Congressional counterpart. The committee would eventually claim that 1,300

Ohioans were members of the Communist Party, and that 700 of them lived or worked in Cleveland.

The public's anxiety level was given an extra jolt at the sight of Civil Defense fallout shelter signs that had popped up all over the city. Seemingly overnight, yellow and black signs with three intersecting triangles appeared on schools, courthouses and other public buildings. School students had their classes interrupted for "duck and cover" drills, in which they were instructed to duck under their desks and cover their eyes, a somewhat dubious means of surviving the detonation of a nuclear device. Families were encouraged to build underground blast shelters and to stockpile food and clothing so they could wait out the aftermath of an attack by the Communists.

Don Wharton, a fellow Ohioan who would later serve as General Secretary Treasurer of the IAM, recalled the situation Wimpy was faced with:

> He became a very, very close confidant of Ernie White, and Ernie would use him for a lot of special assignments, very touchy assignments. Back during that period of time, we had a lot of problems with Communist members. And the FBI would—I would meet with them a lot and they'd say, "Look, you have a Communist sympathizer we think in this plant, don't do anything about it—we just want you to be aware of it, and we want to keep track of him." And he did that with Wimpy I know because we've had discussions about it. So even though our constitution says you couldn't belong to the Communist Party, or fascism or all that, it was hard to police.[1]

Wimpy, acting his new capacity as White's emissary to the embattled local, would conduct meetings of the Warner and Swasey lodge at District 54 headquarters on Euclid Avenue, in the second floor meeting hall. Tensions ran high. When tempers flared, Wimpy would use his gift of gab to try to calm the older, more grizzled members, usually successfully. White realized the volatility of the situation and dispatched Bob Lease, an oversized, hulking mountain of a man from the regional office to watch Wimpy's back.

Don Wharton recalled what Wimpy was up against:

> That was a very rough period of time and I know several times he was threatened with bodily harm. For a while they met upstairs in the hall and they threatened to throw him down the steps and everything. And he would normally bring a couple of guys with him, but if it was an all out [fist fight] he was undermanned. Fortunately, he never really had that problem—not that I know of. He never mentioned it if he did actually have a physical fight with them. But he was close friends with Bob Lease, and they ran together quite a bit, did organizing and special projects.[2]

Wimpy knew he had a potentially explosive situation on his hands with his first assignment, but as he would throughout his career, he used his intellectual gifts and eloquent speech to calm the waters and win the members over to his side.

At the time he was reading a biography of United Mine Workers President John L. Lewis and took some solace at the fact that the situation he faced, while dangerous, was nothing compared to what Lewis had survived. "John L. Lewis had an influence on me," he recalled later. "He was aggressive, had the ability to turn a phrase to fit every situation, tough minded and unbounded by all the traditional horseshit, including the National Guard. That's what I admired about him: stand your ground for better or worse."[3]

Wimpy's ability to stand his ground was put to the test one night at a local meeting in Toledo. His oldest son, Ken Winpisinger, remembered:

> ...one time [he told] me he was at a local lodge meeting...it may have been Toledo...He got up and was talking. Some guy didn't like what he was saying and they got in a big argument. The next thing you know he said the guy had a gun in his face. He said he didn't back off. I don't know if it was Phil Zannella or one of those guys was there and witnessed it and said he couldn't believe it, because my father just stood there and kept arguing with the guy.[4]

By October 1951, Wimpy and Pearl's cramped apartment was too small to house their growing brood. Wimpy was also concerned about his mother, Edith, living alone after the tragedy of her husband's death. He eventually convinced Pearl to make room for Edith, who, like Pearl, had a strong personality. Pearl's condition was that they find a two-family house.

After searching through the area, Wimpy found just the ticket, a three story wood frame two family house at the corner of Cooley Avenue and West 132nd Street. The house was a "double house," meaning Wimpy, Pearl, and the kids could live on the first floor, and Edith could live in a separate unit on the second floor. 13201 Cooley Avenue, which would be home to the Winpisinger family for the next decade, was a charming little house with bay windows on each floor that overlooked a park across the street. It was an older house and would provide Wimpy ample opportunity to show off his skills as a handyman.

Once he got his family settled, Wimpy was on the road a lot, organizing and handling special projects for Ernie White throughout the IAM Great Lakes region, which stretched from Ohio to Michigan and Pennsylvania. His son, Mike Winpisinger, later recalled:

> Once my dad went to work for the union, which was before I was a year old, we very, very rarely ever saw him. He was on the road quite a bit. Then when he was home, it might be like he was there when we got up Saturday morning, and then he would be gone Sunday afternoon.[5]

With Wimpy on the road, Pearl was left at home with the three boys and her mother-in-law. Edith Winpisinger, who had worked in an airplane factory in the First World War and who had effectively raised her brothers and sisters from a young age after her alcoholic father disappeared, was now helping raise Wimpy's children.

Ken Winpisinger remembered her:

> [She was] a strict disciplinarian. A lot of the values my father had directly came from my grandmother. She had a lot of character; a lot of the things that make up character, she had the best and most of it and tried to instill it upon her children. When they weren't listening, she'd bat them upside the head so they would listen…She took a dim view of people that didn't adhere to a good work ethic, didn't display a lot of truthfulness and trustworthiness and stick-to-it-ivness. She had a way of presenting these character things to people and make them aware of them and strive to attain them.[6]

Mike Winpisinger's recollections of his grandmother were similar:

> She was very strong-willed. She was very strict. There was one way that things were going to be done, and that was her way. She was the original "Do it my way or hit the highway," and she didn't put up with a lot of shenanigans.[7]

Pearl Winpisinger, now twenty-four years old, did her best to keep the home fires burning and the kids under control while Wimpy traveled. She did not have her driver's license, so grocery shopping and errands required walking a few blocks to the shops on Lorain Avenue, usually pushing a stroller with the two older boys in tow.

During his absence from family life, Wimpy was cutting his teeth as an organizer and helping the union strive to meet its goal of a million members. George Kourpias remembered:

> He worked hard at his job. It was twenty four hours a day. I remember once when he was given an assignment to organize a plant. He went in. They were hiring, and the company had no idea he was a union organizer. He went in and filled out an application. They hired him. He spent the next month, without anybody knowing he was a union organizer, convincing people they ought to have a union in there, and they finally got the union in the plant.[8]

While Wimpy was organizing and doing special projects for Ernie White, a major change took place in the American labor movement. Sixty-six-year-old Philip Murray, the President of the CIO, passed away on November 9, 1952, and was replaced by forty-five-year-old Walter Reuther, President of the United Auto Workers. Reuther, a dedicated socialist and one of the founders of Americans for Democratic Action, was the son of a German immigrant. He lost his job at the Ford Motor Company during the Great Depression, and he and his two brothers moved to the Soviet Union, where they got jobs at a Gorky car manufacturing plant. After two years in Russia, the Reuther's returned to Detroit. Walter Reuther denounced Communism, but remained a committed socialist. He ran for the Detroit City Council in 1937, as a member of that party and lost. A few years later, attracted by the socially progressive agenda of President Franklin D. Roosevelt, he switched his allegiance to the Democratic Party.

Late in his life, Wimpy recalled Reuther fondly:

> *I admired Walter Reuther because of his social views. I thought the mission of the labor movement ought to be looking out for the guy who didn't have it so good. That's what we're all about. And just because you advance your membership nominally out of those ranks doesn't mean you ought to forget about them. You have a social conscience in terms of what you're doing and drag others along with you if you can. There's nobody else to talk for them. Reuther was also very innovative. He always figured out some way to develop some program to take care of a need that was identified among his members. I admired that in him too.*[9]

Twelve days after Reuther replaced Murray at the CIO, seventy-nine-year-old William Green, the President of the AFL, also passed away. Green's replacement was fifty-eight-year-old George Meany, who had gotten his start as business agent for Local 463 of the New York City Plumber's Union. He was steadfastly anti-Communist and had been head of the New York state Federation of Labor before being chosen to replace Green.

Wimpy and Ernie White continued to organize and to battle Communist infiltration of their union. While Wimpy had no use for communists, he was decidedly more liberal than the average union organizer. Don Wharton recalled how Wimpy, who was fast establishing credentials as a socialist in the Reuther mold, reconciled his political beliefs with the job of ousting communists:

> I don't think he felt those members were in there for any reason other than their own cause. They weren't in there trying to benefit our membership, and that's all Wimpy looked at—the benefit of our own members and the American people. He really—if you had your own agenda, then he had no use for you.[10]

Wimpy also admired Ernie White's willingness to stand up for social justice, even in the face of the anti-Communist hysteria. Late in his life, he said of White:

> He was the only one who put up a fight to keep the "class struggle" clause in the IAM constitution when all the rest of us were cowed under the pressure of "Commies talk like that," and "That's a Commie expression from yesteryear, and it ought to come out." Bullshit! He was right. We're still involved in the class struggle. We're in it up to our eyeballs every day.[11]

Wimpy and Pearl welcomed their fourth child, Vickie, in August 1953, one day after the Armistice ending the Korean Conflict was signed. Wimpy tried to buy Pearl an automobile, hoping she would finally learn how to drive so she wouldn't have to walk everywhere with the kids, but she would have none of it. The following year, Wimpy was thrilled when his beloved Indians advanced, albeit unsuccessfully, to the World Series and the Cleveland Browns won the National Football League playoffs.

He was less than thrilled at a spectacle he and the rest of the nation watched on television that spring and summer. Both ABC and the DuMont network broadcast gavel to gavel coverage of the hearings Senator Joseph McCarthy held to investigate actions taken by the US Army. McCarthy's aide, G. David Schine, had been drafted. When McCarthy's Chief Counsel, Roy M. Cohn, began trying to influence the Army to give Schine special privileges, he was rebuffed. McCarthy was outraged and claimed the Army was holding Schine "hostage" because of the actions the Senator had taken to expose Communists in the military ranks. The hearings were broadcasted for thirty-six days, covering 188 hours of television. 20,000,000 Americans watched with rapt attention as Senators plowed through mountains of testimony, taped telephone conversations, and fake memos.

The spectacle climaxed on June 9, 1954, when Joseph N. Welch, a Boston lawyer representing one of the witnesses, took umbrage at McCarthy's attack on one his young associates, and confronted the Wisconsin Senator. "Until this moment, Senator, I think I never gauged your cruelty or recklessness... Have you no sense of decency, sir, at long last? Have you no sense of decency?" The question struck like a lightning bolt. It crystallized what the majority of Americans felt about McCarthy and his tactics. It was a question many Americans had been dying to ask.

These events solidified Wimpy's anti-authoritarian beliefs and were a watershed in his political education:

If I had any lingering doubts, they were totally dispelled when I witnessed the outrage of McCarthyism. To

brutalize citizens of this country, not withstanding
our provisions for free speech and free expression
just because they wanted to listen to someone else
speak out on what they viewed as injustice just drove
me right up the wall. I made a solemn vow then that
never would I shrink from the responsibility to say
what was on my mind in any given situation whether
I was a worker in a shop, steward, a local union
officer, anything else.[12]

In March 1955, in one of the final assignments he would fulfill as an assistant to White, Wimpy helped oust the Communist-dominated United Electrical Workers from two Michigan Whirlpool factories. After a hard fought campaign at the company's Benton Harbor and St. Joseph plants, members voted 1,317 to 702 for IAM representation. One of the organizers explained the reason for the IAM's overwhelming victory:

The UE makes a mockery of union democracy.
While Whirlpool employees sought to enforce their
contract, eliminate speed-ups and hold incentive
rates, UE officers spent the union's funds and energies
circulating phony Communist 'peace' petitions and in
supporting other Red causes.[13]

Ernie White was jubilant at the victory, which he called "One of the year's most important victories for American trade unions."[14]

After four years of organizing, strategizing, and fighting off Communists while also standing up for social progress and collective bargaining rights, Wimpy was about to make a huge leap forward in his union career.

ELEVEN

CALLED TO WASHINGTON

International President Al Hayes was shaking things up in Washington and always on the lookout for new talent and young blood to revitalize the leadership of the union. He preached his sermon of growth and progress from coast to coast, saying, "A labor union cannot afford to stand still, and the IAM is not going to be content to remain at its present size."[1]

One of the most fertile areas for growth was in the automotive field, where about 1,000,000 people worked at repairing or servicing vehicles without union representation. Automotive Coordinator Howard Tausch, a Cleveland native who had gone to Washington at the beginning of the Hayes administration, needed someone to run a new joint organizing venture with the Teamsters. This was to be one of the union's highest priorities, a significant chance to increase membership and expand their presence in the automotive industry. He needed someone visionary and energetic, yet tough enough to hold his own with the rough and tumble Teamsters. After careful consideration, he chose the thirty-one-year-old William W. Winpisinger as his man.

The IAM was the leading union in the automotive field, but they had been sparring off and on with the International Brotherhood of Teamsters for more than two decades, sometimes operating under jurisdictional agreement with them and sometimes not. When the IAM, increasingly upset over the failure of the AFL to adequately police this and other jurisdictional disputes, disaffiliated from the federation in 1943, the Teamsters immediately pounced on the opportunity and announced they would begin organizing garage mechanics.

The IAM—Teamster battle for automotive industry workers was the fiercest contest between the two titan unions since they had fought over Dave Beck's attempt to raid the IAM's workers in the Seattle aircraft industry in the late 1940's. With so many potential new members to be had, the stakes were enormous.

The Teamsters were growing rapidly, consolidating their hold on the trucking and vending machine industries. Membership, which stood at 75,000 in 1933, had reached 1,200,000 by 1953. Their efforts to grab auto mechanics from the IAM were met with swift and effective resistance at every turn.

In Cleveland, the Teamsters had been organized since 1912, and were a respected member of the Cleveland Federation of Labor. Their leader in the early decades, Edward Murphy, was regarded as tough but honest as he led his union in organizing drives in the laundry, dry cleaning, beverage and newspaper industries. Murphy was a scrupulous trade unionist who did not allow organized crime to get a foothold in the Cleveland union as they had with Dave Beck in Seattle or with Jimmy Hoffa in Detroit. That changed in 1950, when Murphy died and the union was taken over by Bill Presser.

Presser and his partner, a Mafia-connected plug ugly named Louis (Babe) Triscaro, were bad news. Presser was a short, rotund man with thick hands and a jowly face. He had made a name for himself by "organizing" the juke box and vending machine industry in Cleveland and other Ohio cities. His methods included beatings, bombings and vandalism.

Presser and twelve others were indicted by a federal grand jury on June 20, 1951, under the Sherman Anti-Trust Act, for fixing prices in Cleveland's lucrative candy and tobacco trades. He was moving at the time to affiliate his vending machine workers union with the Teamsters and, through the intervention of Dave Beck and Jimmy Hoffa, was granted a Teamster charter despite the pending federal charges.

James Neff, who chronicled the ties of the Presser family to organized crime in his 1989 book, *Mobbed Up*, described Triscaro and his relationship with Presser:

> *Triscaro was a 1931 Golden Gloves flyweight champ, short, with quick hands, slick black hair and olive skin. He held himself ramrod straight, looking taller, and commanded respect. Triscaro and Presser worked as partners. When one of them needed to deal with the underworld, Presser handled members of the Jewish syndicate while Triscaro met with the Mayfield Road Gang, later called the Cleveland Mafia.*[2]

Once he had the Teamster imprimatur, Presser began to branch out beyond Cleveland. An effort in Akron, described by Neff, was typical:

> *One victim of Presser's Akron racket was Robert Holland, who owned Leslie's Sandwich Shop, a small storefront, and the popular Sea Gull Restaurant, a larger sit down place. Presser's Local 410-A insisted that Holland join the union. Holland was also pressured to pay dues to the newly formed Summit County Vending Machine Operators Association, also formed by Presser. Holland refused to do either.*
>
> *On April 15, 1952, at about one-thirty in the morning, a stink bomb was hurled through the window of Holland's Akron home. Holland realized that the racketeers meant business and notified the police. The assistant chief of the Akron Police, John F. Struzenski, assigned detectives to investigate. Within*

hours they had linked Presser and his new union to
the violence.³

By 1953, Bill Presser had managed to consolidate his power
in the Cleveland Teamsters union and was elected President of
Joint Council 41. Babe Triscaro was his vice president.

When Presser, who was always hungry for new territory,
took a run at the Cleveland IAM automotive shops, he ran into
a buzz saw by the name of Phil Zannella.

Tom Buffenbarger recalled what happened:

> They started after the Cleveland dealerships,
> represented by the Machinists. One in particular
> was Marshall Ford. Sam Marshall and Phil Zannella
> had been—they were friends...Anyway, they came
> after him. Phil called [Presser] saying, "Your locals are
> going after one of my dealerships. I don't think you
> want to do that." And Presser says, "Well, what the
> fuck are you going to do about it?" He [Zannella]
> says, "For every member you take of mine, I'm going
> to take five of yours." And he [Presser] says, "Well,
> we'll see about that." About 1,000 members later, Bill
> Presser called and said: "We're out of the automotive
> business."⁴

And so it went across the country. Not everyone was as
successful as Phil Zannella at holding off Teamster raids, but
the IAM managed to more than hold their own. Eventually,
the Teamsters decided that the IAM were better as partners
than as competitors. There were lots of jobs to organize in
the automotive industry and the two unions gradually came to
an understanding that jobs involving assembly or repair were
Machinists jobs and those involving less skill, such as moving,
fueling, or polishing vehicles, should belong to the Teamsters. In
1949, the two unions embarked on a number of coordinated

efforts at auto dealerships across the country and were often met with stiff resistance.

They won a drive in Boston in 1950 at Fuller Cadillac Olds, a huge dealership owned by former Republican Governor Alvin T. Fuller. Fuller refused to bargain, took a strike, and hired thugs from a private detective agency to harass strikers and escort scabs across picket lines. Before long, Secretary of Labor Maurice J. Tobin, himself a former Governor of Massachusetts and a Democrat, called for the FBI to investigate Fuller's aggressive anti-union tactics.

When the IAM and the Teamsters attempted to organize auto dealerships in Nevada, a group calling itself the "Nevada Citizens Committee," and representing resisting employers, sprang into action. According to contemporary accounts, they were "inciting lynch mobs, threatening to tar and feather union men, putting pressure on fair employers to stop recognizing legitimate unions and threatening public officials."[5]

As the IAM ramped up its automotive industry organizing and began to seriously entertain thoughts of a partnership with the Teamsters, the question of whether or not to re-affiliate with the American Federation of Labor loomed large. By the end of 1950, Al Hayes knew the IAM would be better off back inside the federation, particularly if they could get ironclad assurances that their jurisdictions would be enforced by the federation.

IAM historian Robert Rodden wrote the following:

> ...Hayes intended, from the minute he took office, to take the IAM back to its traditional home in the AFL. Like most craft trade unionists of his generation Hayes was emotionally attached to the memory of the incomparable Gompers. He had not only grown up in the House of Labor but, man and boy, had fought side by side with other AFL unions against

*enemies ranging from the NAM and the NMTA to
the IWW and the CIO.[6]*

The membership of the IAM voted by a four-to-one margin
to re-affiliate with the AFL in December 1950.

Now, three years later, a formal jurisdictional agreement
was hammered out with the Teamsters, and signed February
4, 1953, by Hayes and Teamster President Dave Beck. It was
an odd pairing of two former adversaries. Hayes and Beck had
fought a fierce battle for aircraft industry workers in Seattle,
and the usually diplomatic Hayes had let go with a verbal
broadside against Beck, then a Teamster Vice President, when
it was over.

The two unions plowed ahead with their joint committee
under the agreement, signing contracts in many cities, including
Kansas City, St. Louis, and Anchorage.

In September 1955, Hayes and Beck decided to take the
relationship a step further and signed another agreement to
enlarge the joint committee and establish a central office called
the "Teamster and IAM Automotive Coordinating Office."

Each union contributed $100,000 to finance the effort,
to be overseen by Howard Tausch and Harold Thirion, the
Teamster's Director of the Building Materials and Construction
Drivers Division. Members of the committee included Wimpy's
current boss, Ernie White from the Great Lakes Territory,
Machinists General Vice President P.L. Siemiller from Chicago,
and Teamster Vice President Jimmy Hoffa. Tausch asked Ernie
White to assign Wimpy to the project, and White complied.

Wimpy was headed to Washington. He had to move quickly
once he got the call, because this was a top priority for the
union. He left Pearl, the kids and his mother in Cleveland and
took a small apartment in Washington, commuting home on
weekends.

The Coordinating Office got right to work. Before long, victories were recorded and contracts negotiated in Jamestown and Rochester, New York, and in Philadelphia. Some old animosities lingered, but the Coordinating Committee had enough muscle with White, Siemiller, and Hoffa to prod any reluctant field representatives into action.

By July 1956, the Coordinating Office had won first round victories in Eureka, California, and Portland, Oregon. A successful campaign had led to a strike against dealerships in Galesburg, Illinois, when the dealers refused to recognize the unions.

IAM and Teamster organizers developed plans for drives in San Antonio and Dallas, Texas, and St. Louis, Missouri.

One of the benefits of having a Coordinating Committee was that grievances and disputes between the two unions could be hammered out quickly. When the committee held its quarterly meeting at Washington's DuPont Plaza Hotel on July 18, 1956, they took up concerns raised by members in cities across the country, including Baltimore, Omaha, Buffalo, Newark, Los Angeles, Racine, Wisconsin, and Cheyenne, Wyoming.

The Machinists were fully committed to the alliance and adopted a resolution at their 1956 Grand Lodge Convention in San Francisco directing:

> Automotive lodges everywhere shall join state and central bodies and other local councils where possible, thereby getting acquainted with officials of other unions, particularly the Teamsters locals, so that we may get cooperation in fulfilling the pact between the Teamsters International and the IAM.[7]

Wimpy began traveling the country extensively, meeting with local leaders from both unions and encouraging organizing campaigns wherever possible.

1955, the year Wimpy arrived in Washington from Cleveland, had been an excellent time for an ambitious young labor activist to make it to the big time. One of the most significant labor events of the twentieth century, the merger of the American Federation of Labor and its long time rival the Congress of Industrial Organizations, took place February 9, 1955, in Miami, Florida. Al Hayes, a member of the AFL Executive Council, hailed the move as "One of the greatest accomplishments by the organized labor movement in all the years of its history," and proclaimed "This merger will have a profound and substantial effect on the standards of life of the people of the United States, and by the example it sets, on other free peoples of the world."[8]

George Meany, the President of the AFL, was chosen to head the combined organization. Walter Reuther, who had been President of the CIO, would become Executive Vice President, and would continue to serve as International President of the powerful United Automobile Workers union.

Reuther, an avowed Socialist, but staunchly anti-Communist, took the occasion of the merger to point out the benefits to democracy:

> At this time in our history when this country and all the free world are beset by the challenge of Soviet Communist totalitarianism, a united labor movement will best be able to mobilize the working men and women of this country toward the defense of our free institutions and toward the development of full employment and greater security for all the people.[9]

Three months after the AFL-CIO merger, the IAM took a significant step of its own, laying the cornerstone for a new headquarters building at 1300 Connecticut Avenue in Washington, DC. The new ten story building, located six blocks from the White House, on a site previously occupied by the British embassy, was slated to cost $2,500,000. It would rise 110 feet above Connecticut, N, and 19th Streets, and would provide 110,140 square feet of workspace, three ground level stores, a 256 seat auditorium, and parking for thirty-six cars. It would replace the Machinists Building at 9th and Mt. Vernon Place, which the union had occupied for the preceding thirty-six years. That building, which had cost $374,807 to build in 1920, would fetch $750,000 when it was sold.

Far from Washington, two events that would spark the Civil Rights Movement took place in 1955. In August, in rural Mississippi, an African-American boy from Chicago was murdered in brutal fashion while visiting his cousins. Fourteen-year-old Emmett Till was abducted and killed by two white men in their thirties who claimed that the child had been fresh to the wife of one of the men. They savagely beat him, cut off one of his ears, gouged out an eye, and shot him repeatedly with a .45 caliber pistol. They then tied a seventy-five pound weight around his neck and threw his body off a bridge into the Tallahatchie River. Till's outraged and grieving mother insisted that his casket be left open during his wake so that the world could see the inhuman brutality to which he had been subjected.

Four months later, forty-two-year-old Rosa Parks, a worker at a department store in downtown Montgomery, Alabama, made history when she refused to yield her seat on the Cleveland Avenue bus to a white person. Montgomery's busses were strictly racially segregated by law, but when bus driver James Blake demanded that Parks give up her seat, she refused and was arrested. That sparked outrage in Montgomery's African-American community and led to a boycott of the city's bus system organized by a young preacher from the Dexter Avenue Baptist Church named Martin Luther King, Jr.

Wimpy's career in Washington, off to a fast start at a fascinating time, nearly came to a halt less than two years after it started, through no fault of his own. The IAM's partner in the Coordinating Committee organizing automotive workers, the International Brotherhood of Teamsters, underwent massive changes and became the most infamous labor union in history. Beck was ousted as president, replaced by the equally nefarious Jimmy Hoffa. Congressional hearings soon established unmistakable links between the union and the Mafia. The Teamsters resorted to their old tricks and begin raiding IAM at breweries. But Wimpy had no way of knowing all that lurked just around the corner as he scrambled around the country trying to make the coordinated campaign a success.

George Kourpias later recalled:

> I was president of our district lodge, still working at the plant in Sioux City. We got a letter from Howard Tausch, or maybe it was Al Hayes, that said William Winpisinger would be coming to Sioux City as a test pilot to organize the mechanics of Sioux City. Because in Iowa we had [organized] Des Moines, and we had the Omaha area, Council Bluffs. We had the Quad Cities, but we didn't have the auto mechanics in Sioux City. So I was getting ready to meet this guy. The day that he was to come in, we got a telegram from Al Hayes telling us the agreement between the Teamsters and the Machinists is now declared null and void because of the Hoffa situation.[10]

Once again, Wimpy's fate was about to turn on a dime.

TWELVE

THE TEAMSTERS AND THE AFL-CIO

Complicated. That was the best word to describe the relationship between the International Brotherhood of Teamsters and the IAM. The two largest affiliates from the AFL, now both members of the umbrella AFL-CIO, were growing rapidly and constantly adding new members and new areas of jurisdiction. Wimpy's latest project, to which each union donated $100,000 (when the per capita annual income in the country was $1,881), was one of several cooperative efforts.

In 1955, IAM General Vice President Paul LeRoy Siemiller, known to his contemporaries as Roy, had negotiated a deal with the Teamsters to cooperate on vending machines. It was a billion and a half dollar a year industry, employing nearly 300,000 people. The majority of machines, dispensing everything from cigarettes, candy, and soft drinks to sandwiches and hosiery, were located in factories, many of which were under IAM contracts. The Teamsters wanted a monopoly on supplying the machines and their contents, and the Machinists wanted exclusive jurisdiction over their production.

Siemiller, assigned to Chicago as the Midwestern States General Vice President, struck a deal with William M. Griffin, Director of the Teamster's National Miscellaneous Division. The IAM would instruct its shop chairmen and stewards to raise hell if the machines in their plants weren't furnished and serviced by the Teamsters. The Teamsters would in turn refuse to install any machine that did not have the IAM label conspicuously displayed. Within months, vending machine companies started including the IAM logo on their machines, and manufacturers who didn't have an IAM contract scrambled to get one.

IAM districts, councils, and locals across the country were being directed and urged by their leadership to cooperate with their brothers and sisters from the Teamsters on automobile dealership organizing and vending machines.

The two outsized and rapidly growing organizations, which had fought bitter battles over jurisdiction in the aircraft industry, breweries, and the automotive industry seemed to be cooperating with one another more and more with each passing month. But before Wimpy and his fellow auto industry organizers could get fully established in their new jobs, things began to change.

Six months after the merger of the AFL and the CIO, the new federation's Executive Council established a Committee on Ethical Practices. It was vitally important to the success of the new combined organization that they be perceived as completely untainted by Communism or corruption.

Allegations of ties to Communism had long been the bane of organized labor, and most unions, especially the IAM, had taken extensive steps to rid themselves of any Communist infiltrators. That didn't stop anti-labor organizations such as the National Association of Manufacturers or the National Metal Trades Association from hurling accusations at every turn, hoping to weaken the labor movement by tarnishing their public image. With anti-Communism hysteria running rampant in the nation, no labor organization, particularly the governing federation, could afford even a whiff of scandal about their loyalties to the United States.

The third rail for labor was corruption, or more specifically, association with organized crime.

A Pulitzer Prize winning series of newspaper articles from 1948, called "Crime on the Waterfront," was made into what turned out to be the motion picture of the year in 1954. The series, written by Malcolm Johnson for the *New York Sun*, ran for twenty-four days on the paper's front page. It detailed the inner workings of the New York City docks, the Longshoreman's Union, and their direct ties to gangsters Charles ("Lucky") Luciano, Frank Costello, and Meyer Lansky.

The newspaper articles, which brought Johnson the 1949 Pulitzer for local reporting, could not compare with the public outcry that accompanied release of the movie. Director Elia Kazan used an all star cast including Marlon Brando, Rod Steiger, Eva Marie Saint, Lee J. Cobb, and Carl Malden to paint a brutal picture of crime and violence perpetrated on working people by unscrupulous "labor bosses" who were under the thumb of mobsters. The film was a national sensation and won five academy awards, including best motion picture.

The AFL-CIO leadership realized that the perception of infiltration by organized crime was just as dangerous as allegations of sympathizing with Communists. They pledged to adopt a code of ethics and rid themselves of any bad actors. George Meany, the AFL-CIO President, needed a man of unquestionable integrity to head the Ethical Practices Committee. He chose IAM International President Al Hayes.

Years earlier, the IAM had developed an ethics code of its own that covered the conduct of union officers. Hayes would now lead a five-member committee to come up with the rules: himself; David Dubinsky, President of the International Ladies Garment Workers Union; Joe Curran, President of the National Maritime Union; Joseph Portofsky, President of the Amalgamated Clothing Workers; and George Harrison, President of the Brotherhood of Railway Clerks.

Hayes outlined his charge in explaining his new role to the membership of the IAM:

> What labor should do in the field of ethical practices is, of course, to rid itself of every vestige of persons or practices which tend to pervert a union, at any level of organization, from the fundamental reason

*for existence. That reason is the economic and social
well-being of its members and the community at
large.[1]*

Over the course of the next year, the Ethical Practices
Committee came up with five codes that the federation
adopted.

The first dealt with issuing local union charters by national
and international affiliates of the AFL-CIO. Prior to its adoption,
some unions had issued charters to individuals, rather than
to organized groups, resulting in widespread abuse and the
creation of so-called "paper locals."

The second concerned the administration of health and
welfare funds. Since many unions had negotiated generous
benefit packages for their members, the size of these funds was
growing at a phenomenal rate. The possibility for financial
catastrophe due to mismanagement was at least as great as
the threat of criminal fraud.

The third code cut right to the chase: "Safeguarding the
labor movement against exploitation by racketeers, crooks,
Communists, and fascists."

The fourth defined conflicts of interest on the part of labor
union officials. It was no longer acceptable to hold a union
job and also work for the insurance company that wrote the
policies for the union, nor was it appropriate to receive a kick-
back from contractors or vendors.

The final code dealt with the financial practices of unions
and required all affiliates to keep their members informed
about how their funds were managed and invested.

The codes were adopted by a unanimous vote of the
Ethical Practices Committee and submitted to the AFL-CIO
Executive Committee, which also gave its unanimous approval.
The Executive Council then empowered the Ethical Practices
Committee "to take the initiative in making preliminary

inquiries into situations involving corruption, Communism and Fascism, and to recommend formal investigations to the Executive Council."[2]

The AFL-CIO's concern about the taint of corruption proved quite timely. In the United State Senate, Arkansas Democrat John L. McClellan, Chairman of the Senate Permanent Subcommittee on Investigations, no doubt also influenced at least in part by the public outcry over *On the Waterfront*, had begun to sniff around about organized crime in the labor movement. His interest and that of his young, aggressive, chief counsel, Robert F. Kennedy, was piqued by an investigation they conducted in 1956 into dishonesty and corruption in clothing procurement for the military.

In his book *The Enemy Within*, Bobby Kennedy recounted how they got started:

> As we continued our investigative work, we found that some of the leading East Coast gangsters, Albert Anastasia, Johnny Dio and his brother Tommy, and others, were involved directly or indirectly in the manufacturing or trucking of uniforms. We found corruption, violence, extortions permeated all their activities.
>
> We heard from Johnny Dio in executive session in May of 1956 and knew from information furnished us by District Attorney Frank Hogan in New York that other racketeers had muscled into the labor movement in that area. Clark Mollenhoff, Washington correspondent for the Cowles Publications and perhaps the nation's best-informed reporter in the field of labor-management corruption, told me racketeers had moved into the Teamsters Union in the Midwest and elsewhere in the country.[3]

By the end of 1956, their investigation had taken them to Seattle, to Dave Beck's doorstep. Information they uncovered there led to the Chicago offices of a shadowy figure by the name of Nathan W. Shefferman. Using a Senate subpoena, they pried Shefferman's financial records loose from his bank.

Shocked by what they found, the Senate took immediate action. It formed the Senate Select Committee on Improper Activities in the Labor or Management Field, with McClellan as Chairman. Bobby Kennedy would be Chief Counsel to the committee, whose other members were his brother, Massachusetts Senator John F. Kennedy, and Senators Sam Ervin of North Carolina, Karl Mundt of South Dakota, Irving Ives of New York, Pat McNamara of Michigan, Barry Goldwater from Arizona, and the discredited but still active Senator Joseph R. McCarthy of Wisconsin.

The committee was funded to the tune of $350,000 for their first year and held their first meeting on January 31, 1957. The AFL-CIO acted quickly, hoping to head off or minimize any damage. *The Machinist*, the IAM's award winning weekly newspaper, published an article headlined "AFL-CIO Pushes War on Rackets." It began, "The AFL-CIO Executive Council cleared the decks last week for a full-scale war on any bums, boodle boys and bomb throwers who may be using labor organizations as fronts for crime and communism."[4]

The investigation and resulting fall-out would ultimately lead to the resignation of Dave Beck, the rise of Jimmy Hoffa, the expulsion of the Teamsters from the AFL-CIO, and the end of Wimpy's joint organizing campaign.

Al Hayes and Dave Beck had virtually nothing in common except their status as union presidents. Hayes was trim, prim and proper. He comported himself as a gentleman, dressed modestly and rarely raised his voice. Hayes was scrupulously honest and had once fired a staff member for merely accepting a patio chair from a company where the IAM had a contract.

Beck, on the other hand, was flabby, flashy, and flamboyant. His hometown newspaper, the *Seattle Post Intelligencer*, described him as "A jowly, balding man with a temper…a cross between world leaders Nikita Khrushchev and Dwight D. Eisenhower… He didn't drink or smoke but could shout down opposition on the street or in the courtroom in a thunderous manner, his oratory well-spiced with four letter words."[5]

Hayes and Beck had crossed swords in Seattle when the Teamsters tried a raid at Boeing in 1948. A grueling and contentious two year battle ensued and left a very bitter taste in Hayes' mouth for Beck's tactics.

Some of Beck's exploits in his rise to power in the Teamsters were described in David Witwer's book, *Corruption and Reform in the Teamsters Union*:

> *Beck set up collusive agreements with associations of small businessmen. In the laundry industry, for instance, he encouraged formation of an association of laundry owners, which would limit competition in the areas of price expansion. Beck agreed to use his Teamsters to police the laundry industry for this association in return for a solid collective bargaining agreement. He worked out the same type of agreement in other industries—garage owners, bakers, milk dealers, and still others. As had been the case with Teamster leaders from Al Young to Charlie Green, this kind of arrangement had a very hard edge. Violent incidents involving recalcitrant employers often accompanied Beck's organizing campaigns.[6]*

Beck, who was six years older than Hayes, became president of the Teamsters in 1952. Hayes realized the benefits of joint IAM-Teamster efforts in the automotive and vending machine industries and set aside any lingering personal animosity long enough to sit down and sign at least two cooperative agreements with him.

Now, however, as Chairman of the AFL-CIO's Committee on Ethical Practices, Hayes would have to sit across the table from Beck once again, and the outcome wouldn't be as pleasant.

As the McClellan Committee held hearings to delve into the improprieties Bobby Kennedy's investigation uncovered, they prepared to call Beck as a witness. Beck fled to Europe. The committee carried on with other work, grilling witnesses who detailed Beck's corruption, including using union funds to improve his personal home by installing a swimming pool, building his son a house, and "borrowing" nearly half a million dollars in cash from the Teamster's Western Conference fund. Beck finally returned to Seattle from his European excursion but sent word to McClellan that his doctors had advised him he was too ill to travel to Washington to testify. Meanwhile, the Teamster records that would have demonstrated Beck's wrongdoing disappeared. Union officials explained that the records had been stored in a basement and someone must have accidentally thrown them out.

With the records gone, Beck felt it was safe to return to Washington. As soon as the committee found out that he was available, they set a date of March 26, 1957, to hear his testimony.

Thirteen days before Beck was to appear, Teamster Vice President Jimmy Hoffa was arrested in Washington for trying gain an edge in the hearings by bribing a committee staffer, John "Cye" Cheasty, to provide him with inside information. Hoffa had approached Cheasty, an attorney, with a promise to provide him with $1,000 cash, and another $2,000 per month if he would get a job on the staff of the committee and pass along documents and confidential plans. Cheasty instead told Bobby Kennedy about the offer. Kennedy gave Cheasty the job, then provided him with false information to pass to Hoffa. Hoffa and Cheasty met under the watchful eye of the FBI. Cheasty passed along the bogus information, and Hoffa handed him $2,000 in cash. The FBI then swooped in and placed the red-faced Hoffa under arrest.

When he made his initial appearance before the committee, Dave Beck repeatedly invoked the Fifth Amendment of the Constitution as Senator McClellan and Bobby Kennedy started to grill him. The hearing degenerated into a shouting match, with Beck screaming that he was protecting the highest interests of American Democracy by his refusal to testify. Bobby Kennedy, not in the least cowed by Beck's bluster, calmly forced him to admit that, as a regent of the University of Washington eleven years earlier, Beck had denounced some faculty members who had taken the Fifth during an investigation into their possible Communist ties, saying, "Americans who live the American way of life do not have to hide behind technicalities."[7]

The AFL-CIO had a rule explicitly prohibiting union officials from taking the Fifth when testifying about union affairs. When Beck stonewalled the committee, AFL-CIO President George Meany sprang into action and called for a special meeting of the federation's Executive Council three days later.

The Executive Council suspended Beck as an AFL-CIO Vice President and Executive Council member, and instructed the Ethical Practices Committee to initiate an investigation. Al Hayes set May 6 as the date for a hearing. Meany then called for another Executive Council meeting two weeks after Hayes' hearing to give Beck and the Teamsters an opportunity to present a defense.

Beck and the Teamsters were furious. The Teamsters board met in Galveston, Texas, on April 16 and fired off a letter to Meany and Hayes challenging his suspension and calling it "a nullity." Meany and Hayes refused to back down. At the May 6 hearing of Hayes' committee, the staff presented a twenty-two page report listing charges against Beck and Teamster Vice Presidents Frank Brewster of Seattle and Sidney Brennan of Minneapolis. Beck then read a prepared statement: "We deeply resent and we vigorously deny this malicious and unfounded slander of our membership and our official family."[8]

Beck was then summonsed back before the McClellan Committee and again ducked their questions, at one point even refusing to admit that he knew his own son.

When the AFL-CIO Executive Committee met May 20, Beck attended the session personally and heard Meany provide a twenty minute presentation of Al Hayes' report outlining his misuse of union funds to pay personal bills and his profiting personally from real estate and other transactions involving Teamster funds. The committee then voted unanimously to remove Beck from his positions as Vice President and member of the Executive Committee on the grounds of "violating the basic trade union law that union funds are a sacred trust."[9]

Next up for the McClellan Committee was Jimmy Hoffa. Bobby Kennedy, who had little regard for Dave Beck, felt even more contempt toward the pugnacious Vice President from Detroit and the crowd he associated with. He related in his book:

> ...there was no group that better fits the prototype of the old Al Capone syndicate than Jimmy Hoffa and some of his lieutenants in and out of the union.
>
> They have the look of Capone's men. They are sleek, often bilious and fat, or lean and cold and hard. They have the smooth faces and cruel eyes of gangsters; they wear the same rich clothes, the diamond ring, the jeweled watch, the strong, sickly-sweet-smelling perfume.
>
> And they have criminal records to compare with those of the old Capone mob.[10]

Hoffa knew better than to take the Fifth, given what had happened to Dave Beck. When he appeared in August, he testified freely, sparring verbally with Bobby Kennedy and members of the committee. Hoffa's personal business ventures, many of which involved companies with Teamster contracts and his close association with New York mobster John "Johnny Dio" Dioguardi, all came to light under questioning.

Once again, Al Hayes' Committee was called upon to investigate. The staff delivered another report, their third, to the Teamsters on August 27, detailing the extensive violations of the Code of Ethical Conduct and invited Hoffa and Beck to appear before them September 5.

Dave Beck was scheduled to retire later that month. This would be the last meeting between Hayes and Beck as Union Presidents. As they sat facing, perhaps three feet apart, at a table in the AFL-CIO building on 16th Street, news cameras flashed and the two men who had sometimes cooperated, but much more often had fought, stared at one another intently. Beck delivered a prepared statement essentially denying that the Teamsters were sufficiently corrupt to be thrown out of the federation and promising to adopt unspecified reforms at their upcoming convention. The confrontation lasted two hours and fifteen minutes, and Dave Beck departed, disgraced and dishonored.

The Teamsters met in convention in Miami Beach on September 30. The Ethical Practices Committee report calling for reforms was read to the delegates, then immediately expunged from the record. The convention, in other words, had told the AFL-CIO and Al Hayes' Ethical Practices Committee to get lost.

Hoffa was elected to replace Beck as President, a move that George Meany saw as Hoffa forcing Beck out:

That was the old Hoffa muscle working. Beck had no guts at all, and there were a lot of recalcitrant Teamster local unions that didn't care for the international union. When Beck became president, he needed some heavy muscle to keep people in line and the little guy he depended on was Hoffa, because Hoffa was a tough little guy. It was Hoffa who really bulldozed Dan Tobin into quitting [as Teamster president] so Beck would get the job. Hoffa made no bones about the fact that Beck was only there temporarily.

Hoffa had a gangster mentality; he was not a trade unionist in my book. It was a way of life with him; he loved power; he loved to push people around.[11]

The AFL-CIO Executive Committee set a meeting for October 24 in New York City, and gave the Teamsters and two other unions who had been exposed by the McClellan Committee, the Bakers and the United Textile Workers, a final thirty day chance to clean up.

Hayes' sixty-four page report to the Executive Committee on the Teamsters was brutal. He accused Beck and the Teamster Executive Board of "dereliction of duty" for their failure to make reforms, and threw the book at them, detailing seven areas of significant violation of the Code of Ethical Practices.

The Executive Council voted twenty-five to four at their October 24 meeting to follow the recommendation of the Hayes Committee and suspend the Teamsters from the AFL-CIO. The move, essentially the death penalty for a labor union, would require a vote of the AFL-CIO convention to be held in December.

In the meantime, the McClellan Committee continued with its work. IAM members were shocked when they heard the testimony of one of the next witnesses the committee called, Nathan W. Shefferman. It was Shefferman's records that had convinced Bobby Kennedy that Dave Beck was crooked. Shefferman ran an outfit called Labor Relations Associates, a Chicago-based company that helped employers defeat union organizing attempts. His company listed some 475 clients, including two Ohio Whirlpool plants that Ernie White and Wimpy had tried, but failed, to organize. It turned out that while the Teamsters were cooperating with the IAM on auto mechanics and vending machine companies, a man their President Dave Beck considered one of his closest friends, and with whom he had significant financial dealings, was stabbing them in the back. Shefferman's men used goon squads, threats to union members, and phony "Vote No" committees to deprive workers of IAM representation.

On December 6, 1957, the second day of the AFL-CIO convention, George Meany brought the report of the Hayes Committee calling for the expulsion of the Teamsters to the floor for a vote. After surprisingly little debate, the federation voted 10,458,598 to 2,266,497 to show the Teamsters the door.

Wimpy, as Howard Tausch's point man on the Joint Organizing Committee, had been at the axis of the relationship between the Machinists and the Teamsters. Now, with Hoffa and the Teamsters expelled, the assignment that brought him to Washington would soon end.

THIRTEEN

REPRESENTING AIRLINE WORKERS

Wimpy had endured a rough few months at the office he shared with his fellow committee staffers, many of whom were Hoffa's men, as details dripped out about the Teamster's dirty laundry. Despite the distractions, during 1957, the IAM and Teamsters had been successful in organizing auto dealerships in Boston, St. Louis, Washington, DC, and the Northwest.

While much of the country's attention was focused on the hearings in Washington, two other significant events occurred. In late 1956, the Little Rock, Arkansas, school board had voted to desegregate its high school beginning in the fall of 1957. Governor Orval Faubus was opposed vehemently to the idea and deployed his National Guard on September 4 to block nine black students from entering. The move sparked outrage and legal action and prompted President Dwight Eisenhower to summon Faubus to Washington for a meeting. Eisenhower persuaded the Governor to withdraw his guard troops, and the students again tried to enter the school on September 23, only to be turned away by an angry mob. The following day, the President dispatched troops from the 101st Army Airborne Division to Little Rock where they restored order and escorted the students into the school.

And 1957 saw the beginning of the space race. In October, the Soviet Union launched *Sputnik*, the first satellite to reach outer space. News that the Communists had beat the US into space sent shivers down the spine of many in America. Nerves frayed even more when the Russians followed up by launching a second satellite, *Sputnik II*, less than a month later with a dog named Lakia (Russian for "Barker") aboard. The

United States scrambled to respond and, using manufacturers that would soon be represented by the IAM, built a rocket and launched a satellite, *Explorer I*, in just eighty-four days. The first US unmanned space craft lifted off from Florida's Cape Canaveral Air Force Station at 10:48 PM on Friday, January 31, 1958. The space race was on.

Even after the vote to expel the Teamsters, Wimpy kept working for the Joint Organizing Office and commuting from Washington, DC, to Cleveland on the weekends. It was becoming clear that the days of the program were numbered. The Teamsters were no longer part of the AFL-CIO, and it would only be a matter of time before the federation forbade cooperation with them.

Wimpy spent his precious few hours at home each week fixing up the house on Cooley Avenue.

Mike Winpisinger recalled his father's visits home:

> You knew he was home when you woke up Saturday morning and you heard the pounding and the banging and so on and what have you. But he was a hell of a craftsman. Very, very little that he couldn't do…he would do carpentry, concrete work, siding, interior repairs, linoleum tile. [1]

The Winpisinger kids were growing up to be a rambunctious lot. Poor Pearl had her hands full. Said her son Ken:

> We made life hell for my mother. We took off. I borrowed a bike from a guy. He's riding my bike, and I'm riding his bike, and his bike is defective. And I'm going down that steep hill that goes down into Rock River. I hit a tree and broke my neck in four places. I'm laying in the hospital and my father's out of town.

*He's in Buffalo, New York, or somewhere, and my
mom can't get hold of him. She doesn't know what's
going to happen to me. They're saying I could go into
surgery at any minute. Meantime, while she's at the
hospital dealing with all that, my brother Bill was in
the garage playing with gasoline, and he ends up
dumping the gas on this old chair they had stored in
there, and set it on fire. So my mother comes home
from the hospital and there's the fire department
out in front of the house. I'm surprised she didn't
have a nervous breakdown or something.*[2]

The word Wimpy had been expecting came down from
the AFL-CIO Executive Council when they held their mid-
summer meeting in August 1958. By a vote of twenty-two to
one, the council "directed all affiliated unions to cancel any
alliance or agreement, formal or informal, with the International
Brotherhood of Teamsters."[3]

The project that brought Wimpy to Washington was over.
But he had performed admirably, and Al Hayes and his staff
saw great potential in the young man from Cleveland. They
told him not to worry about being transferred back to the
Great Lakes office, that he would be given new duties at Grand
Lodge headquarters.

Since his new job would be in Washington, Wimpy decided
it was time to move the family there. But first, he had to finish
his renovations of the Cooley Avenue house so that they could
place it on the market.

Mike Winpisinger remembered:

*He had to fix that place up quite a bit. Because when
he sold it, you know, he had to split the money with
her [Edith Winpisinger] because she'd help buy it.
So he went out and bought a band saw. My mother*

was all upset. She was convinced, you know, "You're going to cut your hand off." He kept telling her "Aw, be quiet. Only an idiot would cut his hand off." So my mother was downtown shopping one day... [4]

Ken Winpisinger picked up the story:

Bill and I were up on the sidewalk outside the house...and we were taking caps and hitting them with hammers. And he was downstairs running a saw. That's why we were hitting the caps with a hammer, because he couldn't hear it.

And he ran the saw over his fingers and he cut his fingers real bad. He came running up the stairs and he was in a panic. As soon as I saw his face, I figured, oh, man, we're in deep doodoo now. [5]

Mike Winpisinger recalled:

So my brother Bill took off running, just assuming he was in trouble because he was horrible. And my dad had a rag all wrapped around his hand. He'd almost cut off two of his fingers. He was going next door to get the neighbors to drive him to the hospital. The last thing he said before he left was, "Don't say anything to your mother." Well, the cab pulls up and my mother gets out with an armful of bags. She didn't have two feet on the ground and my brother Bill's over there, "Dad cut his hand off! Dad cut his hand off!" [6]

Fortunately, Wimpy's wounds were less severe than his young son thought, and doctors were able to stitch him back together. It took several months, however, before he heard the last of Pearl's comments on the matter.

The Teamsters were gone from the AFL-CIO, but the McClellan Committee hearings dragged on for another year and a half. All told, the committee called 1,525 witnesses, and the transcripts of their work filled several dozen bound volumes. Like all television dramas, the hearings contained heroes and villains, and in this case, it was the committee and their staff who were the good guys and labor unions that were the bums.

The mainstream media, increasingly owned by big business interests, saw a golden opportunity to take some of the wind out of the sails of the entire labor movement. They solicited the inside story from the political figures who were only too happy to oblige. Senator McClellan wrote an article entitled "What We Learned About Labor Gangsters" in one of the most widely read newsmagazines of the time, *The Saturday Evening Post*. Next, Bobby Kennedy wrote "Hoffa's Unholy Alliance" for *Look Magazine*. *Reader's Digest's* September issue included "What Union Members Have Been Writing Senator McClellan."

Many newspapers published by labor unions, which had been open to the committee's investigation at the outset, reacted bitterly to the writings of the committee members and their interim report. *The Machinist* was typical in its early support, at one point saying, "An honest investigation will let the chips fall where they may without fear and without favor. More than that labor cannot and does not ask."[7] That moderate stance turned to outrage once McClellan and his staff used the mainstream press to mount a broad-brush condemnation of the labor movement.

George Meany called it a "disgraceful example of the use of sensationalism in an attempt to smear the trade union movement...Despite the qualifiers that the Committee has dropped in, the net effect of this report is to indict the entire labor movement for the sins of the few and to ignore the great strides labor has made to clean its own house."[8]

Al Hayes shared that view and cut right to the chase:

> And because of the sensationalism with which their hearings have been reported by the daily press, many people have come to believe that corruption and racketeering are the rule in the labor movement Hayes wrote. "So we come now to the critical question...Why?...Why has organized labor been singled out for such sensationalized coverage by the nation's press and radio? I think the answer lies in the fact that the labor movement has made great progress over the past twenty-five years—too much progress to satisfy that small, but vocal, group of economic recalcitrants who yearn for the old days when the boss was the boss—unhampered by the united voice and strength of his employees...We in the labor movement are being attacked on many fronts. We are losing legislative debates now that we would have won five and ten years ago."[9]

Hayes took time out from the public relations battle to figure out what to do with Wimpy. He decided to send him where things were hot and, at that particular moment, nothing was hotter in the IAM than negotiations with the airlines.

By August 1957, the IAM had entered into negotiations with six of the nation's major airlines, looking for wage increases, severance pay, company-financed health benefits, and new regulations on picket lines. Six months of bargaining got them nowhere and members of several of the lines voted to strike. President Eisenhower stepped in and created an Emergency

Board under the terms of the Railway Labor Act in order to avert a work stoppage. The Board came back recommending a nine percent wage increase but suggested the IAM drop the remainder of its demands. The carriers were delighted with the Board's findings and said that was the only thing they'd settle for.

Employees of Capital Airlines, members of IAM's District 144, who had delivered a ninety-nine percent strike vote, gave the airline a deadline of mid-October to sign a new agreement. After last minute negotiations failed to produce a pact, 2,600 members laid down their tools. Capital's flights to seventy-seven cities in seventeen states were grounded.

Wimpy was assigned to assist Grand Lodge Representative L.T. Faircloth, who was coordinating the strike for the International, and working with District 144 General Chairman Robert T. Quick. Winpisinger and Faircloth hit the road, checking picket lines and visiting strike headquarters in Pittsburgh, Detroit, and Alexandria, Virginia.

Capital decided to play hardball and issued an ultimatum through its Vice President, Robert J. Wilson. The company would reduce its offer of a twenty-six cent an hour increase by a penny a day until it reached twenty cents unless the members accepted immediately. District 144 told him to take a hike. By mid-November, the six airlines, including Capital, sweetened their offer. Wimpy, Faircloth, and Quick immediately scheduled a vote, and the new package was turned down by a resounding ninety-four percent of the members. The strike continued.

The government assigned Francis A. O'Neill as a mediator and Wimpy began to attend meetings with him in Atlantic City, New Jersey, shuttling from there to company headquarters at Washington National Airport, where they'd meet with company President David H. Baker, and to meetings at IAM headquarters with International President Hayes.

Members working for other airlines, seeing little movement even with Capital grounded, hit the bricks. 12,000 IAM members struck at TWA and Eastern, bringing those carriers to a halt. Negotiations between Capital and the IAM took on new urgency, and President Hayes and Baker, Capital's President, began to participate in face to face bargaining. Finally, after an all-night session that ended at midnight, the two sides reached an agreement. Members of District 144, who had maintained total discipline throughout the work stoppage, voted 927 to 755 to accept the offer and return to work. Within a week, three more airlines settled, leaving only Eastern on strike. It was finally brought to heel the first week of January 1959, when the company agreed to pay two million dollars in retroactive raises to get back in the air.

Wimpy's first foray into airline representation at the highest levels was a resounding success. He began working out of the headquarters office of Frank Heisler, the IAM Airline Coordinator, following up on the strikes and helping negotiate with other carriers across the USA and Canada. When Heisler was out of the office for two weeks in February, Wimpy took over as Acting Airline Coordinator.

On Monday, April 13, 1959, Wimpy was called in to meet with President Hayes. Bob Quick, the District 144 General Chairman, had been temporarily suspended from his duties and Hayes needed someone to take control of the contentious district where forty-five percent of the members had voted against the settlement and were none too happy to be back to work. Three days later, Wimpy, now thirty-five years old, took over control and supervision of District 144.

The district lodge that Wimpy was charged with running had been chartered in 1946. It represented the workers on Capital and Alleghany Airlines and on two airline service firms. Bob Quick had led the district since its inception, and would return to that post once the charges against him were settled.

As usual, Wimpy was busy as a one armed wallpaper hanger. He was learning the ins and outs of representing airline workers at a difficult time, and establishing credibility with members of the district. Despite the challenging schedule, he chose this time to relocate his family to Southeast Washington, getting them settled temporarily at a house he rented in the city's Oxon Hill neighborhood.

Capital Airlines was a troubled company. In addition to the rocky relationship it had with its employees, its fleet of Vickers Viscount airplanes had suffered a series of crashes. Forty-nine people died in a crash at Saginaw, Michigan, on April 6, 1958. Fifteen died forty-four days later when a Viscount collided mid-air with an Air National Guard training jet in Maryland. On May 12, 1959, a month after Wimpy took over the district, Capital had two accidents on the same day: a plane went off the runway in Charleston, West Virginia; another crashed during a thunderstorm in Baltimore. Another Capital Viscount crashed in Virginia on January 18, 1960.

The public was understandably concerned about flying on Capital, and the company's revenues started to decline as fast its planes dropped from the skies. By the end of April, Wimpy was participating in meetings with company representatives, members of their board of directors, officials from the Civil Aeronautics Board, and members of all the airline's unions about the future of the airline. Vickers foreclosed on what was left of the Viscount fleet, leaving Capital with only its aging, albeit more reliable, Lockheed Constellations. Things looked grim for Capital and the members from Wimpy's district. Fewer airplanes meant fewer passengers. Fewer passengers meant less revenue to stem the tide of red ink. It was a complete downward spiral. Bankruptcy loomed.

David H. Baker, Capital's President, was a stubbornly persistent businessman with a Harvard Business School degree. A graduate of West Point, he'd served as a two star Air Force

General in World War Two and Korea before retiring in 1957 to become Capital's President. He wasn't going to let his company go down without a fight. On July 28, 1960, he announced that Capital would merge with Chicago-based United Airlines, in what would be the largest merger US airline history.

Wimpy was thrilled that his members' jobs were spared and that he was able to hand the reigns of District 144 back to Bob Quick.

FOURTEEN

THE ROY BROWN WAR

The diminution of labor's political clout Al Hayes had warned of when the McClellan Committee issued its interim report became a crisis in 1959. The public parade of corrupt Teamsters and leaders from other unions who had betrayed their members' trust had put an ugly face on the American labor movement.

The National Association of Manufacturers, long labor's biggest foe, saw a golden opportunity to strike a blow against working people and crafted a pernicious piece of legislation. The bill, officially called the Labor Management and Reporting and Disclosure Act of 1959, better known as the Landrum-Griffin Act, for the name of its principal sponsors, was the biggest setback labor had faced since the passage of Taft-Hartley eleven years earlier.

NAM, the force behind the legislation, was founded in Cincinnati, Ohio, in 1895. It grew rapidly into a well-funded and sophisticated lobbying organization that was aggressively anti-union. As early as 1903, it advocated open shops and right-to-work laws. The association strenuously opposed President Franklin D. Roosevelt's New Deal, and went so far as to employ "the father of public relations," Edward Bernays, a nephew of Sigmund Freud, to coordinate its advertising.

From 1934 to 1947, the NAM spent more than $15,000,000 on public relations efforts, including movie shorts and films for schools seen by millions of people every year. Almost 300 newspapers carried a daily NAM column on their pages.

The NAM had been the moving force behind Taft-Hartley in 1947, and now it was the chief proponent of Landrum-Griffin, which the IAM Executive Council denounced as "A fraud on the American People."[1] The IAM did everything it could to block the legislation, dispatching all available hands to Capitol Hill, including Wimpy, to buttonhole as many labor-friendly legislators as possible. Wimpy's own notes from the debate include a copy of the bill with the somewhat whimsical margin notation: "W.W.W., 'Wimp the Washington Wonder.'"

Landrum-Griffin would never have been introduced without the McClellan hearings, but once the public relations apparatus of the NAM drove home the negative stereotype of labor unions, the association's lobbyists managed to ram it through the House with a 229 to 201 vote and the Senate by a single forty-six to forty-five vote margin. The new law made it more difficult for workers to form unions, forbade secondary boycotts and picketing, and restricted the ability of workers to inform the public about the facts of labor disputes. Massachusetts Senator John F. Kennedy, a member of the McClellan Committee who had originally had his name attached to the bill, recoiled in horror when he saw the final result:

> It contains many features inserted by the enemies of organized labor and the general public not to get at the hoodlums and the racketeers who have infiltrated the labor movement field, but to weaken the rights of honest unions to represent their members at the bargaining table.[2]

Landrum-Griffin was a major triumph for the NAM and a serious blow to labor, Wimpy, and the IAM. It was not the last time these powerful entities would lock horns. Yet, the labor movement continued to grow. By 1960, one out of every three workers in America belonged to a union. Wimpy was doing his part to help that growth in his new assignment in the Airlines Department at IAM headquarters.

He attended the 1960 Grand Lodge Convention in St. Louis in September 1960, as the temporary chairman of District 144 and saw history made on two counts. The 1960 convention was the only labor convention in history to be addressed by the nominees of both major political parties. 1,500 IAM delegates were joined at the St. Louis Municipal Center by 10,000 visitors to hear John F. Kennedy. Senator Kennedy received a thunderous ovation and told the assembled mass, "I come here this morning to ask you to join with me in a great common task—the task of rebuilding the strength, the prestige and the vitality of the United States."[3]

Kennedy was followed to the rostrum the next day by Vice President Richard M. Nixon, who told the delegates and a somewhat smaller and less enthusiastic group of visitors, "Too often in this country the idea has gotten abroad that only the candidate of one political party would be welcome to speak to a great organization of labor such as this one. The fact that you have invited me as well as my opponent indicates that you are fair minded."[4]

The delegates listened politely to Nixon's forty minute off the cuff remarks, rewarded him with tepid applause, then voted overwhelmingly to endorse JFK for President.

The other history making event was the challenge to International President Al Hayes' leadership by General Vice President Roy Brown and his allies. Brown, who had a significant following from his California base and had been Ernie White's mentor, was entertaining thoughts of taking on Hayes in the next election. He used the convention as a test of strength. He and his supporters put forth three different attacks on Hayes, each of which the International President was able to defeat. One of his broadsides had to do with the joint organizing campaign Wimpy had coordinated with the Teamsters, which Robert Rodden described:

> The second attack came when the Automotive
> Committee reported on a resolution from a group

of California lodges censuring Hayes and the other Executive Council members for terminating the IAM agreements with the Teamsters. The wording seemed deliberately insulting, accusing the Council of "glossing over factual considerations" and sneering that their decisions "are renown for scarcity of information and facts." Though the resolution was easily defeated after Hayes and Walker explained actions taken towards the IBT, it was plainly calculated to sabotage Hayes' leadership.[5]

Once again, Wimpy found himself at the center of the action.

As soon as he returned from his stewardship of District 144 and his brief stint as an IAM lobbyist, he was given a new task: negotiate the first union contract at Continental Airlines, the largest non-union carrier in the country, with more than 800 employees. The company, headquartered at Denver's Stapleton Airport, had been formed by Walter T. Varney in 1934 as Varney Speed Lines of El Paso, Texas. Within three years, Varney sold it to Robert Six, who moved it to Denver and changed the name. The airline had taken delivery of a fleet of brand new Boeing 707 jets in 1958, and was in the midst of a rapid expansion of their route system.

Wimpy began shuttling between Washington and Denver in October 1960. It was his first significant contract negotiation, and he wanted to get it right. Continental's other major hub was in Los Angeles, so Wimpy often flew from Washington to Los Angeles for a day or two, then on to Denver for the balance of the week before returning home for the weekend. The family had moved into a new house just off the grounds of Andrews Air Force Base on Arbroath Drive in Clinton, Maryland, fifteen miles from IAM headquarters. They celebrated their first Valentine's Day in the house by welcoming a new baby, Linda, their fifth and final child. Wimpy's commute from headquarters to home was considerably better than the weekly drive to Cleveland, but his Continental negations meant he was spending many hours each week flying across the country.

Wimpy took time off from work on Tuesday, November 8, 1960, to cast his vote for the man the IAM convention had endorsed for President, forty-three-year-old John F. Kennedy. After a nail biter of an election night that dragged on into the dawn of the following day, Kennedy was elected President by a margin of less than two votes per precinct across the country. When the 66,000,000 popular votes were tabulated, Kennedy won by just over 300,000, less than one half of one percent.

Kennedy's inaugural parade on January 20, 1961, took place despite eight inches of snow and a temperature of twenty-two degrees. Wimpy was a continent away in sunny Los Angeles where he handled a special meeting of Continental Airlines employees so that they could elect temporary officers for the purpose of processing their charter application to form a new IAM lodge. His months of bargaining were beginning to bear fruit. He managed to conclude negotiations with Continental management by the middle of February and his work was rewarded by swift ratification votes in Denver, Los Angeles, Tulsa, Kansas City, Chicago, and Dallas. After a quick victory lap to each of the stations to congratulate the new IAM members, Wimpy returned triumphantly to headquarters. The auto mechanic from Cleveland was now a hot shot airline representative.

The IAM now represented more than 40,000 employees at fifty-seven different airlines and aviation service companies. There was a tremendous amount of work to do servicing them and fending off constant raid attempts by the Teamsters, who were now free, as a non-federated union, to take their best shot whenever they pleased. Wimpy began traveling extensively throughout the country troubleshooting for Frank Heisler, the Airlines Coordinator.

It was also a contentious time within the union. Roy Brown, who had challenged Al Hayes so boldly in St. Louis, was left off the slate of approved candidates when nominations for the 1961 election of Grand Lodge officers were announced. Brown wanted to take on Hayes directly, but realized he didn't have the votes to beat him. He decided, instead, to challenge the irascible Elmer Walker for General Secretary Treasurer.

Brown's challenge led others to think they could grab power as well. The result was that every position on the ballot was contested, except for International President and the IAM's delegate to the Canadian Labour Congress. Bitter battles ensued. In Brown's race, IAM staffers on the West Coast were put in the awkward position of having to choose between Brown, the man who had hired them and to whom they were loyal, or the International President for whom they ultimately worked, the guy who signed their paychecks. Nine stuck with Brown and openly campaigned against Walker and the rest of the Hayes slate. The IAM, with a hard won and well deserved reputation for democracy was, nonetheless, at its core a very disciplined organization. Hayes, Walker, and their followers campaigned furiously from coast to coast in the United States and Canada. When ballots were cast at the union's 1,700 local lodges, Walker and the rest of the Hayes slate received roughly seventy-four percent of the vote. Roy Brown was out.

Al Hayes, never a man to be trifled with, took note of the role the nine Brown loyalists on his staff had played in the campaign. They were summarily dismissed. Hayes had an Executive Council with three new members on it, and he had major shuffling and house cleaning in mind.

The three new council members were Mike Rygus from Toronto, Floyd E. Smith, known as "Red," of Spokane,

Washington, and the guy who made the telephone call that started Wimpy on his path as an IAM representative, Matt DeMore of Cleveland.

Hayes, who under the IAM constitution had unlimited authority for the assignments of Vice Presidents, sent Ernie White, the Great Lakes General Vice President from Cleveland, back to the West Coast to take charge of the renegades from Brown's operation. White had worked as Brown's administrative assistant as they were growing the region, and knew all the key players and the issues. He had broken with Brown to support Al Hayes. Hayes trusted him to bring any remaining dissenters back into the fold.

Red Smith, who had also worked with Brown but was loyal to Hayes, was sent to Cleveland to take over for Ernie White.

Matt DeMore, who had distinguished himself as a significant power in Ohio's labor and political circles and who had also served for many years on IAM's powerful Law Committee, was sent to New York City to head up the Northeast Territory.

Hayes' decision to fire the nine renegade Grand Lodge Representatives proved to have significant repercussions. Seven of the nine decided to sue Hayes and the union for unlawful termination. They argued that Landrum-Griffin provided "freedom of speech" to all union members, allowing them to express any opinion they wished. Hayes' position was that the right to speak freely protected dissenters at local lodge meetings, not people on his payroll who were campaigning against his hand-picked slate of candidates. The case ended up in the courts for seven years. The US Supreme Court ruled for the plaintiffs, declaring that nothing in the Landrum-Griffin Act distinguished between common union members and "Officer-Members," such as Grand Lodge Representatives, and upholding a lower court's assessment of significant punitive damages against the IAM.

While Wimpy traversed the country servicing airline members, he stopped at automotive and manufacturing lodges to say hello and break bread with his brothers and sisters from other sectors. Some of this was practical—a chance to campaign far and wide for the Hayes slate of candidates in a hotly contested election. Some was just Wimpy's natural inclination to be sociable and to get to know as many people as possible. His old sidekick from Cleveland, Phil Zannella, was reaching out as well. He had campaigned extensively throughout Ohio for Kennedy and the Democrats in 1960 and for the Hayes slate in 1961. Zannella was developing a reputation as a tireless organizer and an effective fundraiser. When they reorganized in 1961, Ohio's AFL-CIO, recognizing what a dynamo he was, elected him their Secretary Treasurer.

Fear of Communism, the space race with the Russians, and a growing Civil Rights movement continued to be the issues of the day. American-backed insurgents trying to invade Cuba to overthrow Fidel Castro were soundly defeated by Castro's Communist backed forces at the Bay of Pigs on April 15, 1961. Four US pilots and a hundred of the Cuban born invaders were killed in what quickly became known as "The Bay of Pigs Fiasco."

Tensions between the US and the Soviet Union were stoked further when the Soviets began building a huge wall to separate the two sectors of Berlin. The "Iron Curtain" Churchill had described fifteen years earlier now had a visible face, with a miles long concrete wall, topped with barbed wire and guard towers, patrolled on the Communist side by jack-booted storm troopers with menacing dogs. The focus of the struggle for civil rights in the United States also resulted in violence in May 1961, when Birmingham, Alabama, Commissioner of Public Safety Eugene "Bull" Connor used fire hoses and snarling police dogs to disperse peaceful black protesters. Connor's violence convinced Dr. Martin Luther King, Jr. to begin a widespread campaign of non-violence against racism.

On a more positive note, America was beginning to pull ahead in the space race. President Kennedy had set a goal in his inaugural address of landing a man on the moon and returning him safely to Earth before the decade was out, and the National Aeronautics and Space Administration was up and running. Workers at Cape Canaveral and in the various aeronautic companies that manufactured the rockets and space capsules were IAM members.

Astronaut Alan Shepard became the first American in space on the IAM's 73rd birthday, May 5, 1961. His "Freedom Seven" space capsule, powered by a Redstone rocket built exclusively by IAM members, launched him beyond the earth's atmosphere. At the beginning of another space mission nine months later, a tense nation watched every move on television as two IAM Lodge 837 members, Tommy Griffin and Cal Moser, scrambled to replace a broken bolt on Lieutenant Colonel John Glenn's Mercury Atlas Six space capsule at T-minus sixty minutes. The new bolt firmly in place, Glenn blasted off, slipped from the earth's gravitational pull, and managed to circumnavigate the globe in space in four hours, fifty-five minutes and twenty-three seconds.

John Glenn was hailed as an American hero, and the IAM was firmly established as America's Space Age union.

FIFTEEN

THE ULTRAS: A POLITICAL AWAKENING

The time Wimpy spent on Capitol Hill lobbying against the Landrum-Griffin Act ignited his interest in politics, not simply the politics of horse trading for votes in the Halls of Congress or the process of getting elected, but the larger picture. What did it all mean? What were the larger forces driving the political process? The Wagner Act, Taft-Hartley and Landrum-Griffin were merely battles in a larger war. Wimpy wanted to understand what that war was, and who was calling the shots. His job in the Airline Department required him to travel constantly, and that meant he had plenty of time on planes and in airports for reading. Wimpy had always been a voracious reader.

He knew instinctively, through personal experiences in bargaining sessions, and on picket lines, that the business community had a coordinated agenda. He had seen it in the strike of 1949, the way the auto dealers in Cleveland fought the IAM. He saw it when the airlines put aside their competitive differences to stand firm against the IAM strike in 1958. And he witnessed it up close when the NAM and other business groups muscled Landrum-Griffin through Congress despite labor's best effort to stop it. Were these shows of unity mere convenience or was there a larger agenda waiting to be revealed?

From his earliest days as a member of Local Lodge 1363, Wimpy believed the union should do more than collective bargaining. He wanted it to be involved in social issues and in trying to level the playing field for all working people. The IAM and other unions shared his vision to varying degrees. Now he yearned to discover if there was a larger agenda for social change.

President Hayes saw the restless intellectual talent of his young Grand Lodge Representative, and in June 1962, sent him to New Jersey for a weeklong leadership seminar at Rutgers University. The high school dropout from Cleveland walked the grassy commons between the ivy covered halls of the prestigious university. He was still a young man, not noticeably older than many of the graduate students. There is no record of the seminar that Wimpy took or his reaction to it, but an article published that same week in *The Nation* by a Phi Beta Kappa graduate of Rutgers, Fred J. Cook, made a lasting impression on him, and he kept it in his desk at IAM headquarters until the day he retired.

Cook's forty-one page article (for the June 30, 1962 issue) was titled "The Ultras—Aims, Affiliations and Finances of the Radical Right." It shed light on some of the most significant battles Wimpy would fight throughout the rest of his career as a trade unionist. Here, in meticulous detail, were the links between the various enemies Wimpy would face over the next quarter century: big oil, big business, big media, the Military-Industrial Complex, the radical right, right to work advocates, anti-socialists, and people opposed to any effort to find common ground with people in Communist countries.

Cook laid it all out. This wasn't merely a series of battles. It was war: big business and the radical right on one side, unions, socialists, and progressives on the other side.

These were the politics in which Wimpy was interested, and Cook was providing a road map.

Like Upton Sinclair, Ida Tarbell or I.F. Stone, Fred J. Cook was a muckraker. He wrote more than a dozen books and was a regular contributor to *The Nation*, which bills itself as "America's oldest and most read weekly journal of progressive political and cultural news, opinion and analysis."[1]

The *Nation* was founded July 6, 1865, and has been published continually since then. It lists among its many stellar contributors such notables as Albert Einstein, Dr. Martin Luther King, Jr., I.F. Stone, and Jean-Paul Sartre. While hardly the type of publication one might expect to find tucked under the arm of the average trade union representative, it was popular on many college campuses.

Fred J. Cook, fifty-one years old at the time, wrote "The Ultras," had been a newspaperman at various New Jersey publications and at the *World Telegram* in New York City. Among the books he wrote were *The Unfinished Business of Alger Hiss* (1958); *The Warfare State* (1962); *Walter Reuther: Building the House of Labor* (1963); and *The Great Energy Scam: Private Billions Versus Public Good* (1982).

In a posthumous tribute to Cook, Ralph Nader wrote, "Cook and McWilliams [his editor at *The Nation*] were possibly the greatest reporter-editor team in post World War II journalism in our country. They stand as a luminous model challenging the trivialization of the news by a press in indentured servitude to corporate supremacists."[2]

The radical right movement was in full bloom by 1962. It was anti-labor, anti-Communist, and anti-Kennedy. It wanted desperately to undo the New Deal and turn the clock back to a "Constitutional Government." It claimed that Supreme Court Chief Justice Earl Warren and even President Eisenhower were either "Communist," or "an arm of the Communist apparatus." *The Nation*, in an introduction to Cook's piece, said their purpose was "…to provide a frame of reference by which the reader may make his own assessment of today's Radical Right as a threat or potential danger."[3]

Cook began "The Ultras" by distinguishing between the "Respectable Right" and the "Radical Right." In his estimation, the major difference was not in ideology as much as in the willingness to throw verbal brickbats in public forums.

Both are at war with their century, with the whole trend of popular government during the last thirty years. For both, representative government has degenerated into virtual mobocracy, and the purity of the American system, as they conceive it, has been lost. The diehard conservative, like the man of the Radical Right, has yet to reconcile himself to the Roosevelt reforms of the 1930's. He is shocked at the extension of Social Security. High federal budgets (except for military expenditures) are anathema to him. The world beyond our borders is a vast and menacing and overwhelmingly hostile conspiracy.[4]

Cook posited that the Radical Right could exist only in opposition to internal and foreign menaces and the notion that "the peril to the Republic was never greater."[5]

"Take away from it its cherished menace and it is a desiccated skeleton. It has no program except the program of opposition."[6]

He claimed they were funded by big business, in cahoots with crusading Christian evangelists, and engaged in a massive propaganda campaign based on racism and fear of international tensions to indoctrinate the nation's military and school children.

He dug up some of their most outlandish quotes such as, "We must let it be known that we are at all times ready for war to keep the peace," and "The stressing of both sides of a controversy only confuses the young and encourages them to make snap judgments based on insufficient evidence. Until they are old enough to understand both sides of a question, they should be taught only the American side."

Prominent among those he exposed as the face of the Radical Right were Robert Welch, who had formed the John Birch Society with substantial support from prominent members of the National Association of Manufacturers; and the Reverend John F. Cronin, who had conducted a major campaign to expose what he alleged was Communist domination of labor unions in the late 1940's.

Welch had been a Regional Vice President of NAM for three years, a member of the group's board of directors for seven years and Chairman of its Educational Advisory Committee. The original governing council of the John Birch Society included three former NAM Presidents.

He went on to introduce the reader to Vance Muse, a Texas flimflam man, financed by a Texas oil millionaire named John Henry Kirby, who formed "Right to Work Clubs," under the name "Christian Americans," and detailed his methods:

> *CIO organizers were branded as "foreign agitators" and "Communist agents." Anti-Negro and anti-Semitic themes were also used. "Christian American's can't afford to be anti-Semitic," Mr. Muse confided to one interviewer, "but we know where we stand on the Jews all right."*[7]

Muse's Christian Americans formed an alliance in Arkansas with the Veterans' Industrial Association, another anti-labor group led by James T. Karam, who was alleged to have played a leading role in organizing the mobs outside Little Rock High School that had denied admission to nine black children in 1957.

Cook went on to detail the propaganda machine of the Radical Right, particularly the work of the National Education Program of Dr. George S. Benson, President of Arkansas' Harding College. Benson became a favorite of big business interests for his virulent anti-labor and anti-Communist writings and soon was heavily endowed with money directly or indirectly from General Motors, Armco Steel, and Pittsburgh's conservative

Falk Foundation. The list of companies whose executives participated in Benson's National Education Program included Monsanto, Swift & Company, Mississippi Power, Washington Water Power, Union Bag, Camp Corporation, and General Electric.

Cook described the themes that so endeared Benson to big business, "They include opposition to all welfare legislation, attacks on unionism as 'monopolistic,' the championing of right-to-work proposals, and attacks on anything that smacks of liberalism or socialism and so can be equated with communism."[8]

The National Education Program began to print brochures for the Veterans' Industrial Association and produced films for distribution to high schools and major employers. One such film, *Communism on the Map,* made the outrageous claim that communism dominated the entire globe, save for West Germany, Formosa, Switzerland, and the United States.

Communism on the Map was a big hit with the business community and soon companies all over the country were showing it to their employees in mandatory "industrial indoctrination programs." Among the companies listed as having foisted this upon their workers were major IAM shops such as Boeing, Lockheed, Western Electric and Aerojet, makers of the Polaris missile.

Wimpy highlighted a section of the article subtitled "Industry's 'Loyalty Board'":

> One major agency, the creature of American Big Business, combines in its person the dual themes that a Communist lurks under every bed at home and the only way to end the threat is to blast the mother lode of communism abroad with every weapon in our nuclear arsenal. This organization carries the high sounding name of the American Security Council...

Apparently its quarry was not just Communists, but anyone who might endorse any "statist" activity—a broad and elastic qualification that could be stretched to include such items as federal aid to education of President Kennedy's current proposal for medical care for the aged.[9]

The article continued on to detail initiatives such as massive anti-communist rallies in California featuring Hollywood stars, politicians, a 15,000 member choir, and the forerunner to today's televangelists; outlandish programs to censor public school textbooks in Texas; and advocacy of "protracted conflict" in the Cold War, including an intensification of the arms race and the branding of any move toward disarmament or mutual disengagement as "defeatism." All of this funded, coordinated and executed by big business, big oil, Christian fundamentalists, and the Radical Right.

Wimpy had his roadmap. Someone had described the war for him. It is unfair to say that this lone article turned Wimpy into one of the most liberal, iconoclastic, and socialist trade unionists of the twentieth century. But it is fair to say this article provided at least part of the score for the tune Wimpy sounded as he led his troops into battle.

SIXTEEN

THE THREAT OF NUCLEAR WAR

"Squadron Of Jets Sent To Florida In Reply To Cuba." This front page headline greeted readers of the *New York Times* on Friday, October 19, 1962. In it, a Pentagon spokesman says there is "no reason to get excited about it."

Within days, Wimpy, IAM members who built ballistic missiles, and the rest of the world would learn this was patently false. The threat of Communist aggression and the possibility of a catastrophic nuclear confrontation were laid bare. Five days earlier, on October 14, a Central Intelligence Agency U-2 spy plane flew a mission over Cuba to gather information about the Soviet military buildup going on there. When the film was developed and analyzed, it revealed the presence of Soviet medium range ballistic missiles (SS-4's) on the ground in Cuba, a mere ninety miles from US soil. During a dinner party he was hosting, McGeorge Bundy, President Kennedy's National Security Advisor, was summoned to the telephone. It was an urgent call from Ray Cline, the Deputy Director of the CIA: "Those things we've been worrying about—it looks as though we've really got something."[1] And so began the Cuban Missile Crisis.

President Kennedy assembled what was known as his Executive Committee, or "Excom," the top people from his administration having responsibility for national defense and diplomacy and began a terse dialogue with Soviet leader Nikita Khrushchev about stopping the military build-up and removing the missiles. The repositioning of the jets to Florida was part of his enhancement of offensive capability in case he decided to invade Cuba, one of several options the Excom was discussing in secret.

By Monday, October 22, word of unusual military activity and the virtual disappearance from public view (in the middle of a mid-term election campaign) of the President, Vice President, and all top level security officials from the administration was raising eyebrows. President Kennedy decided that, as shocking as it may be, he'd have to address the nation and inform them that they were on the brink of a full-scale nuclear war with the Soviet Union.

At 7:00 PM that evening, President Kennedy addressed a nationwide television and radio audience from the Oval Office. He said in part the following:

> *The purpose of these bases can be none other than to provide a nuclear strike capability against the Western Hemisphere...Each of these missiles is capable of striking Washington, DC...This urgent transformation of Cuba into an important strategic base—by the presence of these large, long range, and clearly offensive weapons of sudden mass destruction—constitutes an explicit threat to the peace and security of all Americans...Nuclear weapons are so destructive and ballistic missiles are so swift that any substantially increased possibility of their use or any sudden change in their deployment may well be regarded as a definite threat to peace....American citizens have become adjusted to living daily on the bull's eye of Soviet missiles located inside the USSR, or in submarines. In that sense missiles in Cuba add to an already clear and present danger...It shall be the policy of this nation to regard any nuclear missile launched from Cuba against any nation in the Western Hemisphere as*

an attack by the Soviet Union on the United States, requiring a full retaliatory response upon the Soviet Union..."

He then called upon Khrushchev to remove the missiles immediately, saying:

"He has an opportunity now to move the world back from the abyss of destruction...[2]

Kennedy's address sent shockwaves rippling throughout the country. People came to the stark realization that their worst fear, a full scale nuclear exchange with the Soviet Union, could be at hand. Suddenly all those bomb shelters, Civil Defense centers, and fall-out drills did not seem quite so ridiculous. Parents gathered their children and made emergency plans. People who hadn't been to church or temple in years found themselves deep in prayer.

The *Boston Globe* editorialized:

> *Speaking for all Americans, this forty-five year old President of the United States laid it on the line for the sixty-eight year old Premier of the Soviet Union to hear, read and ponder. From here on, Mr. Kennedy was saying to Comrade Khrushchev, it is your move. We shall risk everything, and life itself, rather than turn back or give in.[3]*

From the *Cleveland Plain Dealer*:

> *The President made it clear he was not temporizing with a critical situation; that he was taking the necessary first steps 'to halt this offensive buildup,' that he was aware of the grave risks involved, and that, if necessary, he was prepared—and the nation should be prepared—to go all the way.[4]*

Members of IAM's District 54, meeting in Cleveland unanimously adopted a resolution, which they sent to the White House: "Although the risks are tremendous, this action by our Commander in Chief represents the only clear answer that the Communists can understand."[5]

Kennedy's first move was to enforce a naval "quarantine" of Cuba (the term "blockade" would legally constitute a war) to turn back ships headed there from Russia with additional weapons. The world watched with baited breath to see what the Soviet response would be to this action. Would they blink, or would it be war?

By Saturday, October 27, as the world stood by on pins and needles, things reached a climax. The Joint Chiefs of Staff were recommending that President Kennedy order the massive bombing and invasion of Cuba the next day. An American U-2 spy plane piloted by Major Rudolph Anderson of the 4080th Strategic Reconnaissance Wing was shot down over Cuba, and the Soviet ship *Grozny* was steaming toward the quarantine line. It would be war or peace within the next twenty-four hours.

Kennedy and Khrushchev had been exchanging letters and engaging in back door diplomacy seeking an end to the crisis. Ultimately a deal was struck that the US would agree not to invade Cuba or support any invasion of Cuba and the Soviet Union would withdraw the missiles. There was an additional secret agreement as part of the deal that the US would remove missiles it had based in Turkey.

The *Grozny* turned back before it reached the naval blockade. Khrushchev's letter and Kennedy's response were released to the media. The crisis was over. A nuclear war that could have destroyed the two most powerful countries on Earth had been avoided by the slimmest of margins.

Wimpy continued to work in the Airline Department, flying all over the country to negotiate contracts, handle disputes and fend off Teamster raids. His travel schedule for 1963 was brutal. He made a total of 105 trips to more than twenty cities, including New York, Chicago, St. Louis, Detroit, Denver, Seattle, Los Angeles, San Francisco, and Honolulu. All told, he flew over 120,000 miles, mostly on commercial jets, but sometimes by prop plane.

When he wasn't in the air flying to some distant IAM station, he was loading Pearl, the kids and a ton of gear into his Chevy station wagon and driving at breakneck speed from Maryland to Cleveland for visits with his mother, Phil Zannella, and the rest of their friends and relatives there. His daughter, Vickie Winpisinger, recalls, "Our vacation was going back to Cleveland. I swear it seemed like every weekend. At that point it was a seven or eight hour drive."[6] Her brother, Ken Winpisinger, added, "There was a turnpike, but there was no good way to get up to it. Cleveland was his home. He was very home oriented. That's where his life was, the way he saw it."[7]

Wimpy considered Cleveland the center of the universe. In addition to family and friends, his baseball and football teams were there. His childhood memories were there and he enjoyed the look, feel, even the aroma of its neighborhoods. It's where he got his start in the labor movement, and it remained a powerhouse in the IAM hierarchy. He understood and loved Cleveland.

Shortly after they had settled in Maryland, Pearl was getting ready to deliver Linda, their fifth and final child. Knowing that the blessed event was imminent, Wimpy begged Pearl to let him drive her to Cleveland so that all of their children could say they were born there. Pearl refused, and much to Wimp's disappointment, Linda was born in Washington.

Several significant events forever altered the course of American history that summer and fall as Wimpy was jetting around the country. Dr. Martin Luther King, Jr., was arrested in Birmingham, Alabama, for conducting a large non-violent protest and wrote his famous "Letter from a Birmingham Jail," in which he shamed fellow clergymen who had written to ask him to quit the protest. Quoting Socrates, St. Thomas Aquinas, T.S. Eliot, Thomas Jefferson, and Jesus Christ, Dr. King crafted a masterful response laying out the theological, political and ethical basis for the Civil Rights Movement, saying at one point:

> We know through painful experience that freedom is never voluntarily given by the oppressor; it must be demanded by the oppressed...Oppressed people cannot remain oppressed forever. The yearning for freedom eventually manifests itself, and that is what has happened to the American negro.[8]

Four months later, Dr. King stood on the steps of the Lincoln Memorial in Washington, DC, before a crowd of more than 200,000 people and delivered the defining speech of the Civil Rights Movement.

Dr. King said in part the following:

> I have a dream that one day this nation will rise up and live out the true meaning of its creed: We hold these truths to be self-evident, that all men are created equal...I have a dream that my four little children will one day live in a nation where they will not be judged by the color of their skin but by the content of their character...Let freedom ring and when this happens, and when we let it ring from every village and hamlet, from every state and every

city, we will be able to speed up that day when all God's children—black men and white men, Jews, Gentiles, Protestants, and Catholics—will be able to join hands and sing in the words of the negro spiritual: Free at last! Free at last! Thank God Almighty, we are free at last![9]

The moving turn of events for Dr. King, from tragedy to triumph in several short months, happened in reverse for President Kennedy.

In June, the President traveled to Berlin, where the Communists had completed a wall separating the great city in half and delivered a powerful speech before a crowd of more than 150,000 people jamming the square in front of City Hall. He reminded Berliners that better days lie ahead:

Freedom is indivisible, and when one man is enslaved, all men are not free. When all men are free, then we can look forward to that day when this city will be joined as one and this country and this great Continent of Europe in a peaceful and hopeful globe.[10]

Five months later, on a campaign trip to Dallas, President Kennedy was shot dead while riding in an open car in a motorcade through the city.

The world was shocked and horrified by the death of America's young President. The United States came to a standstill. Grown men wept as his casket was wheeled down Pennsylvania Avenue on its way to be laid in state at the Capitol in a perverse reversal of the inaugural parade that had celebrated the beginning of his presidency a mere thirty-four months earlier.

All that travel took a toll on Wimpy. Even though he was a strapping fellow and generally healthy, he ran himself into the ground and wound up in the hospital in February 1964, one day before the Beatles made their first appearance on *The Ed Sullivan Show*. He had an abscessed cyst in his lower back and he had developed an infection. The cyst was very close to his spine, making an operation exceedingly difficult. Doctors finally managed to defeat the infection and perform the operation, but he remained hospitalized for three weeks. Wimpy, who had a remarkable constitution and would rarely complain of pain, spent the next ten weeks at home convalescing. Because of the location of the incision, he had to lie on his side the whole time.

Wimpy finally recovered and returned to work in May 1964. During his absence, sixty-two-year-old Howard Tausch, the man who brought Wimpy to Washington to work on the joint organizing campaign with the Teamsters, became seriously ill and took a leave of absence. Tausch's job as Automotive Coordinator for the IAM was one of the truly big jobs, one rung below the Executive Council. President Hayes tapped Wimpy to take his place, with the title Acting Automotive Coordinator. In his new position, Wimpy would be overseeing the representation of more than 100,000 auto mechanics employed in more than 8,000 shops in the United States and Canada. The job also included Tausch's other responsibilities as coordinator of the union's apprenticeship program and as managing trustee of the IAM Labor-Management Pension Fund.

This was a tremendous challenge and a great opportunity for the thirty-nine-year-old former mechanic. The Automotive Department was one of the fastest growing areas of the IAM, having added almost 20,000 members since 1960. Apprenticeships were one of Hayes' pet projects and the four-year-old pension fund, which had started off with the participation of just two employers, was growing by leaps and bounds.

By choosing Wimpy, who was personally very close to Tausch, to stand in as Automotive Coordinator, Hayes bypassed older staffers with more seniority. It would prove to be a major test for Wimpy. He would need to withstand jealousy and prove that he could be effective leading a big and important part of the union.

Wimpy smiled, rolled up his sleeves, and said, "Let's get to work!"

SEVENTEEN

ACTING AUTOMOTIVE COORDINATOR

Shortly after he settled into his new duties as Acting Automotive Coordinator, Wimpy met a young man who would become his friend, confidant, and protégé. Thirty-two-year-old George Kourpias, a slender Greek-American with olive skin and dark, penetrating eyes, was brought aboard as a Special Representative, the newest addition to President Hayes' staff.

The son of immigrant parents, Kourpias had been born and raised in Sioux City, Iowa. His father, John, was a packing house worker, a socialist, and a member of the United Packing House Workers of America. Like Wimpy, George Kourpias quit high school in his final year without graduating despite his father's best efforts to keep him in school.

In George's words:

> I was just about through and I had the idea in my head that I should be making money instead of going to school. I got into an argument with my dad, who was very pro-education. We were very poor and my family was poor, my mother was an invalid and there just wasn't much money. I took off and worked in Chicago for about nine months. I had an uncle there, someplace to go, a roof over my head. He lived about two blocks from Wrigley Field and the first ten days I was there I spent at the ballpark. Finally my uncle sat me down and said, 'You better get yourself a job, you didn't come here to watch baseball.' I went to work for Zenith Corporation at their tube plant. In those days they manufactured the big television tubes and

I worked there for about seven or eight months. I decided to go home and spend Thanksgiving with my folks and my sister. They were in poor health, so I decided to stay. My next job was in Sioux City at Wincharger. They were owned by Zenith, and a union shop. I obligated to Local Lodge 1637 in September of 1952.[1]

Within six months of joining the union, Kourpias became financial secretary of the lodge. A year later, while working operating a grinder, he became Chairman of the Negotiating Committee. He soon was called upon to oversee a seven-week strike against the company and to reach a settlement. When the strike was over, the company offered him a position in marketing, which would have moved him into the ranks of management. Kourpias preferred his union activities to life in the front office. He bumped back into the factory, ran a power press, and happily continued with his union activities.

By 1964, he was active in local politics as a candidate for State Representative from Woodbury County, and was President of the Iowa Council of Machinists.

We were celebrating the 25th anniversary of the State Council and Al Hayes came in and was asking around who the hell I was and what I did…He was questioning an awful lot of people. And I thought, What the hell is going on? A friend of mine who was a Grand Lodge Representative said, "They're thinking of offering you a job, and don't turn it down because they don't offer it much." The following Tuesday I was working at my machine and a foreman came up to me and said, "You've got a long distance call from Washington." So I went and answered it, and it was Al Hayes. He said, "Young man, I'd like to put you on the staff." I said, "Let me ask you a question, can I remain in Iowa? Because I'm running for office." And he said, "No, the job I have for you is in Washington. Here's my home number, I need a call no later than late tonight." Well, the campaign was looking good. I was married to June, we had three young daughters and my mother was living with us. I called June and said, "Listen, I've been offered the job, but it's in Washington. What do you think?" She said, "Well, I think we ought to take it." So I called him that night and said, "I'm coming.".[2]

Kourpias was assigned to handle "Article L" cases, called that because of a clause in the IAM constitution. Essentially, it was his job to investigate the merits of charges of wrongdoing filed against any member or officer of the union by another member—what might be called an Internal Affairs operation.

Not long after he moved to Washington, while June was in town to look at houses with him, he ran into Wimpy. Kourpias remembered:

There was a sandwich shop called Libby's next to our headquarters building at 1300 Connecticut Avenue, and June and I were in there having lunch when Wimpy and Howard Tausch came in. I took June over to introduce her and said, "This is Howard Tausch and Bill…". I drew a complete blank. He looked at me, started laughing and said, "Winpisinger, God damn it!"[3]

A month after Wimpy and Kourpias started working together, President Johnson, fulfilling a mission started by President Kennedy, signed the Civil Rights Act of 1964. The idea of ending the South's Jim Crow laws and guaranteeing equal access to housing, education and jobs to everyone regardless of race, color, religion, sex, or national origin, was not popular among the South's politicians. After passing the House by a comfortable 290 to 130 margin in February, the measure ran into a stone wall in the Senate. While there were enough supporters to pass the bill on a straight vote, it was doubtful supporters could raise the two thirds majority needed to break a filibuster.

Alabama Governor George Wallace was running for President against Johnson in the Democratic primaries, campaigning as a strict segregationist, and if he won, Southern senators knew he would veto the legislation. They began their filibuster, hoping for the best. When Wallace ran well in the Indiana and Wisconsin primaries, their hopes of defeating the bill were bolstered. The filibuster continued. And continued. President Johnson, a masterful manipulator of the Senate, finally persuaded conservative Illinois Republican Everett Dirksen to throw his weight behind the bill. The cloture vote, seventy-one to twenty-nine, ended an eighty-three day filibuster, at the time the longest in Senate history.

A month after President Johnson signed the landmark legislation, three North Vietnamese patrol boats attacked the USS Maddox in the Gulf of Tonkin, twenty-eight miles off the coast of Vietnam. Five days later, on August 7, 1964, Congress passed the Gulf of Tonkin Resolution, giving the President the power to use American forces to protect any Southeast Asian country in danger of falling to the Communists. The measure passed the House unanimously and was opposed by only two members of the Senate.

Six weeks later, President Johnson became the first sitting President ever to address an IAM convention. Speaking to 1,500 delegates and more than 2,500 visitors at Miami's Deauville Hotel, he pointed proudly to his warm relationship with the IAM and called attention to the improving economic climate.

Old records are being surpassed very month. August reports have just come in. I read them last night and they show this—more men and women were on non-farm payrolls last month than ever in American history—59,250,000—up by 1,600,000 more than a year ago. Factory employment reached the highest August level in more than ten years—17,500,000— 300,000 more than a year ago. Average weekly earnings set a new record for August of $103.- $4.50 more than August, 1963, and ten dollars more than August, 1961.[4]

President Johnson went on to urge the delegates to support his efforts to pass Medicare legislation, which would guarantee benefits to Americans when they turned sixty-five. After interrupting President Johnson's speech by applause thirty-two times, delegates voted unanimously to endorse the Johnson—Humphrey ticket.

Six weeks later, the voters concurred with the IAM's choice and granted President Johnson a four-year term with the largest landslide in American history. Johnson drubbed Arizona Senator Barry Goldwater, carrying forty-four states with a total of 486 electoral votes.

Goldwater, who had served on the McClellan Committee, was a darling of the right wing, known as "Mr. Conservative," an avowed enemy of organized labor and a vocal proponent of right-to-work laws. The rapid growth of right wing activist organizations and their extensive propaganda campaign had been noted earlier in the year by *The Machinist*, with the colorful headline: "500 Stations Air Kook Propaganda."[5] The article pointed out that the John Birch Society and other radical groups were producing more than six thousand Right Wing radio broadcasts a week on small radio stations across the country. Extremist groups had spent more than $30,000,000 promoting their agenda in 1963 when the average worker took home about $100 a week.

International President Hayes, who would bump up against the union's mandatory retirement requirement before the 1968 convention, delivered his final State of the Union speech at Miami. He pointed with pride to the union's sixty-nine percent growth during his administration, increasing from 1,734 lodges to 1,942. Membership had climbed from 518,000 to 875,000, and the staff had grown from 168 to 232. More than half the members were covered by pension plans, up from a mere five percent in 1949. The union had a net worth of $29,500,000. President Hayes also sounded a warning and a challenge:

> The ant-labor biases of those who have poisoned public opinion though their ownership and control of the press, radio and T.V. continue to besmirch the image of all of organized labor. The days have long since gone when unions could limit their activities or their aspirations to the bargaining table. The laws, policies and philosophy of government have a deep, immediate and daily impact on our homes, our communities and our jobs.[6]

The staff that President Hayes had assembled at headquarters was a tight knit bunch. They worked hard to grow the union and to prepare for the challenges of a rapidly changing workplace. When the workday was over, staffers often got together socially, to dine, drink, bowl, or play cards. George Kourpias recalled:

> We had a poker game twice a week at Howard Tausch's house. Howard, myself, a guy by the name of Alex Bower, and Al Hayes. We played on Wednesday

and Saturday nights. The stakes were ten or fifteen cents. Al Hayes was always controlling the game, he was "Why don't you make change, George?" "You didn't put the nickel in, George." He loved it. That and bowling. Wimp would bowl. Wimp was a bowler, I'd never seen Wimpy in a poker game.

He was like me. We weren't outstanding bowlers, we drank a lot of beer and booze and a couple of times got snockered at lunchtime and went up and drank some more at the bowling alley. I'll never forget one night we got there and we'd had a few drinks and his team was playing Al Hayes' team. It was the tenth frame and Al needed a spare in order to beat Wimp's team, Wimp was snockered. Al threw the ball and missed. As he was coming back, Wimp looks at him and says, "Man, you sure as shit missed that spare didn't you?" Wimp and I laughed like crazy. Boy was he mad! He looked at Wimp and said, "You're lucky if you have a job when we get back!" We had a lot of fun together in those days.[7]

Wimpy, fortunately, didn't lose his job and continued to serve as the Acting Automotive Coordinator in Tausch's absence. By April of the following year, it became clear that the heart condition that had been plaguing Howard Tausch was not improving and he submitted his retirement papers. Phil Zannella drove in from Cleveland to serve as Master of Ceremonies at Tausch's retirement dinner at headquarters. Standing behind a podium in a tuxedo and black tie, Zannella recounted some of the highlights of Tausch's thirty-one year career, started at Lodge 1363. He brought the crowd to tears with his touching remarks, thick Cleveland accent, and hilarious off-the-cuff jokes and malapropisms. Wimpy also spoke and thanked Tausch for the confidence he had shown in him from the beginning of his days in the joint Teamster organizing project through his service as Acting Automotive Coordinator.

Howard Tausch, who would pass away four months later, accepted the praise graciously despite his poor health, which made it difficult to sit up for any length of time. He realized he didn't have much time, but as he looked at the dais he was immensely proud. His gaze fell on his Cleveland boys, Matt DeMore, who was now the Resident Vice President; Phil Zannella, who was one of the most important local representatives in the IAM; and Wimpy, who had been named to replace him as Automotive Coordinator. The boys from Cleveland had done well, and they were not done yet by a long shot.

EIGHTEEN

GO-GO UNION

By 1965, five of the twenty-seven union Presidents serving on the AFL-CIO Executive Council were so old that they had been given emeritus status. They were no longer allowed to vote, but could attend meetings and conventions "to continue to lend their knowledge and wisdom."

In several unions, the old timers' grasp on the levers of power were being challenged by younger members eager to move up. In one union after another, the young were challenging the old guard, and all could see that holding on to power too long bred dissension in the ranks. I.W. Abel, the General Secretary Treasurer of the United Steel Workers challenged David J. McDonald for the presidency. At the Union of Electrical Workers, Paul Jennings, an International Executive Board member, took on James B. Carney, who had led the 250,000 member union since its inception. Jerry Wurf, who cut his teeth battling New York City Mayor Robert Wagner, ousted Arnold S. Zander, who had led the American Federation of County and Municipal Employees since 1936.

Seeking to avoid such conflict, the IAM took the dramatic step of writing into its constitution a mandatory retirement age of sixty-five for all union officers. When the 1965 election of Grand Lodge officers was held, neither Al Hayes nor Elmer Walker, both born at the turn of the century, were eligible to run for re-election.

Paul LeRoy Siemiller, the General Vice President from the Midwest Territory was nominated for International President, and Cleveland's Matt DeMore, who had been serving as Hayes' chief of staff as Resident Vice President for the past ten months, was nominated for General Secretary Treasurer. Neither had a single challenger, which had only happened twice since 1905.

President Hayes declared the nominees elected and said, "The results of the nominating meetings in our local lodges proves again the unity of our membership. Lack of serious antagonism is a sign of strength in any organization. We also feel it is a result of competent leadership sensitive to the will of the average rank and file member."[1]

Siemiller and DeMore, both sixty-one, would be limited to one term. In his initial remarks to the staff, Siemiller announced, "This is going to be an administration in a hurry."[2]

Bob Rodden described him:

> Christened Paul LeRoy Siemiller was born in September 1904 on a homestead close by the Platte River in central Nebraska. His father was a Civil War veteran who served at various times with the 4th Iowa Infantry and the 51st Missouri Cavalry. While Roy was still a boy his father left the farm to an older brother and began an odyssey that took the family westward and eastward before settling down in Arkansas. Striking out on his own in the old-time "strive and succeed" tradition of a Horatio Alger hero, young Roy left school at an early age to become a Western Union messenger. Spotting an "Apprentice Wanted" sign in the window of a machine shop where he was about to make a delivery, he removed his Western Union cap, went in, fibbed about his age and talked himself into working nine hours a day at eleven cents an hour (with, as he later said "no deducts"). After completing his apprenticeship and serving a hitch in the Navy, he went to work for the Rock Island Railroad in Herrington, Kansas. Though not yet an IAM member Siemiller joined the parade when union members marched out in the big shopmen's strike of 1922. With no other jobs in sight

Siemiller bummed around as a farm hand before finding work as a machinist in Port Arthur, Texas. He was initiated into Local Lodge 823 in September 1929 just in time for his job to be wiped out by the stock market crash a few months later. Again taking to the road he eventually wandered into the Ozark town of Harrison, Arkansas, where he pounced upon a rare opening in the machine shop of the Missouri-Arkansas Railroad.

Having kept up his IAM membership Siemiller tried to find other IAM members. He learned that a few years earlier the only IAM local lodge in the area became defunct following a strike in which a mob of company-incited vigilantes hung the financial secretary from a railroad bridge.[3]

Siemiller eventually organized enough fellow machinists to charter Lodge 1093 and was elected as its General Chairman. He was hired onto the Grand Lodge staff in 1937, and became a General Vice President in 1948, assigned to the Midwest Territory, based in Chicago.

As Vice President, Siemiller had worked closely with the Teamsters, forging an alliance with them on vending machines at the same time Wimpy was working with them on the joint organizing campaign.

Wimpy rolled up his sleeves and got busy in his new role as the Automotive Coordinator. Siemiller made it clear in his inaugural remarks that he intended to continue to grow the union through organizing and that auto mechanics were a key target. Wimpy's job now included two important positions he inherited from Howard Tausch: Co-Chairmanship of the National Joint Apprenticeship Committee and Co-Chairmanship of the four-year-old IAM Labor-Management Pension Fund.

The apprenticeship program gave Wimpy the chance to help scores of young men like him who never completed their formal education land decent, steady jobs. It was a coordinated effort with the American Trucking Association with supervision from the Department of Labor's Bureau of Apprenticeship and Training. Under Wimpy's leadership, the program formed local joint committees, established standards for participation, set wage guidelines, and developed a 144-hour classroom instruction program. Participants were required to be over eighteen, but younger than thirty. The program put apprentices through four years of training. They would be paid at forty-five percent of the journeyman mechanics rate for the first 500 hours and ninety percent after that until they completed the training and became journeymen.

Speaking at the Eastern Seaboard Apprenticeship Conference at Atlantic City shortly after he took control of the program, Wimpy said the following:

> We tend to put a lot of emphasis on our rising college enrollments and we stress the need for everyone to support our colleges and universities. But who is worrying about the far greater number of youngsters who will never see the inside of a college classroom? We must find ways to bring these youngsters—whose potential skills are now going to waste—into contact with training opportunities which will prepare them to play a useful role in society.[4]

Wimpy's other big responsibility, the labor-management pension fund, would expose him to IAM members across the country in all sectors of the union. The thriving fund had an asset base of $5,500,000 and covered 15,000 members working for more than 500 employers. It had added 5,000 members in the past year. Established in 1960, the original intent of the fund had been to provide retirement security to auto mechanics, who tended to be nomadic and who worked in much smaller groups than their brothers and sisters in factories. The IAM would negotiate with the employer to participate in the fund and the employer would pay between forty and eighty cents a day into the fund for each employee. Members vested in one year, and could take the pension plan with them from one shop to another. They could collect benefits when they retired if they were at least fifty-five years old and had at fifteen or more years of service.

The merits of the plan soon became obvious and it spread from auto mechanics to other sectors of the union. Wimpy knew that the bigger the asset base, the more powerful the fund would become, and he encouraged as many units as possible to include the pension benefit in their bargaining for new agreements.

Wimpy himself had some success at the bargaining table, inking a three-year contract for IAM truck mechanics in eleven Western states, the first master agreement in their history. Under the deal he worked out, 3,000 members got a significant raise in pay and an increase in the amount their employers paid into the pension fund on their behalf. The pact also lengthened their vacations and increased the employer's contribution to the health and welfare plan covering the members and their families.

Wimpy pulled off another coup when he managed to get the California Trucking Association to agree to bring its 1,200 automotive mechanics into the pension plan. He followed that quickly with the addition of United Parcel Service and the Century Delivery Company. Under his leadership, the pension grew at a phenomenal rate.

The front office camaraderie that characterized the Hayes Administration was diminished under Siemiller, who spent a lot of time on the road encouraging organizers and trying to bring about change. George Kourpias remembered:

> *Change was easy for Roy. When he became International President he knew it was only for one term. He traveled and tried to change our organizing structure. He also wanted another term if possible. He was the first president to see that if you're going to be closer to your members you have to get on a plane and travel around. He did that. He was very seldom at headquarters. My office was just two doors down from him and he was very seldom around. Roy didn't care about bowling. Roy didn't care about playing cards. Roy got his business done and had his private life.[5]*

While Siemiller was traveling around the country, Matt DeMore rolled out the unions' spanking new computer, a $1,500,000 Univac III, which resided in a specially air-conditioned space in the IAM headquarters. It took a staff of eleven programmers and operators twenty-eight months of training and data entry to get the system up and running. For the first time, a broad array of information vital to organizers and people in bargaining sessions could be had at the press of a button. Industry wage studies that had taken union researchers a minimum of ninety days to prepare were now compiled by the machine in a mere fourteen minutes. The computer also stored terms and conditions of agreements covering workers in more than 15,000 shops and factories, which were punched into 120,000 cards and transferred to magnetic memory tapes. The Univac also made DeMore's life easier by spitting out payroll checks for the 1,000 members of the Grand Lodge staff, ending years of having to prepare individual checks by hand. The Machinists entered the Digital Age.

Nearly everyone in America supported the Vietnam War at the outset. The Cuban Missile Crisis had driven home the message that Communist aggression knew no bounds and had to be fought fiercely at every turn to avoid a nuclear war. Only two senators had opposed the vote on the Tonkin Gulf Resolution, and all across the country newspapers, radio stations and political groups of every stripe put their support behind the President's move. The AFL-CIO passed a unanimous resolution at their 1965 mid-winter meeting endorsing "energetic measures to deter and halt Communist acts of provocation and aggression," and called for the US "to counteract and expose the slanderous international Communist propaganda drive against our country and its role in trying to halt Communist aggression in this pivotal area of Asia."[6]

Gordon Cole, editor of The Machinist, was the first correspondent of the labor press to cover the war from the battle zone. In a dispatch from Saigon published June 17, 1965, he reported that "The Vietnamese labor movement, 300,000 strong and growing, has emerged as one of this war torn nation's unifying forces."[7]

Cole reported widespread labor dissatisfaction with the South Vietnamese government, rampant corruption, and a sense that the Communists were settling in for a long war. In a subsequent dispatch, he reported, "United States military commanders in Vietnam are quick to explain that the fighting there is not for territory, not for 'real estate,' but for the loyalty and confidence of the people." His final report got personal: "I came away from Vietnam proud of the United States' activity there. The war will be long and often perplexing, but I am convinced that it will eventually be won by and for the Vietnamese."[8]

George Meany, the crusty President of the AFL-CIO, saw the war as an opportunity to burnish the patriotic credentials of the labor movement and remove some the Communist tainted stigma that had attached to it in previous years. Speaking to a Virginia AFL-CIO state convention:

> The American labor movement must lead now in letting all of the people know that they have a responsibility to support the Commander in Chief in the war in Vietnam. It's a war for us; it's a war for our freedom as well as the freedom of people all over the world.
>
> We can't let these intellectual jitterbugs who preside over classes in some of our colleges—and God help our children if we don't do it better—we can't let them form public opinion because they don't know anything about this subject.[9]

As Meany was picking a fight with the intelligentsia over Vietnam, Siemiller was re-branding the IAM as the "Go-Go" union, after the latest dance craze at trendy nightclubs. Scantily clad women in white leather go-go boots were gyrating to "Wipeout" by the Surfaris, "Surf City" by Jan and Dean, and the theme from the television show *Batman*. Go-Go was the opposite of the slow ballads and popular dance music of the 1940's and 1950's. It was fast, furious, rebellious, modern, and young—all the qualities Siemiller was hoping to instill in the seventy-seven-year-old Machinists Union. Now the unofficial IAM logo displayed the words "Go-Go". Middle aged business representatives and Grand Lodge employees nearing sixty were donning black and white IAM "Go-Go" buttons.

The Go-Go union continued to grow at a rapid rate, adding an average of 5,000 new members a month. Matt DeMore predicted that at their current rate of growth, the union would obligate its millionth member within a year or two.

The Go-Go union became the no-no union when the airlines came to bargain in 1966. The pact that had settled the strike Wimpy worked on in 1958 was up for renewal and the union was anxious to share in the huge profits the airlines were reaping after upgrading their fleets from prop planes to jets. The five airlines in the pact, United, TWA, Eastern, Northwest and National enjoyed a $500,000,000 surplus. IAM General Vice President Joe Ramsey, who handled airlines and railroads, felt the workers deserved a share. When he was unable to reach an agreement with the carriers, both sides requested the help of the National Mediation Board. After months of back and forth, it was clear the board wasn't going to be successful either, and the union voted to strike.

President Johnson invoked the Railway Labor Act and appointed an Emergency Board to study the dispute, delaying any action that would ground the planes. Johnson was fighting on all fronts to fund his escalating war and was asking all employers to invoke a voluntary 3.2% cap on wage increases to keep inflation under control. The IAM was seeking five percent in 1966 and 1967 and four percent in 1968. The Emergency Board came back with a proposal of 3.5% each year, slightly more than the President's so called "guideline," but well below what the union felt was fair. On July 8, 1966, 35,400 IAM members put down their tools and walked off the job, effectively shutting down air travel on the East Coast.

As the strike entered its fourth week, President Johnson called Roy Siemiller and the negotiators from both sides to the White House and begged them to come to terms with one another. After being locked in a room together for thirteen hours the two sides emerged with a proposed agreement, calling for a 4.5% raise each year. The proposal was put to a vote in sixty local lodge meetings and soundly rejected by a membership vote of 17,251 to 6,587. The airlines remained grounded.

The following week, the Senate passed a bill authorizing President Johnson to invoke the Railway Labor Act and order the strikers back to work for 180 days while negotiations continued. The House then passed a similar measure, raising the prospect of a compulsory settlement. The two sides took their last best shot at settling and after an all night session hosted by Assistant Secretary of Labor Jim Reynolds, reached a compromise which included a cost of living escalator. The members, anxious to get back to work and feeling that they had received some measure of justice, voted 17,721 to 8,265 to accept the pact. Forty-three days after the strike began, the first flight lifted off, staffed by satisfied IAM members.

With the important 1966 midterm elections looming, the IAM realized it had a significant political asset it was underutilizing. Because of the size and age of the union, it had a large, geographically diverse base of retired members. These were some of the same folks who had become political with the 1948 election, and General Vice President Matt DeMore, who had been instrumental in turning the Cleveland Machinists into a fearsome political force, decided to harness their collective wisdom and political muscle. He held rallies for retirees in Oakland, Burlingame, Burbank, San Diego, Chicago, and Miami. The response was tremendous. Retired members jumped at the chance to get together with their old brothers and sisters to help elect labor-friendly candidates. A new force within the IAM had just come to life.

NINETEEN

THE MARCAL MEETING

Roy Siemiller knew when he took the oath of office in July 1965 that, unless he could change the constitution, his career spent rising through the ranks of the IAM would end with a four-year stint at the helm of the organization. It hardly seemed fair to him, or efficient, that things should come to such an abrupt ending. After all, despite his looming sixty-fifth birthday, he still felt young and vibrant, an energetic leader for the go-go union.

But Siemiller was a Southerner and a railroad man, part of the "Mason" element of the Machinists, which was in decline. With the rapid growth of the union since the Second World War, the balance of power was shifting rapidly and decisively toward the Northern and Western "Catholic" element of the union. The decision to begin organizing on an industry-wide basis had brought large populations of factory workers into the union throughout the Northeast's industrial corridor and on the West Coast, where thousands of workers at Boeing and Lockheed outnumbered the workers on the railroads who had started the IAM. The old power center of the union in the rail shops of Atlanta gave way to a new industrial base, and that was centered in Cleveland.

Cleveland was home to or a significant career posting for most of the movers and shakers in the IAM. Matt DeMore had built District 54 into one of the strongest units in the country. DeMore's protégé, and Wimpy's closest friend in the union, Phil Zannella, had turned the once moribund Local Lodge 1363 into a powerhouse. Zannella also led the country in Machinists Non-partisan Political League fundraising and was Secretary Treasurer of the Ohio AFL-CIO. General Vice President Ernie White, originally from the West Coast, had done his first tour as GVP in Cleveland and still had many friends there. Elmer Walker and Howard Tausch went from Cleveland to Al Hayes' staff in 1949, and, of course, it was where Wimpy got his start as a trade unionist.

The latest addition to the Cleveland crew was Floyd Emery Smith, known as "Red," the new General Vice President for the Great Lakes Territory. Red Smith was another of Ernie White's guys from the West Coast. He had taken a very circuitous route to an IAM Vice Presidency. Smith had been born into a sharecropper family in Quimmo, Kansas, in 1912. His family eventually settled in St. Louis, where Smith worked briefly as a machinist's helper in a factory that manufactured land anchors for telephone poles, making twenty five cents an hour. When the Great Depression shuttered the factory, he dabbled at door-to-door sales, bartending and other odd jobs before learning to lay bricks. By 1935, he qualified for a union card as a bricklayer in St. Louis. In 1942, at the age of thirty, he moved his wife and five young children to Las Vegas, which was experiencing a building boom.

The Great Depression and the war had dealt a major blow to the building trades in most of the country, but Las Vegas was humming with the construction of the Hoover Dam thirty-four miles away, the rapid expansion of Nellis Air Force Base to train fighter pilots, and the construction of several new casinos. A local builder named Tommy Hull got the ball rolling with the construction of the El Rancho Vegas Hotel and Casino on what was to become the Vegas Strip in 1941, and within five years, four more new properties opened, including the Flamingo, built by legendary mobster Benjamin "Bugsy" Siegel.

Within two years of moving to the city, Smith became president of the bricklayer's local in Las Vegas. He also befriended many members of Machinists Local Lodge 845, and when the governor of Nevada asked the Machinists to nominate someone for Deputy Labor Commissioner, they chose Red Smith. He was grateful to the machinists for their support and remained close to many of the Nevada members throughout his eighteen months at the agency.

While Smith, a big man often described as "gruff" or "two fisted," performed his government service in Nevada, General Vice President Roy Brown was building his team and hiring more and more organizers for the Machinists in California. Brown's top lieutenant was Ernie White, and Ernie was always on the lookout for new talent. In September 1945, White invited Smith to come to Long Beach, California, to help out with duties at IAM Local 1235. Within a year, Smith won election as a union representative for the local, a post he held until he was appointed to the Grand Lodge staff in 1952, and assigned to represent construction and erection machinists in the seven Northwestern states, including Alaska.

Ernie White and Roy Brown parted ways after White was elected to the Executive Council in 1949. When Brown challenged International President Al Hayes' authority in a couple of nasty floor battles at the 1960 Grand Lodge Convention in St. Louis, White stood by Hayes, giving Brown the cold shoulder. The following year when Brown decided to challenge Elmer Walker for the post of General Secretary Treasurer in order to get into position to knock off Hayes in a subsequent election, White suggested to Hayes that he add someone from the West Coast to the slate of General Vice Presidents to draw support away from Brown, and he had just the candidate: Red Smith. Hayes put Smith on the slate and he was elected General Vice President in 1961.

Ernie White's reward was to be assigned back to his home in California, and Red Smith was sent to Cleveland to take White's place at the helm of the Great Lakes Territory.

The partnership between Roy Brown and Ernie White may have been shattered but the deal Wimpy and Phil Zannella had made in 1951, their mutually beneficial "Master Plan," was beginning to pay real dividends.

Wimpy had gone on from a Special Representative organizing in the Great Lakes Territory to top-shelf appointments in Washington in the airline, automotive, pension, and apprenticeship programs. As Automotive Coordinator, he held one of the union's top jobs and was highly visible and widely respected. Wimpy, to put it simply, got things done. Whether it was a joint organizing program with the Teamsters, ridding a local lodge of Communist infiltrators, soothing a troubled airline district, settling a major strike, building the country's largest portable pension fund or expanding opportunities for young men through apprenticeship programs, Wimpy was the Machinist Union's go-to guy. Smart, brash, energetic, and eloquent, Wimpy was a young man everyone regarded as a true leader.

Phil Zannella, meanwhile, had more than lived up to his end of the bargain. With Matt DeMore in Washington, Zannella was the dominant figure in the union's Cleveland power base. He built the local, made it solvent and positioned it to remain a power for years to come. Whether it was bargaining for an agreement with every car dealership in town, raising money for the union's political action committee, or coordinating a political campaign, Phil Zannella was the man to see in Cleveland.

By the mid-1960's, the office for the Great Lakes Territory had moved from a bank building in downtown Cleveland to an office park on Pearl Road on the Eastern side of the city. The new facilities offered spacious, modern office space, easy access to the new interstate highway, and plenty of parking. It also was just down the road from a quaint Italian restaurant named Marcal's, which quickly became a Machinists Union hang out. It was there that a meeting took place sometime in 1966 that dictated the direction of the Machinists Union for the remainder of the twentieth century. There is some debate about who was at the meeting, but it's pretty clear that Matt DeMore and Ernie White and Red Smith were in attendance. Vice Presidents Charlie West of Seattle and Mike Rygus of Canada may have been there. Phil Zannella, though not a member of the Executive Council, was included, and some speculate that Wimpy was present.

DeMore and White, both sixty-three years old, were major power brokers in the union, and were headed to retirement before the next election of an International President. The first order of business was Roy Siemiller's quest to change the constitution to allow him to serve another term. If the change was made to benefit him, both DeMore and White, born the same year as Siemiller, would be allowed to carry on in their duties as well. The two had worked together for many years in Cleveland when White was Great Lakes Territory GVP and DeMore was President of District 54. White also had a power base on the West Coast as Roy Brown's chief aide and later, as Vice President for that territory. DeMore was the guy who had built the Machinists Union into a major force in Ohio. He also held considerable clout as the number two official in the union and had served as a vice president in the Eastern Region and at headquarters. If these two wanted to work with Roy Siemiller to wrangle votes, they could surely have pulled off a change to the constitution, but they decided that what their million-member union needed was a new generation of leaders.

There would be no amendment to the constitution and Roy Siemiller would be a one term President. They also decided it was high time that the leadership of the International Association of Machinists and Aerospace Workers reflected something other than southern railroad men and the Masons. They plotted a course of action that once and for all moved the center of power in the IAM out of the southern railroad locals to the more populous north and west, the Catholics. It's important to remember that the designations "Mason," and "Catholic" do not refer to organized religion, per se, but rather to a long-standing tension about the view of the role of the union in society, with "catholic" meaning "universal," not specifically the religion.

The deal they worked out at Marcal's gave both White and DeMore an International President as their legacy. White would get his man, Red Smith, as International President for two terms beginning in 1969, when Smith would be fifty-seven years old. DeMore would then get his man as International President when Smith retired in 1977.

DeMore wanted Phil Zannella to take the helm, but realized that his gruff, unpolished shop floor personality and his abject desire to remain in Cleveland were obstacles. Phil's straightforward blue collar mentality and salty tongue were perfectly acceptable in managing the union's power base, but they were ill suited to running the union in the last two decades of the twentieth century. Besides, Phil would be fifty-nine years old by the time Red Smith retired in 1977 and would only be eligible to serve one term.

Zannella was touched by the loyalty his mentor DeMore was showing but resolute in his commitment to his friend Bill Winpisinger. He told DeMore that if he really wanted to honor him he would throw his support behind Wimpy to lead the union. That was not an easy commitment for DeMore to make. He loved Phil Zannella like a son, but he still had his differences with Wimpy. Phil was a fellow Italian-American and was unfailingly respectful to his elders. Wimpy came from a different culture, and while DeMore had nothing but admiration for his intellect, work ethic, and record of accomplishment, he never really warmed to the brash, iconoclastic Winpisinger.

Phil Zannella went to bat for Wimpy as he had done in 1951, when Wimpy needed Matt DeMore's consent and Ernie White's approval to be appointed to the Grand Lodge staff. He pleaded with DeMore to overlook his discomfort and anoint Wimpy the future International President, a choice that would be popular with White, who had become a huge Winpisinger fan. As he had done in 1951, DeMore put aside his personal feelings to do what he thought best for his union in the long run. He turned to Ernie White and said, "Wimpy's my guy."

The deal set at the Marcal's involved many elements and most likely took several bottles of Chianti to settle. Joe Ramsey, the vice president handling airlines and railroads, would reach the magic age of sixty-five the following year, opening a seat on the Executive Council. Wimpy would get the seat. Ernie White would be the next one to hit the ceiling, and his long time number two man, Robert "Pop" Simpson would get his seat. Siemiller's attempt to change the constitution would be defeated, and Smith would be elected International President. Phil Zannella would get the "Cleveland seat" on the Law Committee.

As White and DeMore left the restaurant with a brief two years left in their own Machinists careers, they had assured their legacies. The Machinists Union would survive and flourish well into the next century.

William W. Winpisinger was ticketed to the top.

TWENTY

INTO LEADERSHIP

As expected, Vice President Joe Ramsey announced on April 20, 1967, that he would be stepping down effective July 23 of that year. International President Roy Siemiller, unaware of the meeting at Marcal's and its tightly orchestrated line of succession, was still hoping to wrangle another term out of the 1968 convention. He began to maneuver to place his top lieutenant, Paul Burnsky, on the Executive Council to replace Ramsey, certain that Burnsky would support his efforts to amend the constitution. As he made calls to his fellow council members, it was clear that not all of them would support his choice, but he thought he could muster a majority of the votes.

Burnsky, a Chicago native, had been with Siemiller since his days as General Vice President for the Midwest Territory. He'd gotten his start as an airline mechanic on Capital Airlines, and had risen through the union ranks as a local lodge officer, Special Representative and Grand Lodge Representative. Siemiller had turned to him time and again to handle delicate situations, and was confident he would be a faithful supporter and sure vote for Siemiller's agenda. Wimpy knew that his own backers on the council, particularly Ernie White and Matt DeMore, were going to push for his election. He anxiously awaited the verdict of the ten remaining members of the executive council.

Siemiller announced that the Council would meet at the IAM's Washington headquarters on Wednesday, July 19 to choose a new Vice President.

"Wimp kept me informed every day about what was happening," George Kourpias remembered.

The night before the vote there was another guy in the picture. The Siemiller people were going to support Paul Burnsky, Siemiller's assistant. Matt DeMore had lined up the votes for Wimp, and it was going to be very close. The next morning Matt DeMore went in to see Siemiller with this proposition: "O.K., if you promise me that the next vacancy in the council will go to Wimp, I'll agree with you now [to vote] for Paul." And he said to Matt, "No, I'm not going to give you a promise like that.", and it pissed Matt off. [Matt] Walked into the room, and by a close vote, Wimp won—I think he won by one vote. And I'll never forget, they called him in there and told him, and I came—my office was right by the fountain near where the council was meeting- and he was getting a drink of water. He looked at me and winked. I said "Oh God! We made it!"[1]

Wimpy had to cancel his plans to have a drink with Kourpias after work that evening and instead Kourpias ended up spending the evening with Paul Burnsky, the runner-up. Kourpias recalled:

I went down to a restaurant on Connecticut Avenue. Paul Burnsky and a guy from Chicago were sitting there. He's out, and he knew it. I sat down and had a drink with him. He looked at me and said, "You know what happened, Wimp got the nod. I guess, George, that'll make you happy." He was a little bit hurt, but there were no hard feelings. In fact the next morning Wimp went in and sat down with Paul behind closed doors and had a good discussion with him. We all continued to go to lunch together and Paul and Wimpy got along fine.[2]

Siemiller decided to give his newest General Vice President a unique and challenging assignment. Wimpy would keep his portfolio overseeing the Automotive Department, the pension fund, and the apprenticeship programs, and he'd pick up Joe Ramsey's responsibilities for the airlines and railroads. The new position would be called General Vice President for Transportation, and it would be based at headquarters.

Wimpy had hands-on experience dealing with each of the areas in his new job, except for railroads. The IAM had originated as a railroad union and it was still a vital, albeit smaller, part of the membership. At that moment, railroads were big news, and not particularly good news.

The IAM had struck the nation's railroads on July 16th, three days before the council voted to elevate Wimpy to Vice President. It was the first railroad strike in forty-five years and it caused chaos from coast to coast.

Joe Ramsey had begun negotiations with the rail lines in April 1966. When fourteen months of negotiations failed to yield an agreement, the members voted to strike, triggering the Railway Labor Act's provision that an Emergency Board be appointed by the President to try to avert a work stoppage. That bought the carriers ninety days, during which the President filed legislation that would allow him to appoint a mediation board that could force both sides to accept a deal. The so called "Mediation to Finalization" bill passed the Senate on a seventy to fifteen vote, despite fierce labor opposition. The House passed a similar measure, except that the House version, while giving the President the power to force both sides to keep talking, did not contain the authority to impose a final settlement.

While the anti-strike legislation awaited the action of a joint House-Senate conference committee, the ninety day cooling off period of the Railway Labor Act expired. With no settlement in sight, the Machinists walked off the job and set up picket lines. Members from the five other rail unions honored the lines and within two days 237,000 railway shop workers were on strike. As the trains ground to a halt, 160,000 commuters in New York City had to find a new way to get to work. 100,000 cars loaded with perishable fruit and vegetables lay idle, the mail all but stopped, and Secretary of Transportation Alan S. Boyd said, "Let's not kid ourselves- we've got chaos."[3]

President Johnson fretted publicly about the damage to the nation's health, economy and Vietnam war effort. Secretary of Defense Robert S. McNamara said, "The widespread railroad strike will have an immediate effect on the movement of ammunition and heavy equipment to ports of embarkation for Vietnam and on the movement of supplies and materials necessary for production to support the Vietnam war."[4]

Two days after the strike started, the House-Senate conference committee dislodged the bill, with the mediation to finalization clause intact. The full House approved it by a vote of 244 to 148. The Senate concurred, sending it to the President's desk by a vote of sixty-nine to twenty.

The striking workers returned to their duties and a new Presidential Board was appointed the day the council elected Wimpy Vice President.

Wimpy rolled up his sleeves and jumped right in, meeting day after day with the new five-member rail mediation board, trying to hammer out an agreement. The board had thirty days to mediate, followed by thirty days to hold hearings and issue settlement recommendations. If, after those two steps had been completed no settlement was reached, the board's recommendation became binding thirty days later.

Meanwhile, a growing chorus of criticism rained down on Roy Siemiller and the IAM. Editorial writers across the country scorned his decision to call a strike against so vital a resource as the railroads. Siemiller responded by calling for the nationalization of all railroads, claiming that if they were so important, they should owned by the government and not operated to make a profit.

Newspaper columnist Victor Riesel pointed out that Siemiller had also been behind the strike that grounded the nation's airlines a year earlier: "It should be realized that the president of the International Association of Machinists has now called almost as many dramatic and vital strikes in the past two years as John Lewis actually called in a decade."[5]

By mid-September, the mediation board came through with a shocking finding. The last offer by the railroads had been for an eighteen month contract with a six percent increase plus twenty five cents an hour for journeymen. The board instead imposed a two year contract with a retroactive six percent increase the first year and an additional five percent in the second year of the contract, and a more generous bonus for journeymen, resulting in a rate that was ten percent better than what the operators had put forth. The companies had been caught in their own trap. They had labor peace, but at a cost far greater than they had ever imagined.

Wimpy had his fist victory working on railroad issues, and it was a big one.

"Washington has heard that protest (the strike), make no mistake about it." he said. "Our membership can take pride in the improvement of their position."[6]

One of the tactics the White House had used to build public sentiment against the railroad strike was the effect it would have on the ability to fight the war in Vietnam. Despite increasing restiveness among draft age students and the intellectual cognoscenti, President Johnson's war efforts still enjoyed wide public support. AFL-CIO staff polled delegates to thirteen different union conventions throughout the summer of 1967 and found that seventy-nine percent of delegates wanted to continue the present policy or even escalate action, and only twenty-one percent favored de-escalation or withdrawal. Wimpy himself was supportive of the President's policies early in the war.

"I remember one time he came in and the hippies were doing something." His son, Ken Winpisinger, recalled, "There was some huge protest about Vietnam early on. All these people are on TV screaming and hollering that we're a bunch of baby killers and all this other stuff. I gathered from the way he was talking that he still thought that [the war] was a good idea at that point, early on."[7]

The hippies weren't the only ones protesting in America's streets. There had been widespread race riots in major cities for the past three summers, beginning with a two night affair in Harlem in July 1964 in which one person was killed, 100 were injured, and several hundred were arrested. That was followed by an even more violent confrontation in Los Angeles' Watts neighborhood in August 1965, which lasted five days and nights and saw thirty-four people killed, 1,100 injured, more than 4,000 people arrested and nearly 600 buildings damaged or destroyed. Wimpy's hometown was the site for racial rioting the following July as four people were killed, thirty critically injured, and 240 fires set in Cleveland's Hough's neighborhood.

City officials across the country were wary as the summer of 1967 dawned, and just after Wimpy stepped into his new role as Vice President, a new wave of violence started to sweep the inner cities. Newark exploded into six days and nights of violence from July 12-17, with twenty-three dead, and 725 injured. No sooner had peace been restored to those streets than the most deadly riot yet broke out in Detroit. When the damage was totaled for the city's so-called "Twelfth Street Riot," forty-three were dead, 467 were injured, 2,000 buildings had been burned down, and more than 7,200 people had been arrested.

Black leaders, including Dr. Martin Luther King, Jr., pleaded for an end to the violence, and called for "an end to mob rule in our cities." King, AFL-CIO Vice President A. Philip Randolph, NAACP President Roy Wilkins, and Urban League President Whitney Young said in a joint statement, "There is no injustice which justifies the present destruction of the Negro community and its people."[8]

In an editorial titled "Extremists," *The Machinist* was sympathetic to the plight of inner city blacks and likened the destructive riots to factory workers destroying the machinery at their own place of employment to protest working conditions. However, the editors also took aim at what they saw as dangerous outside influences:

> ...*heavy unemployment, low wages and poor living conditions have made the Negro communities breeding grounds for extremists like leaders of the so-called Student Non-Violent Coordinating Committee with its call for "Black Power," the Moscow oriented Communist Party and the Chinese style Revolutionary Action Movement.*
>
> ...*American Negroes have the sole responsibility for choosing their own leaders. If they let themselves be led around by Communists their suffering has only begun—as the recent riots should prove.*[9]

As 1967 drew to a close, the Go-Go union found itself squarely in the middle of a burgeoning culture war. Vietnam and racial justice were the big issues, fought in often bloody battles on the streets, but long hair, clothes, and drugs were becoming defining issues. Union members were advised to avoid the temptation to take LSD "trips," with warnings of "immature groups" where "LSD is a 'membership card' into 'the group.' Takers are people who are unable to postpone pleasure and withstand the frustrations of daily life." 10 And in a *Reefer Madness*-like screed, a guest columnist in *The Machinist* proclaimed "The truth about marihuana":

> ...*the prophets of the drug experience make fantastic claims for the virtues of marihuana. They would have it regarded as a 'benevolent herb,' which may lead its users to profound philosophic truths, greater intimacy and keener artistic expression. These claims are often accompanied by otherwise valid criticisms of society's ills and hypocrisies.*
>
> *Such observations are designed to enlist the individual's sympathies and thus to convince him that the claims are as justified as the criticisms. However, it takes little philosophic sophistication to recognize that such virtues do not reside in drugs but in men. They are the products of conspicuous labor, and cannot be attained on the peddler's prescription.* [11]

Even mini-skirts might get IAM members in trouble. Union representatives at Lockheed Aircraft in Burbank, California, had to come to the rescue of one comely young member who was ordered off the job for wearing a skirt her supervisor deemed too short. Not one, but two male IAM staff members measured the "tolerances" of the offending garment with a wooden yardstick and made the case to company management that twenty-two inches from ground to hemline was not a danger to the workplace. Hair too became an issue when Northwest Airlines suspended six IAM members for failing to comply with a company anti-sideburn edict. The members were returned to work with full pay when union leaders at the local threatened to make sure that Northwest would be known as the "hippie airline," because all IAM members would stop shaving or getting haircuts until their brothers were back on the job.

Wimpy, who later in his career would become a combatant of note in the great culture war, spent his first six months consolidating the operations of his newly-formed transportation domain.

Frank Heisler, the man he had worked for when the joint organizing program with the Teamsters collapsed, remained as Airline Coordinator. Wimpy appointed forty-year-old Maurice O. Sullivan Automotive Coordinator. He was a Navy veteran who had been Master Mechanic for the city of East St. Louis and a business representative for IAM District 9. He brought forty-two-year-old Harold Bauer, who had been on special assignment to the AFL-CIO's Industrial Union Department organizing factories in Chicago, back to headquarters to take over as Railroad Coordinator.

1967 was a whirlwind, exciting and successful year for Wimpy. He was a member of the Executive Council and on a path to become International President of one of the largest labor unions in the country, with membership fast approaching one million. As he relaxed with friends and family in Cleveland over the holidays, he had no way of knowing he was about to live through one of the most tumultuous years in the history of America.

TWENTY-ONE

1968: THE WHOLE WORLD'S WATCHING

1968 was the year that changed everything. Before it was over, the IAM would realize its goal of becoming a million-member union, Wimpy would oversee tremendous growth in the Transportation Department, Roy Siemiller would be denied his coveted second term, and Ernie White, one of Wimpy's mentors and most ardent supporters, would retire.

The goings on of the go-go union, however, would be the least of it. In the space of twelve incredible months, the world witnessed riots, assassinations, unparalleled civic revolts in the US and abroad, the political abdication of a US President, a sharp escalation of violence in the increasingly unpopular Vietnam War, and the election of Richard M. Nixon. It was a year when society's thin veneer of civility was stripped away, revealing cultural rifts that would last for more than a quarter of a century, forcing people to take sides. There was no safe middle anymore. The rift would separate old from young, moderate from liberal, anti-Communist from anti-war, us from them. The seeds of the evenly split country that revealed itself in the 2000 and 2004 Presidential elections were sown in 1968.

As it does every election year, the IAM began with a conference of its Machinists Non-partisan Political League. The MNPL set a goal of raising $625,000 to contribute to candidates for federal office and looked to mobilize 10,000 members to work on campaigns. Wimpy told the assembled planners that the union would make a concerted effort to target the members of the House and Senate who had voted for the compulsory arbitration legislation that ended the rail strike. In an IAM poll of local lodge presidents, President Johnson received overwhelming support for re-election against three potential Republican challengers: George Romney, Nelson Rockefeller, and Richard Nixon.

A couple of warning notes were sounded by guest speakers at the conference. The first, by an Assistant President of the Ladies Garment Workers Union, cautioned that labor's traditional allies in the liberal community were terribly divided over the Vietnam War, while the African-American community, long supporters of labor's causes and candidates, was torn by internal strife between traditional leaders and supporters of a militant and growing Black Power movement. The Executive Director of the Philip Randolph Institute warned that the country could be looking forward to another summer of inner-city violence.

Less than a week after the MNPL conference, the world was plunged into crisis when the North Korean Navy boarded and seized the *USS Pueblo*, an American intelligence gathering vessel operating off the Korean coast. One crew member was killed and the remaining eighty-two were taken captive in a move the North Koreans claimed was precipitated by the ship violating their territorial waters. Three days later, on January 26, after tense negotiations had failed to get them to release the ship and its crew, President Johnson addressed the nation on television, decrying the action and demanding the North Koreans abandon their "course of aggression."

The Soviet Union (who many years later would be identified as the instigators of the seizure—they wanted to get their hands on a cryptograph machine aboard the vessel) was strongly committed to defending North Korea against any American military attack. The Chinese accused the US of threatening war and leaders around the world feared that a widespread conflict, a ground war involving the United States, the Soviet Union, and perhaps even China could be in the offing.

A week after the seizure of the *Pueblo*, while military saber rattling and desperate diplomatic attempts to resolve the crisis proceeded at full throttle, the Viet Cong launched their most widespread and bloody attacks of the war. Timed to coincide with the lunar New Year, or "Tet Nguyen Dan," the so-called Tet Offensive saw Viet Cong units attack targets in Saigon and throughout South Vietnam. In a brazen attack on the US embassy, five American troops were killed when invaders blew a hole through the wall of the compound and fought their way inside. The attackers there and throughout the country were eventually repelled, and more than 10,000 Viet Cong were killed, but the attacks called into question repeated assertions that America was "winning" the war.

Public sentiment was further eroded by a shocking photograph and film clip showing Brigadier General Nguyen Ngoc Loan, the chief of the national police of South Vietnam, pulling his sidearm and summarily executing Viet Cong Captain Nguyen Van Lem, who had been accused of leading a team that had assassinated police officers and their families.

A war that seemed somehow far away and headed toward victory turned closer, more complicated and far less acceptable. Stopping Communist aggression was one thing, but film clips of dead American soldiers, huge holes blown through the walls of our embassy, and an up close view of one man blowing another's brains out, was quite another. American sentiment toward the war began to turn. Walter Cronkite, the CBS Television anchorman known as the "Most trusted man in America," journeyed to Vietnam for a firsthand assessment of the war and didn't like what he saw. On Tuesday evening, February 27, he ended his nightly broadcast with a personal editorial that dealt a devastating blow to the credibility of President Johnson's portrayal of the conflict.

> We have been too often disappointed by the
> optimism of the American leaders, both in Vietnam
> and Washington, to have faith any longer in the
> silver linings they find in the darkest clouds...For it
> seems now more certain than ever that the bloody
> experience of Vietnam is to end in a stalemate...To
> say that we are closer to victory today is to believe,
> in the face of the evidence, the optimists who have
> been wrong in the past. To suggest we are on the
> edge of defeat is to yield to unreasonable pessimism.
> To say that we are mired in stalemate seems the
> only realistic, yet unsatisfactory conclusion.[1]

Cronkite's devastating pronouncement was as shocking to Americans as the Tet Offensive. Cronkite held a position of prominence, power, and authority unimaginable in today's world of twenty-four hour news cycles and infinite news sources. In 1968, there were only three national television networks, and each offered only one prime-time evening news broadcast. Nearly half the households in America tuned in to hear Cronkite each night. Johnson had to fear that if he lost Cronkite, he would lose the country.

One group the President didn't lose was the Executive Council of the AFL-CIO. George Meany wasn't about to abandon the Democratic President, particularly when his overarching strategy was to use support for the war to demonstrate the labor movement's credentials as anti-Communist. Meany rammed through a pro-Vietnam resolution at the federation's midwinter meeting, asking members and the general public to support President Johnson. Roy Siemiller, as a member of the Executive Council, voted to support Meany's resolution.

Siemiller was still campaigning to amend the IAM constitution and wasn't about to rock George Meany's boat. He was ramping up his public profile, and *The Machinist* carried many front page stories about the brave and statesmanlike International President. One touted his nomination as "Labor Man of the Year" by labor columnist Victor Riesel, and another proudly pointed out that an article in *Life Magazine* had referred to him as a "Bullheaded Leader of Labor." One accomplishment of which Siemiller was justifiably proud was that the union had initiated its millionth member, twenty-four-year-old Timothy Braunstein of Local Lodge 1746 in East Hartford, Connecticut, on his watch. With Meany looking on, Siemiller welcomed Braunstein to the IAM family and recalled the nineteen machinists who had founded the union eighty years earlier. Then he took a swipe at the anti-war and anti-establishment movements. "They organized because they were not getting a fair share of the wealth their labor created, and they knew it. But they didn't set out to burn and destroy and tear down society around them," said Siemiller. "Instead, they built a union—our union. Because they set out to build instead of destroy, millions of workers have enjoyed a better life in a better society."[2]

Attaining the holy grail of a million members meant that the IAM was now the third largest union in the country behind only the Teamsters and the United Auto Workers. The growth under Siemiller had been impressive: 174,312 new members in thirty months.

To service the burgeoning membership, the Executive Council voted to expand the Airline Department, adding five more Special Representatives, bringing the total to fifteen. John Peterpaul, who had been an assistant general chairman of District 147 at Mohawk Airlines, was brought aboard to be the number two man in the department under the supervision of Airline Coordinator Frank Heisler. Wimpy's empire was growing.

Sentiment against the war was growing too, and that could not be welcome news to a President seeking re-election. The New Hampshire Presidential primary was held in March 1968. President Johnson, who adopted the slogan "A strong man for a tough job," was the prohibitive favorite to win the primary even though he was not campaigning there, preferring to stay in the White House to appear "Presidential." He was opposed by long-shot maverick, Senator Eugene McCarthy of Minnesota. In a *New York Times* story a week before the primary, reporter Warren Weaver, Jr., wrote the following:

> Almost no one, including Senator McCarthy, believed, however, that he could put President Johnson's renomination in doubt, even by coming within 20 percentage points of him in New Hampshire. Realistically, the Senator's goal has been to moderate Administration policy in Vietnam rather than replace the President.[3]

Thousands of college age students flocked to New Hampshire to campaign for McCarthy hoping to bring about an end to the war. Not wanting to be off-putting to staid New Englanders, student organizers adopted strict dress codes for volunteers. Boys had to be clean shaven and short haired and girls were encouraged to keep their skirts appropriately long for the occasion. "Neat and Clean for Gene" became their watchword.[4] McCarthy noted the enthusiasm of his young supporters but called for broader action. "This is not the kind of political controversy which should be left to a children's crusade, or to those not directly involved in politics."[5]

Primary day was cold and gray and a late afternoon snowstorm blanketed the state. Despite the foul weather, turnout was higher than expected. When the votes were tabulated, the nation got quite a shock. McCarthy had captured forty-two percent of the vote, and twenty of New Hampshire's twenty-four delegates to the Democratic National Convention. Suddenly, Johnson was vulnerable and opposition to the war was a viable political strategy.

Five days later, Johnson got a real opponent: New York Senator Robert F. Kennedy. In announcing his candidacy before a standing room only crowd in the same Senate Caucus Room where his brother had launched his successful 1960 campaign, Bobby Kennedy outlined his platform in terms that neatly summed up the divisions in the country: "I run to seek new policies—policies to end the bloodshed in Vietnam and in our cities, policies to close the gap that now exists between black and white, between rich and poor, between young and old in this country and around the world."[6]

A Gallup poll conducted before the New Hampshire primary had shown that Johnson and Kennedy were virtually tied for the support of the Democratic Party, as they were in union households. The IAM was torn. Kennedy had been a staunch ally in the legislative battles against binding arbitration and in favor of an increased minimum wage. He was perhaps the strongest supporter in the Senate of collective bargaining and, as Attorney General, had helped draft Executive Order 10988 guaranteeing federal employees the right to join a union. By the IAM's scorecard, he had voted with the union seventeen out of twenty times since 1965. But there remained lingering anxiety about the role he had played ten years earlier as Chief Counsel for the McClellan Committee.

Members and leaders of the IAM also felt he had gone overboard supporting the punitive Landrum—Griffin Act of 1959, even making an appearance on the *Tonight Show* with Jack Parr to ask the public to send letters to Congress supporting the legislation.

President Johnson, the only sitting President who had ever addressed an IAM convention, remained very popular. As the leadership pondered who to support there was yet another twist in the plot. Fifteen days after Kennedy announced his candidacy, President Johnson addressed the nation in a televised speech from the Oval Office. His remarks were about the war, and he surprised many by announcing he would adopt several of the measures Kennedy and McCarthy had been advocating on the campaign trail. At first, it seemed to be a bold political move, co-opting his opponents. But then he put down the prepared text and looked squarely into the camera. He spoke of the heavy burden the Presidency places on those who serve and quoted Presidents Roosevelt, Kennedy, and Lincoln. He paused and dropped his thunderbolt: "I shall not seek and I will not accept the nomination of my party as your President."[7]

Four days after Johnson's bombshell, the Reverend Martin Luther King, Jr. was in Memphis to rally support for 1,300 striking sanitation workers. On the evening of April 4, as he prepared to leave the Lorraine Motel for dinner, he leaned over an outside railing while talking to Jesse Jackson and a musician from Chicago named Ben Branch, who was going to perform later that evening at his rally. A shot rang out. Doctor King fell to the deck, dead at age thirty-nine from an assassin's bullet.

People across the country, black and white, rich and poor, reacted with shock and horror. Fear that racial tensions might lead to widespread violence seemed warranted. Tennessee Governor Buford Ellington immediately declared a state of emergency and called up 4,000 National Guard troops.

Bobby Kennedy, who as Attorney General had worked closely with Dr. King, was flying to Indianapolis for a campaign event in a predominantly African-American neighborhood. Kennedy was informed of the assassination when he landed. A short time later, he was the one who told the crowd of 500 people who had been waiting for nearly two hours for his arrival that Dr. King had been killed. As he waited for the cries of anguish to subside, he gathered himself and spoke solemnly and convincingly, his voice choking with emotion:

> *Those of you who are black can be filled with bitterness, with hatred and a desire for revenge. We can move in that direction as a country, in great polarization—black people amongst black, white people amongst white, filled with hatred toward one another. Or we can make an effort, as Martin Luther King did, to understand and to comprehend, and to replace that violence with an effort to understand, with compassion and with love.*[8]

While Kennedy and mainstream black leaders across the country pleaded for peace, Stokely Carmichael, the former Chairman of the Student Non-Violent Coordinating Committee did just the opposite, urging angry black youth to "go home and get your guns...White America has declared war on Black America," Carmichael said, adding that there was "no alternative to retribution. Black people have to survive and the only way they will survive is by getting guns."[9]

Widespread rioting and looting broke out across the country. The National Guard was called out to quell violence in Chicago; Detroit; Boston; Jackson, Mississippi; Raleigh, North Carolina; and Tallahassee, Florida. Rioting in Washington was so bad that President Johnson called up federal troops to protect the White House and the Capitol as the looting and burning reached within two blocks of the White House. An Associated Press photograph, taken from the roof of the Machinists Building on Connecticut Avenue, showed the nation's capital in flames.

A week after Dr. King's assassination, President Johnson was finally able to wrestle the Civil Rights Act of 1968, which granted equal access to housing out of the Senate where it had been subject to a filibuster. In a White House signing ceremony April 11, the President hailed the third major piece of Civil Rights legislation and called for an end to the violence wracking the country's cities.

> We all know that the roots of injustice run deep, but violence cannot redress a solitary wrong or remedy a single unfairness. Of course all America is outraged at the assassination of an outstanding Negro leader who was at that meeting [discussing civil rights] that afternoon in the White House in 1966.
> And America is also outraged at the looting and the burning that defiles our democracy. And we must put our shoulders together and put a stop to both.[10]

Violence in the streets eventually subsided, but the country remained extraordinarily agitated. The chapped relations among blacks and whites, rich and poor, old and young, academics and working class, had been rubbed raw by the whipsaw events so far in the year. The IAM issued its call for the Grand Lodge Convention, to be held beginning September 3 at the Conrad Hilton Hotel, in Chicago, Illinois. The Machinists would be using the same hotel that the Democratic Party would use as headquarters for their convention in late August.

The race for the Democratic nomination was in full swing with Bobby Kennedy drawing large, enthusiastic crowds as he campaigned across the country, Gene McCarthy continuing to run as an anti-war candidate, and Vice President Hubert H. Humphrey maneuvering to corral delegates using the power of the White House. Roy Siemiller signed on as a founding member of the Citizens for Humphrey Committee claiming he was acting as an individual, not as International President of the IAM.

On June 5, Kennedy won the South Dakota primary handily, receiving fifty percent of the vote to Humphrey's thirty percent and McCarthy's twenty. But California was the big prize, and Kennedy, with strong backing from minorities and the liberal elements in the labor movement, beat McCarthy 1,402,911 to 1,267,608, and captured 172 delegates. It was a day of major triumphs, and Kennedy was beginning to look like the inevitable nominee. Shortly after midnight, he stood at a podium in the Embassy Ballroom of Los Angeles' Ambassador Hotel, flanked by his wife, Ethel, pregnant with their eleventh child, and thanked his cheering supporters, wrapping up with, "Now on to Chicago, and let's win there!"[11]

The Kennedys left the stage through a back door. As they passed through the hotel kitchen, eight shots rang out. Bobby Kennedy sank to the ground, lying in a quickly spreading pool of blood. Bodyguards Rosey Grier and Rafer Johnson pounced on the shooter, twenty-four-year-old Sirhan Bishara Sirhan. Senator Kennedy was rushed to Central Receiving Hospital and quickly transferred to Good Samaritan Hospital. Five other people were wounded in the shooting, including forty-three-year-old Paul Schrade, a Regional Director for the United Auto Workers, who was shot in the head. Surgeons worked frantically trying to save the Senator's life. On Vice President Humphrey's orders, an Air Force jet rushed Doctor James Poppen, head of neurosurgery at Boston's Lahey Clinic, to Los Angeles to assist. Across the length and breadth of the country people prayed, even some to whom a house of worship was not a familiar place.

Twenty hours after he was shot, forty-two-year-old Bobby Kennedy died. Grown men wept openly. James "Scotty"

Reston, one of the most influential journalists of the era, and a confidant of John F. Kennedy, mused about a morality crisis that was threatening the very existence of American democracy:

> *There is something in the air of the modern world: a defiance of authority, a contagious irresponsibility, a kind of moral delinquency, no longer restrained by religious or ethical faith.And these attitudes are now threatening not only personal serenity but also public order in many parts of the world.*[12]

The Machinists were still planning to hold their convention in Chicago, at the Conrad Hilton Hotel. 2,036 delegates had been elected by 876 local lodges, a fifty-three percent increase over the size of the convention held four years earlier in Miami. The Executive Council was to meet in Chicago beginning Sunday, August 18, and the Law Committee would start its work, sorting through the various proposed amendments, the following day.

The IAM leadership was in Chicago so early because it was also the site of the 1968 Democratic National Convention. The Hilton Hotel would be headquarters for the Democratic Party, and the convention itself would be held a couple of miles south in the International Amphitheater, located in the Union Stockyards.

Preparation for both conventions was complicated by an Electrical Workers Union strike that prevented the installation of telephones, and by a second strike: drivers of the city's two major cab companies. There was also a significant threat of mass anti-war protests and of riots. Party leaders and city officials were on high alert. Chicago Mayor Richard J. Daley assembled a huge force: 11,900 police, 5,000 National Guardsmen, and 6,500 federal riot troops.

As the gavel came down to start the Democratic convention on August 26, thousands of young protesters arrived from across the country, a mixed bag of hippies, Yippies (members of the Youth International Party), Students for a Democratic Society, and hard core members of the National Mobilization Committee to End the War in Vietnam. Tensions between protesters and the police built. For the first three days of the convention there was only sporadic violence as protesters goaded the cops, calling them "pigs," and occasionally tossing bricks and bottles at the riot clad officers who would respond by lobbing tear gas and wielding clubs. On Wednesday night, with the convention set to nominate Vice President Humphrey, seen as little more than a surrogate for the hated President, the mob gathered in Grant Park near the Hilton to prepare to march to the convention center. Mayor Daley had denied them a parade permit and had instructed his police to keep them away from the Amphitheater. When the protesters lowered an American flag during their rally, the cops took great offense at the unpatriotic gesture and showered them with tear gas.

The protesters spilled out of Grant Park onto Michigan Avenue, in front of the Hilton, rubbing their eyes and regrouping for the march. As television cameras recorded the scene, the crowd started chanting: "The whole world's watching! The whole world's watching!" Police radioed for reinforcements and squawked over bullhorns that the protesters should clear the street. When the backup forces arrived and the mob of 3,000 did not move, the police attacked. *Time Magazine* reported, describing police tactics:

> *They flailed blindly into the crowd of some 3,000, then ranged onto the sidewalks to attack onlookers...In a pincer movement, they trapped some 150 people against the wall of the hotel. A window of the Hilton's Haymarket lounge gave way, and about ten of the*

> *targets spilled into the lounge after the shards of*
> *glass. A squad of police pursued them inside and*
> *beat them. Two bunny clad waitresses took one look*
> *and capsized in a dead faint. By now the breakdown*
> *of police discipline was complete. Bloodied men*
> *and women tried to make their way into the hotel*
> *lobby.* [13]

Without offering any proof, Mayor Daley told CBS that he had intelligence reports that there was a plot to assassinate him, the three leading Presidential candidates, and others. He called the demonstrators "terrorists," and said they used "the foulest language you wouldn't hear in a brothel hall."[14] Democratic officials, aghast at the violence and the ugly pictures being beamed into every living room in America and around the world, pleaded with Daley to call off his cops. Even Humphrey, who desperately wanted to remain on good terms with the mayor, condemned the "storm trooper tactics."[15]

When order was restored and the tear gas cleared, 650 people had been arrested and hundreds of people had been seriously hurt, including 152 police officers.

The smell of tear gas hung in the air as IAM delegates began checking in to "Fort Hilton" for the convention. Sentiment in the International Ballroom of the hotel seemed to run in favor of Mayor Daley and against the protesters. In his opening remarks, Roy Siemiller condemned the violence he had witnessed:

> *You don't have to be an expert in poll-taking*
> *techniques to know that union members who have*
> *worked so long and hard to build this country are*
> *pretty sick of rioters, looters, peaceniks, beatniks,*
> *and all the rest of the nuts who are trying to*
> *destroy it.* [16]

George Meany, echoing the International President, picked up the theme in his remarks:

> *I was here in Chicago last week, and I saw the invaders who came to this city. They were not invited but they came with the announced intention of upsetting the ordinary way of life of this city, of preventing the people of Chicago from welcoming the guests in their midst. I want to tell you quite frankly that I think the Chicago Police did not over-react, whatever that means. What would you do if some group advertised they were coming in here to prevent you from holding this convention? I know what you would do with the dirty-necked and dirty-mouthed group of kooks. To be frank, you might over-react.[17]*

Despite this harsh rhetoric, not all IAM delegates sided with Mayor Daley. Some, like Wimpy, thought the kids had a point. The analysis that "you're with us or you're a Communist," for the past two decades accepted as gospel, was outdated and wrong. Sure, the kids in the street weren't conforming to the strict codes of society. They wore long hair, beards, beads, tattered clothes and stood in naked defiance of authority. But they weren't the tools of Moscow or Beijing. They were standing up to a President who had sent thousands of their peers to die in a far away land in a war they viewed as unjust and un-winnable. They were shell shocked at the loss of Martin Luther King, Jr. and Bobby Kennedy. To use a phrase that became popular several years later, they were "mad as hell and not going to take it anymore."

Siemiller and Meany may have condemned the kids and everything they stood for, but over the course of the next twenty years, William W. Winpisinger embraced them with open arms.

TWENTY-TWO

RED SMITH TAKES OVER

Once the high-spirited speeches were over and the delegates settled down to business, Roy Siemiller's dream of serving another term was soundly defeated, all but assuring Wimpy's march to the presidency.

Siemiller's gambit to amend the constitution and allow an officer to complete his term of office regardless of age was supported by 199 local lodges. Unfortunately for him, almost 300 lodges argued that allowing officers to serve beyond age sixty-five would only lead to a tougher sell when negotiating early retirement for members in their contracts and instead endorsed amendments that would strengthen the sixty-five-and-out rule.

The 1,850 delegates (seventy-two of whom were women) agreed with that logic and voted a change to the IAM constitution stipulating that any candidate for an elected Grand Lodge office, including incumbents, could not seek that post unless they were young enough to serve at least two full years of the term before reaching the mandatory retirement age. Goodbye Roy Siemiller, hello Red Smith.

As the convention pressed on with its routine business, Vice President Humphrey, the newly-minted Democratic nominee, called in via a telephone hook-up from Redondo Beach, California, where he was campaigning. Humphrey, known as "The Happy Warrior," engaged in his customary banter and humor, which seemed oddly out of place in the mood of 1968. He credited the Machinists for their pluck in fighting political battles and asked for their support, pointing out that there were major differences between him and Richard Nixon.

Some people have said that Hubert Humphrey and Dick Nixon are like, they said, two peas in a pod, and it doesn't make any difference which one is elected President. Well, the other day Mr. Nixon vigorously denied the charge and I am here on the other end of this telephone to tell you that this is the first time he has been right![1]

Despite the subsequent endorsement of the IAM convention and a yeoman effort by labor to carry the Democratic ticket to victory, Humphrey lost the November election to Nixon. Nixon's popular vote margin of 112,803 was even smaller than John F. Kennedy's had been eight years earlier, and he won a bare minimum of 287 electoral votes, only seventeen more than the required 270.

Wimpy left Chicago knowing that he was destined to take the reins of the IAM in eight years, after Red Smith served two terms. His transportation empire was big and growing, and he was about to take on new roles representing the union on governmental commissions and as a delegate to international conferences. The IAM Pension Fund he chaired was growing by leaps and bounds and had nearly 70,000 members at 1,500 employers. The forty-four-year-old son of Cleveland had a full agenda, and a real desire to move the union in a more progressive direction. Although it may not have been clear to people observing him at the time, his personal politics would prove to be far closer to the demonstrators on the streets of Chicago than to the hardnosed speeches of Siemiller and Meany.

There was a nascent dynamic emerging in American politics, the "New Left," based largely in the academic community, which embraced the counter culture and eschewed the "Establishment" of big business, big government, and, now, big labor. The New Left's issues were not only the economic and class issues that had defined the early labor movement; they also supported women's rights, civil rights, improved race relations, and a liberal (if not tolerant) outlook on sexual mores, abortion, hair, clothing, and the recreational use of drugs.

Wimpy himself still looked like the former Cleveland auto mechanic he was, with conservative business suits, white shirts, and narrow ties, shiny black shoes, close cropped hair, what was left of it, and thick horn-rimmed glasses. His kids, the oldest of whom was twenty years old and in the Navy, chose to keep their hair short and their clothing neat. Pearl was still a stay at home mom, caring for their eight-year-old daughter, Linda. The Winpisinger family looked like the same bunch that had moved to Washington ten years earlier, outwardly unaffected by the cultural revolutions of the decade.

Throughout his career, from his early days as a shop steward in Cleveland to the day he hit the mandatory retirement age, Wimpy always valued the participation of youth and promoted education and training. The assignment Al Hayes had given him to work on apprenticeship training programs for the union gave him an opportunity to further those interests.

In October 1968, Wimpy was elected Co-Chairman of the National Transportation Apprenticeship Conference, a joint effort between government, business and labor to find and train the young people who would keep the airlines, railroads, trucking, and maritime industries staffed with the skilled labor they needed. Through the efforts of the IAM and the NTAC, nearly 11,000 apprenticeships in the metal trades were made available to kids graduating high school. Wimpy was proud of the number of opportunities, but objected to the high school graduation requirement. Testifying on Capitol Hill before the Senate Anti-Trust Subcommittee on the shortage of auto mechanics, Wimp was asked by Nebraska Senator Roman Hruska what he thought of the educational requirement.

If a high school diploma were necessary, I would have automatically been disqualified from a satisfying and rewarding occupation. I'm a drop-out and I've got a hunch that a lot of potentially good mechanics are standing around street corners because they have been disqualified by this kind of criteria.[2]

Wimpy was clearly more comfortable with the younger members of his union than with the conservative, seventy-four-year-old George Meany. The rapid growth of the IAM in the 1960's had changed the face of the membership, and more than a quarter of the million plus members of the union were under thirty. The new members were also far better educated than their older counterparts. By 1969, the average member had 12.3 years of formal education. Twenty percent of them had completed college.

When the nomination of officers rolled around in February 1969, Floyd "Red" Smith, the General Vice President from the Great Lakes Territory, was nominated for International President without opposition. Wimpy was nominated for re-election to the council by 973 lodges, and Phil Zannella was nominated for the Law Committee by 967 lodges. The plan hatched at Marcal's Restaurant was right on schedule.

Smith and the new Executive Council were sworn in July 1, 1969, with Smith indicating there would be no significant changes in the way he administered the union.

"I want the Machinists Union to continue to be known across the continent as the Fighting Machinists," he said. "Trade union members have never won a dime sitting still and being patient and turning the other cheek. What we have won is the result of the power that comes from organization and the intelligence to know how to use it. That's the way I hope the Machinists Union will continue to operate."[3]

Eugene Glover, a forty-six year old aircraft mechanic from St. Louis who had been serving as General Vice President in the Chicago office, took over Matt DeMore's position as General Secretary Treasurer. Glover, the father of seven children, was a World War Two veteran, and unlike many of his contemporaries, had managed to graduate high school, even though his mother had been widowed when he was only eighteen months old.

As Smith assembled his leadership team, there was tremendous excitement among the members and the country as a whole about the first trip to the moon. Astronaut Buzz Aldrin, Jr., an honorary lifetime member of the IAM, would be aboard the mission. He had legally changed his name from "Edwin" to "Buzz," and had been granted a gold lifetime membership in 1967 after he became the first "space mechanic," working outside his spacecraft for five and a half hours during the November 1966 *Gemini XII* mission. Upon receiving the gold card at the IAM's Aerospace Conference in Houston, Aldrin said, "I want to assure you that I receive this on behalf of all of the members of the astronaut group. We really appreciate everything your group has done for us in making possible the many events that we have been able to participate in."[4]

Aldrin's comments referred to the employees at Boeing, McDonnell Douglas, Bendix, TWA, RCA, Convair, and Lockheed who had built the rockets and other modules and the nearly 1,500 mechanics who were members of nine IAM locals at the Kennedy Space Center, then called Cape Kennedy, in Cape Canaveral, Florida, and the more than 120 members of Houston's local 1786 who would work on the mission to the moon.

Members at Cape Kennedy received shipment of the components of the *Apollo 11* modules in mid-March and began the painstaking chore of assembling the three stages of the giant *Saturn V* rocket in the center's vehicle assembly building.

Once that was completed they helped move the behemoth to launching pad 39A and began wiring and checking the electrical systems. As the days to the launch ticked away, they completed the mating operation of the *Saturn V* rocket to "Columbia," the *Apollo 11* command module, and "Eagle," the mission's lunar module, which would make the actual moon landing.

Aldrin, who would pilot the lunar module, and his fellow astronauts, Neil Armstrong and Michel Collins, arrived at Cape Kennedy June 26 to begin the countdown demonstration test. IAM members working with the astronauts and NASA personnel began putting in twelve hours a day, seven days a week to conduct the necessary tests.

In addition to the mechanics working on the spacecraft, another team of IAM members installed and maintained the escape chute and wire that would allow the crew to exit the capsule and slide safely to the ground in the event of a mishap during the pre-launch period.

Meanwhile, members in Houston at the Johnson Space Center's Lunar Receiving Laboratory began preparing for the astronaut's return to earth. No one was certain what dangers might lurk on the moon, and the members of the *Apollo 11* crew would be required to spend twenty-one days in quarantine to ensure that they had not brought back any pathogens. Members set up a "biological barrier" and outfitted the decontamination quarters with all the comforts of home. Although no members were scheduled to be quarantined with the astronauts, they were told to be on stand-by in case there were any mechanical problems. NASA had them sign agreements waiving their rights against "wrongful confinement or restraint." They were informed them that if the need arose for them to work on anything inside the biological barrier during the quarantine, they, too would be locked in for twenty-one days.

On Wednesday, July 16, 1969, *Apollo 11* blasted off from Cape Kennedy. More than 1,000,000 people lined the beaches and the streets leading to the compound to witness the event. A worldwide television audience of more than 600,000,000 people, the largest in history to that point, sat riveted to images of the IAM-built Saturn rocket thrusting the intrepid explorers into space. Four days later, on July 20, Aldrin and Armstrong landed the sixteen-and-a-half ton Eagle on the Sea of Tranquility with less than thirty seconds of fuel remaining in their craft. Six and a half hours later, they emerged and Armstrong was the first to set foot on the moon, exclaiming, "That's one small step for (a) man, one giant leap for mankind."[5]

Aldrin followed moments later, becoming the first member of a labor union to make an extraterrestrial appearance. The two spent just over two and a half hours on the moon's surface, where it was about zero degrees Fahrenheit in the sun and colder in the shade, taking photographs and collecting soil and rock samples before blasting off to rejoin the command module for the trip back to earth. By the time they splashed down in the Pacific Ocean and were recovered by the crew of the USS Hornet, they were international heroes. The IAM members who had worked so hard to make their mission a success were bursting with pride, and the nation had a reason to feel good about itself for the first time since the tragic and tumultuous events of 1968.

Wimpy's concerns at the time were more down to earth. Contracts at the nation's airlines and railroads were up at the same time, and the IAM was planning to seek significant increases for its 71,000 airline members and 20,000 railroad machinists, helpers and apprentices. The previous airline negotiations in 1966 had culminated in a 43 day strike, and bargaining with the railroads, while it yielded a shorter strike, had caused Congress to enact new restrictive legislation.

Bargaining with the airlines was delayed by an unsuccessful raid at United Airlines by a rag tag group known as the Airline

Mechanics Fraternal Association. AMFA fancied itself a craft union and was trying to persuade the IAM airline mechanics that they should not be lumped in with other, less skilled, workers. The mechanics didn't fall for AMFA's pitch and voted to remain with the nation's third largest union instead of joining a group that had no members.

Once bargaining with the nine airline companies got underway, a major problem arose when National Airlines chose to lock out 1,004 IAM members because of a work stoppage. The members refused to work because three National employees had been suspended for refusing to taxi Boeing 727 aircraft at Kennedy International Airport with only two operators in the cockpit. A three member crew was standard operating procedure at the busy airport, but National management demanded that only two of the three team members board an aircraft that needed to be moved. As a result, all three refused to board and participate in what they saw as an unsafe maneuver. The plane sat where it had been parked and the three IAM members were suspended.

Informational picket lines went up at airports in New York City, Newark, Jacksonville, Tampa, and Miami. The IAM purchased full page newspaper advertisements in the *The New York Times,* the *Washington Post,* the *Miami Herald,* and the *Miami News* that asked, "Is THIS any way to run an airline?"

Wimpy sent a letter making a personal appeal to every IAM district, local, officer and representative urging support for the locked out members.

> *They deserve and are entitled to no less than the unified all-out support, both morally and financially, of our remaining 70,000 air transport members. Such an effort will result in victory and strike a ringing blow for better contracts, not only in this round of negotiations, but in all those which lie ahead.*[6]

Meanwhile, Wimpy was working feverishly to try to negotiate a pact for the railroad machinists after a full year of frustration. Since he knew a general strike would create a "national emergency" and was out of the question, he devised an ingenious scheme of selective strikes against regional lines that would guarantee that, even though a particular railroad might be shut down, every section of the country would still be serviced by alternate carriers. Once the negotiations stalled and the thirty day cooling off period required under the Railway Labor Act was about to expire, Wimpy announced plans for the selective strikes saying, "We have no desire to create a national emergency by calling a nationwide strike. The four shop unions involved in this effort are convinced that in no sense would this strike be considered a national emergency—not by the most remote fantasy."[7] The improvised strike idea got the attention of the railroad companies like a cold bucket of water to the face. After seventy-two straight hours of bargaining at a session that included the carriers, Secretary of Labor George Shultz and Assistant Secretary of Labor W.J. Usery, an IAM member serving in Nixon's sub-cabinet, Wimpy emerged triumphantly to announce a settlement. Railroad shopmen would receive an 18.8% raise, moving from a base rate of $3.60 per hour to $4.28 per hour.

Justice for the locked out members at National Airlines took longer. Finally, after sixteen months, the members were able to return with a new three year contract. The three members who had been suspended were reinstated with full rank and privileges. Sixty days after the settlement, the Fifth US Circuit Court of Appeals ruled that the locked out members were entitled to full back pay. That meant a full year's salary and benefits, an average of $9,900 per worker, plus any longevity pay, shift differential, license pay, hospital and other insurance benefits or routine overtime they lost while they were idle. Wimpy and Plato Papps, the IAM General Counsel who had litigated the case, were ecstatic. Nearly two years of constant negotiating and legal wrangling had paid real dividends for his members.

While Wimpy was wrestling with the airlines and the railroads, Red Smith was settling into his role as the International President. He made slight territorial adjustments to the IAM regions and tapped sixty-two-year-old General Vice President Charles West to be his Chief of Staff. West had been working at headquarters since 1950, overseeing the IAM's jurisdictional relations with other AFL-CIO unions and supervising organizing among federal government employees.

Smith and West's political leanings seemed to be more closely aligned with Siemiller and Meany's than the more liberal tact Wimpy would take when he became president. FBI Director J. Edgar Hoover was given a full page in *The Machinist* to rail against "fanatic, anarchist revolutionaries" who were planning a "Summer Work-in."

Students for a Democratic Society, an admittedly radical group, were encouraging members to get jobs for the summer and to make personal contact with union members, prompting Hoover to say, "The SDS wants to make personal and direct contact with 'workers,' and 'educate' them in the SDS's philosophy, that is, that this country is 'rotten,' 'sick' and 'diseased,' and therefore must be destroyed."[8]

Charlie West, Red Smith's Chief of Staff, addressed the IAM Southern staff conference in New Orleans in June 1970, and sounded a lot like Hoover, but did at least throw the kids an olive branch.

> Right now the extremists of the left pose the greatest danger to democratic institutions. Such groups as the SDSers, the Weathermen, the Yippies and the Black Panthers have invaded the arsenals of anarchy and

are trying to bomb, loot, riot and burn away the
foundations of faith that hold our democratic society
together.[9]

But West did recognize the need not to write off a generation totally:

> *We must keep lines of communication open—*
> *especially with the nation's youth. There are those*
> *who are turned off by the sight of young people with*
> *beards, long hair and sideburns. There are those who*
> *hate their music and are shocked by their mini-skirts.*
> *But a nation that rejects its young is nation without*
> *a future.*[10]

The seemingly contradictory messages from West's speech (reject the actions and beliefs of the most militant of the young, but listen carefully to what they have to say) reflected the cultural chasm that marked the union and the country. It was to play itself out over and over again in the coming years, particularly as more of those "kids" with the beards, sideburns, and miniskirts became delegates to the IAM's Grand Lodge Conventions.

TWENTY-THREE

1972 GRAND LODGE CONVENTION

The delegates filing into the 1972 Grand Lodge Convention at the brand new Los Angeles Convention Center were remarkably different from their brothers and sisters at the 1968 Chicago convention. On balance, they were younger, more liberal, and there were many more women, blacks, and Hispanics than at previous conventions. Political and economic circumstances were different as well. Sentiment against the Vietnam war, a flashpoint at the 1968 gathering, was now quite mainstream. The country had reacted with revulsion to public reports and graphic pictures of the massacre of more than 300 innocent Vietnamese civilians at My Lai. The largest protest in the nation's history, a mostly peaceful gathering of more than 300,000 people, had paralyzed Washington, DC, in November 1969. People of all ages from coast to coast were sickened when Ohio National Guard troops opened fire on protesting students at Kent State University, in May 1970, killing four and wounding nine, less than forty miles south of where Wimpy had grown up.

A poll of all IAM members conducted in June 1972 revealed that sixty-percent of the membership favored either immediate withdrawal or setting a definitive date for withdrawal once the prisoners of war were released, and only twenty-six percent favored continuing the country's current course. The strong union support for administration policies President Johnson had enjoyed was a thing of the past.

The economy the delegates faced was rapidly deteriorating. Sharply reduced government spending on the space program and the military began to put a damper on defense contracts. Meanwhile, cheap goods from low wage countries were streaming into the country and good paying jobs were beginning to leak out.

The rising unemployment rate had a direct impact on the IAM. Membership had peaked at just over a million in 1969, but by the time the gavel came down in Los Angeles, it was off twenty-four percent to 760,000. Despite layoffs of Grand Lodge staff and other belt tightening measures, the union had lost nearly $4,000,000 of net worth and the strike fund was in the red to the tune of $1,381,763. Because of the precarious financial situation, the convention would be called upon to touch the third rail of union politics: a dues increase.

Wimpy attended the convention as the Headquarters General Vice President, Chief of Staff to International President Red Smith. He had been moved to that position from his post as General Vice President for Transportation in May 1972, following the retirement of Charlie West. The Cleveland plan was working and Headquarters GVP was Wimpy's final stepping stone to the presidency.

As Chief of Staff, Wimpy would be called upon to assume the chair of the convention when Red Smith needed a break, or when particularly thorny issues were being debated. It was in that role that Wimp was about to become widely known and appreciated across the length and breadth of the IAM.

The convention's first speaker was California Governor Ronald Reagan, who figured he could curry favor with a union so heavily involved in the defense industry by decrying spending cuts and calling for a strong military.

Whatever our political philosophy, whatever side of the bargaining table we sit on, we are all Americans, and whatever threatens America's security and prosperity threatens all of us. And the plain truth is that the proposals that have been advanced to cut America's defenses would retard all the progress we have made toward assuring a peaceful world and a prosperous America.[1]

Knowing that there would be a major battle to get the necessary per capita dues increase approved, in his opening address Red Smith appealed to the delegate's best instincts.

Many times it [the IAM] has stood at the crossroads where it could have gone backward more easily than it could go forward. Each time the members of this union, and the delegates to these conventions, have responded with the understanding and inspiration that have kept the IAM in the forefront of the struggle for social and economic justice.[2]

Smith's proposal called for an increase in payment of per capita dues to the international by basing it on twice each member's hourly earnings. The system provided for a base, and allowed locals to scale the rate for journeymen, technicians or apprentices. It also added dues money directly to the strike fund to wipe out the deficit in that account. Debate on the measure was heated. Smith's supporters and his administration pointed out the benefits of a strong, solvent strike fund and the increasing costs of organizing and arbitration. Opponents reacted with skepticism about the belt tightening claims the Grand Lodge was making and demanded to be given details on staffing. As debate continued, Red Smith's lack of skill as a parliamentarian, his quick temper and his battle against a significant respiratory illness nearly led to disaster.

Don Wharton, a delegate to the convention who would later become General Secretary Treasurer, recalled the scene as chaotic:

> *Red was a great trade unionist, but he couldn't run a meeting and couldn't make a speech very well. And guys knew that. If a meeting started to get out of hand, they would see that and just keep putting the knives in, and it would blow. And Red would threaten to come down there and knock the shit out of him. "I'll beat you right in front of the stage!" And he'd have to have Wimpy take it over. He'd just boil and go behind the stage for a while and calm down. He had emphysema so bad he'd get to coughing and he couldn't stop coughing.[3]*

Smith's parliamentary problems came to a head as they debated Proposition 48-J. A motion was made and seconded from the floor to accept the Law Committee's recommendation to change the dues structure. A delegate from Lodge 1400 made a motion to table the matter until the Law Committee developed a more detailed report. Other delegates jumped up and started shouting "second," and "point of order!" Smith, confused, ruled the motion to table in order and then tried to conduct a roll call vote. More shouting erupted from the floor and several delegates rose to point out that a move to table to a time certain was not in order, since it was in fact a motion to postpone. As tempers flared and voices rose, Smith got further into the weeds by trying to explain that delegates casting weighted votes based on the number of lodges they represented would only have one vote since this was a division of the house, and their weighted strength only applied on full fledged roll calls.

The commotion and the decibel level continued to rise as confusion spread through the hall. Paul Eustace, a delegate from Local Lodge 1726 in Boston, recalls the animosity and dissent:

> *A good friend of mine from New Jersey, Ralph Pollicio, is at the mic. I was about four or five rows back. All of a sudden I'm noticing across the hall a guy from Texas, a big son of a bitch, coming streaming across the hall. Ralph is trying to make himself heard, which is a problem in a room with probably two thousand delegates. I'm looking and all of a sudden it occurs to me [that] this guy's coming over to nail Ralph! I went up and just as I got there, about five feet away, this guy let him have it. Blindsided him. Ralph's a pretty tough kid. He's at the mic talking and boom!*
>
> *I grabbed Ralph, sided this guy off—"What the fuck are you doing?!" There was a B.A. from Philly, he grabbed the guy from Texas and pushed him back. He was president of a big local lodge from Texas, kind of a cuckoo.*[4]

George Kourpias remembered:

Guy's up at the mic, a guy by the name of Bertani, I forget the guy from New Jersey's name, Bertani slugged him to get him off the mic. One guy was pro-Red Smith; the other guy was anti-Red Smith. I was in the back of the hall; I really thought everything was going to come apart. But we got through the next half hour and the convention adjourned for the day. And the council got together. Siemiller was going around-he was retired- Siemiller was going around the audience telling people that they had to get Al Hayes, who was there, to get up and chair the meeting. Because Al was a great, great parliamentarian. The council said to Red Smith, we need Wimpy to open up the convention and to quiet those delegates down.[5]

Things would escalate even more outside the hall before Wimpy got a chance to work his magic. George Kourpias explained:

> We used to have a mutual alliance. The mutual alliance, you join once, when you were first delegates, and you were automatically a member if you were a delegate, it meant that when you went to a convention you will always be invited to a dinner with a lot of booze and a lot of fun. Well that crowd was angry. That crowd was pissed at Red and they were pissed at the council, they were pissed at each other, it was a mess.
>
> So they had this banquet, 2,000 people, only delegates. And for years, because of the Masonic type of thing, about fifteen or twenty people would become—I forget what we used to call it, but they used to dress in costumes, and they'd walk around swatting people and having fun. Well this one got out of hand, because what we used to do at those mutual alliance dinners was put a fifth of two or three types of liquor at each table. When I walked in, I was late—I was doing something at the hotel, I walked in—you could tell it was going to be terrible. The council will always sit up front. And they would be introduced and people could jump up and yell at them and say "you son of a,"—but it was a joke all the years, from day one. Boy, I could tell this was—I found a seat—I didn't know anybody at that table. The guy next to me, I put out my hand, he's "Well who the hell are you?!" Well they'd already killed a couple of fifths. I said "George Kourpias." "What do

you do?" I said "I'm a Grand Lodge Representative,"
and he started heckling me. And these guys had
paddles; they'd come by and paddle your butt.

Before the night is over, the band leader got hit
in the eye with a beer bottle. A couple of women
had their gowns destroyed. It was a terrible, terrible
night, everybody got their anger up. In front of the
convention center there was a pool. Delegates were
picking other delegates up and throwing them in,
there was a lot of damage to the place. I think it was
about $100,000, and in those days that was a lot
of money.[6]

The Mutual Alliance dinner was on Friday night, September
8. The following morning the delegates straggled in, many
bleary-eyed and hung over for their Saturday session. The Very
Reverend Patrick McPolin of the aptly named Our Lady of
Solitude Church opened the session, then Red Smith called on
Wimpy to speak.

Wimpy strode to the podium, stood ramrod straight, and
recalling the spirit of founder Tom Talbot and, paraphrasing
President Lincoln, brought order to the unruly proceedings.

...we are the beneficiaries of a great and justifiably
proud tradition. It is a tradition forged by the
founders of the IAM upon the principles of fair
play, achievement of the greatest good for the
greatest number and, above all, firmly anchored in
the principles of modern democracy... This great
convention itself is a testimonial today that ours truly
in our union is a government of the members, by the
members and for the members... Throughout all of
the years since 1888, that tradition has consistently
been built upon by succeeding conventions each

four years and it has been built upon primarily through the sober consideration at all times of all the proposals fostered by the membership or the officers and brought to the convention floor...It has been forged by the intelligent, thorough and often times articulate debate which has consistently resulted in a constitution which is the envy of the free trade unionists everywhere. It has provided the IAM an honored place in the forefront of the trade union movement in all of the areas of our operation. It has benefited our members on the job in terms of wages, hours and working conditions. It has benefited them at home, in the communities and even in the pursuit of leisure, which is more and more available to us...And I believe that it is the preservation and the future building upon that tradition which is the challenge of this convention on Saturday, September 9, 1972, and I say that because reports reaching us seem to indicate that the issues which are central to this convention are becoming very, very confused and an atmosphere of confusion can simply not contribute to productive, beneficial results.[7]

Wimpy, who believed strongly in the proposal, went on to detail the new dues structure and the payment to the strike fund in simple, straightforward terms. There was complete calm in the audience as the delegates hung on his every word. He wrapped up by appealing to them for a respectful debate.

And, in conclusion, as I said before, we have a challenge facing us in this convention and we begin work on that, I think, this morning and I would earnestly hope that every delegate will view this as the serious business which it is; that he will be in his seat and give due respect to all of the speakers as the issues are debated and clarified and create the climate within which the intelligent debate and the dissemination of information will make for the kind of enlightened decisions that have made us a great union.[8]

According to George Kourpias, "The convention settled down, we got our strike fund, we got the dues taken care of."[9]

The proposition carried on a voice vote. When a few of the dissenters questioned the ruling of the chair and requested a roll call vote they could muster only 129 votes, not even half of the 300 votes necessary to trigger a roll call.

The convention then heard from Senator George McGovern, the Democratic nominee for President. McGovern had won the nomination at a bizarre convention in Miami Beach two months earlier. In 1968, the chaos had been in the streets; in 1972, due in large part to rules "reform" implemented by a commission chaired by McGovern himself, the battles moved to the convention floor. Traditional delegates from labor unions and other core Democratic constituencies saw their influence diluted by the addition of hundreds of "diversity delegates," representing women and racial minority groups. Sessions began in the evening and lasted until the crack of dawn. The traditional focus on economic issues that were the bedrock of the party gave way to divisive debates on social issues such as reproductive rights, gay rights, women's rights, and civil rights. The young liberal activists in attendance felt empowered. Some of the staunch old-line Democrats felt uncomfortable and others were outright disgusted.

McGovern selected Missouri senator Thomas Eagleton as his running mate. Shortly after the announcement, it was revealed that Eagleton had checked himself into the hospital three times in the past decade for mental or physical exhaustion, and had twice received electro-shock treatment. Hours after saying he stood behind Eagleton "One thousand percent," McGovern accepted Eagleton's resignation from the ticket and named Kennedy cousin Sargent Shriver to replace him. McGovern was wounded and limped through the campaign. IAM members, eager to replace Nixon, were nonetheless skeptical about his labor record. At the Los Angeles convention, McGovern addressed that head-on, saying his Republican opponents were lying about him.

> One of the biggest whoppers they have in circulation is the preposterous charge that if George McGovern becomes the President of the United States, there are going to be fewer jobs for the working people of this country and especially for the Machinists and Aerospace Workers. If that were my intention, do you think I would show my face at the convention here today? Would I be going into the aerospace plants at San Diego and Seattle and meeting with the workers of those plants?[10]

McGovern's plea for the IAM's help ultimately worked. After a floor debate, the delegates voted, albeit not unanimously, to endorse his candidacy.

But even labor endorsements couldn't overcome this inherently weak Democratic ticket, which was culturally at odds with a majority of the country. McGovern got swamped on Election Day, carrying only Massachusetts and the District of Columbia. The country braced for four more years of Richard Nixon.

TWENTY-FOUR

RESIDENT VICE PRESIDENT

Wimpy's move to Resident Vice President in May of 1972 signaled to even the most casual observer that he was next in line to be International President. It also freed him from the arduous and time consuming responsibilities of representing members on the airlines, railroads and in auto repair shops. George Kourpias recalled:

> It was a promotion. Because you're chief of staff to the president, and the signal went out quickly when Wimp was moved from transportation to Resident Vice President. Meaning he's the next guy. I think everybody knew that when Charlie West retired Wimp was coming upstairs, everybody couldn't wait. Wimpy wanted the staff to run things, and he wanted to be out with the people. West wanted to know everything that was going on, Wimp didn't care for the scuttlebutt. He kept looking at the big picture.[1]

Red Smith, due to failing health and personal inclinations, ran the day-to-day operations at headquarters. No detail was too small to escape his personal attention. That left very little of the traditional chief of staff function for Wimpy, so rather that stay at headquarters and butt heads with Smith, he used his position to hit the road, meet members, serve on government panels, travel overseas, establish a vast network of important contacts, expand his knowledge of politics and the economy, and hone the communication skills he had demonstrated at the Los Angeles convention to a formidable edge.

While Wimp and Smith remained friendly, there was a bit of an edge to their relationship due mostly to their different views of the role the union should play in the community at large, and a bit of jealousy on Smith's part. George Kourpias observed:

> One very big difference was dealing with and being part of the community at large. Wimpy was involved all over the place in different groups that were not necessarily union groups. Red did not welcome that. Wimp loved to be interviewed and loved press conferences. Red Smith wanted nothing to do with those. It was a real difference of philosophy as to how to promote the union. How do you put us on the map if your leader refuses to go to the public? So that was the big difference between the two of them. I would say Red came from the old school and Wimp represented a new way of thought. At times because Wimp could get up and make a marvelous speech and handle himself beautifully in a press conference, it would be impossible for Red. He was jealous of Wimp, and it showed on his face. He would say to me, "Oh there he goes again!" But he also understood Wimp's intelligence, and he understood what Wimp could do what he couldn't. Red knew that but it teed him off. So it was two different characters, two different ways of life.[2]

The political waters that Wimp waded into were roiled by two significant events that would have long term effects on American society. At 2:00 AM on June 17, 1972, during the presidential campaign, Washington, DC, police responded to what they thought was a routine burglary call at the swank Watergate Office Building on the banks of the Potomac River.

Inside the office of the Democratic National Committee, they encountered five men with electronic bugging equipment, walkie-talkies, mace, and fifty-three sequentially numbered $100 bills. One burglar, James W. McCord, proved to be Security Director for the Republican National Committee and the Committee to re-elect the President. All five had CIA connections, and three of them had in their wallets the White House telephone number for E. Howard Hunt, a former CIA operative who had helped hatch the Bay of Pigs fiasco.

Months of follow-up investigations by the authorities and the *Washington Post* revealed that the break-in had been directed from the White House. By May 1973, the US Senate convened a Special Committee and held hearings to get to the bottom of the matter. For nearly four months, the nation watched the daily television coverage of the hearings and became more and more outraged as the complicity of the President and his staff in the break-in and subsequent cover-up became clear.

The other significant event was an oil embargo imposed by the Organization of Petroleum Exporting Countries that began on October 17, 1973. It came in response to America's support for Israel in what soon became known as the Yom Kippur War. Egypt and Syria attacked Israel in an effort to recover land they had lost in the 1967 Seven Day War. The ministers of OPEC banded together in support of their Arab brothers and sent the price of oil skyrocketing from five dollars a barrel to more than twelve dollars. Gasoline prices nearly doubled. The cost of fuel to heat homes and run factories spiraled out of control.

The American economy, already racked with rising prices and high unemployment, took a major beating. As gasoline supplies dried up, long lines began forming at service stations. Anxious customers waited hours to buy the fuel they needed to get to work. But not everyone felt the pain. Oil companies made out like bandits; their profits shot up as much as sixty percent. The IAM surveyed its members and found that one out of five had experienced layoffs in their shops as a result of energy shortages. Union leaders were astonished to learn that seventy-five percent of their members reported that they could not get to work using public transportation; cars had reached a new level of necessity.

As Wimpy traveled around the country meeting with management groups, government officials, college professors, reporters, authors, and television interviewers, he realized he needed a steady hand back at headquarters to watch over things on his behalf. He tapped his close friend and confidant, George Kourpias, to be his Administrative Assistant. The forty-one-year-old Kourpias would also provide staff assistance to Red Smith, continue in his role as director of the union's older members and retirees program, and serve as Vice Chairman of the Machinist's Non-partisan Political League. Wimpy and Kourpias were constant companions, and close as brothers. They formed a solid team with Wimpy always looking at the big picture and Kourpias keeping him grounded and paying attention to the details. They socialized frequently, with Wimpy and Pearl often going to George and June's house for dinner. The trip over from the Winpisinger residence was sometimes as exciting as the dinner itself.

George Kourpias remembered

> He was something when he was in a car. He was an excellent driver and he drove with both feet, his right for the gas, his left for the break. He would tailgate everybody, get within an inch of the car in front of him and try to get them to move faster. At one point he even had a speaker in his car and he'd yell out and tell people to move it! He was a fast driver. He loved to drive. When he was around nobody could drive but him. They came over for dinner one night,

I opened the door and Pearl took one look at me and said, "George, there were only ten 'son of a bitches' from my house to yours."[3]

As Wimpy traveled the country giving speeches and offering "Labor's view" on the issues of the day, he began to find his political voice. Whether it was a speech to the Great Lakes Territory staff conference, a lecture at the Carnegie-Mellon Institute or a place on a State Department panel on the transfer of technology, Wimpy sounded consistent themes. He quickly developed a reputation as a maverick, unafraid to make waves. He spoke of the "three legged stool" that kept American manufacturing humming-scientists to develop an idea, engineers to design the means of production, and skilled machinists to make the product. He disdained a society that looked down its collective nose at people who worked with their hands. In a speech to the Great Lakes Territory staff conference in Cincinnati, in March 1974, he lamented that "... something very deep and fundamental is bothering American society as a whole today."[4]

He went on to summarize his view of the past four decades:

> *For four decades we have neglected our most pressing needs. During the 1930's we couldn't afford to meet the needs of the American people. During the 1940's we were too busy saving democracy, including the skins of the French and a few others who now feel it's safe to thumb their nose at Uncle Sam. During the 1950's complacency and the Eisenhower philosophy of do-nothing government was in the saddle. During the 1960's we squandered money, manpower, and materials, including God knows how many hundreds of millions of barrels of petroleum products, in and over the jungles and rice paddies of Southeast Asia. And now, in the 1970's,*

*as the personal gift of the Abby Hoffman's and Jerry
Rubens and David Dellinger's and all the rest of that
pack of hippies and yippies who tore Chicago up
before the TV screens of a watching nation, and who
shouted down one of the most humane and decent
men who ever graced the political scene, with their
obscenities and insane chants of 'dump the Hump,'
we are now stuck with one of the worst afflictions
the American people ever put into the White House.
Whether or not Richard Nixon stays in the White
House remains to be seen.[5]*

He railed time and again in his speeches for more
apprenticeships, respect for the working class, and attention
to the on-the-job hazards that claimed lives through accident
and job related diseases. In the first period of American history
where energy was no longer plentiful and cheap, he began
calling for the development of alternative energies: solar, wind,
geothermal, and hydroelectric, and touted what a boon they'd
be to the economy.

But even as he pointed out to group after group that the
productivity of American workers had doubled since World
War Two, and decried the notion of an "acceptable level of
unemployment," he still did not fully embrace the socialism
he'd become known for in later years.

In a speech at the Carnegie-Mellon Institute defending
labor's support for free enterprise, he took aim at socialists
and the New Left:

*Even today a motley crew of small splinter groups—
such as the Socialist Workers Party and the Socialist
Labor Party—reject capitalism in its entirety. However,
when they send their emissaries into the mills,
mines, factories and workshops to radicalize what*

> *they consider the "proletariat," the reaction mostly*
> *runs from derision to a punch in the nose. Though*
> *the radicals of the New Left have infiltrated a few*
> *union halls, they haven't accomplished much beyond*
> *making a nuisance of themselves by harassing union*
> *reps trying to carry on the day to day functions of*
> *basic trade unionism.[6]*

Wimpy took great exception to the export of American technology and jobs, pointing out that the vast majority of the cost to develop new technologies was borne by taxpayers. He felt that private industry should not export the technology and jobs it made possible while receiving as little as ten cents on the dollar.

In an outline of remarks for a speech almost a year before he ascended to the presidency, Wimp tried to explain the differences between his generation and the "newer" generation that was swelling the membership rolls of the IAM:

> *My generation, the generation that fought World War*
> *II, views economic—social environment differently*
> *than the newer generation.*

* Highly patriotic ("I fought for this country")
* Associates beards and long hair with hippies, yippies, gays, etc.
* Seeks security, stability, order (based on Depression memories)
* Usually has no more than high school education (probably less)

Newer generation (sometimes called "Lordstown" generation)

* More bearded, beaded and black

* Not only more women—but different roles—apprentices,
  union stewards, local lodge officers
* Better educated
High percentage have some college
* Less willing to accept things as they are[7]

In addition to his domestic travels and speech making, Wimpy used the freedom of his new position to travel overseas for the first time since his days in the Navy. He led an eight-man delegation to Stockholm for the International Metalworkers Federation Convention in June 1974, that elected the first American as Governing Secretary of that conglomeration of 115 trade unions from sixty-eight countries. Then he became so interested in labor's role in Scandinavia that he returned a month later to spend the balance of the summer in Sweden, Norway, Switzerland, and England. The following summer, he skipped a trip to the AFL-CIO convention to attend the IMF convention in Japan.

Wimpy also began to accept appointments to boards and commissions. In August 1974, he was appointed to the Federal Committee on Apprenticeship by Secretary of Labor Peter J. Brenan. His appointment, announced the day before President Nixon resigned, came as somewhat of a surprise. The Watergate probe had revealed that Nixon held the IAM in very low esteem, and had even placed Red Smith on his infamous "enemies list." Wimpy was elected to the Democratic National Committee as a delegate from Maryland. As a prominent labor leader, he was immediately appointed to the organization's finance committee. In 1975, he was elected President of the Institute on Collective Bargaining, a not-for-profit organization supported by trade unions, a select few industries and Theodore W. Kheel, a venerable labor lawyer and collective bargaining expert. The organization was a spin-off of an effort started in 1962 by Al Hayes and an industrialist named John Snyder.

Snyder's company, US Industries, Incorporated, manufactured a robot they called the "TransfeRobot," which performed many menial manufacturing tasks and reduced the need for manual labor. The company rented the machines to manufacturers for twenty-five dollars a week, less than half what they were paying the workers it replaced. Snyder, however, realized the catastrophic effects his machines could have on employment and joined with Hayes and the IAM to form an institute based in New York City they called "Automation House." The institute, which studied the future impact of automation on employment, was funded by royalties from his machines.

Snyder died in 1965, and his successor as President of US Manufacturing withdrew funding for the effort. After several years of casting about for a new sponsor, Roy Siemiller finally managed to recruit Frank Gallucci, a Vice President of Essex Wire Company to serve as Co-Chairman. They eventually spun off an institute devoted to studying collective bargaining based at Automation House. Ted Klassen, President of American Can Corporation, and subsequently the Postmaster General of the United States, was the first chairman. The AFL-CIO's Lane Kirkland, George Meany's right hand man, served as the first President. Seven years later, Wimpy was elected to replace Kirkland and Colonel Frank Borman, President of Eastern Airlines, replaced Klassen as Chairman.

The Collective Bargaining Institute position injected Wimpy into yet another high level circle of movers and shakers and required him to spend significant time in New York City. It also allowed him to develop a close working relationship with the influential Kheel, who was very active at Cornell University. At Kheel's suggestion, the board of trustees of Cornell University elected Wimpy to serve on their Advisory Council for Labor and Industrial Relations, and he maintained a close working relationship with the university, returning there to speak several times in later years.

As the calendar pages turned toward Red Smith's sixty-fifth birthday and Wimpy's ascension to the highest office in the union, he became the best prepared individual ever to assume that office, skilled at representing members from every trade and discipline, battle tested in campaigns and the halls of Congress, and welcomed in union halls and the ivy clad lecture halls of major universities. As he might have said (and probably did say): "Not bad for a high school drop-out from Cleveland."

TWENTY-FIVE

PROGRAM FOR PROGRESS

Wimpy's eventual elevation to International President had been determined by the deal cut at Marcal's Restaurant in 1966, but now, ten years later, as the 1976 election for President of the United States ramped up, a more formal series of events that would lead to his ascendancy began to unfold.

By February 1976, Wimpy was openly commenting on his likely election as the next International President. He told the Illinois Council of Machinists at their February 7, 1976, meeting that, "I hope I do not sound immodest or overconfident in saying that come July first, I expect to become the eleventh individual in the almost eighty-nine years of IAM history to have the honor of serving as International President."[1]

In that address, Wimpy said he did not seek the office for personal glory or ego gratification. He had a deeply held belief that as international president he could contribute to the members, the future of the union itself and the "long-range good of the nation and the economy."[2]

He outlined his beliefs that the American workforce was the best and most productive in the world, that the government was shortchanging those workers by encouraging high rates of inflation and unemployment at the same time by allowing a massively disproportionate distribution of wealth and income, and that there was a conspiracy among the well-to-do to promote unemployment as a way of keeping the workforce docile and compliant.

He closed with a quick list of his priorities and words that would prove prophetic: "I've always looked forward to a good fight!"[3]

The IAM Wimpy was about to lead stood at nearly a million members, making it larger than all but the Teamsters and the

United Auto Workers. The union had an excellent relationship with the Auto Workers and was on at least passable terms with the Teamsters. The sizeable membership of the IAM, roughly one out of every two hundred people in the entire country, gave it enormous political clout. The Machinists Non-partisan Political League was one of the biggest and best funded political funds in the country. The union had 1,891 locals, 152 districts, 250 Grand Lodge Representatives, Auditors and organizers, 692 elected union representatives and general chairmen, 17,360 officers elected at the local lodge level, and a Grand Lodge support staff of 269. IAM contracts were in effect with employers across the continent, 12,300 in all. The IAM Pension Plan, which Wimpy chaired and had been instrumental in growing, covered 133,000 members at 2,465 employers and had reserves of $155,635,000.

The eighty-nine-year-old union, once known only for representing Southern railroaders, was now the dominant union in all phases of transportation except trucking. It represented a broad range of workers in the aircraft, aerospace, metal manufacturing and auto repair industries. As Wimpy had pointed out in a speech about a new generation of IAM members, the union was more "bearded, beaded and black" than at any time in its history. And it contained a sizable and rising number of female members, many of whom were being elected to positions of leadership at the local lodge level.

For all its strengths, the union also faced challenges. Inflation, high energy prices, stagnant wages, and the loss of manufacturing jobs to other countries were taking a major toll. Membership was declining from its peak of just over 1,000,000, and the IAM had run at a deficit of $6,806,270 between 1972 and 1975.

The 1972 convention, despite its often chaotic proceedings, had raised dues and put local lodges and the strike fund back on sound financial footing. But the plan adopted at the Los

Angeles convention did not share the wealth with the Grand Lodge and the districts. As a result, the union was hurting at those levels.

At Wimpy's behest, the Executive Council would bring a proposal to the 1976 convention called the "Program for Progress," which would establish an automatic distribution of dues and income among the local lodges, district lodges and Grand Lodge.

Wimpy, rolling up his sleeves and getting ready for the Presidency, began to collate the observations and aspirations he had developed into a plan of action. His IAM would be the most militant, aggressive, and progressive union in the United States and Canadian labor movements. He would put the IAM on the map and make it a household name.

Women and minorities would be given roles of power and prominence and accorded the respect and support necessary to be successful in those positions. He'd get out of headquarters as much as possible and spend time with the members, teaching, preaching, and hearing what they had to say. He would turn the Grand Lodge offices into a beehive of activity, crawling with young, talented, creative people, whether they had come up through the ranks or not. Some were not even members of the IAM until they started working at headquarters. Among his passions were apprenticeships and the education of his members. He also intended to become a proponent of every new form of technology he could get his hands on. Freed of having to carry out the goals of someone else's presidency, he planned to stake out positions and become a forceful advocate on the pressing issues of the day, including energy, the reform of labor laws, and the image of organized labor. And in a major departure from the ways of Red Smith, he wanted to build coalitions with myriad groups which had common interests but were not labor unions. Wimpy's IAM would be a reflection of their new president: bold, brash, intelligent, energetic, honest, decent, and just downright *interesting*.

As Wimpy prepared to assume the Presidency of the IAM, a pitched battle was underway for the Democratic Presidential nomination. With the party seemingly poised to recapture the White House in the wake of the Watergate scandal and Nixon's resignation, nine candidates tossed their hat into the ring. The MNPL did a casting call at the Shoreham Americana Hotel in Washington, DC, in late January, and each aspirant paid his respects and made a pitch for the IAM endorsement.

Wimpy's first choice was former Oklahoma Senator Fred Harris, a liberal populist who railed, as Wimpy so often did, against multinational corporations, monopoly industries, and high unemployment. As much as Wimpy liked Harris' politics, the pragmatist in him knew Harris was too liberal to win the nomination. His second choice was Washington Senator Henry "Scoop" Jackson. Standing at the MNPL podium, Jackson connected with the conference attendees by recalling his vote against Taft-Hartley, his support for the Kennedy-Corman health security bill, and his bedrock commitment to full employment.

Indiana Senator Birch Bayh, Texas Senator Lloyd Bentsen, Pennsylvania Governor Milton Shapp, Arizona Congressman Mo Udall, former North Carolina Governor Terry Sanford, and Sargent Shriver, the 1972 Vice Presidential nominee, all made brief presentations and were met with polite attention.

Jimmy Carter, the former Governor of Georgia and the eventual nominee, was the darkest of dark horses when he spoke. No one suspected that later that evening, his well organized political machine would pull off an upset finish in the Iowa caucuses. He rattled off the same laundry list of labor concerns the other candidates did, and then touched on a subject that would come back to haunt him: "Any time a repeal of Taft-Hartley or 14 (b) can be passed, I will be glad to sign it. I'm not going to take it on as a crusade…but I would be glad to see 14 (b), the right-to-work laws repealed."[4]

Carter went on to place second to "uncommitted" in the Iowa caucuses, receiving almost twice as many votes as his next closest challenger, Senator Bayh. Although he polled a relatively small number of actual votes, approximately 13,815 to Senator Bayh's 6,580, Carter became the instant front runner. His strategy was to win in Iowa and New Hampshire and use those as a springboard to the nomination. In New Hampshire a month later, Carter edged out Mo Udall by 4,315 votes. Scoop Jackson, labor's favored candidate, won the primary in the more populous and industrial Massachusetts a week later, but Carter's momentum soon forced Jackson to drop out.

In May, when it was apparent that Carter would be the nominee, Wimpy appeared before the Democratic National Committee Platform Committee. He urged the Democrats to emphasize jobs, health care, and a more balanced tax system. As he did almost everywhere he spoke, he ripped the multinational corporations that were shipping American jobs and technology overseas. He lambasted the big oil companies that racked up record profits while paying little or no taxes.

In late July, the IAM sent fifty-four members as delegates to the Democratic National Convention at Madison Square Garden in New York City. Unlike the disastrous conventions of 1968 and 1972, this was an orderly affair, with a party united for victory behind Jimmy Carter.

The IAM convention in Hollywood, Florida, running from September 7–16, was another matter. Tensions were about to erupt on a number of issues, particularly the new Program for Progress which would change the allocation of dues monies, sending forty percent to the Grand Lodge General Fund and ten percent to the Strike Fund. Member's average hourly earnings had increased twenty-five percent since the Los Angeles convention of 1972, but the cost of living had increased 29.6%. Therefore, members were feeling an economic pinch and the leadership of the union would face stiff opposition to their proposal.

The layout of meeting rooms at the Diplomat hotel, where the convention would be held, only added to the already tense situation. The room for the main session was a huge "V" shape, with the main stage at the bottom of the "V." Because of the unusual configuration, one half of the convention couldn't see the other half. There were twelve floor microphones, twice the usual number. Once again, Red Smith lost control of the convention and had to turn to Wimpy to settle things down. Phil Zannella, Jr., son of the legendary Phil Zannella, was at the convention as a sergeant at arms:

> I'm twenty years old and I'm wide-eyed and everything else. Red lost control. It was a huge convention. We had so many delegates that it was set up in a "V," so one side really couldn't see the other. And the sound didn't carry well, especially when you had voice votes. You had people with different opinions and different agendas, and with all the microphones set up, certain people were trying to take them over to get their point across. Some factions there were obviously against anything, anti-Grand Lodge, anti-International. …You even saw a lot of, I don't want to say fights, but I would say very heated discussions amongst friends. Ohio was seated way in the back of the hall. Red was getting frustrated. They had switches for the microphones and when people started really getting on him, you could see Red up there trying to switch them off, and he's totally losing it. And then he probably didn't say the right things, either. And then,

as usual, cool, calm and collected, Wimpy stepped in. Nobody's going to take Wimpy to school, he just took over and the convention calmed down.[5]

After two hours of more orderly debate with Wimpy at the podium keeping the discussion under control, the Program for Progress was put to a vote. It carried by twenty-nine votes, 3,872 to 3,843.

With the union's finances on a path to solvency, Wimpy started dreaming of ways to achieve his goal of putting the IAM on the map.

Don Wharton remembered:

Just before he was elected [International President] and just before he actually took office, I was with him in Indiana at the Indiana State Council of Machinists. Wimpy was great for getting a group of guys together and sitting around talking about what ought to happen in the union. One of the fellows who had been around quite a while was a Grand Lodge Representative, and he said, "Wimp, let me tell you what our problem is, we're not as big as the Steel Workers, the Rubber Workers, the IUE and different unions, and so we don't get the recognition." Wimpy looked at me and I didn't say anything. Then he said, "Don, which of those unions are bigger than us?" And I said, "Well, the Steel Workers are not bigger than us. IUE's certainly not bigger than us. Rubber Workers are about half our size. The UAW's bigger than us, that's the only union that's bigger than us." He said, "Well, how do they get on the news all the time?" I said, "The Rubber Workers get on the news because if they strike they shut down all the rubber and the whole world knows about it, they've got the

*tires. The IUE, if they have Westinghouse on strike,
or GE, you hear about it. That's the only reason." And
Wimpy said, "Let me assure you. When I become
International President, you will not ask that question
after a year or two. We're going to be heard. We're
going to be out front. I might not always be right, but
I'm going to be heard."⁶*

Wimpy soon hit on a unique strategy to begin to increase
the IAM's visibility. A former auto mechanic and a hellacious
driver, he was a big fan of automobile racing, preferring the
Indy cars to NASCAR. Always a shrewd operator, Wimp did
some research and found out that Indy racing was the second
most popular sport in the country at the time and pulled
in the second highest television ratings, right behind horse
racing.

In mid-1976, he and Pearl attended a banquet in Las Vegas
with Bud Melvin, a close friend who was a railroad General
Chairman from California. Melvin had a relationship with
Steve Waldman, the sales director for the Frontier Hotel, who
invited the Melvin's and the Winpisinger's to catch a show after
dinner.

Bud Melvin recalled:

*We all saw Buddy Hackett together, and we were
jolly and having a real good time. On the way out
to the car, Steve said, "When are we going to go
see Indianapolis?" And I said, "Well, I can get us pit
passes," because my brother had a radiator shop
that made radiators for the race cars. Steve said,
"Well, I can get us the hotel." Wimpy said, "Well,
if someone can find the tickets, I can pay for the
tickets."*

So I went to a friend of mine, and he bought the tickets from Rowe Shock Absorber Company. They always hold big blocks of seats. So we got the tickets through them, and Steve took care of the hotel.

So we went. We all had a marvelous time. He was Joe Super Fan. He had cameras and binoculars and everything around his neck. We went into the pits, and we really thought we had hit the big time.[7]

Wimpy was thunderstruck by the atmosphere at Indy. Cars, power, speed, the low throated growl of the sleek cars, the roar of the crowd. The pits were the place to be, and they were chock full of mechanics. Just like the mechanic Wimpy had been back in Cleveland, and just like the 100,000 mechanics the IAM represented. He hit upon an idea: an IAM racing program.

It would raise the profile of the union and he and the members could have a hell of a lot of fun in the process.

He devised a three stage strategy for getting the IAM into the Indy racing circuit. First, he'd have the union sponsor trophies and cash prizes for the top mechanics at major races. Other people sponsored trophies and prizes for drivers and owners of the cars, so why not salute the guys who turned the wrenches?

At Wimpy's urging, the Executive Council approved the race recognition program, to begin in the 1977 racing season, awarding a check for $1,000 to the chief mechanic of the car that won the Indy pole position and a huge trophy and a check for $5,000 to the mechanic of the winning car. They also committed to present checks to winning mechanics at the Milwaukee 150, the Pocono 500, Norton 200, Texas 200, Milwaukee 200, Ontario 500, Michigan 150, and Phoenix 150 in the inaugural season of the program.

His second phase was to have the IAM sponsor its very own Indy car class race, a 150 mile contest at New Jersey's Trenton International Speedway.

His third and final phase of putting the IAM brand on Indy racing was the boldest and most expensive: the union would sponsor a race car to be known as the "Machinists Union Special."

TWENTY-SIX

PRESIDENT IN WAITING

As the 1976 campaign drew to a close it appeared the country would elect a Democratic President for the first time since 1968. Yet what had started out as a sure thing was beginning to look a bit too close for comfort. The labor movement and a sizeable portion of the Democratic Party were less than thrilled with Jimmy Carter but recognized that electing him was far better than four more years of Republican control under President Ford.

Wimpy traveled to an Indiana State Council of Machinists meeting eleven days before the election to give a speech intended as a rallying cry for Carter's election. It soon became apparent that he was going through the motions, but his heart was not in it. The candid notes he prepared for the speech began: "As campaign limps to a listless conclusion—more people than ever turned off—say it doesn't matter who wins—pollsters predict less than 55% turnout."[1]

He mentioned Carter's name only twice in his remarks, once at the beginning and again at the conclusion. Gerry Ford's name came up in a negative context nine times. Wimpy, like many people in the country, was preparing to hold his nose, vote for Carter, and hope for the best.

Labor did what it could to elect him. The MNPL raised a record $1.4 million for the election cycle. Machinists local lodges played a significant role in the voter registration and get out the vote drives. 20,000 union phone lines made calls on Election Day. More than 80,000,000 letters, leaflets, and postcards were distributed to union households, and more than 120,000 union workers volunteered in the final hours of the campaign.

On Monday, November 8, 1976, the day before Carter would be elected, another vote took place in Washington.

The Executive Board of the International Association of Machinists and Aerospace Workers was called to order by International President Red Smith at 9:30 AM. After disposing with the routine matters of a report on the ladies auxiliary, dues payments by members affiliated with the Grand Lodge, a reading of the financial statement, and a brief report on ongoing organizing campaigns, the President called for nominations for elected officers.

Gene Glover was nominated without opposition for General Secretary Treasurer.

Smith then smiled at Wimpy, looked around the table and called for nominations for International President.

Twenty-nine years, three months, and twenty-four days after he was initiated into Cleveland's Local Lodge 1363, William Wayne Winpisinger was nominated without opposition to lead the Executive Council's slate and become the eleventh International President of the IAM.

The next day, Jimmy Carter eked out a victory over President Ford by the slimmest of margins, fifty percent to forty-eight percent. He carried the states of the Old South, including Texas, but did not win any other state west of the Mississippi. Carter carried only eight industrial states north of the Mason-Dixon Line. Exit polling revealed that it was union households and African-American voters who put him in the White House. Carter received fifty-nine percent of the votes of union families and eighty-two percent of the Black vote.

While plans for Carter's inaugural moved forward, the IAM ran its own nomination and election campaign. Wimpy's claim on the presidency of the IAM had been common knowledge and a popular idea throughout the union for many years. Now the constitutional I's were dotted and T's crossed so that he could succeed Red Smith to become the union's eleventh President. General Secretary Treasurer Gene Glover distributed "Official Circular Number 681" in January 1977 listing the slate of candidates approved by the Executive Council and calling on local lodges to submit nominations. When the returns were submitted in February, Wimpy was nominated for International President by 824 of the union's lodges. He faced two token opponents, F.P. Meagher of Lodge 1327 in San Francisco, who received the nomination of twenty-two lodges, and C.D. Troia of Lodge 837B in St. Louis who was nominated by just one lodge. Neither of Wimpy's challengers won the nomination of their home lodge, and neither reached the threshold required to hold an election. Wimpy was elected by acclamation for a four year term to begin on July 1, 1977.

On April 19, 1977, shortly after the results of the IAM election became official, Wimpy delivered a Patriot's Day address to the American Arbitration Association in New York City, in which he outlined some of his immediate concerns and goals as a union President-elect. He noted that the labor movement as a whole was in a catch-up mode on wages since years of inflation and high unemployment had eroded their relative economic position. He outlined plans for a major push to reform the country's labor laws.

"One of my personal priorities when I assume the presidency of the Machinists Union will be to increase lines of communication with the membership. One of our problems, as I see it, is that too many union members have lost sight of the direct line that runs from the ballot box to the bread box."[2]

Wimpy praised the efforts of the International Ladies Garment Workers Union in using television commercials to educate the public to the value of unions, an effort in which he was immensely interested. Television had become the most powerful vehicle for molding public opinion, and Wimpy was fascinated with the notion of taking the IAM message directly to the viewing public without the filter corporate America applied to news coverage.

As he continued the process of transitioning from Vice President to President-elect and mapped out his battle plan for the initial phase of his Presidency, Wimp spoke out on economic issues, becoming more and more sophisticated and erudite. Suddenly the high-school-drop-out auto mechanic from Cleveland was quoting and discussing David Ricardo's Law of Comparative Advantage, from *The Principles of Political Economy and Taxation,* published in 1817, Adam Smith's *An Inquiry into the Nature and Causes of the Wealth of Nations,* published in 1776, and the controversial Phillips Curve, established by New Zealand economist A. W. Phillips in his 1957 work *Relationship Between Unemployment and the Rate of Change of Money Wages in the United Kingdom, 1861–1957.*

Wimpy also began to build coalitions beyond the labor movement. In a speech at the annual Americans for Democratic Action Roosevelt Day Dinner in Baltimore on May 1, 1977, Wimp cited the common bond the ADA and the labor movement had as they fought side-by-side for "health, housing, education, consumer rights, equal opportunities, tax reform, energy, ecology, and a wide range of other public issues."[3] Far from content to sing for his supper, he proceeded to blast them for walking away from labor on the fights against multi-nationals, and labor law reform, and the repeal of Section 14-b of Taft-Hartley:

> It seems that many liberals and liberal organizations have swallowed the stereotype by which unions are portrayed in the media. According to this stereotype, unions have become too big, too powerful, and too selfish. Many of our liberal friends mourn that unions

have become part of the system and have lost the idealism of earlier and more romantic days when brave little bands of workers went forth to do battle with the might of entrenched corporate power.[4]

Wimpy went on to urge them to support labor's efforts to strengthen the Wagner Act and to back off their policies in favor of free trade. He hinted at what he perceived as an elitist attitude and issued a call to arms:

To me the essence of liberalism is desire for a just and equitable society. But it is not enough for liberal organizations to go out and do battle for the poor, the old, the handicapped and those disadvantaged because of their race, creed, sex or color. It's time that somebody felt some compassion for the millions of men and women who go into the mines, mills and factories and do the hard, dirty and dangerous jobs that make life easier for everyone else.[5]

Similarly, in a speech to the A. Philip Randolph Institute, an organization of Black trade unionists formed to fight for racial equality and economic justice, Wimpy laid out three goals for labor and took his first public shots at two men who would become frequent targets of his criticism in the months to come: George Meany and President Carter. Explaining that labor wanted three basic things, the chance to organize, a new morality in the economic scheme of things and improved public image, he set his sights on the elderly chieftain of the AFL-CIO:

Power does not come with only twenty-two percent of the workers in America organized...Regrettably, I note that in the years 1973–1974, and 1974–1975,

> *the latest years for which figures are available,*
> *the AFL-CIO spent slightly over $400,000 for its*
> *Organization and Field Services Department, yet*
> *during the same years, [it] spent over twice as much*
> *—$919,000 on International Affairs.[6]*

His assault on Meany and his stewardship of the AFL-CIO sharpened as he mentioned him by name and accused him of sabotaging George McGovern's Presidential campaign, and of walking away at critical times in the civil rights movement:

> *Nixon set up labor at the [1972] AFL-CIO convention*
> *to make is look like a howling mob. Then brother*
> *Meany appeared on Burning Tree Golf Links in a not*
> *so subtle move against Senator McGovern....After*
> *years at the forefront of the civil rights movement,*
> *the AFL-CIO chose to maintain an almost invisible*
> *profile during the civil rights march of 1963, and*
> *again during the poor people's campaign of*
> *1968...Too often we find ourselves depicted as war*
> *mongers, dupes of the CIA, cavorting with merchants*
> *of death in the arms race, roaming the streets in*
> *packs of hard hats looking for some kid's skulls*
> *to crack or some blacks to rough up on a yellow*
> *school bus.[7]*

He also took the first of what would become many public shots at President Jimmy Carter, a mere six months into his administration. Accusing Carter of being disingenuous in his support of labor law reform, Wimp rhapsodized about a day when a majority of American workers would belong to unions and said, "...Then the President of the United States won't wink at Congress and tell us, 'You get it passed and I'll sign it.' He'll be leading the charge..."[8]

Alluding to Carter's professed moral certitude on the way he dealt with issues, Wimp took a whack at him:

> *We thought we elected a humanitarian and compassionate man. So we're not asking him to trade favors. But we do ask him: Where's the morality in twenty-five million people deeply and rigidly embedded in poverty? Where's the morality in three million people being forced to labor for poverty wages? Where's the morality in an economy of scarcity that gives four percent of the people nearly two thirds of the nation's wealth?*[9]

Red Smith presided over his last Executive Council meeting, a three day affair at headquarters in Washington, from June 20–22, 1977. In a preview of the expansive view he would take of the IAM's public role, Wimpy brought in a sales representative from an advertising agency to make a presentation on using television advertising to promote the IAM. Inspired by the ILGWU's television spots, he now wanted the council to approve a budget for his proposal. But the Council was shocked at the cost of producing and airing network commercials, and voted no.

Two days before he was sworn in as International President, Wimpy took another shot at Carter in front of another largely black audience. Addressing the St. Louis National Association for the Advancement of Colored People, he said outright that the new president had disappointed him:

> *Last November the American people, and especially the nation's blacks and union members, served notice that they wanted something different than what Jerry Ford was offering. That's why we went out in great numbers and elected Jimmy Carter. If we*

had wanted more of the Jerry Ford philosophy and economics we would have stayed home, and Jerry Ford would still be president. We showed by our votes that we wanted something different, but what we're getting from Jimmy Carter, I'm sorry to say, is more of the same.

Jimmy Carter isn't going to solve the real problems that confront working people, which included most of the blacks in this country, by appointing a few more blacks to high positions in government...As I'm sure you've gathered by now, I'm frankly disappointed in Jimmy Carter.[10]

Wimpy was speaking out. He no longer had to be the faithful Vice President to a conservative Red Smith. He could pick his fights and make his own mark. Now it was time to get the message across to the headquarters staff that a new day was dawning.

He instructed George Kourpias, his administrative assistant, to draft a memorandum summonsing everyone who reported to the International President to a staff meeting to begin at one minute past midnight on the day he was sworn in to office.

Wimpy had a lot to do, and there wasn't a moment to waste.

TWENTY-SEVEN

A NEW DAWN

Wimpy's midnight meeting to mark the beginning of his term as International President caught the staff at headquarters off guard. George Kourpias, who sent out the notification as Wimpy's second in command, later recalled the reaction:

> We put the memo out, and I had staff people coming into my office laughing. Saying things like, what the hell's going on here, midnight, are we all supposed to be drunk when we get there, that'll be a hell of a meeting. And my advice was I wouldn't be drunk, and I'd be there. I can remember taking four or five of the staff out to my house, and we barbecued and didn't have a drink.[1]

The meeting started promptly at midnight. All present were sober and attentive, anxious to find out what their new leader had planned. Wimpy made it clear the old way of doing things, by the book and by the bell at headquarters that signaled the mileposts of each workday, was over. Years later, sitting in his office at IAM headquarters relating his recollection of the evening to an interviewer, Wimpy said the following:

> My final exhortation that night was, "I'm going to be gone a lot because my predecessor had sat with his big ass in this chair for eight solid years, and if we hadn't printed his picture in the newspaper every month, nobody would have even known him..." The last thing I told them was, "When I'm gone, and there's nobody around when something happens

and you confront a problem, you think of the most
liberal thing you can do and do it. If you screw up,
we'll come back and redress it later. But at least we'll
be off and running for 90 percent of it."[2]

On his first day as International President, Wimpy instructed the maintenance staff at IAM headquarters to disconnect the bells that signaled the rhythms of each workday. The move had significance in two ways. First, Wimpy wanted a staff that planned, thought and acted on its own, not one that waited for a signal to act. He also wanted to be clear that the IAM's workday didn't end at a specific time just because a bell rang. It ended when the day's work was done.

The IAM headquarters staff, like the membership of the union and the leadership of the country, was undergoing a massive demographic change. It was becoming younger, more racially diverse and more gender-balanced. Fifty-two-year-old Wimpy had replaced the sixty-five-year-old Red Smith, and Wimpy's executive council had an average age of forty-eight, with the youngest member forty-two years of age and the oldest fifty-seven. Over the course of his Presidency, Wimpy would become famous throughout the labor movement for his bold initiatives in hiring and promoting women, young people, and people of color. Leadership in the White House was younger as well. The sixty-four-year-old Gerald Ford had been replaced by the fifty-four-year-old Jimmy Carter, who made significant progress in naming a cabinet that was younger and more ethnically balanced. One place where the youth movement had not taken hold was at AFL-CIO headquarters. George Meany, who had obligated to a New York City plumber's union in 1917, was still leading the federation at age eighty-three. While Wimpy respected his elders, Meany's age, autocratic style, and conservative political philosophy rankled him to no end, and he didn't hesitate to say so.

At his midnight staff meeting, Wimpy stressed that stopping the decline in membership and adding new members to the IAM was his top priority. He told the staff that in his opinion, the best opportunity to improve the success of organizing campaigns was to be found in labor law reform legislation that was being drafted by the Carter Administration. The battle to get it enacted would force him to work closely with both President Carter and President Meany, and would ultimately lead to his belief that both men had to be vanquished from their positions, Meany because he was to old, too slow and too conservative, and Carter because he was incompetent, ineffectual and untrustworthy.

By the time Wimpy took the reins of the IAM, the gains the labor movement had realized since the 1935 passage of the Wagner National Labor Relations Act were receding rapidly. The 1947 Taft-Hartley Act, big business's initial assault on worker's rights, had been followed by the punitive Landrum-Griffin Act of 1959, passed largely in response to corruption by a handful of unscrupulous labor leaders uncovered by the McClellan Commission. Business had also become more sophisticated at gaming the system to defeat organizing drives and neutralizing those that succeeded. Gone were thick-knuckled goons who beat up union supporters. Enter the slick attorneys and buttoned-down psychologists who used delaying tactics, artifice, and outright illegal strategies to ward off organizers, thwart elections, ignore certified bargaining units, and fire union activists.

Testifying before the House Labor subcommittee considering the Labor Law Reform legislation, IAM General Vice President George Poulin described a five step sequential strategy employers would use to defeat workers' attempts to organize. According to Poulin's testimony, at the first sign of union organizing the employers resorted to intimidation.

Spies were employed to infiltrate organizing meetings or to sit across the street from the union hall photographing workers entering or leaving an organizing meeting. Workers were told flat-out that they would be fired for any attempt to organize a union, and, in due course, the employer made good on that threat. During the run-up to a vote, intimidation gave way to offers of bribery. If workers rejected the union, the employer promised to sweeten the pot by providing whatever additional pay or benefits were at issue.

Poulin went on to describe how the employer's next move was screening to identify workers sympathetic to the union so that they could be culled from the workforce. New hires were people unlikely to buck the company and support a union. Well groomed young people walked the shop floor, clipboards in hand, to conduct "worker attitude surveys." While they took pains to tell the workers there was no such thing as a "wrong answer," anything but the "right" answer was a ticket to the unemployment line.

As the screening process continued, the employer brought in high priced legal help skilled at anti-union campaigns. Then the fun would begin in earnest. Delay was the name of the game, and they excelled at it. Any organizing drive was challenged at every step of the process. All of the administrative and judicial tribunals established to see that workers got a fair shake were used against them. The appeals simply overloaded the system. Employers then challenged one aspect of the election, perhaps the card count, and lost. But as the sheer volume of challenges mounted, the staff to deal with them did not. The adjudication of the matter took months, months the screeners used to identify troublesome workers and see that they were replaced with more compliant new hires.

Even the legal battles after a union had been voted in by workers dragged on for months or even years. Finally, after all of the delaying tactics were exhausted, management simply refused to bargain in good faith, or often times, refused to even meet with union representatives.

The National Labor Relations Board eventually caught up with them, forced them to bargain, fined them for the delay, made them reinstate workers fired for union activity with back pay and otherwise slapped their wrist. In the meantime, pro-union sentiment evaporated as attrition plus the screening process weakened the union activist's standing. To add insult to injury, any monies the employer had to cough up to repay workers they had fired illegally was a tax deduction for them, just another cost of doing business.

Over the years, this took a toll on the ability of unions to organize and attract new members. The percentage of the American workforce that belonged to unions had slipped from a high of twenty-eight percent to twenty-six percent by 1977, and it was continuing to decline. Organizing campaigns that made it to a vote had an eighty percent success rate in 1946, but a sixty-two percent win rate in 1967. By 1976, when 8,638 elections were held to determine union representation, the success rate had slid to forty-eight percent. Unions were winning less than half their organizing battles.

The most prominent bogey man for labor organizers was the notorious J.P. Stevens and Company, a textile manufacturing conglomerate with plants throughout the South. Founded in 1813, the company had grown from a small family-owned Northern textile mill, turning out consumer products, to a multi-national conglomerate with 45,800 employees and 1977 revenues of $1,400,000,000, ranking it 160th on the *Fortune* 500 list. The company was run from a new skyscraper on the Avenue of the Americas in Manhattan, and in addition to its US plants had manufacturing facilities in Canada, Mexico, France, Belgium, New Zealand, and Australia. By 1977, textile consumer products represented less than thirty percent of its total revenues, and the company had branched out into the sale

and maintenance of Beachcraft Airplanes and the publishing
and printing of telephone directories. In 1977, Stevens turned
a $41,100,000 profit. It had been locked in a fierce battle with
the Amalgamated Textile and Clothing Workers Union since
1963. Management had employed every trick in the book to
keep the union out of Steven's plants. By 1977, the AFL-CIO
called Stevens "The nation's #1 labor-law outlaw."[3]

It was against this bleak backdrop that Wimpy, Meany and
the rest of the AFL-CIO executive council started working
with President Carter and his legislative staff to draft a labor
law reform package. By August 1977, Senate 1883 and House
8410 were filed by the Carter Administration with labor's
backing.

In his message to Congress introducing the measure, Carter
talked about the weakness of the National Labor Relations
Board:

> The problem of delay has been compounded by
> the weakness of the Board's remedies. One of the
> reasons the regulatory process has worked so slowly
> is that a few employers have learned, because of the
> problems the Board has in enforcing its decisions,
> delay can be less costly than initial compliance with
> the law. In one case, for instance, workers who were
> illegally fired in 1962 are still awaiting payment for
> lost wages. Because of these problems, workers are
> often denied a fair chance to decide, in an NLRB
> election, whether they want union representation.[4]

Carter's bill was rather mild given the egregious abuses
he cited in his cover message. It increased the National Labor
Relations Board from five to seven members, and stipulated
that two members, as opposed to the whole board, could rule

on routine disputes. It imposed strict deadlines for scheduling representation elections, and provided for automatic court enforcement of board orders within thirty days unless there was an appeal. It also doubled the back pay for workers wrongfully dismissed; blacklisted companies that broke the law from government contracting, and established a compensation fund for workers whose employers refused to bargain after the union had been certified.

The tepidness of the bill reflected a conscious decision by labor unions to proceed cautiously after a stunning defeat in the new Congress that March. A bill that would have permitted common situs picketing at construction sites, which had been passed by the previous Congress, but vetoed by President Ford, was defeated 217-205 in the House of Representatives. Eighty-eight Democrats defected on the bill, and its sponsor, Democratic Representative Frank Thompson, Jr., of New Jersey, placed blame squarely on Carter and his administration for providing only lukewarm support. This time the AFL-CIO, wanting to encourage Carter's support, and hoping to avoid a potentially crippling filibuster in the Senate, agreed to forego the chance to repeal Section 14 (b) of the Taft-Hartley Act, the dreaded "right to work" clause.

Wimpy was disgusted by what he viewed as Meany's capitulation to Carter's weakness on labor issues. In a speech before the Industrial Relations Research Association, he outlined what he would have done:

> In my opinion the AFL-CIO is seeking no more than the bare minimum in labor law reform. If it were my decision I would have demanded and gone in and fought like hell for a lot more than the kind of minor reforms that the AFL-CIO is seeking. I would have stuck to my guns and demanded at least treble

> back pay, without offsets, for workers unjustly fired
> for union activity. I would have demanded that if a
> union gets authorization cards from a majority of the
> work force, it would also get automatic certification
> without going through the delay and expense of an
> election. But most of all I would have insisted on
> repeal of that lousy Section 14 (b) which gives anti-
> union state legislatures the right to enact right-to-
> work-for-less laws.[5]

Wimpy may have preferred to go with stronger legislation, but he knew that under the circumstances, getting even the relatively modest proposal passed into law would be no mean feat. In an open letter to members that was published on the front page of *The Machinist*, Wimpy called his troops to arms:

> Now, I am asking your help in one of the most difficult
> undertakings the IAM and the entire American
> labor movement have ever attempted. With the
> support of President Carter, we are seeking a major
> overhaul of the nation's laws governing the rights
> of employees to organize in a union and bargain
> with management. Only through changes in the
> laws can union organizing become effective. Thus to
> spur organizing, labor law reform must be our top
> legislative priority in Congress.[6]

Wimpy deputized his Executive Assistant and confidant George Kourpias as Chairman of the IAM Task Force on Labor Law Reform, a sign that this was truly a top priority. Kourpias immediately appointed eight regional coordinators to mine their territories for support and to work with their respective Vice Presidents to hold meetings in each territory to gear up the lobbying campaign. During an initial planning meeting with the coordinators, Wimpy and Kourpias heard from General Vice President George Poulin about the volume of anti-labor reform mail business interests were generating to members of Congress. In response, Wimpy, Kourpias, and Poulin hit on a plan. They would print IAM postcards to members of Congress and get the nearly one million IAM members to sign them. But their plan had a twist. Rather than relying on the union members to send the cards directly to their Congress member, Wimpy and George instructed them to return the cards to headquarters. Then, at the appropriate time, the union would deliver the hundreds of thousands of cards to Capitol Hill all at once, demonstrating clearly to each member just how many IAM votes were at stake in his or her district.

In his instruction to the coordinators, Wimpy said, "If every member does his or her part to notify Congress of their support for labor law reform, we will overcome the blizzard of hate mail. This mail is pouring into congressional offices from those whose aim is an oppressive society where working people toil without the benefits of protections provided by a strong healthy union."[7]

The battle had begun. The IAM was going to flex its considerable political muscle.

With the plan in place for the lobbying campaign, Wimpy left for Europe to attend the annual meeting of the International Metalworkers Federation. General Secretary Herman Rebhan, formerly the International Affairs Director for the United Auto Workers, and the first American to ever hold the post, invited Wimp to do a sort of "victory lap" through Europe, meeting with many of his counterparts from other countries. The tour took him through Dublin, London, Rome, Athens, Vienna, and Geneva.

Back in the United States, Wimpy called his first IAM Executive Council session on Tuesday, September 6, 1977. His first order of business was to remind council members of the mandate of the convention that they establish a Civil Rights Department, a Community Services Department, and an Organizing Department. These efforts were to be a top priority for him and the entire IAM leadership.

The council meeting lasted until Friday, and Wimpy explained in detail how he planned to spend most of his time on the road meeting with members, opinion leaders, the media, and anyone else who could help put the IAM and its agenda firmly in the public eye. Council members also discussed a proposal to build on the Machinist's choice Connecticut Avenue property, as well as free trade versus protectionist policies, and the federal government's upcoming decision on whether to withdraw from the International Labor Organization.

Both the AFL-CIO and the US Chamber of Commerce favored withdrawing from the ILO because of what they viewed as Communist domination of the body, but Wimpy favored staying in and battling for control. President Carter's own cabinet would split on their formal recommendation to him a month later, with Secretary of State Cyrus Vance and National Security Advisor Zbigniew Brzezinski agreeing with Wimpy that the US should remain involved, and Labor Secretary Ray Marshall and Commerce Secretary Juanita Kreps advocating withdrawal.

At the council meeting, Wimpy argued that labor is not a commodity, that all workers should enjoy freedom of expression and association, and that poverty anywhere constituted a danger to prosperity everywhere. He also expounded on the US exporting jobs and technology to foreign countries, and on the Carter Administration's failure to do much to reverse these trends. The Council appropriated $60,000 to fund a film on the problems of imports and their effect on IAM member's jobs.

Out on the stump, Wimpy continued to sharpen his economic message. In a lengthy series of comments to the annual meeting of Americans for Democratic Action, which elected him to its board of directors, Wimpy sounded his first of many calls for what he termed a "reconversion" of the American economy. He argued that much remained to be done to shift the American industrial and economic systems from production of arms, munitions, and materials for the Vietnam War to the peacetime goal of improving the country's infrastructure and producing consumer goods.

The economy under Carter still had all the problems of the Nixon years: high unemployment, 7.1 percent, high inflation, 6.5 percent, and rising interest rates, with prime ranging from 6.5 to 7.75 percent. Wimpy stressed that the Carter Administration had not yet articulated a direction for its defense policy. The trend indicated that Carter would accept the Defense Department's argument that reduced defense spending in the future relied on a continuation of heavy defense spending in the present.

Wimpy once again blasted the Phillips Curve, calling it "an esoteric term which says there must be a trade-off between full employment and price stability." He claimed that the "result of Phillips Curve-Zero-growth syndrome is stagflation, with the rich getting richer, the poor getting poorer, and middle income receivers becoming poorer too. [It] looks very much like a scheme to redistribute income and wealth to the top of the economic pyramid."[8]

He called on the ADA to form a coalition with labor to fight for reconversion and suggested they consider establishing a parliamentary style "shadow cabinet," to monitor congressional and executive policies in the interest of working people.

Meanwhile, the battle over labor law reform legislation raged. As George Kourpias whipped his troops to produce postcards to their legislators, Wimpy campaigned across the country for passage of the legislation. He saw the forces he had read about in "The Ultras," Fred Cook's 1962 *Nation* essay, lining up to defeat labor's last best hope at gaining a bigger share of the American workforce. In a speech in San Diego, he shed light on what he saw as the right wing conspiracy:

> *...such newspapers as The New York Times, the Los Angeles Times and even the Chicago Tribune have carried editorials assuring employers they have nothing to fear from this little bit of labor reform. That hasn't stopped the right wingers—from the John Birch Society to the National Right-to-Work Committee—from going into hysterics. They've already raised millions of dollars to defeat these few mild reforms. They are also counter-attacking with bills which would make union-busting easier than it already is.*[9]

At the AFL-CIO, George Meany finally heeded Wimpy's advice and solicited the support of civil rights groups, feminists, religious leaders, environmentalists, consumers, and other community groups in the fight for the legislation. This was "all hands on deck" time.

The AFL-CIO also rented seventy-five kiosks in the vicinity of the Capitol and plastered them with posters showing Uncle Sam with his arms around two workers, a man and a woman, under the headline: "UNCLE SAM Protects You! You can't be fired for joining the union." A sticker saying "VOIDED BY BIG BUSINESS" was shown across the bottom half of the three figures, and the tag line at the bottom of the poster said: "SUPPORT LABOR LAW REFORM."

The October 1977 issue of *The Machinist* carried a lengthy article:

> *Examining the opposition's tangled web, Who's Who in the Right Wing," which pointed out: "The popular myth about our opposition is that it is a loose organization formed spontaneously to counter 'big labor.' Nothing could be further from the truth. The right wing is one of the most powerful, well organized, and best financed elements of our society.*[10]

On October 3, the IAM delivered 255,724 postcards to members of Congress. The delivery, made to the offices of all but four members, ranged from 300 cards in the smallest rural district, to a high of more than 6,200 in urban districts. Any member confronted with the signed wishes of that many voting families from his or her district had to take that into consideration before casting a vote. The day before the vote in the House, Wimpy held a news conference to report on the success of the card drive and laid out what was at stake. "It's all on the line on this one," he said. "This is not a litmus test, it's the absolute test."[11]

That night, on the eve of the House vote, the AFL-CIO hosted a massive dinner in Washington, at which Vice President Walter Mondale spoke and urged the troops on to victory. The following day saw the end of two days of debate and five roll call votes that defeated more than 250 potentially crippling amendments to the bill. After beating back a final last ditch effort to substitute a bill that would have set restrictions on strikes and organizing, the House, on its sixth and final roll call, passed Labor Law Reform by a vote of 257 to 163.

The vote in the House was a tremendous victory for Wimpy, the IAM, the AFL-CIO and workers across the country. Now the battle would move to the Senate. Although labor felt confident of a majority, there was concern about gathering the sixty votes it would take to overcome a filibuster. One danger sign lurked in the House vote: the ten-member delegation from Carter's home state of Georgia, all Democrats, voted against the measure.

Wimpy once again used the front page of *The Machinist* to rally the troops for the upcoming Senate battle:

> *Getting labor law reform through the House of Representatives was a big step, but we're still only half way home. We now have to get it through the Senate. And that isn't going to be easy. Though we can probably muster a majority of the Senate in favor of labor law reform, it will take an even greater effort to get the sixty votes necessary to break the anti-labor filibuster that's expected.*[12]

The business community, stunned at their defeat, rallied to derail the measure by whatever means necessary in the Senate. They formed the National Action Committee for a Fair Labor Law, and even adversaries within their ranks, such as the National Association of Manufacturers and the United States Chamber of Commerce, put aside their rivalries to kill the bill.

Harold P. Coxson, Director of Labor Law for the Chamber called the bill "nothing more than phony reform," that would "push employees into compulsory unionism."[13]

James M. Sprouse, Executive Director of the Association of General Contractors, blasted the bill as a measure that would "force the union way of life on all Americans." He vowed, "We will redouble our efforts to see that this bill is defeated in the Senate. This legislation must be stopped."[14]

There was a concerted effort throughout the labor movement to rebuild the labor—liberal coalition that had existed prior to the upheaval of the 1968 Democratic National Convention and ensuing unsuccessful presidential campaign. Wimpy was at the vanguard of that movement and preached constantly to his own staff and executive council and to the heads of other unions that the key to their ongoing success lay in gathering support for their issues beyond the walls of the union hall.

In a speech to the Citizen's Action Coalition of Indiana, at Purdue University in November 1977, Wimpy, in an almost whimsical fashion, called for cooperation between the two movements and displayed his liberal chops.

> *There are four reasons, which come to me immediately, why we should cooperate. The first three are not altogether irrelevant thoughts, which I will mention in passing.*
>
> *First, it occurred to me, how do we expect to curb the international arms race, when we cannot even control the sale of cheap handguns within our borders?*
>
> *Second, fiction is reality. The neutron bomb is Mary Shelley's Mad Scientist; it is Dr. Strangelove; it is Kurt Vonnegut's Ice Nine. We should ponder when will a clean bomb be one that preserves life rather than destroys it.*
>
> *Third, in observance of Veteran's Day, how many leaders of our veterans organizations will speak out for international peace, rather than resistance to the Panama Canal Treaty and SALT agreements? How many of our veterans organization leaders will recognize the moral courage of ostracized Vietnam war resistors, as well as salute the courage*

of those who served and died there? How many
veterans' organization leaders will condemn the
CIA and the FBI for un-American and criminal conduct
and drug abuse as they have many private citizens
and individuals.

Fourth, Adolph Hitler solved Germany's chronic
unemployment with the Wermacht and nihilism.
Russia solves it with forced labor and forced military
service. Is America destined to copy the same mad
methods?[15]

Wimpy was fast becoming recognized as a new breed of cat among labor leaders. His intellectual discourse on economic theory, his red hot rhetoric on social justice, and his militant advocacy for working men and women were making him a go-to person for media representatives looking for a quote, and groups looking for an electrifying speaker. Wimpy truly believed every word he said, and that point came across to his audiences loud and clear, in person or through the news media.

The IAM, as one of the nation's largest and most powerful unions, had been represented on the AFL-CIO Executive Board since the inception of the federation. As the group's twelfth annual convention approached in December 1977, there was some question as to whether or not Wimpy would be elected to the council in the seat Red Smith had held, because he was openly and colorfully opposed to George Meany. In those days, the AFL-CIO was a one-man band, and Meany called the tunes.

Wimpy didn't make matters any easier, referring to the eighty-three-year-old Meany with quotes like "We've got an image problem, and that's the image." Or "I'm fed up with seeing the attributes of this labor movement summed up in a labor leader about whom you can only say he's mentally sharp, sprightly of step and alert."

As the convention in Los Angeles approached, Meany sent word to Wimpy that he would be elected to the council and Wimpy cooled things down a bit, noting publicly that while he didn't support Meany, he had enormous personal respect for him and what he had done for the labor movement over the decades. But Wimpy being Wimpy couldn't resist the chance to get in one last dig.

"In those days it was a practice that if you were new on the council," George Kourpias recalled, "you'd throw a reception for the delegates—and the Machinists threw a reception, and we were betting as to whether or not George Meany would show up."[16]

Maria Cordone remembered that Wimpy "asked one of the guys to go out and get a wheelchair. And when George Meany came to visit our reception, he wanted to wheel George Meany out. 'This is time for you to retire. This is your wheelchair, go.' That shocked me, but that's Wimpy's personality."[17]

"George [Meany] was the first one there," Kourpias recalled. "He had a cane and he looked at Wimpy and he said 'Well, I bet you didn't think I was going to come.' Meany came, he took the first table, and he sat there for two and a half hours making sure that everybody knew that he was there."[18]

Wimpy was elected to the Executive Council, Meany was re-elected to a new four-year term, and the first six months of Wimpy's term as International President went into the books.

The new day he described at his midnight staff meeting had indeed dawned.

TWENTY-EIGHT

LABOR LAW REFORM

Wimpy now had a seat at the big table, as one of the thirty-five cardinals of the labor movement. His views carried tremendous weight, even though he was frequently and publicly at odds with its ancient leader. His colleagues on the AFL-CIO Executive Council granted him grudging respect because they knew he was a true trade unionist at heart.

When asked to give his views on the future of the labor movement at a management seminar hosted by General Electric in January 1978, a month after his election to the AFL-CIO governing body, he agreed:

> *Unions rose in America in response to very specific needs in the work force. We have survived, despite opposition and adversity, because we have managed to meet those needs. Though many so-called experts are hopefully and happily predicting a continuing decline in the strength and influence of unionism, I do not see any decline in the kind of problems that made unions necessary in the first place... We must continue to demand that our government provide its own work force the kind of trade protections that are taken for granted by the European Economic Community, Japan and other industrially advanced nations. That means protection against job destruction by multi-national corporations who have all too freely been exporting America's capital, technology and jobs.[1]*

He was even more militant and direct in addressing his first MNPL Planning Committee meeting in his new role:

> We're going to find ways to use every bit of capacity we've got. I didn't aim to become I.P. to carry on business as usual. I don't intend to try to win the approval of the press, the politicians and employers as a 'labor statesman.' We are a union, and by God, we are going to make that plain to both our friends and our enemies. But first it seems I have to make it plain to our members and to some business representatives and grand lodge representatives. If acting like a union means we lose some members who would prefer to belong to some kind of fraternal marching and chowder society, so be it! I'm interested in building a union made up of muscle, not fat. If necessary, we'll get rid of the fat, and build from there. We're going to have a program of organizing, political action and collective bargaining that's going to produce trade unionists and not just dues payers.[2]

As part of that legislative and political battle, Wimp once again marshaled the forces of the IAM to push for Senate passage of the Labor Law Reform package. At the January 1978 meeting of the IAM Executive Council, he outlined a seven-step plan to duplicate and expand the lobbying program that had helped nudge the legislation through the House. All members were to be encouraged to sign a postcard to both of their senators. Anyone drawing an IAM paycheck was to write personal letters and follow up with phone calls to their senators. Retirees were asked to help, and the IAM planned to reach out through central labor bodies to increase the number of postcards pouring into Washington in favor of the labor law reform legislation.

Wimp began presenting labor law reform as a long overdue natural progression that would not cause a great deal of pain to business interests. He argued that it was inevitable and that it had begun on February 2, 1960, when a committee chaired by Archibald Cox told the Senate Committee on Labor and Public Welfare that union members were being denied justice because of long delays of NLRB proceedings. He also recalled fifteen days of House hearings in 1961 that revealed that businesses got little more than a slap on the wrist as a result of Labor Board decisions.

The business lobby moved into high gear. Its representatives descended on the Senate in droves. New Jersey Senator Harrison A. Williams, Jr., chairman of the committee responsible for the legislation described "an atmosphere of near hysteria surrounding the labor reform act."[3] Wimpy responded by holding a press conference where he proclaimed, "While we sit at the bargaining table trying to make the system work, our employers are knifing us behind our backs and setting the stage for a return to class warfare and the law of the jungle in the workplace."[4]

A week later, President Carter invited 102 members of the MNPL Planning Committee to meet with him at the White House to thank them for their support in 1976 and to urge them to rally around Democratic congressional candidates in the upcoming off-year election. Wimp met privately with the President in the Oval Office, then they joined the larger group in the East Room. The President made brief remarks and then circulated among the attendees, shaking their hands and posing for pictures. According to an account in *The Machinist*, "He thanked them for their support and hard work that helped put him at the helm of our government. And he pledged closer coordination and cooperation moving toward the realization of mutual goals like Labor Law Reform, full employment,

energy, tax reform, fair trade, health security and more."[5]
A front page picture of the event shows a crowd of machinists,
and the two Presidents standing nose to nose, about three feet
from one another. Both men have their hands in their pants
pockets. President Carter is standing on a small riser, speaking
into a microphone. Wimpy is standing with his coat open, his
jaw firmly set and his eyes narrowed. He appears more to be
taking the measure of the man than listening to his speech.

The East Room meeting would prove to be the last time
the two men ever exchanged civil words.

Wimpy had reason to doubt Carter's resolve on Labor
Law reform, since the President had quickly ruled out asking
for the repeal of Section 14 (b) of Taft-Hartley, and had failed
to deliver a single vote from the Georgia delegation when the
House voted. But it was another topic Carter had mentioned
in his East Room remarks, energy, that would prove to be the
real breaking point between the two men.

By the time Carter took office, the United States was
deep in an energy crisis. As demand skyrocketed, domestic
production of oil and natural gas were dropping at about six
percent a year. Imports had doubled in the five years preceding
his presidency and, while the gasoline lines that had plagued
the country in 1973 were gone, very little had been done to
promote conservation. Prices were escalating quickly, fueling
inflation. Carter took to the national airwaves on April 18,
1977, and declared "the moral equivalent of war," in dealing
with the situation. He described the situation as "a problem
unprecedented in our history," and "likely to get worse through
the rest of this century." "The oil and natural gas we rely on for
seventy-five percent of our energy are running out."

Admitting the program he was about to introduce to
Congress would be "unpopular," and cause people to "put up
with inconveniences and to make sacrifices," he claimed, "the

alternative may be a national catastrophe."[6] But one problem Carter faced was public opinion: surveys revealed that more than half the American people did not believe there was an energy crisis, and thought that to whatever extent a problem existed, it had been manufactured by the energy companies to raise profits. Trying to bolster his credibility, Carter took the unprecedented step of releasing a CIA report that predicted that the price of oil, then about $8.20 per barrel, would face "sizeable increases," and could reach as much as $13.00 per barrel if demand continued to rise and production was not increased dramatically.[7]

His legislative package, based on what he termed ten "principles," was filed on Capitol Hill the next day and was immediately besieged by lobbyists and special interests. By mid-March of 1978, when Wimp and the MNPL planners met with him at the White House, the energy package (not labor law reform) was Carter's number one legislative priority. A major element of it was the deregulation of natural gas prices. Natural gas prices were capped by federal law at eighteen percent above all costs of production and distribution, except for gas sold within the boundaries of the states where it was produced. This resulted in plentiful gas at higher prices in Texas and Louisiana, and shortages in heavily industrial states like Ohio, New York, and Massachusetts.

To his dismay, Wimpy realized that Carter's energy program would have as much impact, if not more, on his membership as labor law reform. If factories in Ohio couldn't get enough natural gas to run their plants, members would be laid off. On the other hand, if prices were deregulated and allowed to soar to new levels, members across the country would be hit hard in their wallets as they cooked and heated their homes.

Wimpy looked closely at what was behind Carter's "energy crisis" and didn't like what he saw. In a speech to Americans for Democratic Action in Boston, he described the unmitigated power of the "seven sisters" of big energy. Through an arrangement with the OPEC cartel, Exxon, Mobil, Gulf, Standard of California, and Texaco the companies cleverly conceived joint ventures; interlocking directorates; and the use of common banks, financial institutions and accounting firms. Together, they wielded unassailable control over America's energy supply.

"To put it bluntly," Wimpy said, "the multinational energy corporations have control, have the power, and the government and the people do not."[8] Wimpy was learning the ins and outs of energy policy just as he had with economics. The more he learned, the more he came to believe that there was a cabal of powerful players off-stage influencing the government and sticking it to the little guy.

In the words of George Kourpias:

> When the whole issue of natural gas came into the picture, President Carter had another meeting at the White House with a select few people. Wimpy was included. At which time Wimpy told the president his thoughts on natural gas, and that deregulation should not happen. He told the president that he would be violently opposed to deregulating the industry. Wimp came back from the White House, and he said, "I've had it with this son of a bitch. He's not for working people, and we've got to be prepared to run somebody against him." And that's when the thought began forming in his mind that Teddy Kennedy should take him on.[9]

About the same time as the Carter meeting, Wimp was approached by a thirty-three-year-old community organizer from Chicago named Heather Booth. She had created a training center for organizers around economic issues called the Midwest Academy, an attempt to re-establish the coalition of progressives, consumers, and labor groups that worked effectively together before the Vietnam War, and before the fallout from the Democratic convention violence in 1968. Her academy was a place where people from many backgrounds came together to learn communication and advocacy skills and share the history and try to create the future of the progressive movement. Booth had made a strategic decision that the energy crisis presented a first-rate opportunity to rebuild the coalition. To do that, she would need support from labor. Her husband, Paul Booth, worked for the American Federation of State County and Municipal Employees (AFSCME), and had met Wimpy through their shared membership in the Democratic Socialists of America. Heather convinced Paul to arrange a meeting with Wimpy.

In Heather Booth's words:

> We called him and asked to meet him. And he agreed to the conception of building a national consumer rights organization on energy that would link labor, community, religious, and public interest groups. And be involved in both Washington lobbying and direct action in the field of grassroots lobbying and organizing. I didn't have all parts of it worked out, it was a general idea. He agreed to housing for Citizens Labor Energy Coalition (CLEC) in the Machinists [headquarters]. I lived in Chicago. He agreed to pay a certain amount of money I don't know what it was at first. It became thirty thousand dollars, which was actually a lot of money then. He also subsidized everything in the building for CLEC. It was a great deal of money.[10]

Suddenly, a number of Wimpy's strategic goals began to converge. He recognized an opportunity to further integrate the Machinists Union with movements for social justice outside of organized labor, to garner non-traditional support for labor law reform, to bring talented and energetic women and young people into the building, to take a stand on energy issues that affected his members, and, ultimately, to promote Ted Kennedy for President.

Wimpy hosted a luncheon in Washington, DC, on March 16, 1978, to try to persuade the unions of the AFL-CIO federation to join his cause and help create a citizens—labor energy coalition. Among those in attendance were representatives from the United Auto Workers, the Steelworkers, AFSCME, the Chemical and Atomic Workers and the Sheet Metal Workers. He began by outlining what was at stake: new jobs created when energy production from alternative sources ramped up, jobs that ought to be ripe for organizing—and what he hoped the coalition could accomplish.

In Wimpy's words to the crowd:

> We must insist on full regulation of natural gas and oil prices. It is these prices more than any other that are feeding the fires of inflation. It is not wages. It is not labor. It is the energy companies who are responsible for the soaring cost of living. Energy is basic to the whole production process. The only way to bring energy inflation under control is to control the companies themselves and their prices and rates.
>
> We are here today to find out if we can commit ourselves to build a national energy coalition to fight the hydra-headed energy monster. If we are going to do this, we need to pursue the strategy that has begun on the labor law reform issue. That is, we will have to work with a broad spectrum of organizations who

*are willing to ally themselves with us. Senior citizens,
the Consumer Federation of America, Energy Action,
farm organizations, statewide citizen's action groups,
Environmentalists for Full Employment—are all
potential members of the coalition. Now would seem
to be the time to begin building such a coalition. The
energy bill is in Congress and we can focus on that.
We can go to those congressional districts where the
oil lobby has greased the palms of its minions, or is
greasing the skids for our friends, as the case may
be, and develop some grass root support on our side
of the issues.[11]*

While some of his fellow union presidents saw the merits
of what Wimp was proposing, others retreated to their cold
war mentality. Heather Booth remembered her impressions
at the time:

*So all of this was new, risky, and fraught with problems.
Winpisinger understood it, drove that alliance, let
nothing stand in the way. He took enormous risks
over it. Before the conference started, and I hadn't
known him that long, maybe three months, I get a
call. He says he needs to meet me - that he got a
call from the AFL-CIO, from [Lane] Kirkland saying
he shouldn't work with me. So I fly into Washington.
I am panicked. I am just totally in panic. I don't
know Kirkland. I don't know the history. I sit down
in Wimpy's office, and Wimpy says, "I got a call from
Kirkland saying I shouldn't work with you. You're a
Communist."*

*I was taken aback and floored. I didn't know
what to say. I could have expected many things. I
didn't expect that. I mean I was part of the New Left,*

which really was what they were upset about. And what was part of the New Left is that it was new. It wasn't part of the old left. So Wimpy says this, and I'm there with my mouth open. No words coming out. And Winpisinger says, "So Kirkland says I shouldn't work with you because you're a Communist. So what do you believe?"

And I'm trying to formulate an answer, saying, "Well, I believe that working people should have their rights in this society. I believe democracy is a good…" I tried to start fumbling with an answer just to say what I believe in, because it was his question to me. What do you believe? So Wimpy cuts in. He says, "Because I believe," I don't remember the figures, I'm sure he had the right figures, "I believe that eighty percent of the wealth of this country is owned by ten percent of the people, and ten percent of the wealth of this country is owned by eighty percent of the people. And we've got to do something about that. What do you think?" So I said, "I agree." He said, "Okay, let's work together."

Well, every part of this is an extraordinary situation. He's willing to take on the leadership of the AFL-CIO. He doesn't really know me. He does it on the basis of trust and relationship…He believes the vision and the idea is so important that it's worth breaking with some of these politics of the past, building bridges across these lines. Anyway, it was just amazing. To me it was transforming.[12]

Appropriately enough, it was on Patriot's Day, April 19, 1978, that Wimpy and Booth convened more than 150 leaders from labor, citizen's action groups, politics, and academia at Washington's DuPont Plaza Hotel for the first planning conference of what was to become the Citizens-Labor Energy Coalition. Besides Wimp and Booth, the keynote speakers were Barry Commoner, a Columbia University professor and noted energy expert and environmentalist, and Senator Edward M. Kennedy.

Wimp opened the conference with a lengthy discourse on the insidiousness of the big energy companies, the failure of the political system to adequately deal with them, and the power that the assembled groups could wield for reform if they worked together. He concluded his remarks by introducing Booth, calling her "our own Mother Jones."

In Heather Booth's words:

> We had a very complicated structure. Labor had one third of the votes on the board, citizen groups had one third of the vote, and public interest and religious groups had a third of the vote, which reflected their sort of numbers in the organization. But it meant that no one could veto anyone else. That you couldn't be forced into a policy you didn't agree to. So we get to the conference, and everything has been worked out. There's these three documents. The AFL-CIO has reviewed them. Everyone who came into the conference reviewed these documents: principles, program, and structure. And they really were a reflection of compromise and a great deal of work. We get to the conference and there's lots of tension…Also, we had questions. Was the energy industry going to come and sabotage the conference? They were meeting in DC at the same time. We had all sorts of concerns. [13]

One of the major concerns, which almost proved to be a deal breaker, was what position, if any, the coalition would take on nuclear power. The environmental groups were vehemently opposed to it. Some of the unions, particularly the building trades and the Atomic Workers, were strongly in favor of building more reactors. Both sides dug their heels in, and it appeared that the infant coalition might die in the crib.

Again, Heather Booth:

> So we take a break. We adjourn the meeting for several hours. It was at least two hours. And about five of us go up to a conference room to figure out what we are going to do about it... And with Wimpy, we write an agreement... I went down and told someone to pick up a bottle of whiskey because I know that always helped in these conversations... How we resolved it, we decided not to deal with nuclear power. Groups could do what they wanted on it... So everyone had to sign their name on the statement. Now for Wimpy to have invested his energy, his reputation, his insight, his stature to do this and to take on a very foreign issue.[14]

Once the thorny issue had been addressed, Senator Kennedy spoke to the gathering, predicting the coalition would not let the Department of Energy set the coalition's agenda. "It's time we started getting down to fundamentals," he said. "It is time we started getting serious about breaking up the power of the oil companies, a power which is growing every day. The oil and gas companies have a stranglehold on two of our fuels, now they want control over coal as well."[15]

Then the Massachusetts Democrat zeroed in on President Carter's scheme to de-regulate the price of natural gas: "We'll fight deregulation and we will let the American people know that we are not talking about more gas, we're only talking about higher prices. I say we shouldn't deregulate under any timetable."[16]

Wimpy was on a roll. He had his coalition, and it had a champion in Senator Kennedy. Thirty-one year old Barbara Shailor was soon appointed as its Washington representative. She had served on the staff of former Oklahoma Senator Fred Harris, and had an encyclopedic knowledge of the energy industry. Wimpy gave her office space with the Machinists Legislative Department.

In Barbara Shailor's words"

> *At first he hired me as a consultant. When I say he hired me, it literally was he who hired me. I didn't get buried in the indifferent kind of departments. I really was reporting and working directly with him and his administrative team. And he watched at a very high level exactly what was going on, how the groupings were coming together. He was almost fatherly about saying "I'll do this," which meant, Wimpy, "I'll deliver the United Auto Workers and the Steelworkers, and SEIU. I will call and deliver this significant trade union base…And then not only conceptually and strategically did he see this, but then he put the resources of the union behind it…So you told him an idea and he said, 'That's terrific!'" "That sounds right to me!" And so there was a kind of thousand flowers quality, in the best sense of the word, about his engagement and openness to working with movements. There was just a kind of almost youthful enthusiasm to do things. Not to talk about them but to do them…The fact that he would not only lend his name, but lend his union's sort of institutional support to these fledgling, experimental projects was—there's just no way to overestimate*

how important it was. It might have taken another decade to do if it had not been for his vision, his enthusiasm, his support. He was just terrific.

When I first got out of college I was a flight attendant for United Airlines. When Wimpy was about to actually hire me full time working for the Machinists Union after doing the consulting work for probably the better part of six or nine months, he said to me, "I would never have hired you if you hadn't been a worker."...Wimpy, at his core, was very much a seat of the pants intellectual, [he] really believed that you had to have had working experience. You had to literally work for an hourly wage and see both the challenges and the abuses of what a real workplace looks like.[17]

As he worked with the Citizens Labor Energy Coalition, Wimpy's public statements about Jimmy Carter started to become more strident. In a speech to the Democratic Socialists Organizing Committee in Chicago, Wimp let the President have it with both barrels:

It is the working people and everyone else who lost when the Carter Administration caved in to the blackmail of the oil and gas lobby and meekly agreed to deregulation of natural gas. In effect Jimmy Carter has told the working people "you lose" on employment, "you lose" on inflation, "you lose" on energy.

I may be a high school dropout, but I've debated enough college professors to know all about the Phillips Curve and I say the Phillips Curve is an economic bean-ball. The Kennedy-Johnson years proved you can have stable prices along with low unemployment.

*The Nixon-Ford years just as conclusively proved
you can also have high unemployment and rising
prices. But apparently what's plain to a high school
dropout is too subtle for some double-dome, dingbat
economists who insist that the cure for inflation
is more unemployment. That's like saying that the
remedy for a fever is a broken leg.*[18]

That red-hot rhetoric caused Wimpy's fame and popularity
to grow by leaps and bounds. The June issue of *Fortune* magazine
carried a glossy profile of him by A. H. Raskin, who also wrote
for the *New York Times*. Raskin opened his piece, called "Labor's
Bogeyman," with a fawning description:

*He is the Stanley Kowalski of American Labor, a
counterpart in every external of the hard hats who
chased long-haired students through the canyons
of Wall Street at the height of US involvement in
the Vietnam War. His beefy frame, hamlike hands,
barroom gregariousness, and earthy language all seem
to add up to the stereotype of an old-line union boss.
But the reality of William W. Winpisinger, president
of the International Association of Machinists and
Aerospace Workers, hardly corresponds to his
corporeality.*[19]

Meanwhile, the battle for Labor Law Reform raged on in
the Senate. Big businesses used their corporate jets to fly small
business owners to Washington to meet with their senators
and ask them to vote against the measure. One corporate
lobbying organization, the Business Roundtable, was particularly
aggressive, and drew Wimpy's ire. The Roundtable was made
up exclusively of chief executive officers of the 180 largest
corporations in America. Anyone below the rank of CEO, or

any company not in that top 180 in revenues, need not apply. Meetings to set their agenda, discuss strategy and develop lobbying plans were closed and secret. No records were kept, and if the CEO of a company could not attend personally, no substitute was allowed. Members of the Roundtable would then personally call on legislators in private meetings to make their pitch. The secretive and collusive nature of the group really rankled Wimp as he explained to a professional association in 1978:

> If 180 prominent Italian-Americans behaved so surreptitiously, the FBI would be interested. If 180 Croatian, Greek, Polish or Slavic- Americans met in such secrecy, the CIA would be tracking them. If 180 Afro Americans held such a meeting, probably all intelligence agencies would have them covered. And if 180 American trade union leaders attempted secret parleys, investigative journalists would be on the hunt.[20]

When the Senate finally began debate on Labor Law Reform on May 16, Republicans and conservative Democrats from the South were loaded for bear. They knew they lacked the votes to kill the bill outright, but they began a filibuster and were confident that the Democratic majority couldn't muster the sixty votes needed to invoke cloture and pass the bill over their objections. Utah's Orin Hatch led the effort, working closely with Senate Minority Leader Howard H. Baker, Jr., of Tennessee and Senator Robert J. Dole of Kansas. Hatch and his cohorts droned on and on, sometimes reading endless passages from books to keep from yielding the floor. By May 24th, as the mind-numbing speeches continued, the Senate chamber was often empty except for Hatch and either New Jersey Democrat Harrison A. Williams, Jr., or New York Republican Jacob K. Javitz, the principal supporters of the legislation.

The first vote to try to end debate came on Wednesday, June 7th when forty-two senators voted to end debate and forty-seven were opposed. By the following day Democrats managed to pick up seven votes and the second cloture vote was forty-nine to forty-one in favor. Senator Baker then made a motion to recommit the bill to committee, which would have effectively killed it, and was defeated on a vote of fifty-one to thirty-seven.

By June 17, when a fifth attempt to invoke cloture failed, nerves were badly frayed. Senators opposed to the measure asked pointedly when proponents might give up the ghost and allow the Senate to move on to other business. From the *New York Times:*

> *Whereupon the Majority Leader, Senator Robert C. Byrd of West Virginia, told the story of the Scottish patriot, Robert Bruce, who while fleeing the English, watched a spider fail six times in trying to spin a web between two widely spaced rafters.*
>
> *Bruce concluded that if the spider tried again, he would too. The spider tried the seventh time and succeeded.[21]*

And so the debate dragged on. At the peak of labor's efforts, they mustered fifty-eight votes, only two shy of the magic number needed for passage. Finally, on June 22, after nineteen days of debate, the Senate held a record breaking sixth cloture vote, with fifty-three members voting to end debate and forty-five still opposed. Senator Byrd and the labor forces admitted defeat and unanimously adopted a motion to send the bill back to committee.

Labor Law Reform was dead.

TWENTY-NINE

WIMPY'S VISION

Wimpy took the loss of labor law reform hard. Maria Cordone recalls, "He was disappointed. He was angry. But it was momentary. He just realized that you can't stay that way. You need to move on, and try to find some other way. He was never defeated. He knew, O.K., this didn't work out, let's move on to the next step."[1]

Wimpy used the summer lull to return to Europe, this time taking George Kourpias along as they toured Scandinavia and Vienna. Kourpias recalled that while the formalities and protocol of meetings with foreign labor leaders were a breeze for Wimpy, the trip presented problems of a more personal nature. Kourpias had been raised in a Greek immigrant family, loved Greek food and sophisticated cuisine in general, but Wimpy was strictly a meat and potatoes man. In George Kourpias' words:

> There were many moments, especially overseas, he had trouble eating. He couldn't wait to get into a town where they had a McDonald's. He's order two Big Mac's, a double order of French fries, and a Coke. If we were going to a fancy restaurant, he'd order a steak, or maybe a little fish once in a while, and not too often of that. When we were in Vienna and the Scandinavian countries, deer and reindeer were very common. So we had been to a couple of countries and when we got to Vienna we had been served reindeer, which he wouldn't touch. Our labor people there took us up to the Vienna woods to a beautiful restaurant overlooking the mountains. And we were

standing there having a martini and they roll in this
table with a beautiful white cloth over this thing and
our host says, "Wimpy, the cook went out today and
shot a deer." And there's this beautiful deer, it's about
three feet long, just a baby. Wimp took one look at
that and they took it back to carve. He turned to me
and said under his breath, "Now, damn it, don't you
laugh!" Then he said to our host, "I have tremendous
high blood pressure. I'd love to eat it, I love deer,
but it's too rich for me. Damn, I'd love to eat it, but
I just can't." I wanted to laugh in the worst way but
somehow I kept a straight face. And they went out
and got him a Goddamn steak. I'll never forget the
three of us sat there and ate lentils and reindeer
while Wimp enjoyed his big thick steak.[2]

It was hot, eighty-seven degrees to be exact, when Wimpy
gaveled the International Staff Conference to order in
Cincinnati on September 9, 1978. It was the first time the field
staff had been assembled under his leadership, and he would
deliver two lengthy but spellbinding speeches that outlined his
hopes, fears, goals and aspirations. Together, the two speeches
would serve as a blueprint for Wimpy's tenure as International
President.

The September issue of *The Machinist* had landed in
member's mailboxes about the same time he was meeting with
the staff. In it, he addressed the entire membership in a full
page typewritten letter, letting them know what he felt about
the setback in the Senate:

There is great joy now in the boardrooms and
banking chambers of the nation. Their sway over
the US Senate has been confirmed. Their continued
possession of the lion's share of the nation's wealth

has been assured. Their immunity from penalty for violating the rights of workers seeking to organize and bargain collectively through representatives of their own choosing has been verified.

The violators of the National Labor Relations Act are congratulating themselves today. And well they might. They are now freer than ever to scoff at the law of the land.[3]

His two Cincinnati speeches continued in that feisty vein, covering a broad range of topics and, in Wimpy's uniquely unvarnished way, outlined the goals and philosophies that would guide his entire twelve year term as president. He explained how and why he had reorganized the headquarters staff, why organizing was his top priority and why he would be spending so much time on the road meeting members. He sharpened his attacks on George Meany and Jimmy Carter, and talked about the major political battles of the day, natural gas regulation, out of control oil companies, and corporate America's stranglehold on the economy, public opinion, and the electoral process. His call for economic conversion from a manufacturing base geared to war to one that would support a sustainable peace-time economy echoed through the room. He explained why he was aligning the IAM with so many diverse outside groups and spoke in a straightforward manner about what it meant to be a "seat of the pants socialist." He told them why that should never be confused with being a communist. Finally, he made clear, after hours of exhorting his troops, why this job represented the culmination of his life's work, how much fun he was having and why he would always be proud of the Fighting Machinists.

Wimp began his speech to the opening session on Wednesday by praising the changes that the Program for Progress had wrought since the last convention and hinted that the IAM was about to make some noise.

> *It seemed also that we would have to quit the penny-*
> *pinching past that has been a trademark or hallmark*
> *of the IAM, since we were going to be operating in a*
> *trillion dollar economy...*
>
> *And above all, the Program for Progress recognized*
> *that in the real world today, this real world in which we*
> *defend ourselves every day, minnows don't compete*
> *with sharks, and that under my stewardship, the focal*
> *objective of the IAM must be to do battle with those*
> *sharks—not just to do battle, but to beat the hell out*
> *of all of the sharks, all of which every day are around*
> *us preying on our labor, our union, our pocketbooks,*
> *and our principles and moreover, to beat the hell out*
> *of sharks on our terms and not theirs.[4]*

He went on to express pride in the establishment of a Civil Rights Department, a Community Services Department and a Bylaws Department to better serve the membership.

Wimpy took particular joy in pointing out that he had dramatically expanded the International Affairs Department, in part as a response to what he termed "the ever increasing attitude of isolation that we seem to find developing in the AFL-CIO over on 16th Street in Washington," and the appointment of yet another highly talented young woman, Helen Kramer, to work on trade adjustment assistance cases.[5]

One of the major organizational changes he trumpeted was the integration of the Legislative Department and the MNPL.

> *For years, as you all know, we ran those as two*
> *separate and distinct activities, often time far removed*
> *from each other and oftentimes one not knowing*
> *what the other was doing. We always regarded that*
> *as a necessity—at least our predecessors in the*

IAM considered that a necessity under the various statutes to control such activity, and did not take very kindly to integrating them. Well, we've decided over the past year to live a little more dangerously in the present and we've integrated them, and we are telling anybody that doesn't like it to go to hell.[6]

He was also militant about the need to ramp up organizing; casting verbal brickbats at both self satisfied labor leaders and the powerful corporate hands he had seen operating behind the scenes on labor law reform:

In the 1960's, it seemed that there were a lot of people in the trade union family who were fat, happy and rather clubby in their outlook about their existence, and a lot of them seemed to be more at home on the golf course than they were down in the pits with the unorganized and the working poor of whom there are still millions in this country. It seemed to me that the chieftains of labor were more contented with full rosters in the big plants than they were with the lean existence of the unorganized, whose low standards were cutting the floor right out from under all of the agreements that we were managing to negotiate for those who were organized.

In effect, I think that neglect-absolute neglect-in organizing has meant that we've abandoned that field to a bunch of anti-union hucksters who are all around us today, very prevalent, and all of you have met them. They've erected themselves as a multi-million dollar a year industry manipulating the fears, frustrations and torments of unorganized workers and especially the working poor. They have virtually declared class warfare. There's no doubt in my mind that they have declared class war, and that they think that they've got the tools to prevent us from representing those whom we have historically benefit of trade unionism to—and that's all those less fortunate than us in the nation's work places.[7]

After saying that the IAM would hone its skills, and that he would monitor organizing efforts personally on a daily basis, Wimp empathized with the difficulty of the task:

We know that it's a tough job, we know it's the toughest job in the trade union arsenal. Nobody relishes the idea of operating out of the backseat of their car or some lonely motel room out in Squeedunk Junction somewhere. But believe me, survival is the issue and uncomfortable as it may be and as old fashioned as some of us think it may be, the only way we are to survive this current round, this current wave of anti-unionism, is to put our principles and our standards up front—to do the hard nitty-gritty work of organizing the unorganized, punching the doorbells, running a mimeograph machine, making speeches, kidnapping the community leaders— whatever it takes to get them organized.[8]

Wimpy went on to explain his philosophy of being visible and raising public awareness of the Machinists Union as organizing tools:

I run around a good deal trying to create whatever activity I can, name recognition, organizing opportunities of whatever type, anything that we can get out of a very high level of activity and visibility.

All of that is designed to make your job every day a little bit easier if that is possible. That means I'm away from headquarters a great deal. I think that's as it should be. I think our membership is entitled to and wants to see what that big dope is that's running this huge enterprise and I believe in letting them get in not only eyesight, but a few darts in if they're prone to do it, so I am out there with you and your membership as much as I can be.[9]

He let loose a few darts of his own toward George Meany and the "elderly statesmen" who sat with him on the AFL-CIO Executive Committee:

I have been accused from time to time of being critical of President Meany. That is true. I think I have always been a constructive critic. I've never made any attempt to denigrate in any way, manner, shape or form this great trade union movement that we all serve. I've tried to be constructive. But, I was satisfied long before I sat down in that chair [as an Executive Council member] that the AFL-CIO simply is not in step with the times of contemporary USA and Canada today.

That bunch of elderly statesmen, who sit around that table seem to me, as personified by the leader himself, more concerned with the cold war overseas than with the hot war we're having with Corporate America right here in the United States and Canada. A lot more concerned with that cold war over there than the flourishing right-wing reactionary movement that's in full swing on this continent today. He seems to me to be more concerned about molding trade unionism in his image than in responding to the needs and the desires of this country's working people. And he seems to me a lot more sensitive to criticism from the White House and the Congress than he ever was to any criticism, limited though it may have been, from people like me or any other affiliated International Union.

And I, for one, have never believed, and I don't believe now, that surrounding yourself as a chief executive with a bunch of yes-men or even entirely like-minded people is necessarily a good way to lead an organization.

It seems to me over the years that in the absence of any criticism of Meany or his policies, except behind his back and out of earshot, of course, I decided somebody had to start challenging some of his assumptions, and I nominated and elected myself. Simply because nobody else would do it.

So, I just decided that when the stuff hits the fan, I'll put it up front, speak my mind, tell them how it is, and let them know when I disagree with them. And you know something? I think sometimes the old misfit actually likes it."

The whole point of it is that I'm critical of Meany because the AFL-CIO has to be somehow brought damn near full circle when we talk about the problems of the trade union movement and workers in our countries today. I don't know yet how we will accomplish that, but be assured, anybody asks me what I think, I shan't be a shrinking violet. I'll tell them. And hopefully, if I'm doing my job half way correctly, I'll be telling them what our membership is saying on the shop floor. And criticism of the AFL-CIO today, within my earshot, is higher on the shop floor from where you come, than at any time in the history

of the movement. I think our members are at an all
time high in having had enough.[10]

He blasted the AFL-CIO's decision to boycott the International Labor Organization and expressed thanks and glee that the IAM would still be able to participate because of its Canadian membership.

> *...I think it is a damn shame when the labor movement of this country gets so eaten up with catch words that end with isms, everything except trade unionisms, that they boycott the only United Nations organization that is capable of representing workers all over the world and is responsible, if for nothing else, minimum labor standards all over the globe. Nothing is more important today when you talk of trade balances and the foreign competition problems that workers in this country face as a threat to their jobs. We have walked away from the only forum of world opinion in existence that promotes minimum labor standards, and I think it is a damn tragedy and I'll be continuing to agitate to get back in at the earliest possible time.*[11]

Supporting domestic organizations was important as well:

> *Beyond that, we are involved in and support about thirty other organizations, many of which are outside the trade union movement, but all of which in one way or another impact upon it. And it's more than some flaky PR that you see around in the newspapers, even though we do benefit sometimes from the PR fallout.*

We support all those organizations for several basic and important reasons. First, each of them represents a worthwhile democratic cause. Secondly, they're usually threatened with survival on the issues for which they stand, just as we are, and third, they sponsor campaigns and or legislation which, for the most part, nicely dovetails with the legislative and political programs of the trade union movement and more particularly of the IAM.

Fourthly, high postage rates, and we are all familiar with that, and the mailing costs, have driven their message out of the marketplace of ideas and thoughts just as its driven The Machinist *paper from a weekly to a monthly.*

And fifth, they usually have a very limited constituency, and they are not funded by the private foundations of the corporate fat cats which are gimmicks of the wealthy. They have to go out and scratch up dollars the hard way the same way as we do. And we are in a position to help and we do, and in exchange they give us effort, talent and manpower and what have you.[12]

He then spoke of the work of the Citizen-Labor Energy Coalition and the forthcoming battle over the deregulation of natural gas and chided his staff for a seeming lack of passion:

Basically, the job is to fight the oil octopus, those seven giants of energy that are systemically raping our paychecks. Try to keep the lid on natural gas prices that threatening to run through the roof and prevent the thirty-five to fifty billion dollars natural gas rip-off which is being cooked up for us on the hill right now.

I am sometimes appalled when I look at the range of problems we have, and some that I think are readily and easily identifiable, and I don't hear from you any outcries or rage, any screaming on behalf of your members, and in fact almost a disinterest in many cases. Let me tell you something, if these birds get away with what they are cooking up down there right now and which will probably go to a vote in the Senate next week, the American people are going to be about fifty billion dollars worse-off for the experience by 1985, and God can only predict how much after that.

This administration has declared war on our ass, my friends, and they are going to jam five percent down your throat one way or another if they can, and if we sit still for these rip offs, without crying out with every bit of vitality we have, we are going to be saddled with them. I'm offended by that.[13]

He then spoke of the need to convert to a peace-time economy and how the business community would continually ask labor to support things that would work against that.

They ask us to support the development of nuclear power on an unlimited basis even though nobody knows yet whether it will finally extinguish the whole human race.

We spoke out quite loudly as did the Federation against the sale of jet fighters to the Mid East and Israel.

It might have been a threat to Israel, and that's a legitimate concern, but I thought it represented a hell of a lot more of a threat to peace in the world. Selling airplanes in the most volatile theatre of

*political activity—the scene from which every expert
figures if World War III comes it's going to start right
there, and these god-damn employers in this country
go there and sell all of this highly sophisticated stuff
to hasten a day when it will happen, and turn right
around and sell an equal amount to the other side,
on the basis that they will preserve the balance of
terror.*

*It's our kids that go out and fight these wars and
the whole thing that gets lost in this picture all the
time is the human equation. That Senate Committee
sits over there and deals with a bunch of hardware
'who could shoot up what' and 'what do you have to
shoot back' and who lives and who dies in terms of
national interest, and nobody ever talks about the
people. And you got some of those damn fools that'll
try to tell a guy wounded and bleeding in the desert
that that was a defensive weapon that shot him for
Christ's sake.*[14]

He wrapped up his Wednesday speech by explaining his
heightening public profile and taking on the question of his
identification as a socialist head-on:

*If anybody has any curiosity about what we are
trying to do to refurbish the image of the IAM, and
hopefully the trade union movement, some of the
new programs we have undertaken to give exposure
to our name, we will be delighted to answer them
if you care to ask. We are involved in a lot of things,
we write a lot of articles for periodicals, magazines,
newspapers. You see them publishing my puss liberally
in a lot of publications—newspapers primarily,
particularly when they can use all of the catch words*

to scare Americans to death because of our biased culture—our anti-union animus that is inherent in American life.

I am sure all of you have seen recently where they say this is an 'ass in the pants' Socialist—not doctrinaire- Socialist. And when I was asked that question by that reporter, I said I never was told that that's a dirty word. I knew he was going to try to make it one. But I know too that public ownership of essential means of survival in monopoly production in this country is about the only way we are going to stop them from owning us and really have corporate America on our laps.

As long as we permit this myth of 'free enterprise,' monopoly free enterprise, to exist and it's a catch-all for everything that's good, and public ownership manifests everything that's bad, we are in for a hell of a hard time and I will talk more about that Friday morning, too. Meanwhile I'm going to keep using those words because the only way our membership is ever going to understand the difference and get away from the notion that Communism and Socialism are synonymous, or that even related, is to use them and to depend on you to tell them, because if our performance is right, it won't make any difference what they call us. Our members will understand the difference. If we never do it at all, they will still think of us as a bunch of god-damn Communists the minute somebody calls us a Socialist.

So, I don't intend to deny it. I don't even intend to explain it particularly.[15]

He finally wrapped up his opening speech, which had gone on for more than an hour, by telling them how much joy he took in leading their union: As you can tell, I find it as exciting as hell. My life is constantly on the move, and something new and exciting every day, and I wish, hope all of you can enjoy your job that much too."[16]

Wimpy's speech to the closing session on Friday morning was a broad ranging indictment of the American corporate state, and set the underpinning for many of the fights he would undertake in the coming years: his battles with the energy companies and OPEC, a monopolistic corporate system, the vast disparity of wealth distribution, negative public perceptions of labor unions, and an unpopular Democratic President.

The speech began with the need for the IAM to act quickly to defend itself from corporate America:

> I think this much is clear: we can't sit around and wait for the rest of the labor movement. It seems content to act much like a sleeping dog, lie around and snooze, than to act like a sheep dog, wake us up and hurl us into the future, or away from disaster's brink. I can tell you from first-hand experience, that while AFL-CIO leadership sits down there and fiddles and deals with Congressmen and Senators, a hundred of them are alienated while most came to Washington ready to do something on our behalf. And we alienate them because we support the wrong programs. The leadership is out of touch with what the hell is going on, not only among our membership, but all across this country. While we lose our friends, the right wing coalesces among themselves, with the Republicans, with corporate America, small business and they proceed, all together, to put their arm on wavering moderates, liberals, and anyone else they can ensnare.[17]

He talked about the control corporate America exerted on the news media:

> We see the corporate state in full control of the media and corporate acquisitions of publishing houses, newspapers, magazines, and all of the trade press are in abundance every time you pick up the financial page. RCA owns NBC and Random House. CBS owns Mergenthaler Press and Prentice Hall. ITT owns a publishing empire and wants to own ABC. Electronic sounding names like Raytheon, Xerox, GTE, bought old line printing firms all over the country by the score over the past fifteen years. Time, Inc., owns the Washington Star. The Washington Post owns Newsweek Magazine. Only half a dozen major cities in this country have a competitive daily press. Only two wire services feed all of the press there is left, as well as the radio and TV stations around the country. And newspapers in their entirety are exempted from anti-trust laws.[18]

He linked the domestic energy companies to OPEC:

> You see the corporate state very visibly in the energy industry, where major American companies are part and parcel of the OPEC Cartel. Big oil, without any shadow of a doubt, today means big gas, big nuclear, big coal and big bank tie-ins and we even see the octopus reaching out to buy up priceless commodities, indispensable commodities, that contribute to the solar program, if we could ever get it, in the development of photo voltaics. They bought up copper stocks by the jillions in recent months to get a strangle hold on copper plumbing and things of that kind that are

indispensable to those type of installations so that they can price those out of our reach as we go along. Their aim is to keep them competitively priced with oil to keep their interest forever in the forefront. If they could hang a God-damn meter on the sun, we'd have it today, and they would not be messing around like this, but they haven't figured that one out yet.[19]

He then recounted a confrontation he had had over natural gas deregulation:

We saw the corporate state in action very recently in those secret deliberations between the House and Senate Conferees on natural gas price deregulation. I was there firsthand. Representatives of our government meeting in secret and I took a busload of people over to the Capitol and we climbed stairways and back halls of that place that I didn't even know existed, way up in the top somewhere. I couldn't find it today, again, if my life depended on it, but we found the meeting. I accosted one of the Representatives as he came out, while Jim Schlesinger, Mr. Nazi in our government, was just finishing up a press conference. As I arrived, Harley Staggers, the Representative of West Virginia, who is chairman of the House committee, came out to meet me and ask what did I want and I said we wanted into the meeting, Mr. Chairman. He said, "What on earth for?" and I said, "To find out what the hell is going on. That's what for." He said, "Well, you can't get into this meeting. Nobody is getting into this meeting." I said, "Since when?" I said I want to see what kind of deals were being made. And he really got furious, jumping up and down, said there were no deals being made, that everything they did in that room would be reenacted on the floor of the two houses of Congress whenever they finished up and there was no necessity for anyone to be in there. And I said, "Since when do we conduct the business of the American people in a free democracy in the secret rooms of the Capitol building, out of earshot of the check and balance system that the taxpayers think they have?" "Well," he said, "We have to do it on this one." About that time an old friend of mine from the Wall Street Journal walked up and he said, "Wimpy, (this is a fellow I got acquainted with back in my days on the pay board—as President Smith's alternate) Wimpy, Schlesinger is down the hall and he is livid with rage." And I said, "Pray, tell why?" He said, "Because you're here." "Well," I said, "I'll be God-damn, a cabinet minister of the United States of America enraged because somebody had the audacity to come up to find out what's going on and I just saw him take the microphone out of his mouth, telling the nation's allegedly free press what the score was." That is not a system of checks and balances—that is the ultimate corporate power.[20]

He even railed about the corporate state's offshore influence:

We see the corporate state in action overseas. We can't even contain it within our own borders. We see them rape economic and human rights in the Third and Fourth Worlds—all the underprivileged and underdeveloped parts of the world—in Argentina, South Africa, Brazil, Chile, Nicaragua, Rhodesia, and Ben Sharman [from the International Affairs Department] could probably give you a longer list than that. It always boils down to the ruling elite versus the powerless masses. And that, if nothing else, is living proof that they are the same animals they always were and always have been. It is kind of a replay, what we see around the world now, of what life was like in this country before unions and what life will God-damn well be after unions if we let them get away with it.[21]

Invoking the words of Adam Smith, Wimp then summed up the corporate state and took a swipe at "the Holy Trinity of free enterprise."

This corporate state is almost like an invisible hand, like a shadow government that is always there. And they mask themselves behind the myth of the free market and free enterprise. Ah boy, the Holy Trinity of free enterprise. God forbid anyone should every say anything other than it is everything of everything. In the name of supply, demand, the mystical marketplace, competition and the profit motive—those are the Ten Commandments. National advertising on TV, the Chamber of Commerce preaching at every Rotary Club, Lions Club, and Odd Fellows Hall in the country.

Look at our economy. You live in it every day, it is all around you. Where do you see competition? Where do you see competition? Where do you see free enterprise? Not in automobiles, sure as hell. Not in baby foods or breakfast cereals; not in chemicals, not in light bulbs, not in energy, not in health care, not in housing or lumber, not in meat packing, not in mining, not in steel. Free enterprise is a myth and you better start acquainting yourself with the fact that it is. Competition today is a myth. For what it's worth, in this economy today, in my humble judgment, in the real economy, is the general full blown collision— a collision of ethics, of economics, of the values of equity and fairness and the greed of profit and plunder. The free market today offers no priorities, no values, no end and no human purpose.[22]

The economic disparity which drove his socialism was next:

...if you happen to think you are rich, or if you happen to think that anyone you represent is rich, or if you happen to think anyone you live around is rich, consider this: Only four percent of the adults in this country have assets of $60 thousand or more. (And I would like to see some pencils moving right now.)

And that counts everything they own. Only one-fifth of a percent of all American adults own twenty percent of all the corporate stocks, sixty-six percent of all tax-free state and local bonds, forty percent of all the bonds and notes—that is one-fifth of one percent. The richest one percent, to get to a whole number, own fourteen percent of all real estate in the country, more than half the corporate stocks, all the trust assets outside the pension funds and fourteen percent of all the cash in every check and savings account in the pocket and purse of every American. One percent has all of that—the rest is shared by all the rest of us.

The richest one percent own one quarter of the combined market price—market worth of everything owned by every American. And that is exactly what the richest one percent of Americans owned the eve of the Civil War in the United States.

Down at the bottom where the vast majority of people, including our members, live, down where we have to act like mad dogs, snarling and snapping at each other to see who gets the last scrap, over twenty-five million people live below the poverty level of $6,190. per year. Nine out of every ten could sell everything they own, pay off their debts, and have no more than thirty thousand bucks left. Worse than that, more than half of all Americans could settle up with a total net worth of no more than $3,000—half of our people.[23]

Wimpy then invoked the memory of his mentor, Ernie White:

A few years ago, with some lamenting by some of your officers, I remember it well, I was a fledgling officer myself, we engaged in a convention dialogue to take the words "class struggle" out of the preamble of the IAM constitution. One officer, now deceased, for whom I have great love and affection, argued strenuously not to make that move and he was more right than the majority. His name was E.R. White, one of the most knowledgeable and articulate officers this union has ever had. And he saw the picture more clearly than the majority, because what we are reaping now are the fruits of the corporate state in the class struggle that it generates.

What is happening to us is class warfare in its finest hour. And I wish those words were back in our preamble, because that is our mission: To engage in *the class struggle in order to lift our membership out of it.*[24]

Wimpy elaborated on the way the class struggle played itself out:

> *We have been stuck for a long time now, where we are taught in schools, the instruments of the corporate state, that we should save all the contempt that we can muster in our bellies to heap on those who are beneath us on the economic totem pole. And as a consequence, that is exactly what happens. When in reality, we ought to save up a full measure of that same contempt for that richest four or five percent up at the top that makes it all happen and creates welfare clients and those less fortunate than we.*[25]

He then took on the widely held impression that the hard won economic gains of labor unions were to blame for the inflation that most people considered the nation's most pressing problem.

> *If we took four items out of the cost of living index calculation of the past couple of years, you would see an index expanding about only three tenths of a point annually.*
>
> *Those four items are energy, food, housing and health care.*
>
> *You take those out and we live in a decent non-inflationary economy. The cost of those four basic necessities of life rose fifteen percent alone in the second quarter of this year.*

Labor costs are not the cause of this inflation. During the same period that those basic necessities were ratcheting up by fifteen percent in a single quarter, real earnings of our people, adjusted for inflation and taxes, dropped by three percent. Disposable pay went down three percent. We're not even making a fair game of playing catch-up. We're falling behind systematically.[26]

Wimpy then exhorted his staffers to hit back whenever labor got blamed for causing inflation and took a swipe at President Carter:

We have to come down hard as we can on the impact and causes of inflation. Every utterance you make to your communities on these four basic necessities has to focus on the real causes. We've got to turn this inflation argument away from labor, away from paychecks and pin it on those who are really responsible for it and that's that top four percent again. We make a doctor an automatic millionaire when we walk him through the graduation door of the institution, college or medical school. And we have a President who has just betrayed us on a solution to health care and cost as a problem, as he points to a voluntary cost containment program by the hospitals. More hog wash.[27]

He then issued a call to arms:

Okay, that's the whole range of the problems and there are probably some I didn't even discuss. But these are the most grievous, the most aggravating and the most immediate ones.

What are we to do about them? Are there solutions? Well, I guess maybe the quickest one would be just push a button and self destruct, but I don't think we can in good conscience subscribe to that theory. Besides non-violent anarchy, which is what we have now, is getting us nowhere, and I don't think violent anarchy will be any better.

So first we have to determine to work with whatever there is that is available. And that means reaching out externally and build coalitions with all like-minded groups, because there are a lot of other people who understand these facts of life. All you have to do is go find them. I find them by droves, and I find them at the national, state and local levels all across the country. And they can be on single issues or many issues; we're doing it with the energy coalition as one example. We're doing it with this defense dependency and conversion issue on another. In the very near future, I expect to be doing it with the Presidential nomination issue, too.[28]

Wimp's plan of action had eight elements: reaching out to likeminded groups; supporting local public employees in their bargaining efforts; supporting other private sector unions; cultivating the news media; refusing to cooperate with the corporate state and not falling for job blackmail; putting political candidates to a litmus test on labor law reform and natural gas deregulation; forgoing any pretense of being socially acceptable in favor of outright militancy; and most importantly, get ready for some big changes with the 1980 election.

His instructions on dealing with the news media rolled back years of informal IAM policies:

...cultivate your local news media. Reach out to them too. Go visit the editors and reporters. We've ignored them and cussed them and everything else for years. Find out what their problems are. Give them the facts of yours. Reporters for the most part are workers, you know. They're not all finks. They are not all wishy, washy intellects; they are not all hired guns. Most of them put their pants on the same way we do, one leg at a time. And they have the same kind of work related problems as our members do. So make an effort to know them to contact them, because it can make a significant difference in public opinion where you live. I've done it and I know it works, so don't let fear hold you back. Even if they bad mouth you, that gets the IAM right out front and when somebody wants to join up when they got a problem, if they know we are fighting, they'll come to see us.[29]

Wimp brought his speech to a close by as he put it "trying to save the good wine for the last," by making it clear he wasn't going to be supporting Jimmy Carter's re-election:

President Carter has abandoned his constituency, his party's platform, and his own campaign pledges. Carter may be the best Republican President since Herbert Hoover.

I didn't see him publicly flog anybody the way he is publicly flogging people today on the God-damn energy bill, when it came to Labor Law Reform. I didn't see him deliver either Georgia senator's vote for cloture, and if I was the ex-Governor of Georgia and the President of the United States I'd have some kind of whip to crack on that Georgia mafia to get at least one of their votes. One vote would have made the difference.

To me, President Carter is through. He's a weak, vacillating and ineffective President. And I know as well as anyone that those are dangerous words and they are going to invite a lot of attention on our union but I don't give a damn.[30]

Wimpy and the Fighting Machinists were fixing to pick a very big fight.

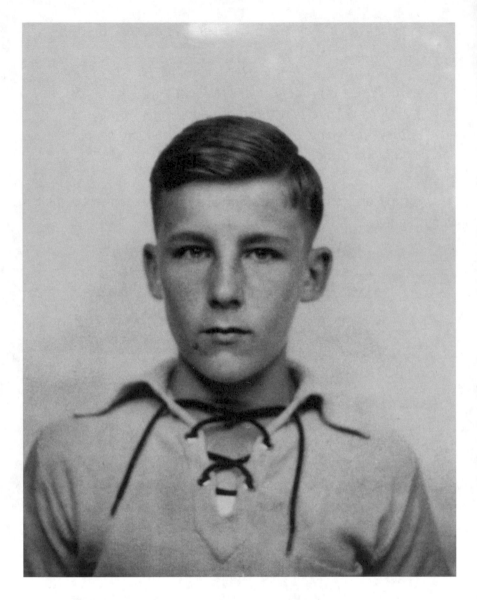

**Wimpy was a talented but restless youth
who went from President of his freshman
class to high school drop-out**

**Wimpy participated in D-Day and the invasion of
Sicily as a crew member of the US LST 310**

**He married Pearl Foster shortly after
returning from the war**

Phil Zannella and Wimpy would meet through Cleveland's Local Lodge 1363 and remain life-long friends who joked often of their secret "Master Plan."

Wimpy was a skilled, if somewhat accident-prone, craftsman.

The Cleveland Connection: Wimpy poses with Matt Demore, Phil Zannella, and Red Smith

Wimpy helps a floundering Red Smith regain control of the 1972 Grand Lodge Convention

**Al Hayes administers the oath of office to
William W. Winpisinger as the eleventh
International President of the International
Association of Machinists and Aerospace
Workers as a proud Matt DeMore looks on**

IAM Headquarters building at 1300 Connecticut Avenue, NW, Washington, DC

IAM Legislative Director Jerry Thompson shows Wimpy some of the thousands of postcards generated by members in support of labor law reform legislation

The venerable but aged George Meany was the first guest to arrive at a reception Wimpy threw upon being elected to the AFL-CIO Executive Council

After Carter failed to deliver on labor law reform
Wimpy began the "ABC" (Anybody But Carter)
movement, and was directly responsible for nudging
Ted Kennedy to challenge Carter in the 1980
Democratic Primary

Unforseeable foreign events and an uneven Kennedy campaign dashed Wimp's hopes of electing a labor-friendly Democrat to the White House

Wimpy was a key figure in the development of the NFL Players Association. Above, he speaks in support of their 1982 palyer's strike

Soviet Premiere Uri Andropov (left) used a Kremlin meeting with Wimpy to respond to President Reagan's characterization of the USSR as an "Evil Empire"

Wimpy was friendly with fellow Cleveland native Paul Newman, Often dining with him during the Indianapolis 500

**The IAM Racing Program put the union before
millions of sports fans**

Wimpy was the most outspoken labor leader of his generation, appearing constantly on television, radio and in print. He made himself a household name and was profiled on "60 Minutes." He did back-to-back appearances on "Donahue"

Soviet Premiere Mikhail Gorbachev (left) used a Kremlin meeting with Wimp to signal to the first Bush Administration that he was serious about arms control

Pope John Paul II thanked Wimpy for all he and the IAM were doing to support the Solidarity trade movement in his native Poland

Nobel Peace Prize winner Lech Walesa credited Wimpy and the IAM with helping spread the word of their labor movement by providing much needed funds to buy printing presses

Four Ohioans who had a major impact on the IAM (left to right) Phil Zannella, Sr., Wimpy, Robert K. Buffenbarger and his son Tom Buffenbarger, who would eventually become the International President of the union

**Wimpy leads 2,000 members on a picket of the
Wolfe Manufacturing Company in Cincinnati, Ohio.
Company officials tried but failed to have the march
halted**

**Wimpy was one of the first civilians ever to see
the intenet, as a participant in a Pentagon DARPA
project**

A life-long supporter of civil rights, Wimpy delivered Jesse Jackson's nominating speech at the 1988 Democratic National Convention

Wimpy shares a light moment with the IAM high command (left to right) Tom Buffenbarger, George Kourpias, Wimp, Don Wharton

**Wimpy and Pearl pose by the statue of IAM founder
Thomas Talbot**

**Wimpy was thrilled that his long time confidant
George Kourpias (far right) was able to succeed him
as International President**

**Fellow union president Ed Asner, famous as
television's "Lou Grant," was a close friend and
staunch supporter**

Retirement dinner: Wimpy was joined by his brothers Ray (left), his mother Edith, and Bud (right)

THIRTY

SUIT AGAINST OPEC

Wimpy fired the first shot in his declared war against Carter by sending the President a scathing letter. Dated September 25, 1978, and hand delivered to the White House, it hit Carter for his many flip flops. It listed the disappointments Wimpy had been railing about to audiences across the country for the past year, and informed him in no uncertain terms that he should not look to the Machinists for help as he geared up his campaign for re-election.

Addressed simply "The President, The White House, Washington, DC," and not dignifying the man by mentioning his name, the letter was an indictment of Carter's tenure as President. Wimpy's tone on a range of issues was blunt:

> ...you have been instrumental in gutting Humphrey-Hawkins Balanced Growth and Economic Development bill.
>
> In fact, your anti-inflation program is merely a continuation of the Nixon-Ford labor scapegoating charade...then caved-in to medical profession and insurance carrier vested interests, which brought forth a program destined to make still-born the prospect of decent health care as a matter of right for every American.
>
> We met your objections to a strong Labor Law Reform bill and sponsored a mild and weaker proposal, but your refusal to employ the parliamentary and presidential powers of persuasion in behalf of the measure, when it was before the Senate, was an omission of fatal consequences...your turn-around

*on the Natural Gas Deregulation issue defies logic
and reason.[1]*

Wimpy went on to say that the President had "retreated," and done "a complete about-face" on the matter. He closed with a direct notice to Carter that the union had a "thirst for honesty" and that disappointing its members would have consequences:

> To sum-up, the Machinists Union is determined to take a stand against the chicanery and vacillation that infects the body politic today. We will take that stand on principle and on the merits of the issues involved. We will no longer support those office holders who insist on playing shuttlecock politics with issues of grave concern to our members, their families and working people in general.[2]

Wimpy, never one afraid to speak truth to power, had just done the equivalent of slapping the most powerful man in the world across the face with a glove. President Carter and his political operatives responded in kind in early December. The Democratic National Committee barred Wimpy from serving on the energy panel at the party's 1978 mid-term convention in Memphis. Wimp then circulated an open statement to the delegates: "We witnessed the Democratic Party's capitulation to Republican Party principles of the corporate state,"[3] and calling for the resignation of Energy Secretary James Schlesinger.

When the MNPL held its annual legislative conference in January 1979, Wimp was fully engaged in doing battle. The United States Conference of Mayors, representing the Chief Executives of approximately 800 cities across the country, held a press conference while the MNPL was meeting. It released an eighty-seven page analysis attacking Carter's domestic policies using the exact language Wimpy had been spouting about Carter's misdirected economic policies.

"Most economists now believe that inflation is more effectively countered through targeted efforts to reduce price increases in food, energy, health and housing costs, and through other policies rather than through cuts in social programs."[4]

The broadside and its eerie similarity to Wimpy's rhetoric did not go unnoticed at 1600 Pennsylvania Avenue. Addressing the MNPL conference, Labor Secretary Ray Marshall attempted a spirited defense of the President that same afternoon: "If our commitment to help the disadvantaged is to be credible," Marshall intoned, "we must convince a skeptical public that we can manage social welfare programs effectively. There is nothing more duplicitous than to portray the President as heartless and callous because he tries to cut programs that we all will admit privately are ineffective and wasteful."[5]

Wimpy was not buying and he had an important announcement to make. He held a press conference the following day in The Rayburn House Office Building, and with Democratic Congressmen Toby Moffett, Harry Waxman, and Senators John Culver, Tom Eagleton, Pat Leahy, George McGovern, and Ted Kennedy. Wimpy lambasted Carter for his cuts to social programs and his increase in defense spending. "In order to make certain we get a recession, President Carter has announced he's going to cut federal spending for social programs by $14 billion next year. That's austerity," Wimpy exclaimed. "At the same time, he's going to increase defense spending at an annual rate of nearly ten percent. No austerity here."[6]

Citing a report the Machinists Union had commissioned from Marion Anderson, a nationally recognized research expert and director of Employment Research Associates of Lansing, Michigan, Wimpy argued that the capital intense nature of military spending and the Pentagon's increasing use of off-shore procurement was actually costing Machinist's jobs. But the news media was most interested in a resolution that had been passed by the IAM Executive Council urging Ted Kennedy to run for President. The resolution was blunt and described the President as "incompetent," and "piously hypocritical."

While Wimpy and the IAM nudged Senator Kennedy closer to a Democratic Primary challenge, events halfway around the world would have immediate and long term effects on both the presidential race and Wimpy's next ten years as president of the union.

On January 16, 1979, and in the face of growing civil unrest and massive street protests, Shah Mohammed Riza Pahlavi, the fifty-nine-year-old monarch of Iran, and a staunch ally of the United States, fled that country. The Shah had been an important strategic partner for US interests. Iran was located on the Persian Gulf and the Southern border of the Soviet Union. Its prodigious oil production fed America's thirst for crude oil and Pahlavi had instituted a broad reaching modernization program. The most controversial element of that program, by far, was the installation of a civil government, a breach of the ancient balance of power between the monarchy and the country's conservative Islamic religious leaders. That balance was about to shift because of seventy-eight-year-old Ayatollah Ruhollah Khomeini, the country's preeminent religious figure. Khomeini had been exiled by the Shah in November 1964 and taken up residence in Najaf, Iraq. By 1978, the Ayatollah's agitation for the removal of the Shah and the establishment of an Islamic republic in Iran was gaining popular support on the streets of Tehran. Iraqi Vice President Saddam Hussein forced Khomeini to leave Iraq. He fled to France using a tourist visa. From Neauphle le Chateau, outside of Paris, the Ayatollah continued to rail against the Shah and to call for his overthrow.

Claiming that his health was in decline, the Shah and his wife, Empress Farah, left Tehran and flew to Cairo, Egypt, on an

Iranian Air Force jet that the Shah himself piloted. He insisted that his return to Teheran depended on his physical recovery. News of his departure brought loud, boisterous crowds into the streets, waving placards with Khomeini's picture and chanting, "Death to the Shah."

On February 1, 1979, two weeks after the Shah's departure, Khomeini made a triumphant return to Teheran. He was greeted by millions of Iranians who thronged the streets to welcome him back. Within ten days, the Ayatollah's forces had neutralized the army, disbanded the monarchy, and dismissed the government. Iran had turned back the clock of modernization and would become a strict Islamic theocracy. Oil prices skyrocketed. Gasoline in the United States pushed past a dollar a gallon, and the dreaded gas lines had returned.

Rampant inflation, particularly the explosion of energy costs, was now a dominant topic of conversation in the US. The thirteen-nation Organization of Petroleum Exporting Countries (OPEC) kept re-setting a fixed price for oil that was escalating far faster than other costs in the economy. OPEC, based in Vienna, Austria, had been established in 1960. It had increased prices 300 percent in 1973, fifty percent in 1974, ten percent in 1975, five percent in 1976, fifteen percent in 1977, and ten percent in 1978.

With the crisis in Iran, OPEC members considered a whopping increase for 1979. Higher oil prices not only hurt IAM members in their pocketbooks, they posed a direct threat to the many members whose work involved transportation. Higher jet fuel prices meant higher ticket costs and fewer airline passengers. Higher gasoline prices meant fewer miles driven and less need for mechanics to repair and tune-up automobiles.

Already deeply involved with the fight against what he termed "the energy octopus," Wimpy was very receptive in late 1978 when he was presented with a radical idea about how to fight back. The proposal came at an unusual place: an automobile race. A California attorney wanted someone to challenge OPEC's actions in court, and considered the IAM, with nearly a million members being hurt by the oil crisis, as a great potential plaintiff.

In George Kourpias's words:

> Our car was racing in Long Beach. Bud Melvin, who was close to Wimp and general chairman of District 19 in those days, picked us up at the airport. This attorney was driving. Bud wanted Wimpy to meet the attorney. And that was the beginning of the suit against OPEC.
>
> So we got back to Washington and Wimpy picked up the phone and asked Plato [Papps, the IAM Chief Legal Counsel] to come up. Plato came up and Wimp said, "We're going to sue OPEC."
>
> Plato said, "God damn it, Wimp, you're crazy. Don't do it Wimp. Who is this attorney, anyway? God damn it, don't do it." And Wimp says, "We're going to sue."
>
> I think that down deep in Wimp's heart, he knew we couldn't win. But also, he felt the action had to be taken. Then again, what the hell? It was Jimmy Carter's Justice Department.
>
> Wimp never hesitated. He wanted us, in all phases, to be on the attack, and not on the defensive.[7]

The Machinists filed their suit against OPEC in Federal Court in Los Angeles on December 29, 1978, seeking a temporary restraining order to prevent OPEC from carrying out any further price increases until the federal court could hold a hearing to determine if the cartel was acting in violation of the Sherman and Clayton Anti-Trust Acts. At the time, prior to the

Iranian revolution, OPEC was already predicting a fourteen-and-a-half percent price increase for 1979.

Wimp held a press conference and explained what he was up to:

> *If the price hikes are not prevented, American consumers will be forced to pay over six billion dollars in artificial prices within the calendar year 1979, as a direct result of the conspiracy among the OPEC members to raise their prices. OPEC members have been able to create revenues of approximately $100 billion per year in recent years. From 1974 through the present, it is estimated OPEC members' revenue due to fixed prices has been approximately $450 billion. It's time somebody fought back against these price fixers. They've been able to get a stranglehold on American consumers.[8]*

The suit drew little attention at first; nobody took it seriously. At the January MNPL Legislative Conference, Wimp mentioned the suit. He was asked if he was afraid that it might backfire: OPEC members might refuse to sell badly needed oil to the United States. He dismissed the concern, saying that under international law, any such boycott would be considered an act of war.

"Given the world situation, OPEC would not declare war on the US. They tried four boycotts in the past. Three fell flat on their faces! One succeeded because at that time there was a state of war between Israel and the Arabs. But that is not the case now."[9]

Wimpy brought up his OPEC suit again in a speech to the Consumer Federation of America in Washington, DC, on February 8, 1979.

We are suing OPEC. All fourteen nations and the seven sisters who do their bidding. We're asking for injunctive relief from the last round of price-fixing and for damages for previous rounds of price-fixing. We've found a pinhole of light in the darkness of the anti-trust laws. We believe big oil can be prosecuted for anti-trust violations. We believe we can challenge the assumptions of oil diplomacy.[10]

Asked by editors and broadcasters visiting the White House the following day if he thought the United States had it within their power to break OPEC's stranglehold over oil prices, Carter responded, "I think it has now become such an institutionalized structure that it would be very doubtful that anyone could break it down."[11]

President Carter lacked Wimpy's zeal for combat.

As the OPEC litigation slowly made its way through the federal court system, another catastrophic event occurred eleven miles south of Harrisburg, Pennsylvania. On Wednesday, March 28, at approximately 4:00 AM, the emergency core cooling system at the three-month old Three Mile Island Nuclear Power Plant was turned off prematurely, causing a dangerous drop in the water needed to cool the nuclear core and keep it under control. By 11:00 AM, the plant was releasing steam into the Pennsylvania countryside with above normal levels of radiation. Plant operators waited until after the releases were halted at 1:30 PM to report the incident to local authorities.

There was widespread shock and alarm at what was quickly termed the worst accident at an American nuclear power facility. While the plant's operators and even the White House scrambled to downplay its severity, the public grew more and more concerned as details dribbled out. Concern turned to near panic two days later, when the Nuclear Regulatory

Commission told Congress that there was an imminent risk of a core reactor meltdown. A large hydrogen bubble had formed in the reactor.

Seven days later, when the NRC had finally declared the incident over and the plant stabilized, Wimpy spoke to more than 65,000 people gathered on the Washington, DC, Mall, in the largest anti-nuclear protest ever staged. He pointed out that working people had an even greater stake in the safety of nuclear power generation than the general public because they made the nuclear fuel, operated the plants and transported the nuclear waste. Taking full aim at both Energy Secretary Jim Schlesinger and President Carter, Wimp declared:

> Carter and Schlesinger are mad scientists in service to an energy industry that has brought us soaring prices, nuclear power and the brink of disaster at Three Mile Island. All we have to show for it is a technology which, at best, will be a 100,000 year poisonous curse upon this planet. We must convert our energy program from centralized oil imports and dangerous radioactive fuels to low cost, renewable and safe alternatives, such as solar, coal, hydro and biomass energy production.[12]

Wimp was still on an alternative energy tear the following month as the OPEC suit was argued in Federal Court.

The lead editorial in the Sunday New York Times for June 24, 1979, cited Wimp's suit, picked up on his themes, and accurately predicted the suit's outcome in a piece headlined: "The Moral Equivalent of the Gas Line." The editorial read in part:

> For one poignant moment last week, between grandiose journeys to foreign summits, Jimmy Carter had a chance to experience the humiliation that

the OPEC cartel daily inflicts on this country. For a President, it should have been the moral equivalent of the gas line.

The President's men were telling him about a law suit to be heard in Los Angeles tomorrow. Brought by the International Association of Machinists, it charges price fixing by the Organization of Petroleum Exporting Countries, which meets in Geneva on Tuesday to fix some more. Legally, the case against OPEC looks substantial. But economically, a court victory over OPEC would be disastrous. To avoid fines and damages, the oil nations would wreck American banks and ruin the dollar abroad by withdrawing billions from their short term accounts. They could also stop investing in the United States or further hold down oil production. They have not even bothered to answer the charge in court.

So while the lines are growing at pumps charging more than $1 a gallon, the President was asked what to do. Did he care to appear in court in the politically absurd role of OPEC's defender or trust the California judge to grasp the stakes and find a pretext for dismissing the suit? No one at the White House could even afford to worry about the legal merits. Probably it was decided to explain the national interest to the judge by some unofficial means.[13]

Officials from the State, Treasury and Justice Departments met twice in a panic to review the suit and decide whether or not to file an amicus "friend of the court" brief on behalf of the oil cartel. After much squirming, they decided reluctantly to sit the case out. "It would kill us with the public to have the Government siding with OPEC when people are waiting in lines and paying more than $1 a gallon for gas," an unnamed "Administration official" was quoted as saying.[14]

Los Angeles attorneys James H. Davis and Richard I. Fine, representing the IAM, brought the case before Judge A. Andrew Hauk of the Federal District Court of Los Angeles on June 25th. Fine claimed that the Foreign Sovereign Immunities Act of 1976 applied, meaning that even though the members of the cartel were foreign governmental entities they could be held responsible under federal anti-trust laws because their conspiring to fix prices had an impact within the United States. He also cited a 1945 case handed down by Judge Learned Hand of the Second Circuit Court of Appeals that established that a Canadian subsidiary of Alcoa Aluminum was restraining American trade by limiting the flow of raw materials. If the law could be applied to aluminum, why not oil?

Judge Hauk, noting that none of the named thirteen member nations of the OPEC Cartel had representatives in court, continued the case until August 20 and issued a thirteen page order instructing that OPEC members be informed again of the suit and requesting a response. Two days later, OPEC met in Geneva. Iran and Libya led a charge for an unprecedented increase in the cost of a barrel of oil, from $14.55 to $23.50, more than a sixty percent increase. An escalation of that magnitude would be devastating to the American economy. Saudi Arabia, one of the most influential players in the cartel, played the "good cop," and held out for a mere twenty-seven-and-a-half percent increase. But the dominant topic of conversation was what to do about the IAM antitrust suit. After a full morning of discussion, the members decided not to respond. Asked by members of the news media what position OPEC would take on the suit, Venezuela's oil minister, Humberto Calderon-Barti answered cryptically, "We will be having contact with certain people."[15]

The Arabian members of OPEC weren't the only Middle Easterners taking note of William W. Winpisinger. The state of Israel, which Wimpy had visited the previous July, bestowed the Prime Minister's Medal, their highest civilian award, upon him for his "continuing support of the free state of Israel and its free trade union movement."[16] At a Washington, DC, banquet attended by more than one thousand people, Israel's ambassador to the United States, Ephraim Evron, draped the medal around Wimp's neck as a beaming Secretary Treasurer Gene Glover and an even prouder US Senator Howard Metzenbaum looked on.

Wimpy's acceptance speech, said in part:

> The tenacity of the people of Israel has always been an inspiration to me, and a model for the American Labor Movement…Israel is a nation of workers. It had to be. The people started with nothing but desert and swamps, and with nothing but their own labor and sweat. But Israel is a nation of workers who are determined, despite many differences, to work together to build for themselves a secure, democratic nation…Before I visited Israel last July, the country seemed somehow unreal to me. It was almost a fabled, legendary place, a nation of giants trying to bring democracy to an area of the world where it was unknown, and trying to shape desert sand into a garden paradise… But when I got there, I found that Israelis are men and women like men and women everywhere. All they want is to make a decent living, and to raise their families in security… Everybody I spoke to, from Prime Minister [Menachem] Begin to workers in the factories, showed me their tremendous love of their country, and the tremendous joy they felt in building their land with their own hands…

*And everybody I spoke to, from Prime Minister Begin
to workers in the factories said that their one dream
was peace... Well, today, Mr. Ambassador, Americans
rejoice with Israelis because their dream of peace
seems to be close... These are exciting times. Peace
in the Middle East not only means that the sky's the
limit for humanly oriented development of that area.
Peace in the Middle East also means that the world
could be spared another World War which could
threaten the destruction of the planet.*[17]

In spite of his forays into international politics, Wimpy was
still at the thick of things in American politics. He led the dump
Jimmy Carter and dump George Meany forces. He continued
to refine his pitch for a more equitable social contract.

At the Rural American Conference at Washington, DC's
Shoreham Americana Hotel on June 26, 1979, Wimp laid out
what he defined as four basic rights of all Americans. This was
his vision for a new political system and what his union held as
its political goals.

First, our program must be based on four basic rights.
Those are:

- The right to a fair share of the nation's wealth and
  income
- The right to full employment opportunities
- The right to organize and participate in private and
  public investment decisions
- The right to peace.

How do we achieve them? What sorts of structural
changes are needed to accomplish our goals? Simply put, we
need socialized central planning, similar to that which we put
in place when the nation mobilized for World War II. We had

a War Production Board then, to determine priorities and allocate resources. We need a similar agency for socially useful peacetime production.

We had mandatory price and profit controls. We didn't need wage controls, because trade unions knew they couldn't demand more than the Treasury held. In return for wage restraint, workers were guaranteed real wage gains. The economy was inflation proof.

We need similar mandatory controls in all forms of income today, with a guarantee that worker's real incomes will be permitted to rise incrementally each year.

This is a social contract that makes sense, is fair and will work.[18]

Early in the summer, news reports of the impending OPEC price increase spread panic throughout the American economy. Voters reacted with outrage. Pat Caddell, President Carter's pollster, was getting disturbing numbers back from his surveys. Carter's overall approval rating had dipped to twenty-five percent, lower even than the support for Nixon during the Watergate scandal. An independent survey of Southern states, conducted by Darden Research Corporation of Atlanta, found the President trailing Ted Kennedy by eleven points in the region.[19]

President Carter, at Caddell's urging, cancelled plans to vacation in Hawaii on his way back from the Tokyo economic summit. Instead, he flew to Camp David in Maryland's Catoctin Mountains to prepare for his fifth major speech on the energy crisis on July 5. But as Americans celebrated the nation's 103rd birthday with parades, cookouts, and fireworks, Carter abruptly announced that he was canceling the speech.

News analysts suggested that Carter's reason may have been the steep drop in the number of people willing to listen to him. While he had drawn an audience of 80,000,000 people for his April 1977 "Moral Equivalent of War" energy speech, a mere 30,000,000 people tuned in two years later when he delivered his fourth energy speech on April 5, 1979. Jimmy Carter was becoming irrelevant.

He spent the next twelve days hunkered down at Camp David, figuring out how to save his presidency. He summoned his top aides, his cabinet officials, and a steady stream of visitors from a broad range of disciplines. All together, 130 leaders from business, labor, political, and civic organizations made the pilgrimage to Camp David. Carter attended each of the discussion, often sitting on the floor and taking notes.

On July 15, Carter finally returned to Washington and announced that he would address the nation the following night. His Sunday evening speech, which aired at 10:00 PM East Coast time, would become known as "Carter's Malaise Speech" even though he never used the word. Instead, he talked of a "Crisis of Confidence" of the American people. Sounding more like a Southern minister than a President, Carter read excerpts from his Camp David notes. After reciting nineteen individual observations or snippets of advice, the President turned to his main focus.

> I want to talk to you right now about a fundamental threat to American democracy.
>
> I do not mean our political and civil liberties. They will endure. And I do not refer to the outward strength of America, a nation that is at peace tonight everywhere in the world, with unmatched economic power and military might.
>
> The threat is nearly invisible in ordinary ways. It is a crisis of confidence. It is a crisis that strikes at the very heart and soul and spirit of our national will. We can see this crisis in the growing doubt about the

*meaning of our own lives and in the loss of a unity of
purpose for our nation.*

*The erosion of our confidence in the future is
threatening to destroy the social and the political
fabric of America.*[20]

He went on to speak of "paralysis and stagnation and drift,"
and claimed, "We are at a turning point in our country."[21]

Before revealing the revamped energy policy that originally
had been the focus of his speech, he spoke directly of OPEC.

*In little more than two decades we've gone from
a position of energy independence to one in which
almost half the oil we use comes from foreign
countries at prices that are going through the roof.
Our excessive dependence on OPEC has already
taken a tremendous toll on our economy and our
people. This is the direct cause of the long lines which
have made millions of you spend aggravating hours
waiting for gasoline. It's a cause of the increased
inflation and unemployment that we now face. This
intolerable dependence on foreign oil threatens our
economic independence and the very security of our
nation. The energy crisis is real. It is worldwide. It is
a clear and present danger to our nation. These are
the facts and we simply must face them.*[22]

Two days later, Carter demanded the resignation of his
entire cabinet and all of his top aides. Fifteen cabinet or sub-
cabinet officers and eighteen assistants and special assistants
tendered their resignations. It was the only time since 1842
that there had been a mass resignation in the middle of a
Presidential term. Carter ultimately kept most of the officials

on board, shuffling a few here and there, but he did accept the resignation of Griffin Bell, his Attorney General, and that of Wimp's nemesis, James Schlesinger, the Secretary of Energy.

Public attention now shifted to Wimpy. His battles against the status quo of the corporate system and two of the most powerful political figures of the day made headlines. Noting that Wimpy had signed 50,000 direct mail fundraising letters urging support for the draft Kennedy movement, reporter Michael Kernan of the *Washington Post* profiled him (in its Saturday, July 7, 1979, edition), under the headline: "William Winpisinger: A leader of the Dump-Carter Movement." Calling Wimpy: "a leader, perhaps *the* leader of the Dump Carter movement," Kernan described Wimpy:

> *What we have here, in brief, is an American original, the self-made man, the guy who pulled himself up from the crowd with nothing but his good strong arms and his fox-quick mind, a hang-in-there fighter who learned all the tricks growing up on the streets in Cleveland at an age when some of his future peers were taking boxing lessons at Andover.*[23]

In the profile, Wimp downplayed his importance to the anti-Carter effort:

> *All I did was breathe it, and it raced like wildfire across the country. The problem with this country is not the people. It's the leadership. If I didn't respond the way I did on Carter, my people would have the same contempt for me that they have for him.*[24]

He continued on with his now familiar indictment of the Carter presidency.

Asked about those who'd labeled him a socialist, Wimp was direct:

> I have never called myself a socialist, but people keep asking me if I am, and I don't deny it. If a guy who believes America can never fulfill its promise to its people without somewhere coming to grips with public ownership of its essential resources and or services, or production that's absolutely essential to the welfare of our people, then I'm a socialist and I think everyone should be.[25]

While he had the reporter's ear, he decided to take a shot at George Meany as well:

> My basic quarrel with the old man is, if he were a bright-eyed liberal I wouldn't give as—if he was ninety-five, I'd be for him. But Meany continues at eighty-five to come down with the same degree of dogmatic heavy handedness as he did at forty-five. And meanwhile the country's forty years down the road.
>
> People at a certain age seem to develop a stake in the status quo, and retrench in their beliefs, and if you can't upgrade your mind or will or vitality to address the new issues and positions, then you owe it to yourself to get the hell out. That's my quarrel with Meany: He doesn't get the hell out.[26]

It was a hot, sticky, eighty-five degree day in Los Angeles on Monday, August 20, 1979, when the IAM suit against OPEC finally made it into court. Judge Hauk informed those gathered in his courtroom that he was going to finish hearing the case that week, even if it meant holding court until midnight each day. "We're going to finish this week. It's my inclination to rule from the bench."[27]

The Machinist's case had drawn widespread support from across the country. Eighteen states, the Washington Legal Foundation, Gulf and Western Industries, a San Francisco advocacy group called Public Associates, and the cities of Cleveland, Ohio, New Haven, Connecticut, and Pueblo, Colorado, had also filed suits against OPEC, hoping to be joined with the Machinist's case. Jude Hauk ruled that the cases could not be joined and that the merits of the subsidiary cases would depend upon his ruling in the Machinist's case.

Although the courtroom was packed, not a single representative of OPEC was present. Instead, Saudi Arabia, Kuwait, Indonesia, Nigeria, Qatar, and Venezuela, had filed "notes of substance" with the United States State Department, claiming they could not be sued in US Courts because of sovereign immunity.

Judge Hauk immediately tossed out OPEC as a defendant ruling that, because the cartel was unable to be served with a complaint since they were located in Vienna, Austria, they did not have to answer the Machinist's charges. The case would have to proceed against the individual member nations. The judge also ruled that it was not within his power to assess damages against any of the named defendants.

Despite these setbacks, attorneys for the IAM pressed forward. The testimony they elicited would lead to some shocking revelations.

Judge Hauk had appointed Dr. Morris A. Andelman, an economics professor at the Massachusetts Institute of Technology, as an expert witness. Andelman revealed that there was a secret agreement in place since 1960 between the multi-national oil companies and the US Justice Department that allowed big oil to "fix prices, divide markets and limit imports into the United States, if so directed by national governments or by a 'supra-national' body."[28] Andelman said the secret arrangement gave Judge Hauk just the excuse he was looking for to dump the case. After musing about the fact that the US government had not filed a friend of the court brief in the case, Judge Hauk admitted that he had discussed the case with Griffin B. Bell, Carter's former Attorney General.

"I asked him why they hadn't filed a [friend of the court] brief on this. He told me that 'We [the Justice Department] wanted to, and so did the Treasury Department, but the President didn't want us to.'"[29]

Judge Hauk, who was nothing if not frank, then delivered the death blow to the Machinist's suit. Referring to Dr. Andelman's testimony he said, "It seems to me, if you are right, [the executive branch] has approved fixing of prices by OPEC. It's a strong indication to this court that I shouldn't be sticking my judicial nose into the Federal Government or the Carter Administration because if I do, I'll get it clipped off."[30]

And so the suit against OPEC died in a stranglehold of collusion between President Carter, the big oil companies, and the powerful cartel. In an almost comic postscript Judge Hauk defied all logic and credibility two months later. In a statement he made while refusing to re-open the case, his logic was completely illogical. According to the New York Times, "District Judge A. Andrew Hauk said that OPEC's price fixing had 'no direct impact' on the price of gasoline in the United States and the oil cartel raised crude oil prices only after gasoline prices had jumped in this country."[31]

Wimpy did not prevail in his suit against OPEC. He did force the government to admit in court that they were in bed with big oil against the best interests of the consumers of America.

Wimpy had many more battles to fight including a desire to rejuvenate the Labor Movement. It didn't take long for him to get his wish. George Meany's health declined quickly. After being hospitalized twice in the early months of 1979 for a bronchial ailment and then bursitis of the knee, Meany missed a meeting of the AFL-CIO Executive Council in May. It was only the third time in his twenty-three year tenure that happened. He paid one more brief visit to AFL-CIO headquarters in August, using a wheelchair and crutches to maneuver around the building, but he was not well enough to attend the August council session.

On the evening of Thursday, September 27, Meany telephoned his second in command, the ever faithful Secretary Treasurer of the AFL-CIO Lane Kirkland, with an important message. According to Meany biographer Archie Robinson:

> ...Meany telephoned the expected word to Kirkland: He would attend the Executive Council meeting the next day and tell the members that he was not going to seek re-election. But he was too ill even to attend the meeting, and Kirkland, in an emotional encounter, had to deliver the message himself.[32]

THIRTY-ONE

ANYBODY BUT CARTER

Wimpy started 1979 with the goal of ridding Washington of Meany and Carter. Now Meany was on his way out, and Carter seemed likely to follow him. Officially, Wimp's line was "ABC," Anybody But Carter. In truth, his heart was set on convincing the telegenic and charismatic Ted Kennedy to take on the unpopular president.

"Draft Kennedy" committees sprouted up all across the country, more often than not led by a local representative of the IAM. Wimpy enlisted fellow labor leaders Jules Bernstein of the Laborer's International, Vic Kamber of the AFL-CIO Building and Construction Trades Department, and Sandy DeMint, of the National Resource Center for Consumers of Legal Services, to form a group named "National Call for Kennedy."

"Our job," Wimpy said, "is to start the ball rolling on this unique, first in history draft of a candidate to the Presidency."[1]

Wimpy brought a draft Kennedy resolution before the 300 delegates of the 32nd Annual Convention of Americans for Democratic Action, and had the crowd roaring with laughter when he said, "In the Machinists Union we no longer ask, 'Jimmy Who?' [Carter's famous self effacing crack from the 1976 campaign], We say, 'Jimmy Hoover!'"[2] The convention passed the resolution. But Wimp had stuck in a catch-all clause just in case he couldn't get the Massachusetts Senator into the race: "If Senator Kennedy chooses not to run, we further commit ourselves to seeking an alternative progressive candidate who can uphold the principles of the Democratic Party and offer effective, progressive leadership."[3] By September, IAM members were heading draft-Kennedy committees in nineteen states.

Wimpy was on the road hopping from state to state, railing against the failed Carter presidency and urging support for Kennedy. He spoke at Yale University on September 13, and outlined his reasons why Kennedy should be drafted:

> Remember, thirteen percent fewer people call themselves Democrats than the day Jimmy Carter took office. Senator Kennedy will bring these disaffected Democrats back under the umbrella. We believe Senator Kennedy realizes the fallacy of perpetuating the free market myths and will be willing to modify and alter it in order to promote full employment and price stability. Senator Kennedy has a seventeen year record in the US Senate. He's been able to do in that millionaire's club what neither of his brothers, with all due respect, were never able to do. Namely, successfully sponsor and move a broad range of humanitarian legislation, on economic, social and foreign policy fronts. National health insurance is Senator Kennedy's bill. Divestiture of Big Oil is Senator Kennedy's bill. Prevention of acquisitions and mergers is Senator Kennedy's bill. Refugee relief is Senator Kennedy's bill. Energy alternatives and conservation is Senator Kennedy's bill. Minimum wage, increased Social Security benefits, Medicare, Medicaid, legal services for the poor, health maintenance organizations, labor law reforms, those are Senator Kennedy's votes. No political leader in America is more respected overseas than Senator Kennedy. Part of it is the legacy of his brothers. But the important part is his tireless efforts to promote peace and international economic and social justice. The Democratic Party demands a return to its humanitarian, liberal and progressive principles. We

believe Senator Kennedy meets those tests on all count.[4]

Between stumping for Kennedy, working with a vast array of activist groups on social justice issues, and continuing his pledge to meet with members across the United States and Canada, Wimpy was constantly on the road. He began to log the kind of hours at airports and on commercial flights that had landed him in the hospital in 1963, when he flew more than 100,000 miles and ended up being hospitalized for three weeks and laid up for another ten weeks. Making matters worse, airline deregulation meant that carriers were raising ticket prices and canceling less traveled routes, effectively cutting off Wimpy's air access to IAM members in many smaller cities.

The IAM Executive Council decided to take action. At their September meeting at San Francisco's Jack Tar Hotel, the council voted to lease a Learjet 25 for a year and to purchase a brand new $2,000,000 Learjet 35A outright.

The Learjet 25, introduced in 1967, was a workhorse of the business jet fleet. Powered by two General Electric CJ 610-6 turbojet engines, it carried eight passengers and two pilots, with a top airspeed of 545 miles per hour and a range of 1,770 miles. It wasn't as fast, fancy, or versatile as the sleek new Learjet 35-A the union ordered, but it provided a much needed reprieve from the drudgery of commercial travel.

Jim Thomas was hired to serve as chief pilot, and Ed Lambert was brought aboard as his co-pilot. Meanwhile, members of District Lodge 70 in Wichita, Kansas, began assembling the 35-A for delivery in December 1980.

One trip Wimpy wouldn't be taking with the leased jet was a long-scheduled trip to the Soviet Union. The IAM had agreed to send a delegation to Moscow in furtherance of

East-West détente. However, on the night of August 3–4, 1979, KGB agents swooped in and arrested three members of the Executive Committee of the Free Interprofessional Association of Workers, a fledgling trade union. Wimpy informed Nikolai Zinovyev, President of the Heavy Engineers Worker's Union in Moscow that the trip was off because of "systematic harassment, imprisonment and exile" of trade unionists in the USSR.

In Wimpy's letter:

> As abhorrent as the conditions under which Scharansky, Orlov, and others are imprisoned in strict regime labor camps are to us, nothing quite matches the horror of the KGB's abuse of psychiatry. The definition of protest as a mental illness and the physical and mental torture of political prisoners in Soviet psychiatric prison hospitals such as the Serbsky Institute are now quite well known in the West.
>
> Under the circumstances, we cannot pretend that a visit of a trade union delegation to your country is an ordinary event without political significance. We will not permit the presence of an IAM delegation to dignify the fiction that workers have the rights of free association and organization in the USSR.[5]

Wimpy had no problem traveling to Communist countries to promote free trade unionism, despite the AFL-CIO ban, but he wasn't about to let the IAM be used to soften the appearance of KGB brutality. And while relations with the USSR remained frozen, there began to be a bit of a thaw in his relations with the rest of the AFL-CIO Executive Council. Lane Kirkland, the Secretary Treasurer and Meany's heir apparent, brought forth a proposal at the August meeting of the Executive Council, which he chaired due to Meany's illness, supporting Wimpy and the IAM in their battle against OPEC and the big oil companies.

In the words of Kirkland biographer Arch Puddington:

> The proposal was far reaching, calling for a government agency to import oil, negotiate its price, and "allocate it throughout society to best meet the needs of all segments of society." It then went even further, urging legislation that would prevent oil companies from acquiring or merging with companies in other energy-producing fields, in order to forestall the oil giants from dominating the burgeoning renewable energy sector. Never in its history had the AFL-CIO called for a federal takeover of a major segment of the economy; to do so would have violated labor's long-standing acceptance of America's commitment to the market economy. But many labor officials had come to believe that the OPEC cartel was primarily responsible for an energy crisis that was in turn driving up the rate of inflation; furthermore, they were convinced that American oil companies were in connivance with OPEC and acting against the American national interest.[6]

Wimpy's campaign to raise the profile of the IAM and its causes was showing real progress. He was becoming a recognizable face to many Americans as the colorful, controversial voice of the radical wing of the labor movement. Where older labor leaders shied away from the media spotlight, Wimpy basked in it. And where more cautious labor leaders, still cowed by the stigma of being labeled "communist," went to great lengths to avoid any hint of socialism, Wimpy proudly claimed the socialist label. In a movement that valued seniority and a toe-the-line mentality, Wimpy was the unabashed iconoclast. He laughed at convention and took delight in poking his cigar in the face of the biggest icon of them all, George Meany.

His rising profile caught the attention of producers at the country's leading news show, *Sixty Minutes*. Created by veteran CBS newsman Don Hewitt, the show had debuted on September 24, 1968. Now, eleven years into its historic run, it was the top-rated show on television. It had a coveted time slot at seven PM Sunday evenings, and each program started with ticking from a Tag Heurer stopwatch. In the days when there were only three networks, a commercial on *Sixty Minutes* was among the most expensive advertising in the world.

A CBS television crew spent a week following Wimp from coast to coast in late August, for a profile in their fall lineup. Forty-eight year old Dan Rather did the interview. He was their chief White House correspondent who would soon replace demigod Walter Cronkite as the anchor of their prime-time news broadcast.

Rather and his crew accompanied Wimpy as he joined Albert Wydick, the Directing Business Representative of District 751 to inspect a Boeing 767 being assembled at the company's Everett, Washington, plant. Next followed a stop at the Amber Light Tavern, a watering hole favored by the district's members, where Wimpy and several members engaged in a spirited discussion over a few cold beers about the SALT II Treaty and the effects of defense spending on IAM employment. Wimpy then took the crew back to Washington where they filmed him meeting with his staff at headquarters and relaxing with his family at his home in Silver Spring, Maryland. They finished in Chicago, where Wimpy met with members from Local Lodge 1487 and attended an AFL-CIO Executive Council meeting.

Rather's October report, titled "Wimpy," noted that it was Wimpy who started the draft Kennedy movement. He portrayed Wimp as a man who fought hard not only for the collective bargaining benefits of his members but also for social issues that affected society as a whole.

"He has been so outspoken about this that he is considered the only card carrying radical among labor union presidents."[7] Rather intoned and then zeroed in on Wimp's political philosophy:

> You say you're not a Marxist, never have been, never will be —
> No way.
> - and denounce that, but you don't back away from the word "socialist."
> People tend to think that anything that's publicly owned or operated in the public interest is a socialistic institution. If that is, I'm a socialist, because I believe we have to do that. I don't see how we solve some of our problems, until we manage to work up the national will to do that.[8]

Rather concluded his piece by noting that Wimpy dismissed his critics who claimed his solutions were overly simplistic: "Wimpy will have none of it. What is simplistic to others he sees as simple common sense. By and large, he thinks Americans see things the same way. The people, he says, are smarter than their leaders, and they're crying out for leadership."[9]

Reaction to the "Wimpy" segment was overwhelmingly positive. Viewers commented on how authentic he appeared and applauded his willingness to take on tough issues even when they seemed to present a short term problem to some of his membership. And because of the broad reach of the show, millions of people across the country now knew that it was Wimpy who had started the draft Kennedy movement. All across the country people were responding to Wimpy's "Call for Kennedy," and by August, 1979, a *Time* magazine poll had shown Kennedy, at the time an undeclared candidate, with a commanding thirty-three point lead over President Carter. A *New York Times* / CBS poll taken in early November, just before he entered the race, put the lead at thirty-four percent, with fifty-four percent support for Kennedy to a mere twenty percent for the President. By the end of October, Kennedy had decided to enter the Presidential race. He began to assemble a campaign staff and raise campaign cash.

In early November, three weeks after *Sixty Minutes* ran its interview with Wimpy, CBS aired a special news program called "Teddy." The Kennedy campaign was hard at work making arrangements to announce his candidacy three days later, and this news documentary was supposed to give him a jump start. The network sent newsman Roger Mudd, a respected veteran of political coverage and someone the Kennedy's considered friendly, to interview the senator at his seaside home in Hyannisport, Massachusetts.

As much as the "Wimpy" interview had been a success, "Teddy" was about to turn into an unmitigated disaster. Sitting on the back deck in unseasonably warm late fall weather, the Senator and the newsman seemed relaxed and cordial. After some introductory banter, Mudd asked the softest of softball questions: "Senator, why do you want to be President?"

What came next was stunning and largely inexplicable. Kennedy froze. He simply stared at Mudd in silence for what seemed an eternity, saying nothing and looking like a deer caught in the headlights of a speeding eighteen wheeler. Slowly, unsteadily, with long pauses and in rambling sentences that lacked verbs, Kennedy began to stammer out an answer. By then it really didn't matter what he said, the damage was done. Viewers were left with the unsettling impression that he had no idea why he was running or what he hoped to accomplish.

Kennedy caught a slight break. The show was on opposite the first television showing of the movie Jaws, on ABC, which attracted record audiences. But Mudd had inadvertently done as much damage to Kennedy's candidacy as the great white shark did to the residents of Amityville.

Another incident that occurred that day would also have a profound effect on the Kennedy campaign. On October 22, the Shah of Iran, who had fled his country in January, had been admitted to the United States for treatment of his cancer at New York's Cornell Medical Center. News of the Shah's presence in the US inflamed student protesters in Teheran, and on November 4, several hundred attackers, many of them armed, stormed the US embassy there, and took sixty-six Americans hostage. The Iranian Foreign Ministry issued an official statement that further outraged Americans: "Today's move by a group of our compatriots is a natural reaction to the US Government's indifference to the hurt feelings of the Iranian people about the presence of the deposed Shah, who is in the United States under the pretext of illness."[10]

Kennedy announced his candidacy for President on Wednesday, November 7, at Boston's historic Faneuil Hall instead of at the Senate Caucus Room his two older brothers had used. He used the Revolutionary War era venue to illustrate that he was more than a creature of Washington. The forty-seven-year-old Senator, speaking to a standing room only crowd of nearly 2,000 and 300 press people jammed on a three tier riser while thousands more thronged nearby streets, said he would offer a "forceful, effective Presidency," and that he would get the nation "on the march again."

"I question no man's intentions, but I have a different view of the highest office in the land—a view of a forceful, effective Presidency, in the thick of the action, at the center of all the great concerns our people share.

I believe in the hope and daring that have made this country great. The only thing that paralyzes us today is the myth we cannot move."[11]

Wimpy's months of hard labor had paid off. His ideal candidate to vanquish Carter and return true Democratic ideals to the White House had just tossed his hat into the ring.

THIRTY-TWO

TED KENNEDY COMES UP SHORT

As Kennedy geared up his campaign, yet another event in a far off land threatened to derail his candidacy. On Christmas Day, 1979, Jimmy Carter got an unexpected political gift from the Soviet Union. Six thousand Soviet combat troops marched into Afghanistan. Five additional divisions massed on the border. It was the first time the Soviet Union had deployed ground troops outside the Soviet bloc or Cuba since the Second World War.

Americans were still reeling from the taking of hostages at their embassy in Teheran. Now the world power perceived as the single biggest threat to American interests was invading a neighboring country. Carter immediately labeled the move "a grave threat to the peace," and "a major matter of concern."[1]

Two days later, citing the invasion and the ongoing crisis in Iran, the President signaled that he might withdraw from the scheduled Presidential debate with Kennedy in Iowa on January 7. It was the first step in what would come to be known as his "Rose Garden Strategy."

Kennedy campaigned across Iowa in early January in anticipation of their caucuses later that month. Wimpy accompanied him to a stop at Iowa State University where, despite sub-zero temperatures, the Senator managed to draw an overflow crowd of students, labor people and local activists to the largest theater on campus.

As Wimp and the enthusiastic crowd hung on his every word, Ted Kennedy offered, "I'm delighted to be here in Iowa with all you hard working *fam farmilies*."[2] The campaign, and the Senator's tongue, were having a difficult time finding their bearings. A protester in the balcony caused quite a stir. She was a young woman wearing a wedding gown, her face covered with ghostly white makeup, and a sign around her neck saying "Mary Jo Kopechne," calling out "Teddddeee...Teddddeee..." until campaign staffers hustled her out.[3]

Kennedy pressed on in Iowa, campaigning in Des Moines, Cedar Rapids, Iowa City, in small towns and on farms across the state. His candidacy floundered. The natural tendency of Americans to rally around the President in a time of international crisis came into play with the twin crises in Iran and Afghanistan. Kennedy's inability to express himself clearly drew unfavorable press. A carefully orchestrated series of questions about his role in Mary Jo Kopechne's death ten years before on Chappaquiddick Island did not help.

By mid-January, a Des Moines Register poll showed President Carter holding a better than two to one advantage over him, fifty-seven to twenty-five percent, which represented a drop of fifteen points for Kennedy in a single month. While giving him points for improvement, a political reporter from *The New York Times* pointed out:

> *His stump speech this time out was considerably smoother than before, with little of the broken syntax and hesitation that marked his pre-Christmas appearances.*
>
> *After two months on the campaign trail, the Senator still does not mesmerize audiences the way his brothers did. His speeches seldom were interrupted more than twice by applause.*
>
> *Separating himself from the President on a broad spectrum of issues has been difficult for Mr. Kennedy. On domestic matters for example, he has been boxed*

in by his record on Capitol Hill, which was basically
one of solid support for most of Mr. Carter's policies
up to the time the campaign began.[4]

After his Iowa appearance, Wimpy traded the frozen tundra for the tropical breezes of Havana. Once again ignoring the AFL-CIO ban on travel to Communist countries, Wimp joined a delegation going to Cuba to discuss labor and trade issues. While he didn't advertise the fact that he was breaking AFL-CIO protocol, he would soon be found out.

> *Wimp had gotten an invitation to go to Cuba,"*
> *George Kourpias remembered, "and in those days*
> *to go to Cuba was a no-no. First of all, most labor*
> *leaders, when they traveled, if they were going to*
> *a Communist nation, always sought out Meany or*
> *Kirkland's permission to do so. He went with nobody's*
> *permission and while he was in Cuba, George Meany*
> *died. And I'm trying to reach him—in those days the*
> *phone lines between here and Cuba were terribly*
> *bad and finally, I must have reached him about—he*
> *called me back and it must have been about 11:00*
> *or 11:30 at night, and I said, "Wimp, George Meany*
> *died today." And he said, "Jesus Christ! Meany's dead,*
> *and I'm in Communist Cuba!"*[5]

Wimpy packed up and headed back to Washington. He couldn't bring himself to attend Meany's funeral, and delegated the task of paying the IAM's respects to Kourpias and Gene Glover. Meanwhile, it was beginning to look like his handpicked presidential candidate's campaign would soon be as dead as George Meany. The same day Wimpy returned, Kennedy and his wife Joan held a press conference in Sioux City, Iowa, to address burgeoning questions about his marriage. (It was reported that he and Joan Kennedy had lived apart for the past two years.) Rumors surfaced about his alleged involvement with other women. And both the *Reader's Digest* and *The Washington Star* carried stories about Chappaquiddick. A *New York Times / CBS News* poll indicated that only twenty-two percent of the public believed Kennedy had told the truth about Chappaquiddick. To make matters worse, the campaign was low on funds and being outspent significantly by Carter in Iowa. News accounts said that Carter had committed $700,000 to Kennedy's $480,000.

Monday evening, January 21, was clear and mild in Iowa, with temperatures in the thirty's, as nearly 100,000 Democrats from one end of the state to the other gathered in fire houses, school gymnasiums and living rooms for their Presidential Preference Precinct Caucuses. Only fifty convention delegates were to be elected, but the stakes were much higher. This was the first time real voters would have a say in the epic battle between the controversial President and his famous challenger. President Carter won handily, fifty-nine percent to Kennedy's thirty-one percent. Late that night Kennedy appeared at his campaign headquarters in downtown Washington and told the disappointed crowd: "We could have done a little better in Iowa and we congratulate President Carter for his win."[6]

Three days after Kennedy's defeat in the Iowa Caucuses, Wimpy sat for an interview with Alan Thompson of his hometown *Cleveland Plain Dealer* and got a few things off his chest. Thompson was quite impressed with the former Clevelander's moxie, and informed his readers, "You leave an interview with Winpisinger feeling like you have been fifteen rounds with Muhammad Ali or Joe Frasier. Ideas fly like scattershot, all from the basic premise that the little guy is getting shafted and the big guy is doing the shafting."[7]

On the Carter—Kennedy race, Wimp insisted that the media was to blame claiming that they were ignoring Carter's performance and were ganging up on Kennedy. "Carter is not running against Ted Kennedy, he's running against Russia, and the media is not telling anybody that."[8] His own view was that the Russians were welcome to have Afghanistan if they wanted it. "I think it's ludicrous to argue about a bunch of snow capped mountains and a bunch of tribesmen that will drive the Soviet soldiers crazy. Let them experience some casualties. Let them use their tax dollars to support a foreign population and all the other things that go with these kinds of adventures, such as we learned in Korea and Vietnam and a few others. Let them get a dose of it for a change."[9]

Wimp also talked about his hero in the labor movement, John L. Lewis and drew an unfavorable comparison to Lane Kirkland, George Meany's replacement at the AFL-CIO. "Lewis had a very profound impact on what 'stand-up-ism' means to me. He was the kind of guy who wouldn't cut and run when somebody turned the burner up."[10]

And as for Kirkland: "There's no reason in the world organized labor has to be the biggest hawk in the country. Lane Kirkland is worse than George Meany. Meany made the comments, but Kirkland was behind most of them."[11]

Thompson warned his readers that the full bore Wimpy was not for the faint of heart: "Dialogue is one thing Winpisinger is exceedingly good at, although anything but a sanitized version would not be suitable for a family newspaper."[12]

While Wimpy was at full steam, the Kennedy campaign looked like it was on its last legs. A week after Iowa, his campaign staff was working without paychecks and there was barely enough money to travel. A Boston Globe poll showed that Kennedy's one time forty-eight point lead in New Hampshire had completely evaporated. He now trailed Carter by twenty-five points, fifty-six percent to thirty-one percent. Operatives were also reporting significant difficulties in Illinois, where Kennedy's troubles were compounded by his close association with the increasingly unpopular mayor of Chicago, Jane Byrne. Kennedy cancelled a scheduled swing through Maine, New Hampshire, and Rhode Island and announced that he would deliver a major campaign address the following Monday at Georgetown University. Speculation ran rampant that he would quit the race.

In George Kourpias' words:

> Kennedy's campaign was not going so well. Some elders from the John Kennedy campaign—one of them was [Sargent] Shriver—encouraged him to make a speech and lay out some real strong points of why he wants to be President.
>
> Wimp and I went to that, and sitting in front of us in the third or fourth row, was Shriver. He turned around to Wimp and shook his hand, and said, "I think we've got the kid going now."
>
> Teddy, I don't think at the beginning, was listening to the people that made John Kennedy president. And then [after the Georgetown speech] it just started turning, but it was too late, and Wimp was tremendously upset.[13]

Kennedy's Georgetown speech was impressive. He managed to explain why it was fair to run against the President even in a time of international uncertainty, and finally provided the ideological underpinning that was so sorely lacking in the Roger Mudd interview.

> The 1980 election should not be a plebiscite on the Ayatollah or Afghanistan. The real question is whether

America can risk four more years of uncertain policy and certain crisis, of an Administration that tells us to rally around their failures, of an inconsistent non-policy that may confront us with a stark choice between retreat and war. The political process has been held hostage here at home as surely as our diplomats abroad. Before we permit Brezhnev and Khomeini to pick our President, we should pause to ask who will pay the price.

Today I reaffirm my candidacy for the Presidency of the United States. I intend to stay the course. I believe we must not permit the dream of social progress to be shattered by those whose promises have failed. We cannot permit the Democratic Party to remain captive to those who have been so confused about its ideals.[14]

Kennedy retooled his campaign staff. He replaced Herbert Schmertz, a Mobil Oil Company public affairs vice president who had been charged with crafting his television image, with Charles Guggenheim who had won an Academy Award for his film *Robert Kennedy Remembered*. The campaign then made a major commitment of $200,000 for television advertising in New England. The Carter camp countered by putting up a flight of negative radio ads. They called Kennedy a weak leader who had lost his leadership position in the Senate and a flip-flopper who called for increased military spending and then voted against it. Each ad featured the tag line: "Every time Senator Kennedy talks about his vision of America, his record gets in the way."[15] The gloves were off.

Maine was next up with their little publicized caucuses. The Carter White House did the equivalent of driving a Brinks truck loaded with federal cash up to the Maine state house, delivering a whopping $75,000,000 in new federal grants in the month before the February 10 caucuses. Despite this largess, Kennedy was narrowing Carter's lead day by day. By the time folks "Down East" cast their votes, the President managed to eke out a six point victory, forty-six percent to forty percent, with California Governor Jerry Brown claiming thirteen percent.

Political pundits took note of Kennedy's campaign gaining traction. Carter and his political operatives played up his statesmanship in trying to resolve the hostage crisis, while the Georgia Democrat remained firmly rooted in his rose garden. Meanwhile, ABC News began airing a nightly update on the crises in Iran and Afghanistan in a program called *Nightline*. It began each broadcast with stark music and the graphic: "America Held Hostage, Day 'X,'" with the "X" representing the ever increasing number of days the diplomats had been in captivity. The show first aired on day four of the hostage crisis.

As the New Hampshire primary approached, it looked like Kennedy might be able to close the gap. Four days before the primary, Ayatollah Khomeini stuck his nose into the situation again, issuing a statement that the hostages wouldn't be released any time soon, and citing "past United States interventions in Iran's internal affairs through the blood-letting Shah regime."[16] America rallied around its President again— and Kennedy's momentum evaporated. Carter beat Kennedy in New Hampshire by 12,046 votes, forty-nine percent to thirty-eight percent. Kennedy was zero for three in electoral contests.

On the Republican side, former California Governor Ronald Reagan disposed of his main challenger, former Congressman, diplomat, and Director of the Central Intelligence Agency, George H.W. Bush.

As March dawned, Kennedy limped into his home state of Massachusetts. There, for the first time in the 1980 race, a sizeable population of union households awaited him. That, coupled with his natural base of support and a newly invigorated political machine, allowed him to rack up a 326,468 vote margin of victory over Carter, sixty-five percent to twenty-nine percent. Carter prevailed in Vermont by a seventy-four percent to twenty-six percent margin, although he only had an 18,795 vote plurality. A strange phenomenon was developing. After five contests, Carter had won four to Kennedy's one, but overall Kennedy had received half again as many votes as the President, 681,351 to 415,343.

The race then turned to Illinois where quirky election laws meant a two-track system of popular voting and delegate selection. Carter beat Kennedy better than two to one in the popular vote, 758,455 to 349,395, but absolutely slaughtered him in the race for delegates winning, 165 to Kennedy's fourteen. As it became clear that Kennedy would not quit the race despite losses in primary after primary, attention turned to the delegate count necessary to secure the nomination. By mid-March, before the primaries in New York and Connecticut, Carter led with 692 delegates to Kennedy's 218. Kennedy carried on determinedly, hammering the President about inflation and the economy in speech after speech. Carter remained holed up in the White House, never venturing out on the campaign trail, a strategy that stymied Kennedy and infuriated Wimpy. Speaking at the IAM Aerospace Conference in San Diego, Wimp vented his frustration:

> Dumb-like-a-fox, Carter hides from the people. He refuses to come out in the full daylight of the political campaign. He slinks away from open forum and refuses to debate the issues that are wrecking the nation.

Dumb-like-a-fox, he makes his appearances at night,
remotely, by telephone or television, into those states
where it's politically expedient for the moment.

When we do see him, he is craftily addressing
one crisis after another, which he himself has either
manufactured or blundered into.

Behind iron locked gates and the thorny thicket of
the Rose Garden, the President of the United States
escapes reality in a suicidal attempt to save his own
predatory ass.[17]

Despite Carter's refusal to engage in the campaign, the tide began to turn. By late March, Kennedy defeated Carter soundly in the New York and Connecticut primaries and trounced him in accumulating delegates in those two states, 284 to fifty-four. Kennedy's red hot rhetoric on the economy was working in the large industrial states. He managed to eek out a narrow victory in Pennsylvania after a bitter and hard fought primary. Carol O'Connor, a television actor and liberal Democrat, was the star of television's top rated show, *All In The Family*, in which he played Archie Bunker, an angry, racist, and sexist comic figure who wore his blue collar angst on his sleeve. He did a television commercial for Kennedy appealing to working class voters. Kennedy was cobbling together an odd coalition of liberals, labor, and conservative blue collar voters who disliked Carter so much they were willing to vote for his more liberal opponent.

On April 25, 1980, news from overseas further muddied the electoral waters. On that evening, an RH- 53D Sea Stallion helicopter operating at a temporary remote desert base in Iran called Desert One collided with a C 130 Hercules transport plane, and killed eight American crewmen. The troops had been deployed to Iran by President Carter as part of "Operation

Eagle Claw," an attempt to rescue the hostages that failed when a desert sand storm fouled the American equipment and made a push into Teheran impossible.

America was shocked and embarrassed. The latest blunder made Carter look incompetent and the US military look weak and ineffective. Voter sentiment turned sharply against Carter, who was seen as bungling the one job, Commander in Chief, that Americans counted on him to do.

Despite a precipitous decline in his favorability, Carter was winning the race to the magic number of 1,666 delegates. He still managed to beat Kennedy 47 percent to 38 percent in Wimpy's home state of Maryland, but Wimp prevailed in his own race to be elected as a delegate, becoming one of the twenty-six delegates Kennedy picked up there to Carter's thirty-two.

With only ten days left in the primary season, Carter had amassed 1,533 delegates to Kennedy's 820. Kennedy needed to run the table on "Super Tuesday," June 3. Eight states would hold their primaries that day, including Ohio, New Jersey, and California. Since none of the states were winner take all, it seemed certain that even if Kennedy won handily, Carter would still accumulate enough delegates to secure the nomination.

Kennedy pressed on, criss-crossing the country and reducing his stump speech to the very message Wimpy had been delivering for the past two years: Carter, a closet Republican, has abandoned the Democratic Party and its principals; he's allowed the country to slide into a recession; he's failed to create jobs or stop inflation; and a direct appeal to labor voters: "If Jimmy Carter wins the nomination, you lose."[18] Kennedy's final stop on the campaign trail was at a Lockheed plant in Burbank, California, where he addressed a cheering crowd of IAM members. Despite falling far short of where he had hoped to be, a combative Kennedy told the crowd: "We haven't come to the end of the campaign. We're just beginning one, and it isn't a campaign. Let's make it a crusade."[19]

Wimpy's candidate carried the popular vote on Super Tuesday, 2,600,000 to 2,400,000, winning in New Jersey and California, but lost Ohio to Carter despite carrying Cleveland, Akron, Youngstown, and Toledo. Carter had finally left the White House to make his one and only campaign appearance—in Ohio—and took Columbus, Dayton, Cincinnati, and the rural swath of the state by enough to ensure victory, putting him over the top in the hunt for delegates.

The Democratic Party had a candidate Wimpy, and a majority of the American people, would ultimately judge to be unacceptable.

THIRTY-THREE

NFL PLAYERS ASSOCIATION AND PLACID HARBOR

Wimpy still had a lot of irons in the fire. His hand-picked presidential candidate would not defeat the President he loathed, but there was a great deal to do on other fronts, and Wimpy was moving full speed ahead.

IAM headquarters on Connecticut Avenue bristled with activity. In addition to the reorganized and highly energized union staff, young people worked on Wimp's community outreach programs including the Citizen Labor Energy Coalition. Wimp had given free office space to other groups striving for social improvement, including Ralph Nader's consumer organization and the National Football League Players Association.

Wimpy was a fanatic football fan. He retained a lifelong soft spot for his hometown Cleveland Browns, but his first love was the Washington Redskins.

"He was a Redskins fan and a Browns fan," George Kourpias recalled. "He grew up with the Browns, but he was really a Redskins fan. I think the first couple of years he was President, Wimp and I probably made every game out at RFK Stadium. He really got into it, and he knew the game. I mean he really knew the game. You'd sit in a room with him and he'd curse, and jump up, and call them bastards."[1]

Like automobile racing, Wimpy saw another opportunity to leverage his love of the sport and build the labor movement. The NFL had surpassed horse racing as the number one spectator sport in America, and its television broadcasts set records for the number of viewers. The league's players had their own union, the National Football League Players Association, that had been founded in 1956 by Don Shula of the Baltimore

Colts, Frank Gifford of the New York Giants, and Norm Van Brocklin of the Los Angeles Rams.

Despite a membership of famous players, the NFLPA was a rag-tag operation with only a skeletal staff and a very limited operating budget. Owners of the NFL franchises refused to participate in collective bargaining with the union, forcing them to seek justice by taking matters to court and to the National Labor Relations Board. It was a management tactic Wimpy was all too familiar with as the President of a sister union. He had addressed the NFLPA convention in January 1977, at the height of their battle with the owners, telling them, "...your fight is our fight. If the owners could defeat *your* right to bargain, they would establish a precedent that would weaken *our* right to bargain."[2]

The players managed to prevail in court after a three year battle and signed a new agreement in March 1977, just before Wimpy took over as International President. As the newly empowered union started to gain traction, Wimpy helped them get established. He approached Ed Garvey, the union's Executive Director, and proposed a joint IAM-NFLPA program to reach out to inner city youth. Dubbing it "Unions for Youth," the program eventually expanded to include sixteen unions and was able to get recognition and funding from the US Department of Labor. All across the country, boys and girls were invited to union-funded summer camps where they got to rub elbows with their gridiron heroes and learn a little about the labor movement in the process. Wimpy was proud of the effort, calling it, "the kind of progressive action that IAM members and other union working people will support to the fullest in order to provide hope and challenge for thousands of disadvantaged boys and girls. The important combination of youth, education and athletes will help to provide a positive image for organized labor."[3]

Wimpy also helped the financially strapped union by offering them free space at Machinists headquarters. It was a move that would pay a huge dividend in a quite unexpected fashion: the advent of Placid Harbor. In the words of George Kourpias:

> *In 1978 Wimp and I and our wives toured all the Scandinavian countries. He was primarily interested in education. In each of the countries we went to the educational centers. He would sit there and listen and ask questions. Here's where they were bringing people in from the shop floor. This is where it was born. I'll never forget Wimp saying to me one afternoon, "We're going to have one of these, because that is the thing that's going to keep the unions in America from dying. We've got to educate our membership, and we've got to put the money out there."*
>
> *He advised the Executive Council that that should be something the council should be thinking about. Garvey, who was head of the football players association—we gave them room in our building; we gave birth to that union; they had free space and rent for years and years.*
>
> *Ed Garvey came into my office one afternoon and said, "I have to get hold of Wimp. I've found a piece of property. I want him to see it. It's now owned by the Food and Commercial Workers. They want to sell it."*
>
> *I got hold of Wimp right away. Garvey wanted to go down. He said, "Wimp, I'll buy half, you buy half." Hell, he didn't have a pot to piss in. He had nothing. He was living on us. They went down to Placid Harbor. Wimp came back that night, and he*

said to me, "Listen, we found it! For $1.1 million I can
buy that land. We can start our school."[4]

The property Garvey found was actually owned by the Retail Clerks Union, a forerunner of the Food and Commercial Workers. It was located on Clark's Landing Road in the small town of Hollywood, Maryland, about sixty-five miles from IAM headquarters in Washington. The facility was stunning. It featured a brick Georgian Colonial mansion fronted by a graceful portico with four Doric columns on a bluff overlooking the Patuxent River, a tributary of the Chesapeake Bay. The estate had been owned at one time by conservative radio commentator Fulton Lewis, Jr., a staunch critic of labor unions, the New Deal, and social progressiveness of any stripe. Best of all, the property had sixty-seven acres of gently sloping lawn, enough land to construct new classrooms and dormitories. The Retail Clerks had already begun the process of turning it into a training facility and had installed classrooms, dining and recreational facilities, and a completely equipped sound studio with closed circuit TV capabilities. There would be a certain poetic justice in having the summer playground of one the leading shills for the American corporate state become the training ground for effective union representation. The Executive Council voted to approve the purchase at their May 12, 1980, meeting.

It took a while for some of the IAM membership to come to grips with the notion of the union operating a cutting edge training facility.

"The rumor started going around that he's buying this as a playpen for himself," George Kourpias said. "'What is this education stuff?' 'They're going to have no education.' 'They're going to all take their girlfriends there.' It was that type of mentality. And he was just bent on proving everybody wrong."[5]

Wimpy and the rest of the IAM leadership were rocked by tragedy a few days after the vote to purchase Placid Harbor. Plato Papps, the brilliant, hard charging, hard drinking Chief Legal Counsel for the IAM, died suddenly at age sixty-two. Papps had been a close confidant of Wimpy's since his first days at headquarters and was a constant companion for lunches and after work cocktails. Tough as nails, with a quick mind, a sharp tongue, and an encyclopedic knowledge of labor law, Papps had once suffered a heart attack while he was on the phone negotiating a contract. Allison Beck, who worked for him in the Legal Department recalled that he toughed it out, finished the negotiation and then allowed himself to be bundled off to the hospital for treatment.

Three hundred of Papps' IAM brothers and sisters gathered for his memorial service in the IAM auditorium on June 2, 1980. A somber William W. Winpisinger delivered a touching eulogy for his departed friend.

> No matter how burdened, Plato invariably found time to listen with infinite patience…It was on those occasions that his gentle manner, his genuine kindness and his sincere concern were most evident, and it was an almost endless demonstration of those qualities that helped all who were acquainted with Plato to more easily bear the burden of life.[6]

Ted Kennedy kept plugging along on the "crusade" he had mentioned to the IAM members in Burbank just before the final primaries. He continued campaigning around the country, trying to solicit support from uncommitted delegates, political operatives and campaign donors. At one point, he even met with Congressman John B. Anderson, who was running for President himself as an independent. Kennedy knew that Carter had all the delegates he needed for the nomination, but he also realized that things had changed since the early days of the campaign when voters rallied around their President because of dual foreign crises. Americans were less apprehensive about the Soviet position in Afghanistan, and were growing impatient with the Iran hostage situation. Many were furious with Carter for his bungled rescue attempt. The economy was in shambles, wracked by high interest rates, joblessness, and runaway inflation. Kennedy sensed that if he could just keep his movement alive, he might yet convince the party to put him on the ticket.

Wimpy, while perhaps a bit more rational about the chances for victory than Kennedy, soldiered on dutifully, urging his troops to stay the course. Addressing the IAM District 98 Annual Meeting in Harrisburg, Pennsylvania, in May, he made his position clear:

> *Anything is possible. The Des Moines Register called for Carter to get out of the race because he's letting politics interfere with his decisions. Less than half the voters will go to the polls in the Carter—Reagan contest. The Anderson hoax could throw the election into the House of Representatives. As the economy worsens and foreign policy blunders lead us down the war path, Carter delegates may take a walk on the first ballot at the convention, then go to Kennedy or a dark horse candidate. We have to preserve that body of ideals, ideas and humanitarianism that the Kennedy wing of the Democratic Party represents. Otherwise we're left with a three headed calf on the right wing, and corporate America is the cow that calved it.*[7]

Carter's political fortunes took another hit three weeks before the Democratic National Convention when his reprobate younger brother, Billy Carter, was found to have extensive financial dealings with the Libyan government of Colonel Muammar Qaddafi. Until this point, Billy Carter had been little more than a minor embarrassment to his brother, with his country bumpkin persona and his promotion of the quite undrinkable "Billy Beer." Now it was revealed that he had received two payments from the Libyan government, $20,000 in January and $200,000 in April, as part of what he called a $500,000 "loan." No paperwork existed to back up the loan and no interest rate or schedule of repayment had ever been established. A Justice Department complaint against Billy Carter said he "was held out by Libyan officials to the US business community as a commercial intermediary through whom US business entities could deal with Libya."[8] The revelations caused a major storm. Kansas Senator Bob Dole filed a formal request that the Senate Judiciary Committee hold hearings as soon as possible to delve into the matter. He addressed his letter to the Chairman of the committee, Senator Kennedy.

Meanwhile, America's big oil corporations released their second quarter profit statements. Mobil was up sixty-four percent, to $2,000,000,000 for the quarter. Exxon announced a quarterly profit of $1,030,000,000 billion, a twenty-four percent increase. Getty was up seventy-four percent, and Sun Oil Company was up twenty-seven percent. Americans were paying through the nose for gasoline and the big oil companies were laughing all the way to the bank.

Carter's support among the delegates began to waver. New York Mayor Ed Koch, one of the President's earliest and most vigorous supporters, began questioning the viability of his continued candidacy. He told reporters that he doubted Carter could carry New York City or the state in November, and noted that the city's large Jewish population was stung by Billy Carter's dealings with Libya: "I am very disturbed that the

President's brother could be used in any form to work with a terrorist, a murderer."[9]

Political operatives started calling for an "open" convention at which delegates would be relived of the responsibility to back the candidate on whose slate they were elected on the first ballot. Many wanted to turn to Kennedy, who still had a huge block of delegates, while others started floating names of potential compromise candidates, such as Senator Henry "Scoop" Jackson, Secretary of State Ed Muskie or even Vice President Walter Mondale.

President Carter realized he had a major problem on his hands. He held a White House press conference on August 4, a week before the convention, to try to diffuse the Billy situation. Under pointed questioning from the press corps, Carter asserted that his brother had done nothing illegal. He made it clear that he didn't approve of Billy's activities but that he still loved his brother.

Carter's hold on the nomination continued to be shaky. George Gallup, Jr., conducted a poll just before the convention and found that only thirty-nine percent of Democrats wanted to ride the Carter horse into the fall election, and fifty-two percent favored dumping him and finding someone else. "Never before in the nearly fifty years of Gallup polls has an incumbent President entered a convention with less grass roots support from his own party than will President Carter," said Gallup.[10]

Kennedy's last remaining hope was that he could prevail in a rules fight on the first night of the convention. If he could get the delegates to suspend the rule binding them to the slate on which they were elected, and thus "open" the convention, he just might be able to steal the nomination.

Wimpy was skeptical. He wanted Kennedy to be the nominee, but he knew Carter's back room operatives would never let that happen. They might be totally incompetent at running the country, but they had proven time and again over the past year that they were plenty competent in hand-to-hand political combat.

Wimpy held a press conference and announced that he would support Kennedy's efforts to open the convention. He also said that should those efforts fail, he would lead a massive walk-out of labor delegates and that he would back Barry Commoner, the candidate of the little known Citizen's Party, rather than Carter.

The air was thick with tension as delegates filed into Madison Square Garden on Monday, August 11, for the first night of the convention. CBS News reported that twenty-six percent of the convention's 3,331 delegates were members of a labor union, including fifty-nine Machinists. The first order of business was the fight to change the rule binding the delegates. Despite a hard fought battle, the Kennedy forces came up short. Jimmy Carter would be the nominee. Ted Kennedy announced that he was quitting the race.

Wimpy resolved to lead a walkout when Carter actually received the nomination. Suddenly "Walk with Wimpy" buttons started appearing on labor delegates and others from the liberal activist groups Wimpy had been courting. Despite his withdrawal, Kennedy kept up his fight to include four minority economic planks in the platform. The platform battle made it to the floor on Tuesday evening and Wimpy spoke in favor of the Kennedy amendments, especially the one calling for the creation of new jobs. Some of Wimp's bitterness toward Carter seeped into his rhetoric as he addressed the delegates.

> *This may be the last chance for the Democratic Party to hold the allegiance of working people in general and of ordinary trade union members in particular…We must have an honest commitment*

to the minority plank, calling for a twelve billion dollar, 800,000 jobs program...The unemployed can't eat promises or survive on broken ones, and neither can either of our major political parties... In politics, all we have going for us is a candidate's word. And a man's word is his bond. And during the past four years we have seen words and bonds broken time after time...This leads us to doubt that this convention honestly intends to change the Democratic Party's economic policy. And this debate, if it's merely sleight of hand which will give the voters only the lesser of two evils in November, then that we cannot accept...What America needs is jobs, jobs, jobs.[11]

Wimpy was followed to the podium by Ted Kennedy who ostensively was there to speak for the minority planks, but in reality was rallying his troops. As he tried to speak, all across the stadium loyalists waved blue and white "Kennedy for President" signs and chanted "We want Ted." A band played "McNamara's Band," as the vanquished Kennedy supporters danced in the isles for thirty-five minutes until Speaker Tip O'Neill, the convention Chairman, finally restored order so Kennedy could speak.

He echoed Wimpy's jobs speech, saying, "Let us pledge that there will be jobs for all those who are out of work. And we will not compromise on the issue of jobs," before closing with the memorable line: "The work goes on, the cause endures, the hope still lives, and the dream shall never die."[12]

Wimpy pressed on with his plan to lead a walkout when Carter got the nomination on Thursday evening.

"Wimpy started it and it kind of mushroomed," recalled Paul Eustace, the Massachusetts Secretary of Labor who was a member of the IAM. "He said 'Screw them.' We met with Wimpy and he said, 'Get with the other [liberal] groups and your delegates, and see if we can empty the whole convention.'" "There was a whole lot of, if you leave, you'll be arrested, all kinds of rumors floating around. There were a hell of a lot of people that walked out. Most of labor—I won't say all of labor because some stayed in that weren't enamored with Wimpy—but there were a hell of a lot of non-labor delegates who were supportive."[13]

The Carter operatives turned down the stadium lights and tried to jam the isles to thwart the walkout. They didn't want the television cameras showing the President giving his acceptance speech to a partially deserted hall.

In Paul Eustace's words:

> ...it was a bitch to get out of the hall. They had people jamming the isles. The lights were not off, but very close to off. A lot of pushing and shoving. To keep people from walking out and get this so-called message. A lot of people who probably wanted to get out—older folks—didn't because the move to keep us on the floor was well orchestrated.
>
> We walked out the door and there were rumors floating around—and I don't know whether they were made up or not, but they said we're going to get out that door, and the friggin' cops are out there, and they've got billy clubs. I turned to Maria [Cordone] and said, "Here we go."
>
> When we went out the door, Wimpy was right up front, and he's leading the parade. I looked out, and I see Maria standing right beside him, and I figured if the shit hits the fan she's in the wrong place. I went up and told her, "Maria, get back in the frickin' crowd. We don't know what the hell is going to happen here. Now, across the street, or up the street, there's

a whole line of cops, a lot of them on horses. You know, the face masks down, and all." And they said, "We've got a problem here." And a lieutenant put up his hand and he said, "Gentlemen, hold one minute." And he came up and spoke to Wimpy, and he said, "Sir, could you bring your guys over to a place we have set up, and there will be no problems?" He was very nice about it. Of course there was murmuring going on in the back, people don't know what the hell is going on.[14]

Maria Cordone, Wimp's secretary, remembered:

Wimpy said he's going to walk out. He cannot stand this anymore, so he gets up an all these other people get up. So I'm following Wimpy, and his daughter Vicky's right behind. Paul [Eustace] grabbed a hold of us to protect us because Jimmy Carter turned all the lights off in the convention hall. We walked outside and we had a place in front of the Post Office. So Wimpy got on the platform and I turned around—there was like 250 people that followed us out of the convention hall.[15]

It was a muggy eighty-three degrees as Wimpy used a bullhorn to address his band of protesters, telling them that walking out of the closed convention was not walking out on the Democratic Party, it was walking out on Jimmy Carter, because he had been walking out on working people for the past four years.

Back inside the less crowded convention hall, things weren't going smoothly for Jimmy Carter. When he mentioned that he had called for legislation to reinstitute the draft after the Soviet invasion of Afghanistan, he was booed. A few minutes into his speech, the Secret Service sprang into action when a woman set off a string of firecrackers. Just as they were getting that disturbance settled, a woman in the balcony began screaming and shouting about her husband being killed during a protest march.

Carter had the nomination, but he didn't have control of the party.

THIRTY-FOUR

2,000 MACHINISTS WALK THE LINE

A week after the Democratic Convention, the AFL-CIO Executive Council, with Wimp abstaining, endorsed Carter for re-election. Their statement was as lukewarm as their support, noting that Carter had proposed and fought for labor law reform, signed the highest increase in history of minimum wage, vigorously opposed a youth sub-minimum wage, and effectively administered OSHA. The summation of their endorsement was "President Carter and his administration recognize the legitimate role of the labor movement in American society."[1]

Wimpy still wasn't buying. He recognized Carter as a loser who would have difficulty holding together the shaky coalition that had won him election in 1976. In a letter to all IAM members explaining his actions at the convention, Wimpy had this to say:

> When we walked out of that closed convention, we didn't walk out on the Democratic Party—we walked out on Jimmy Carter, because, for nearly four long years, he has been walking out on us.
>
> We were told by some that we had to support the Carter candidacy, because we had nowhere else to go. To that, we replied we're sick and tired of being forced to choose between the lesser of evils.
>
> Ronald Reagan may be the nightmare candidate and John Anderson a hoax not a hope, and we have no intention of working for them, but they are not the only enemies in politics today. The real enemy is a Democratic President who believes and behaves like

a reactionary Republican and along with him, those
who uncritically follow him—like sheep—down the
rutty road of reaction and retrenchment.[2]

Nearly three weeks after the Democratic convention, Wimpy ran his first IAM Grand Lodge Convention in Cincinnati, drawing on the same confidence and planning he had employed at Madison Square Garden. Bob Kalaski, who served as Wimpy's Communications Director, described his preparation:"I watched him prepare for conventions. That was his ultimate trademark, the way he ran conventions. And he would prepare for months. Months. They would go away, he and George Kourpias and our legal staff, and practice every possible question on constitutional issues, on, you name it. And when he went into that convention, he was in charge, and there was never, never a single doubt."[3]

Having been called upon to quell disorder at the 1972 and 1976 conventions, Wimpy was determined that the first convention of his presidency would run like clockwork. His friend and confidant, Phil Zannella, would keep a close eye on things in his dual roles as chairman of both the Host Committee and the Law Committee. When Zannella, serving as Temporary Chairman, gaveled the 30th Grand Lodge Convention to order on Tuesday morning, September 2, 1980, he began with a description of his friend:"When I first met him he was a cocky young shop steward who feared neither man nor beast. Now, after all these years, he's a little older and a little fatter, but he's as cocky and fearless as ever."[4] After recounting many of Wimp's accomplishments, Zannella issued a humorous warning to delegates to behave:

He has come a long way since those early days in
Cleveland but he's proven, at past conventions, that

he can swing a gavel just as expertly as he can overhaul an engine. And for this convention we have had a couple of gavels especially made just for him. We not only have a wooden gavel, which rests upon a stand carved in the shape of the State of Ohio, but, in case any of you guys get too rough we also have a brass gavel, specially handcrafted by members of Lodge 1108, which is suitable for knocking on some of the hard heads we sometimes get at Machinists Conventions.[5]

Wimpy, when he took over as Permanent Chairman of the convention, was effusive in his praise of Phil Zannella.

Phil godfathered me into Local Lodge 1363 in Cleveland a little over thirty-three years ago, and for every day since, he's been a loyal, faithful and trusted friend, confidant and advisor. Despite that gruff and sometimes callous exterior, I know him to be a warm and thoroughly dedicated human being with whom I am very proud to be associated.[6]

Wimp knew his union was facing enormous challenges, and would have to change the way it did business to survive. The number of manufacturing jobs in the country was declining steadily as World War Two era plants aged out. Some fled the country to take advantage of lower paid workers without union representation in foreign lands while others retooled their factories using robotics and other labor-saving technologies. The airline industry was in one of its down cycles with bankruptcies and mergers on the horizon and other areas of the transportation industry were being rocked by escalating fuel prices. The result was a declining number of members, now down substantially from its peak of one million in 1968.

Wimp used his opening speech to focus on the future, extolling the virtues of two of the recent acquisitions which had some delegates grumbling - the Placid Harbor education center and the spanking new Lear Jet.

Our educational programs will dramatically expand when the new IAM Labor Studies Center is opened sometime next year—the site, having been acquired a few months ago, at a bargain basement price because, fortunately, we had the resources to commit.

We need only add seventy-five sleeping rooms to inaugurate classes which are programmed to run approximately forty-eight weeks per year. It is our hope that we can thus insulate local lodges all across the country from the tremendously high costs which are currently associated with the conduct of classes and seminars either at our headquarters in Washington or in other urban centers across the country and do it in an atmosphere most conducive to learning.[7]

And on the airplane:

This is an investment in capital equipment, much like real estate, furniture, computers or other property owned by the organization.

Utilization of the aircraft means instant mobility in handling emergency situations; it means we are no longer a prisoner of rapidly deteriorating airline schedules in the post-deregulation era, and it has meant that during the past year, your International President has been able to expose himself to more of our members—both in the lodge halls and in their place of employment—than any officer in our history.

> *It must also be remembered that with the rapidly*
> *escalating cost of airline travel, this investment will*
> *grow more significant and once our real property*
> *is fully developed and fully producing revenues,*
> *once that time arrives, the aircraft will never cost*
> *our membership a single penny of per capita*
> *tax.[8]*

Wimp also let the delegates know that he had begun to explore the possibility of a merger of the IAM and the United Auto Workers, who at the time were still outside the AFL-CIO federation. He termed the relationship of the two unions "cordial," and "cooperative." He had less kind words for the Teamsters.

> *Our relationship with the International Brotherhood*
> *of Teamsters organization can only be described*
> *as stormy. After signing our most recent no-raid*
> *agreement, they continued to indulge in violations*
> *and to assert claims to our jurisdiction that were*
> *never included in the pact.*
> *   Since no self respecting Machinist is going to be*
> *intimidated by the Teamster bully, you should prepare*
> *now to counter-attack should that circumstance*
> *arise.[9]*

The first guest speaker at the convention was AFL-CIO President Lane Kirkland, who began with a very diplomatic description of his sometimes tormenter, the IAM President:

> *If everyone does not always agree with Bill Winpisinger,*
> *it does not result from any confusion as to where he*
> *stands, nor is there any confusion about the solid*

*trade union credentials that Bill Winpisinger brings
with him.*

*On labor law reform, minimum wage, foreign
trade, your union under his leadership did more than
its share in the battle.*[10]

Kirkland knew that he couldn't get away with promoting
Jimmy Carter's re-election in Wimp's house, even though the
AFL-CIO had endorsed him, so he retreated to the age old
dodge of "I'm not going to, but if I were..."

*If I were going to talk about Presidential politics, and
I am not, I might be tempted to point out that Ronald
Reagan shares none of your beliefs or principles.*

*If I dared, I might mention the concern I have
about a conservative anti-union Supreme Court
majority appointed by Ronald Reagan and because
the Supreme Court Justices and the work that they
do for good or ill, will remain with us long, long after
the next Administration leaves Washington. Or I
might talk about how Ronald Reagan is a strong
supporter of right-to-work laws which, as you know,
are nothing more than devices to cut wages and
destroy unions.*[11]

Wimp was pleased that the first day of his convention
had gone as planned. He still had seven long days to go and
several contentious issues to deal with but he knew from
past experiences that conventions developed a personality
of their own, and so far this one was behaving nicely. The
Wednesday session began with a speech from the Secretary
of Labor, Ray Marshall, a man Wimpy liked personally despite

his association with Carter. The convention hall was packed and abuzz because Marshall would be followed to the podium by Wimp's darling, Senator Ted Kennedy. Marshall did his best to make the case for Carter's re-election, and was met with a polite but diffident response. He was barely off the stage when the house erupted with a ground shaking, ear splitting, ten minute demonstration welcoming the Massachusetts Senator.

Delegates applauded, stomped their feet, whistled and walked up and down the aisles waving signs saying, "We're still with you, Ted," and "Kennedy in '84," and "Ted Instead." Wimp beamed as he shook hands and welcomed Kennedy to the rostrum. Kennedy opened with, "I want to thank you, distinguished President, for escorting me to the podium. As I proved in the 1980 Democratic primaries, I was always ready to take a walk with Wimpy!"[12] The delegates showered him with laughter and more applause. "And it is a pleasure, as always, to see Wimpy again. I remember the last time I saw him in New York, in August and at the end of that long week he said, 'Don't worry, Ted, the real convention is next week in Cincinnati.'"[13]

After citing IAM history and calling it an "action union," he thanked them for being the spark that ignited his campaign:

> In 1980 we have all taken a long journey together. It has been eighteen months since the IAM sponsored the first Draft Kennedy meeting in Iowa.
>
> And no one was a better or truer friend than your President, William Winpisinger. Wimpy is a tough, unyielding, blunt spoken fighter for causes about which he deeply cares. His concern reaches to

*all the members of this union and to all the working
people and all those who have been left behind in
America.*

*And across all the months and all the miles, he
never got tired or discouraged; he never gave in or
gave up. He insisted that a political party, like a labor
union, must truly stand for the people it represents.
He said he was "proud" to support me. Let me
say to you, Wimpy, how proud I was to have that
support.[14]*

Kennedy went on to sound the themes he had stressed
in his campaign of social justice, a more balanced economy
and a United States that would be welcomed and respected
around the world. He spoke of what the Democratic
Party stood for in contrast to the Republicans, but did not
explicitly ask the delegates to support Jimmy Carter in the fall
elections.

He closed with words that seemed to leave the door very
much open for another run in 1984:

*Programs may become obsolete, but the ideal of
progress must be pursued. Circumstances may
change, but the work of compassion must continue.
The poor may be out of political fashion, but they
are not without human needs. The middle class may
be angry, but they have not lost the dream that all
Americans can advance together.*

*This is the dream that shall never die. It is the
cause that brought us into the 1980 campaign, that
kept us in it, that will continue to move us in the
months and years ahead.[15]*

The delegates again gave Kennedy a rousing ovation. Wimpy stood with his arm around Kennedy's shoulder, beaming like a proud father. The 1980 Presidential race was lost, but he knew Kennedy would continue to champion the causes he held dear as an influential member of the Senate, and just might be the candidate in 1984. When the demonstration wound down, Wimpy went to the microphone.

> *Senator, that demonstration tells you more eloquently than any words that I could muster the affection that this convention and the membership of our entire union feels for you. I think the senator believes that I am a man, rumors to the contrary notwithstanding, of very few words. Because for nearly a year and a half now, every time we discussed current events, my simple rejoinder was, as it was today when he arrived, "Hang in, Senator, hang in there, hang in." He knows that when the IAM signs on, we do not sign on for part of the journey or almost all of the journey and we do not sign on to run out, but, above all, we stay all the way.[16]*

Kennedy departed with emotions still running high. A delegate moved that the convention go on record as supporting the Democratic Party platform, particularly as it applied to congressional races, while making no endorsement in the Presidential race.

After brief debate, the question was called. Wimpy asked unanimous consent to make a statement before the question was put. He then launched into a spirited defense of his actions in the primaries and at the convention and defiantly claimed that he would not be "caved in," and forced to accept the "lesser of two evils," when it came to casting his vote.

We have a decision to make which comes as a result of a long and tortuous path down which we have all walked together as an organization. We went to the convention after having fought our hearts out the length and breadth of this land, after having seen a fairly good sized bag of political tricks pulled in the 1980 political season: took some very strong positions, because they came from the guts and from the hearts of all the people who make up this great organization.

I never attended a convention in which there was such heavy handed arm twisting and knee busting as there was in New York City a month ago. Never. And I did not appreciate it. Not one bit.

...there was an overwhelming support for the proposition that the only way we could preserve our integrity was to walk out of that convention with our heads high, to protest the kind of politics which pleads our party, the party of Ted Kennedy, guilty to the repetitive sin of always coming up with the lesser of two evils.

I, for one, am sick and tired, in the American political scene, of having us revisited time after time with a candidate who is presented from his own podium as the lesser of two evils.

I reject that as the politics of my party. I have been very vocal about that because if no one protests that politics, then we invite it to be done to us again four years from now. And I have said it in meeting room after meeting room, ever since, in forums as lofty as the Executive Council of the AFL-CIO, and I have watched them go around the table, each one in turn, with a ball bat in his hands, determined to cave in my knees and the knees of this great union, and I resisted.

I will not be caved in.

I have an abiding faith in the intelligence of every member of this organization to do the right thing in the voting booth because after all, in any election and in every election, when the curtain goes closed behind you, you vote your conscience, and I am satisfied that is what our members will do this year, and they will vote their conscience and their self-interest and I am comfortable with that.[17]

With those emotional words, Wimpy put the 1980 Presidential race behind him. He had devoted much of his time and energy to ousting Jimmy Carter and installing a liberal Democrat in the White House. He had managed to convince the heir apparent to the Kennedy legacy and darling of the liberal wing to step forward and challenge a sitting President of his own party. And if not for circumstances beyond his control in foreign affairs and a mystifyingly slow start to the Kennedy campaign, he might well have succeeded in changing the course of American history.

The convention hummed along, passing a resolution in support of the Polish labor rebellion against that country's Communist government, encouraging their efforts and inviting the elected leaders of the free Polish unions to visit with members of the Machinists Union in their homes, their union halls, and on their jobs as guests of the International Union. By the second week of the convention, Wimpy had completely channeled his boundless energy back into IAM affairs, flexing the union's muscle to make a point to a recalcitrant employer.

Tom Buffenbarger, at the time a rookie Special Representative, later recalled what had happened months before the convention that led Wimpy to make such a bold move.

He was in Cincinnati earlier in the year and had given a speech at the convention center. It was a convention of engineers and the topic was obstacles to minority involvement in the engineering community. I watched that speech. Wimp had every minority engineer in there, 3,000 or 4,000 people, nodding their heads agreeing with him. He was just saying all the right things. He gets done. We leave. We're heading out of town, and it's about lunchtime. He asked if there was a Bob Evans restaurant and I said, "There sure is." We're having lunch and he asked if there was anything going on in town. I said, "The strike we've got at the Wolfe Machine Company. It's one of the oldest companies in Cincinnati, a hundred plus years old, and it's a terrible situation. We've been filing decerts ourselves so we can lock in the rights of our current members to vote. We beat management two times in a row, but we're still on strike." He says, "Well, we've got time, let's go walk the picket line with them."

This was before cell phones, so I go to a pay phone. I get hold of the guy that was doing the picket lines for them. I said, "The International President's coming out to walk pickets with you in about an hour."

So Wimp went and talked with them. Stayed for about two hours. We had a great time and they appreciated his support. These guys had been on strike for about two years. As we were driving to Columbus, for the State Council meeting, Wimp says, "Well, if this strike's still going on we know what our activity for the convention's going to be."[18]

The strike was still going on as the IAM met in September, and Wimpy was good to his word. The banner for the convention that year said, "The Future is in Our Hands," and Wimpy was about to show the owners of Wolfe Manufacturing just what the hands of 2,061 delegates looked like.

On the sixth day of the Grand Lodge Convention, Wimpy took the entire convention to the gates of the Wolfe plant. He gave a final set of instructions before the delegates boarded busses at the convention center. The weather was clear and very hot for early September, a good day for a picket.

> When we picket this afternoon, I am going to be out there ahead of you, and we are going to keep it as orderly as we possibly can. Each bus will be met by a picket captain, and you will be shown what to do, where to go, and so on.
>
> Please do not involve yourself in any altercations with anybody. If that should occur, I want to be the one to handle them and we will take it from there. You just be nice, peaceful pickets.
>
> If anyone has to get pinched, I want it to be me, so we can really embarrass that community.[19]

Tom Buffenbarger:

> We had the entire convention out there for this. Eighty busses. We parked them in a little park, and there was this phalanx, there was no end to it. Marched down the street in this industrial park where Wolfe Machine was, shut down that industrial park. This phalanx walked down the street people hooting and

hollering, signs, banners, supporting these forty guys on strike at Wolfe Machine. At the head of the line was Wimp, council members, and Joe Manners, our Chief Legal Counsel. Also at the head of the line with Wimp was Dan Teahan, the Hamilton County Sheriff.

Out of the plant came the plant manager, a guy named Dick Reedy, and their lawyer from the Taft Law Firm, Pat Stanton, a former military JAG officer and a real son of a bitch. And they came running down the street, shouting: "This is illegal! You can't do this! We have an injunction!" Shaking this thing in Wimp's face. Wimp takes it from him very gently. He reads it and hands it to Joe Manners, and says, "Is this an injunction, like I think it is?" And Manners puts on his glasses, reads it, and says, "Wimp, this does appear to be a validly drawn restriction in the number of strikers we can have. So I think you know what we need to do." And he handed it back to Wimp, and Wimp proceeded to tear it up into tiny pieces and blew the pieces out of the palm of his hand—poof—and said, "So, arrest us."

The local jail has maybe room for two drunks. We have thousands, and all they were waiting for was Wimp to say "Sic 'em," and these guys are history. The look on Pat Stanton's face was priceless. I thought his head was going to explode.

The entire parade just exploded with "Yeah!" I thought for a moment, this is going to get ugly here, but it was perfect. They all just continued their march, at which point Dan Teahan, the sheriff, explained to Mr. Stanton that if he had been doing his job *he would have known that we had arranged for a parade permit, which was granted by the Democratic judge, and there was not a goddamn thing he could do about it. It was a great day.*[20]

Wimpy was back, and he was loaded for bear.

THIRTY-FIVE

MEDIA MONITORING PROJECT

Wimpy had always been fascinated with the power of television to shape opinions, and the experiences he had with the Kennedy campaign reinforced his interest. He saw how one painful moment in an interview with Roger Mudd had set a tone for the whole campaign, and he complained later about how the media, particularly television, had shifted the country's focus away from Carter's failed economic policies and toward troubles in far off lands.

He also was a keen observer of how television was used to mold the public's perception of the labor movement. As the point man in a massive cooperative effort with the Teamsters to organize auto dealerships, he had watched with a mixture of fascination and outrage as corruption in the Teamsters Union was exposed in day after day of live television coverage of the McClellan hearings. He took note of how Bobby Kennedy had used an appearance on the *Tonight Show* with Jack Parr to rally support for the Landrum-Griffin legislation.

He was also keenly interested in the television advertising the International Ladies Garment Workers Union was doing to promote itself, and how their jingle, *"Look for The Union Label,"* had become familiar to millions of Americans. One of his first acts as International President—elect had been to ask the IAM Executive Council to appropriate money for a similar advertising campaign, a move the council balked at when they learned its cost. Wimp was thoroughly convinced that television was the best way to get the labor movement's point across and rally support for organizing efforts, and he was tireless—and wildly successful—at getting himself onto the tube.

He also came to realize that the networks, and to a great degree local stations, were owned by large corporate interests

that were skilled at playing the image making game and weren't
about to give labor a fair shake. They were there for wall to
wall coverage of the McClellan hearings, but did not give one
moment of air time to the role unions played in creating the
great American middle class. Wimpy established the IAM race
car program, booming by this point, not as a personal toy but
as a means of getting the union positive coverage on television
sports reports. Since the IAM represented the mechanics who
kept America's cars and trucks rolling, why not have them
compete wheel to wheel with cars sponsored by big corporate
interests?

He also realized that there were two components to
television: what the news programs reported and the content
of the entertainment shows. He had gotten the Executive
Council to approve a small amount of money to participate in
a joint production of a labor-oriented entertainment program.
The effort stalled when the networks would neither give them
a time slot nor sell them one. By the end of the 1970's, Wimpy
was desperate to crack through the corporate control and get
his union into the living rooms of America's television viewers.
He summoned Bob Kalaski, his new Communications Director,
and asked if he had any ideas.

"Well, I'd like to make a movie," Kalaski remembered
answering. "That was before video. 'I'd like to make a movie
about this union that we can use in organizing and to introduce
ourselves to new members. And he liked the idea right off the
bat.""

"I was able to get Ed Asner who at the time was the President
of the Screen Actors Guild [to star in the production]. He was
also the star of Lou Grant, the most popular show on television
at the time."[1]

Kalaski was adamant that the IAM should work with a
sophisticated production company, not the usual union training

film people, and with Wimpy's encouragement, he hired a Hollywood company to produce the film. Corporate Productions, Incorporated, created a lively movie that used Ed Asner in three scenes. The fifteen minute mini-documentary focused on the skills of IAM members, the benefits of membership, and the pride members felt in their union. Asner's scenes were shot in California, at Engs Trucking in Pico Rivera, Lockheed Aircraft in Palmdale, and at Weber's Bakery in Glendale. The segment at Engs Trucking was shared with Wimpy, who walked through the parking lot with Asner and then was shown sitting with him as Asner praised his leadership: "If it's true that the only effective leaders are those who are willing to get out among the people, to share their feelings, to understand their hopes and their anxieties, then the Machinists have the most effective leadership in trade unionism today," Asner said.[2] He closed the film by walking through massive doors at a Lockheed assembly plant, looking right into the camera and summing up his case: "In established industries and in new technologies," the star said, "it is the role of the union today, as it has always been, to see that the American worker is not intimidated by threats or mislead by half-truths. The union is on the job to see that every member gets a fair shake. And wherever the Machinists Union is at work, people are better off."[3]

"Everybody loved it," Kalaski recalled. "It was a big hit. The organizers used it. It was a big help in everything."[4]

While Wimpy was making the film and scheming for ways to get the IAM onto television, the National Parents Teachers Association, a six million member advocacy group with members from coast to coast, was trying to get something *off* television: violence, particularly when it could be viewed by young children. The PTA had hired William Young, a Chicago-based Ph.D. who was a market research specialist, to conduct a massive survey of television content. Young mobilized the PTA membership and trained them in how to monitor and keep a record of what came into their homes. They used the results of that survey to force television networks to cut back on the violent programming during hours children were watching or face challenges to their licenses. The project was remarkably successful in reducing violence *and* also yielded an unexpected finding.

William Young:

> As we analyzed television, we discovered that sixty-six percent of the American public was relying almost exclusively on television for local, national and international news and that seventy-five percent of the population was using television for their prime source of news. As we began to analyze the news it was apparent to us that labor unions were not being portrayed on television nor were many of the public policy issues with which organized labor was con.. cerned being discussed on television.
>
> I talked this problem over with many people in the labor movement, asking what union realized the problem? What union had the leadership to solve the problem? What union had the funds to work on the problem? And, what union had members throughout the United States who wanted television to address the concerns and activities of unions rather than only for television cameras to come out when there was a strike. Only one union met these conditions, and that was the IAM.[5]

Bob Kalaski:

> I was down in Florida at the AFL-CIO meetings. I met this guy, he was the Swedish labor attaché. Bjorn Peterson. Bjorn was fascinated by our race

car program. He said, "Why the hell are you getting involved with race cars?" So I explained about the image of an auto mechanic as Wimpy saw it, and he thought that was fascinating. And he said to me, "I have a friend, I met him in Sweden, he was there on an education trip, and he's a fascinating man."[6]

About a month later, Peterson introduced Kalaski to William Young, who thought the racing program was very interesting.

He said, "I'd like to propose a program where we monitor television and see how American workers are portrayed, specifically union members." He showed Kalaski the PTA program and said, "This project will take us through all the phases of understanding TV, from monitoring the local stations to looking at their public records and talking to them about their news coverage. We'll go to the writers, the producers, directors, all of them, and present the results."[7]

Kalaski brought the idea to Wimpy, who liked it and convinced the Executive Council to give it their approval. Soon after, Wimpy held a press conference at the National Press Club in Washington to announce that the IAM would embark on a year-long, $100,000 - program to monitor how labor was portrayed on television. Terming labor's current public image as "lousy," and "steadily deteriorating," Wimpy outlined what he saw as the challenge facing the movement.

> *As I've said in the past, a lot of that blame for that poor image must be placed on the labor movement itself. But much, perhaps most of the blame should be placed on the television broadcast industry.*
>
> *In the last two decades, television has grown into the single most influential force in our lives. The impressions, feelings and ideas held by most young*

Americans today were molded within the perimeter of a television screen.

Television has dominated their lives from early childhood to such an extent that most of their impressions of many elements of American society are based almost exclusively on what they've seen on TV. Many of those elements of our society— unions, religious groups, minorities—have not been portrayed fairly on TV.

And, as a consequence, these institutions and groups, which have played major roles in the growth and progress of this great nation, are now suffering from sagging images, reduced effectiveness and less or no growth.[8]

While public reaction to the announcement of the IAM Television Monitoring Project was generally favorable, network executives blasted it as an attempt at censorship. Roger Mudd, the anchorman who had done the fateful interview with Ted Kennedy, reported the goals of the project on the *CBS Evening News*, but his straightforward account was followed, perhaps not coincidentally, by a report on the low productivity of American workers.

Under Kalaski's supervision, the monitoring project sprang into action. Thirteen regional training sessions were held to train 400 members of the IAM staff to supervise the project in their areas. The day-long sessions familiarized Grand Lodge Representatives, Special Representatives, Business Representatives, and other staff with the ins and outs of the broadcast industry and taught them how to train the thousands of individual monitors who would be needed for the project.

Monitors would watch a single television station in their area, focusing on the local evening news, network evening news, prime time entertainment, and late local news. Using scorecards developed by Young, they would note how often unions were mentioned in news broadcasts, what was said about them, and how they were portrayed in pictures. They would also screen entertainment programs for whether and how blue collar workers were portrayed and whether they were specifically identified as members of a labor organization.

The training materials Young developed for the program cut right to the chase. Television was about money. Networks thrived by selling audience attention to advertisers who paid on a per capita basis. Costs were passed on to viewers in the form of higher consumer prices. The license to run a television station was, in essence, a license to print money, and the one thing television executives feared most was any challenge to that exclusive franchise. If networks or local stations violated any of the rules that governed the industry—the Fairness Doctrine, the Personal Attack Rule, the Equal Time Rule, or regulations governing political editorials or endorsements—they could be held accountable through the Federal Communications Commission. But first, documentary evidence was required to make a case.

After training sessions in Portland, Seattle, Dallas, Atlanta, Chicago, Kansas City, New York, Cleveland, Louisville, Hartford, Los Angeles, and Washington, nearly 3,000 IAM monitors were put to work. They would monitor one month of programming, February 1980, and report what they saw. By the end of the month, 150,000 report forms were turned in from nearly 200 cities where monitors had watched news broadcasts, fifty-three television series, twenty-four movies, and twenty-four television specials, including a two-part Bob Hope special. Each character within the entertainment programs was identified by name and occupation and classified as having a major, minor, or background role. The characters were then rated for twenty-two personal traits, such as friendliness, intelligence, and explicit or implied education.

For news broadcasts, monitors checked to see how often the IAM's top five legislative priorities, inflation, energy, foreign trade, health care, and tax reform, were reported on, and whether the report showed a bias toward the position of corporate America , or if it was objective.

After months of tabulating and analyzing the survey forms, the IAM came to an inescapable conclusion: television was the "Voice of Corporate America." CBS favored the corporate position on the key issues by a ratio of three-to-one. At NBC, it was five-to-one, and ABC's *World News Tonight*, anchored by Max Robinson in Chicago, Frank Reynolds in Washington, and Peter Jennings in London, took the corporate side by an amazing seven-to-one ratio. The union issue that got the most attention was strikes. Monitors found that the networks just reported the stoppage of work, never what had led the workers to take that action.

Monitors also took note of the fact that visual impact dominated coverage far more than content. Violent demonstrations and fast moving sports got top play, stories of substance got short shrift. Character in motion even dominated political coverage, where politicians were most often shown shaking hands, climbing into or out of cars or waving to crowds. The substance of what they said or their positions on key issues was severely lacking.

If the bias of news broadcasts was obvious, the content of entertainment programs was shocking. Unions were all but invisible. In the rare instances they were portrayed, they were shown to be violent, degrading, or obstructive. The only show on television where a labor union was explicitly portrayed was "SKAG," whose title character was a member of the United Steel Workers Union. The show was dreadful and short-lived, and portrayed officials of the USW as brutal, uncaring bullies. Skagg, the title character, sometimes appeared as a foreman, sometimes as a shop steward, and other times as some other officer of the union. He and his fellow trade unionists were unfailingly portrayed as ruthless, power hungry mobsters.

Other shows were less explicit but just as demeaning. Blue collar workers were clumsy, oafish, largely uneducated, quick to anger, and given to smoking and drinking. The proportion professions was wildly out of whack with reality. Prostitutes outnumbered machinists by twelve-to-one. Butlers outnumbered government office workers by two-to-one, and there were twice as many witch doctors as welfare case workers. And if viewers wanted help figuring out why things were so distorted, they had plenty: private detectives outnumbered production line workers by twelve-to-one.

Wimpy was outraged with the findings. They confirmed the theories he had believed since reading Fred Cook's *Nation* piece eighteen years earlier. In a speech to the Western Labor Press Association just before the study was made public, he vented his frustration.

> *Commercial print media has consistently favored our employer's viewpoint over ours. That's because employers buy advertising while we place only occasional want ads.*
>
> *Television is no different. Money talks. And our employers have lots of money. Folksy folks like United Technologies and United Airlines. The top 100 defense contractors in America, among them most big energy companies, are our employers.*

They not only get their value system expressed gratis in TV entertainment programs, they get to propagandize directly through paid commercials.

We've tried to buy time—prime time—on TV through the networks. It can't be done.

A few producers make up their schedules, based on their loyal and best paying advertisers, prioritize the list, let inner circle and privileged producers develop the shows and programs, and, if there's any time left, we can sponsor a program, at the rate of $35,000 to $70,000 per minute.[9]

Wimp also pointed out that viewers in most markets had a choice between only three or four channels, with very similar programming. In the days before cable, if you couldn't crack the lineup of the three big networks, it was impossible to reach the American public. The IAM Television Monitoring Project made the case. Corporate America had it in for labor unions, and they were using their most powerful weapon, television, to help make *their* case.

THIRTY-SIX

THE PATCO STRIKE

American voters were about to accomplish what Wimpy and Ted Kennedy had not been able to do: banish Jimmy Carter from the White House. As the fall campaign came to a close, Carter trailed sixty-nine-year-old Republican nominee Ronald Reagan by as much as twenty percent in some polls. The former Hollywood B-movie star hammered Carter for his stewardship of the economy and promised both a stronger defense *and* lower taxes. Carter tried to paint Reagan as belligerent on defense and irresponsible on the economy.

The two candidates agreed to one debate, in Cleveland, on October 28, 1980. Two days before the debate, Wimpy co-authored an op-ed in *The New York Times,* "Biting the Bullet." Written with SANE Executive Director David Courtright, the piece ridiculed the rush by both parties to increase defense spending at the cost of social programs. It made it clear that the president of one of the country's largest labor unions was still less than thrilled with Jimmy Carter: "Americans face a roster of incumbents and challengers who seem to outdo each other in support of programs designed to bankrupt the country," they wrote. "While our pathetic social programs are minutely scrutinized for waste, inefficiency, and misappropriations, the military gets off virtually scot-free."[1]

Carter was trying desperately and with limited success to rally the coalition that had elected him in 1976. He had the tepid support of the AFL-CIO, but the Machinists and a couple of other recalcitrant unions sat the race out. The Teamsters and the Professional Air Traffic Controllers Organization (PATCO) endorsed Reagan. Carter's campaign tried to continue to play the Iran and Afghanistan card, stressing his leadership on foreign affairs as it touted his proposed five percent a year growth in the arms budget.

Reagan was using people's misgivings about the Carter economy, still rife with inflation and unemployment, to make the case that had begun to resonate during Kennedy's late surge in his primary challenge. Looking relaxed and dapper on the stage of the Cleveland Convention Center, Reagan managed to project a much folksier image than the President. At one point, he ignored Carter altogether and addressed the audience directly, asking a question that would become famous in political discourse: "Are you better off than you were four years ago?"[2]

Most Americans answered "no." A week after the debate, they sent Carter packing, fifty-one percent to forty-one percent, with Independent John Anderson getting seven percent. The race for Electoral College votes was nowhere near as close, with Reagan trouncing Carter 489 to forty-nine.

The outgoing President, who had shredded the traditional Democratic coalition, managed one more affront to his party on his way out the door. He delivered his concession speech while polls were still open on the West Coast and in Hawaii. As the news of his surrender spread, lines of Democratic voters in Oakland, Los Angeles, and Seattle dissolved. Los Angeles Democratic Congressman James Corman, a staunch labor ally, lost his seat by a mere 864 votes. What had started out as a bad night for Democrats turned into a rout.

In addition to the Presidency, the Republicans picked up thirty-three seats in the House and eleven in the Senate, which meant that Senator Strom Thurmond of South Carolina, an avowed enemy of the IAM, would be president pro tem, and Utah Senator Orin Hatch, who had led the fight against Labor Law Reform, would chair the Senate Labor and Human Resources Committee.

Even before Election Day, Wimp had begun thinking about bolting to establish a third party. Speaking to a symposium at the University of Massachusetts three weeks before Carter lost, Wimp took on the subject of alternative political parties. After running through a historical analysis of third party movements such as Eugene Deb's Socialist Party, the American Communist Party, the Non-Partisan League, and the Farm-Labor Party, he came to the conclusion that these movements, while occasionally viable on the state level, would take too long to become successful, if ever, in electing a President. He pointed out that war or the fear of war tended to drive voters back to traditional parties and away from alternatives, and that contemporary labor leaders, whose near unanimous support would be critical for any successful third party effort, were not the pioneering sort.

Wimpy was dismissive of the existing alternatives, saying of the Libertarian Party: "Forget it. They represent what the Republican Party used to be: isolationist, anti-government, and for self-reliance and individualism."[3] Socialist parties weren't much better in his view: "The Socialist Labor Party is an old romantic group left from the days of Daniel DeLeone at the turn of the century. The Socialist Independent Party is a closed group of political theologians, and the US Labor Party is a right wing front group."[4] He had more sympathy for the Citizen's Party, calling them a "Well meaning and good intentioned group of intellectual activists and frustrated Democrats"…"novices and innocents when it comes to nuts and bolts politics."[5] He concluded his speech by discounting the possibility that Ted Kennedy would lead a third party movement. Instead, he held out hope that their senator would rise from the ashes of defeat to reclaim ownership of the Democratic Party: "It is only remotely possible that Kennedy would forgo capture of the Democratic Party in an attempt to lead an alternative party movement. Only the most obstinate and obtuse resistance on the part of Carterites to prevent the Senator from gaining control of the party and to deny him the 1984 nomination might cause him to bolt."[6]

Wimpy continued to use the threat of leaving the Democratic Party to form an alternative movement as a means of prodding the Democrats leftward from time to time. In 1981, he warned Iowa Democrats: "We can begin to build our own progressive party with a hardcore trade union constituency." And, "At this point we're not saying we're ready for that, but it is the way we'll go, rather than waste our franchise further."[7] But, heading his own advice, he pretty much resigned himself to making do with the existing system.

George Kourpias:

> Forming a third party was always on his mind. But he also knew the Democratic Labor Party in Canada has been around a long time, and the best it had ever done is probably seventeen, eighteen, twenty seats in Parliament. We had this discussion many times, he didn't want to wait an eternity. He wasn't the type of guy who said, "OK, we're going to start a third party, and fifty years from now we'll elect a president." So that's why he joined with groups that would talk about a third party. He never pushed for a third party. He knew that the road would be too long.[8]

As the reality of the 1980 election set in, Wimpy was became despondent. Speaking to an audience at Florida State University a week after the election, he lamented the situation.

> The voters of this country have thrown the brigands out.

Everyone to the left of Henry Kissinger is running around trying to figure out what it all means. And if we wanted to believe the corporate media, we'd all be climbing on board the militarist bandwagon rolling down the Pentagon's road.

But as we see it where I come from, the political leadership of this country has not changed direction at all. Reagan and his advisers and Carter and his advisers are many heads of the same monster, a monster that seriously threatens domestic well-being and the future of the globe itself.[9]

At the January 1981 meeting of the IAM Executive Council in Washington, Wimpy asked the group to appropriate $40,000 to fund the Progressive Alliance. This, he hoped, would be a cooperative effort with six other unions to keep the left wing grass roots of the party alive. The council diplomatically tabled the suggestion, saying more study was needed. Wimp then delivered a long soliloquy in which he said that as a result of the 1980 election, there was no organized Democratic Party. He lamented that the labor movement had not been persuasive in making their case to re-elect Democrats to the Congress and talked of the possibility of a "New Alternative Program," something short of a new party. He asked that the council to let him present the idea to the MNPL Planning Committee, which was then meeting.

Wimpy's fears about the direction of the new administration were further confirmed when Reagan chose fifty-year old Raymond J. Donovan, a New Jersey contractor who had raised $600,000 for his campaign, to replace Ray Marshall as Secretary of Labor. Conservative groups, including Reed Larson's National Right to Work Committee, cheered the appointment. Larson was quick to point out that Donovan was a staunch supporter of Section 14-B of the Taft-Hartley Act. "For the first time in more than thirty years, the American people are going to be represented by a labor secretary who agrees with the right to work."[10] Defending his pro-business stance, Donovan remarked, "You don't bite the hand that feeds you."[11]

It was going to be a long four years.

Meanwhile, Wimpy had to attend to political business closer to home. He was nominated for re-election as International President for another four year term to begin July 1, 1981. He received the nomination of 829 of the 831 lodges participating. Mike Rygus, the General Vice President for the Canadian Territory, was nominated by Lodge 1922, in a symbolic gesture. K.W. Benda received a nomination from Local Lodge 2225 of Sunnyvale, California. Gene Glover, Wimp's General Secretary Treasurer, was nominated by all 831 lodges. Since neither of Wimp's challengers came even remotely close to the requirements of the IAM constitution to qualify for the ballot, he and Glover were re-elected unanimously.

Despite the national pride that had led Lodge 1922 to nominate Rygus as a favorite son, Wimpy was very popular among the Canadian members. He was extremely proud that the IAM included Canadian trade unionists.

Tom Buffenbarger:

> The Canadians loved him. They were more progressive than us, anyway. They were liberal. So he was probably more in tune with the Canadian membership than he was with much of the American membership. Remember, Wimp had always been a proponent of national health care. They had that in Canada. He was a proponent for an organizing system where instead of the procedures we have in the United States, if you demonstrate that you've got a majority of people, you shouldn't have to have a vote.[12]

When the New Democratic Party of Canada invited Wimpy to deliver the keynote speech at their 1981 convention in Vancouver, he was only too happy to oblige. IAM membership in Canada was about 63,000, and most were members of the NDP. He called his speech "The New Dawn in an Era of Darkness" and used it to applaud Canadian social progress. He accurately predicted that the US under Reagan would be taking giant steps backward.

> *The United States is in a period of darkness.*
> *We do not have a pro-labor party in the US and we do not have a genuine two party system.*
> *We have unisex politics bought and paid for by corporate eunuchs and administered by a tight knit cadre of nouveau riche Neanderthals.*[13]

He credited the New Democratic Party for offering a model of success in such dire times.

> *We are visualizing alternatives to the Corporate State and its unisex politics skewed to the right of center.*
> *We are looking toward the Canadian NDP model.*
> *We are looking toward the Scandinavian and West European social democracies for experience and guidance.*
> *We are heartened by the Solidarity Movement in Poland.*[14]

Wimpy was relentless at trying to get the IAM before the American public. Although the council wouldn't allocate the funds for network television advertising, he kept doing newspaper and magazine interviews and was a frequent guest on television talk shows. At the February IAM Executive Council meeting in Hollywood, Florida, he presented another unique idea: co-producing a movie. If he couldn't move American culture to a more positive view of labor through network television, maybe he could do it in a more subtle way by making them heroes of the silver screen.

Actor Cliff Robertson had won an Academy Award for his portrayal of Charly Gordon, a mentally retarded factory worker who temporarily became a genius after undergoing a controversial experimental treatment. *Charly*, released in 1968, had been a huge success and made a lot of money for Robertson who had bought the rights to it in 1961. He was thinking of making a sequel and looking for a partner to finance it—for $7,000,000.

Bo Kalaski:

> *Wimpy and I talked about it with Cliff Robertson, about forming a holding company. After producing one film and making money on it, we would produce another film that would be worker and union friendly, and just keep going from there. Charly Gordon could have become a Machinist working at a bakery. Wimpy wanted that so badly. He wanted the council to approve it.*[15]

Robertson made his pitch to the council with Wimp's blessing. The IAM would put up seven million dollars for production, and Robertson would star in the sequel. There would be no return for the twelve to eighteen months it would take to write, shoot and edit the film and he and the IAM would then split the proceeds fifty/fifty. After a lengthy discussion, the council decided that $7,000,000 was far too much money to gamble on the highly volatile film business.

Wimpy, however, did get the council to approve the establishment of a new IAM department to service older workers and retired members. As the World War Two generation started to hit retirement age, the number of IAM retirees skyrocketed. By 1981, there were more than 140,000 retirees receiving union benefits. George Kourpias, had been trying his best to meet the day-to-day demands of this ever growing group but it was clear that he needed help. One of Kourpias' other affiliations was as second Vice President of the National Council of Senior Citizens, where he got to know the hard driving director of membership, a thirty-year-old who had helped grow that organization's membership from 273,000 to 312,000 in just a couple of years. The NCSC staffer was also quite familiar with the IAM - his father was the International President. In April 1981, with the council's blessing, Michael Winpisinger was hired to head the IAM's newly constituted Older Workers and Retired Members Department.

By mid-summer, 1981, the Reagan Administration was hitting its stride. Reagan's first budget, which he got through Congress with a heavy dose of personal lobbying, dramatically reduced social spending while re-allocating the money to defense. It was the complete antithesis of what Wimpy had been preaching his whole adult life. Meanwhile, Reagan was about to take on his first battle with organized labor, one that would have far reaching consequences.

The nation's 15,000 air traffic controllers were federal workers, employed by the Federal Aviation Administration. They had founded a union in 1968 with the help of famed trial lawyer F. Lee Bailey called the Professional Air Traffic Controller's Organization (PATCO). After a protracted battle that included a sick-out, they were recognized as a collective bargaining agent. The scrappy band's tactics and Bailey's bargaining prowess had garnered them pay increases that, in some cases, more than doubled what their members were paid. Flush with success, they affiliated with the AFL-CIO.

Now, PATCO was back to negotiate their next contract. They had significant demands. Claiming that their jobs were inordinately stressful, they wanted their work week reduced from forty to thirty-two hours. The members, who averaged $33,000 per year, were also demanding an increase of $2,300 per employee above a scheduled $1,700 increase for all federal workers. If they stopped work, 14,200 daily airline flights were at risk of being grounded. Union leaders and federal negotiators came to a bargain just before the strike deadline that gave PATCO members some, but not all, of what they were asking. The membership rejected the offer by a lopsided twenty-to-one margin and authorized a strike to begin August 3, 1981.

13,000 of the union's 15,000 members walked out, but since they were barred by federal law from striking, this was immediately termed illegal. President Reagan took a personal interest in their action and held a Rose Garden press conference. He announced that he had ordered PATCO members back to work under the terms of Taft-Hartley, and that any who didn't report for duty within forty-eight hours would be fired and permanently barred from federal service. He viewed the matter as an opportunity to show labor that there was a new Sheriff in town. The fact that PATCO had been one of the handful of unions to endorse his candidacy for President just a few short months ago was all the better. If he wouldn't give ground to them, what could other unions expect?

The AFL-CIO Executive Committee was holding their summer meeting in Chicago when the strike started. The situation presented a dilemma. Since PATCO members were barred by law from striking, their action was not technically a strike. If other unions who worked at airports such as Machinists, Pilots, or Flight Attendants encountered PATCO picket lines and refused to cross, they risked violating their own contracts and possible termination. On the other hand, if they backed off and let PATCO go it alone, the Air Traffic Controllers would almost certainly lose. Reagan would have a big feather to stick in his cap at labor's expense.

Wimpy saw a chance to flex labor's muscle by shutting down the airlines. Getting Reagan to blink would far outweigh any possible consequences. He tried to convince Captain J.J. O'Donnell, President of the Airline Pilots Association, to join in the battle. O'Donnell, who had had several run-ins with PATCO leadership, viewed them more as adversaries than fellow trade unionists, and would have none of it.

If the 40,000 ramp workers, mechanics, and maintenance people represented by the IAM stopped work, there would be no airline flights. But it was a tough call. Most of the PATCO workers already made significantly more money than their brothers and sisters in the IAM. They had protection as federal government workers against layoffs or cutbacks, unlike IAM members who faced those threats constantly in the volatile airline industry. PATCO workers tended to be far more conservative than IAM members, and had even endorsed Reagan. It was clear that while there was sympathy for their action, it would be asking a lot for PATCO to expect IAM members to walk off the job with them.

Lane Kirkland, troubled by the illegal nature of the action, was concerned that PATCO had failed to build sufficient public support for the strike. He was miffed that union leaders had rushed into it without telling him as he headed to Chicago. After lengthy discussion, the federation declined to take collective action. Adjourning from their meeting, the union leaders were asked to comment to the press. Kirkland said the matter was up to individual unions, not the federation. His comments, though, left little doubt where he stood: "It is all well and good to be a midnight gin militant, to stand up and call for general strikes, but member unions will have to make their own decisions."[16]

Wimpy, aware that his union was being watched closely as negotiations continued, stopped short of saying the IAM would shut down the airlines. Unlike Kirkland, Wimpy made his sympathy for the strikers clear: "I expect our people to act like trade unionists. I expect them not to cross a picket line if they confront it."[17]

The IAM Executive Council in a meeting the following day at the union's new Placid Harbor facility decided that joining PATCO wouldn't be fair to the IAM members who could lose their jobs. PATCO had not only failed to build public support for their action, they had also failed to do the spade work necessary with their fellow trade unionists. Knowing that the Airline Pilots and the Flight Attendants had already decided not to honor the strike, the IAM council somewhat reluctantly concurred.

IAM members would continue to work at the nation's airports, but no union official or employee would fly until the matter was settled. Wimpy padlocked his shiny new Learjet and gamely fired up his black Pontiac Trans Am, long before he knew how decisively Reagan would win this round.

THIRTY-SEVEN

THE RUSSIANS ARE COMING!

One of the first places Wimpy drove his Trans Am was to Chicago to appear on *Donahue*, the country's top rated television talk show. Created by television personality and Cleveland native Phil Donahue, it's generally acknowledged to have been the first of the daytime talk tabloid genre. Donahue started his television career at Dayton's WHIO TV, where he gained national attention as their morning anchor when his contentious interviews of Teamster President Jimmy Hoffa and Texas swindler Billie Sol Estes were picked up for national syndication. He established his own talk show, *The Phil Donahue Show,* at WLWD TV in Dayton in 1970, taking on controversial social and political issues of the day. His first guest was Madeline Murray O'Hare, an atheist who was about to embark on a mission to ban prayer in public schools. The Dayton base proved to be a disadvantage when trying to attract top flight guests from the worlds of politics and entertainment, so in 1974, he moved his show to Chicago's WGN TV, and shortened the name to *Donahue.*

The show, which dealt with controversial issues rather than focusing on celebrities and scandal, was a huge success, particularly among women. In 1980, it had won a Peabody, the most prestigious award in broadcast journalism. The producers invited Wimpy to come on to defend labor's position in the PATCO strike and labor stoppages in general. He jumped at the opportunity. This was his chance to take the movement's message to an audience of millions of people.

The show was taped before a live audience of about 100 people, mostly housewives from affluent Chicago suburbs. The first segment involved Donahue and Wimpy seated at a small round table on a stage at the front of the studio, with Donahue interviewing his guest on whether unions had the right to inconvenience large segments of the public by withholding their services during a strike. The show quickly devolved into a larger exploration of union power, corruption, and public anger (conveyed by the audience) that unions were overstepping their bounds.

Donahue, though he was a liberal sympathetic to the labor movement, played devil's advocate, goading Wimpy about unions causing inflation. As he so often did in smaller groups, Wimpy took the bait and used the opportunity to smack his audience right between the eyes.

"Let's take the white collar junior executive," Donahue said. "Here's a guy in this company trying to work his way up, just like his folks taught him...values, work hard, and so on, and the plumber comes out with *solid gold wrenches* to fix the toilet. *Costs you twenty-five dollars, and the guy's there for seven minutes with his little roto-rooter.!*"

"That's the ultimate whiner!" Wimpy responded. "I have no time for any man or woman in this society who wants to sit around and whine about how well union members do, when all they have to do is go join one and get their piece of the action!"

The audience went crazy, screaming at Wimpy and booing him. A glint appeared in Wimp's eyes and a small, tight smile graced his face: his arrow had hit its mark. He continued, "If it's more important to be anti-union and starve, then that's exactly what you have a right to do. But if it's important to assert your economic welfare as a priority for your family or yourself, if it's important to assert your worth to society for what you do as a job within it or to your employer or anything else, then it ought to be worth getting together and doing something to make that decent and fair."

Wimpy went on to offer a spirited defense of blue collar workers, pointing out that when there were more plumbers than jobs, the cost of hiring a plumber would drop. He maintained that as long as parents, guidance counselors and society as a whole looked down their collective noses at people who worked with their hands, there would be fewer plumbers and that they therefore had every right to be fairly compensated. This was an important concept, and his white collar audience, few of whom appeared to have ever toiled for hourly wages, began to see his point.

Conceding Wimp's point, Donahue moved on, saying it seemed only natural that parents would want their children to move into white collar jobs if they could, and that might explain their lack of sympathy for strikers.

Wimpy wasn't buying: "It's not just white collar. You heard that audience a moment ago. There is in the United States of America—save for the dictatorships in the most backward countries of the world—the most vicious anti-union bias of any country in the world. It's been inherent in our history, it's still here and it continues because it is promoted by all those who stand to lose something if that animus is reduced." There was more grumbling of disapproval from the audience. Donahue leaned close to Wimpy and said, "They're getting ready to attack in just one moment. Watch me and just do what I do."

"Just let them. I'm ready!"

Next, Donahue hit on one of Wimp's favorite topics, excessive defense spending, prompting one of the funniest moments of the show. Donahue asked Wimpy how he could be against defense spending and call it inflationary when so many IAM members were involved in the defense industry. After insisting that he favored reasonable expenditures for defense, Wimpy pointed out that the Reagan budget made a direct transfer from domestic to defense spending. "...whacks out, with a meat axe, slices out of social programs and makes a dollar for dollar transfer of all those funds over to the pentagon, plus a bonus on top of it, and says, 'Go play! Here's *billions*, go play."

"Where are you gonna be when we're all in line here," Donahue prodded, "with little tattoos on our arms, and the Russians are running us?"

"Well, if I thought that there was the remotest possibility that that was true right now, then I would go turn in my cap and badge. You know that's not true, and so do I. Every time this country, *this government of ours*, wants to diffuse the attention of the American people from the real, nagging, aggravating problems of this society, they start the old chant. This has happened several times in the last several decades: *The Russians are coming! The Russians are coming! The Russian are coming!* And I keep lookin' around (turning his head slowly, side to side) *They ain't here yet!* It's been chanted for a long time now—and every American has that patriotism well up in his breast—he snaps rigidly to attention, salutes the flag (mimicking attention and raising his right hand to his forehead in a crisp military salute), and says, 'I will do my part, sir!' And all the while he's standing there rigidly at attention, they're picking his pockets! Raising his taxes, reducing his wages, busting his union. And it's going on right under our noses all the time. And that's why the chant gets started as often as not."

Wimpy was holding his own in front of a tough crowd.

The next segment was a question and answer session. Wimpy moved to the edge of the stage, where he sat perched on a large cushion as Donahue roamed through the audience with a hand-held microphone. One woman said that strikes were losing their effectiveness because they were becoming so common and even suggested that the reason for many strikes was so that labor leaders could get the attention of television audiences.

Wimpy shot back that it was the workers who went without a paycheck during a strike who were hurt the most.

He countered the notion that "union bosses" called strikes by pointing out that it took a majority vote by the members, and in the case of the IAM, a two thirds majority, before any strike occurred.

Donahue interjected to say that often in labor stoppages the unions were making demands that the average person thought were unfair. Wimpy pounced on him.

"Demands," Donahue said, "that we as reasonable taxpaying people think might be unfair…"

The audience applauded.

"See, you're a perfect microcosm of the problem," Wimpy said. The audience hooted in disbelief and laughter. "Because even you refer to it as *demands*. Why doesn't anyone refer to the boss's position in negotiations as *demands*? Everyone pities the boss, because he's *asking* for something. The unions are always '*demanding*.'"

Next, a woman complained that her husband, a plumbing contractor, was stymied because of union regulations. Wimpy listened patiently, then said if her husband didn't like the union regulations he should change them. The woman didn't seem to grasp that unions were a democracy. "Who's going to fight the unions?" she asked.

"I'll take you to union halls all across the country," Wimpy replied. "I see it every day, all kinds of turmoil. People changing their own rules. That's what unions are all about!" Now Wimpy was up, strolling across the stage from one end to the other, peering closely at his questioners, ready to take them on.

"If everyone does what you say, and joins a union to get their piece of the action, who's going to pay us these wonderful wages?" asked the next questioner.

"There are some societies in the world where everyone does belong to a union," Wimpy replied. "They get higher wages and they have more benefits, like free health care."

"Their taxes are higher!" shouted someone in the audience.

"They've got more benefits, too!" Wimpy shot back and soon steered the discussion to another of his favorite topics, the top heavy nature of American capitalism. Striding around the stage, waving his arms for emphasis and raising his voice like a television preacher, he asked, "How many of you believe in free enterprise?" Almost every hand in the room shot up. "And how many of you believe we've got it?" Fewer hands went up.

"I see that fewer hands went up when you asked if we've got free enterprise in America," Donahue noted.

"They're the smart ones," Wimpy replied. "They realize that twenty percent of the corporations in this country control eighty percent of the business and the rest are left to fight like dogs for the scraps." He went on to detail the power of the large corporations that ran the country and dismissed any notion that there was true market competition where they held sway. The audience listened somewhat respectfully. He was making his point and beginning to win them over.

A Roman Catholic priest commented on the magnitude of a billion dollars: "I learned just yesterday how much money a billion dollars is. If you have a billion dollars and you spend a thousand dollars a day, it would take you three thousand years to spend the whole billion. Wouldn't we be better off taking forty billion dollars away from defense spending and using it to feed the poor and provide health care?"

Wimpy saw his opening. "That's what I meant about 'the Russians are coming.' It's time we got back to putting *people* before profits!" For the first time, he actually got applause from the audience.

He had Donahue put up slides that illustrated the costly nature of defense spending based on the research project he had funded in his first year as International President. The graphic showed that when defense spending was increased by $1 billion in 1975, 4,000 IAM jobs had been lost. In 1977, it increased $3 billion and 8,000 jobs disappeared. In 1978, the increase was $5 billion and yet 12,000 more IAM members were put out on the street.

This was new information to his audience, most of whom seemed to be under the impression that military spending created more jobs. Wimp came back with another slide that showed that even though 88,000 jobs were created by the $124 billion defense budget, 118,000 IAM jobs were lost on the civilian side, for a net job loss of 30,000.

The show seemed headed for a timely conclusion. Wimpy had tamed much of the initial hostility and had made several critical points. There was a little time left. The next questioner claimed that his small business had been forced to close because of the cost of dealing with the union. "I could spend hours on union abuses, but what I'd like to know is why have union workers lost pride in the products they produce? Why is it that when we buy an automobile, the door doesn't close, or the window crank comes off in your hand?"

Wimpy took a broad approach to answering the man's question, further riling the audience. "Let's get right back to the beginning. You introduced me as a powerful guy. I'm not that powerful, sometimes I can't even get my own wife to do what I say. Unions are nothing but a collection of Americans. If you're unhappy with unions, the way they work, the way they conduct themselves, the products they produce, then you're really unhappy with America."

The audience didn't like that take on things and got their blood up again. "Unions just want more money! They're not doing anything to try to improve the product!" a woman exclaimed.

"We have been trying for years to get management to be more efficient," Wimpy shot back. "Because if we don't become more efficient they just replace our jobs with a machine."

"My son worked part time for a grocery store and he was forced to join the union," complained a middle aged woman. "His paycheck was thirty dollars and they took out ten dollars in union dues every week. Why can't it be that people who don't want to join the union don't have to?"

The audience was in full revolt, supporting this poor woman. Music started to play and a graphic came up on the screen telling viewers where to send for a transcript of the show. Wimpy stood at the edge of the stage and shouted back at the woman, "I'm not going to let you get away with that ten dollar thing. That's utter nonsense!"

The credits rolled across the screen and suddenly television viewers were confronted with a Volvo commercial. Unlike every other talk show they'd ever watched, this one had ended in chaos.

In those days, that wasn't done. Donahue and his producers realized they had a problem...and an opportunity. This was great television. Passion, controversy, and a guest right out of central casting. A quick decision was made to keep the discussion flowing and to air the rest of it the next day as "Part Two."

Wimpy, who had battled long and hard for money to advertise the IAM on network television, was about to get another full hour of the nation's attention, free of charge.

Donahue, as cranked up with emotion as Wimpy and the audience were, opened the "second show" immediately and eliminated any pretense that it was about the PATCO strike. It was about the labor movement in general.

"I am pleased to welcome you to part two, that is to say the second show featuring the International President of the International Association of Machinists and Aerospace Workers, Mr. William Winpisinger.

"Mr. Winpisinger, as we established on our first program, is the president of one of the largest unions in this country, claiming almost a million members.

"During Mr. Winpisinger's first appearance on this show we were rather surprised by what appears to be an almost unanimous feeling in this studio audience that unions have gone too far. That unions concentrate more on benefits and their own job time and retirement than they do upon the quality of their work. And the feeling also was that unions abuse young people, that maybe we are asking young people in part time jobs to pay union dues that really don't benefit these folks that are going to go back to school anyway.

"How sensitive are unions? How much are unions responsible for how we got here in this country? Why is union membership decreasing per capita in this country? And what is the labor man's responsibility to get us out of wherever it is we are now in this country? *And how come plumbers are so expensive?!*

"This audience is mad, and they're not going to take any more of it!" Donahue claimed.

"Oh, yes they are!" Wimpy shot back.

The gloves were off. Audience members kept pelting Wimpy with questions and their own biases against unions and strikes, then they began to battle one another. One woman complained that PATCO and other unions had no right to strike because it inconvenienced the public. A woman a few rows behind her replied that she had been a registered nurse, and that they'd struck as a last resort, when working conditions became a danger to them and their patients. They squabbled over which unions could strike, and over the morality of nurses walking off the job and possibly endangering patient's lives.

"Don't you talk morality to me!" The former nurse screeched. "Sometimes a strike is the only way you can call attention to a dangerous situation. That strike *saved* lives!"

Donahue added fuel to the fire by describing an outrageous case of featherbedding on television and movie productions, including a union requirement of someone to turn the pages when union musicians played.

Wimpy shot back that Donahue was using the extraordinary example of something a union of 15,000 members may have done to unfairly portray 15,000,000 working men and women performing legitimate jobs.

Donahue wouldn't let up: "You've got a problem. And the problem is right here in this audience. The perceived image is a union guy sitting on top of a skid waiting for the clock to strike four so he can get out of there. I know that making that point insults a lot of hard working, taxpaying union people in this country, some of whom fought in the war and even sent some of their sons, and I'm sorry about that. You still have an obligation as one of the most influential labor guys in this country to speak to this feeling that these people have."

"Every time I speak to it they go AHHHH!!" Wimpy shot back. "Because they obviously think they know more about it than I do!"

"Can we have your admission that there are union abuses and union laziness?"

"Yes."

"And bad attitude."

"A little while ago I said I was a devout believer that power corrupts and absolute power corrupts absolutely," Wimpy replied, "and I therefore don't propose that the unions run the country. Let me ask you: How many in this audience know that my union founded, paid for, has nurtured, and just completed to the tune of more than two million dollars a facility that breeds, trains and provides free of cost to blind people of this country guide dogs? How many people know that?"

"It's about time!" an audience member called out.

"It's been going on, madam, since nineteen hundred and forty-eight. But who knows it? The good things the unions do, *nobody knows about.*"

Donahue tried to pin America's frustration with Detroit's horrid automobiles of the time—the late '70's and early '80's—on the unions. "Is labor at least in some degree responsible for what we believe to be the less than efficient automobiles that are produced in this country?" he asked.

"No. The guys that build them have nothing to do with the efficiency of the product. Nothing whatsoever."

"How can you say that? They make them. They put them together. They're the guys on the line with the big pneumatic tools."

"Efficiency is determined by fuel consumption, horsepower, and the worker's don't design that, all they do is assemble it."

"O.K., we'll give you that one. Now, how come the door doesn't close? How come the handle falls off?" The audience roared its approval. "How come there are so many rattles in it?"

"Alright. Now we're going to get right down to it," Wimpy responded. "Because American managers have never learned to manage the way that Japanese managers do. (Gasps and disapproval from the audience) Why doesn't the American worker stand up at attention, happily sing the company song and dash madly into work to compete like a beaver for eight hours? Maybe because we don't have the same benefits that the Japanese worker does. (Loud grumbling from the audience) *"Alright! Alright, wise guys!"* (Nervous laughter from the audience) "Let me ask you a couple of questions. What's the number one thing that looks over a worker's shoulder every day of his life?"

"The foreman?" Donahue wondered.

"There's an evil far greater than that. It's called *fear*. You know what the fear is? It's a fear that the next day you won't have a job!"

(The audience moans)

"Unemployment stalks the American worker every day of his life. What do the Japanese do? Are you aware there's no such thing as losing your job, no such thing as being laid off in Japan? You go through the Japanese employment office at Toyota and go in there and take a job, and if you get hired you have a job for life! You never have to worry about losing that job."

Wimpy was turning the tide. He was scoring point after point by challenging the audience to look beyond their narrow perceptions, *to think*, to consider the plight of the working man and woman. Responding to a woman who implied that the country couldn't afford union wages because they were inflationary, Wimpy swung for the fences: "Wages, ladies, whether you like it or not, are not the cause of inflation in this country today. Union wage rates, and every other wage rate paid in this society today are falling *behind* the rates of inflation. There isn't a responsible…"(Loud groans and mummers of dispute from the audience) "Well, I'm here to tell you that's an absolute fact, from the *federal government*, not my head! Wages are falling behind. Purchasing power of the members of my union today is at 1967 levels. Now, that's flat-out positive proof that wages are not keeping pace with inflation. Those who believe that wages are the engine of inflation in this country are those who, whether they realize it or not, are saying that workers must suffer reductions in their living standards in order that the multi-nationals can make more money, move less overseas, or wreak less destruction on our economy. It's time if we really believe in *democracy* in this country, it is time that we democratize corporate decision making so that six guys can't get in a paneled room somewhere and decide what you're and my lifestyles are going to be like for the rest of our lives. And *that's* what's happening now!"

The audience roared with approval and applause. Professor Winpisinger was bringing his class along nicely, though the question of union corruption still seemed to be a sticking point. Wimpy took the issue on directly. "Let me ask you one more question, because it's burning in my gut now. How many of you know, for example, that the Teamsters Union has been accused of stealing pension funds?"

Most of the audience raised their hand.

"Certain officials, right? O.K., now I think every American knows that. You know why? Because it's been emblazed across the front page of every newspaper in the country day in and day out. Not once, but over and over. How many of you know that the officers of Grumman, Northrop and Lockheed were guilty of bribing customers all over the world to the tune of *millions* of dollars? How many of you know that?" A few raised their hands tentatively. "Quite a bit fewer than the Teamster indiscretions, right? Which got the most publicity? Who got punished the most? Bottom line: There are fiduciary laws in this country that govern union officers that are as severe as for any class of citizens in this country. Deliberately enacted by the federal Congress in response to the abuses alleged. Absolute fiduciary standards that are almost identical to those faced by bankers. And yet in a recent year I saw that thirty-four union officials, of the multitude of thousands of them that there are in this country, were charged with and convicted of violations of those fiduciary responsibilities, prosecuted and punished. Thirty-four, of the thousands and thousands of them. And by the way, I read about every one of those thirty-four on the front pages of America's newspapers. In the same year, over 1,500 bank officers in this country were convicted of exactly the same thing. And I have people say to me all the time: 'Well, we don't like your union because of all them crooks.'

I don't see anybody runnin' down to pull their money out of the banks! Double standard!"

The audience roared its agreement. Wimpy had turned the hostile crowd completely around by disabusing them of the notions they'd been spoon fed by the media. As his second hour in the national spotlight drew to a close Wimpy left them with one last thought—that most of their concerns about strikes and labor stoppages were really about public employees, and that as the taxpaying public, the audience really was the employer of those workers. "You didn't see the attitude that exists in this room and elsewhere in the country until public employees began to organize and make citizens a little bit uncomfortable because they were such lousy employers," he intoned. "They had to pay a couple dollars more taxes to make working conditions tolerable for those who serve them. That's when all this set in. As long as it was outside somewhere, in an industry, nobody needed to worry too much. Everybody got their back up for the public employees."

The two hour Donahue appearance was a solid home run for the man who had been preaching the gospel of organized labor his entire adult life. Wimpy had turned hard bitten critics into people at least willing to give labor a fair hearing, performing for an audience of millions.

Could he parlay that success into a revitalization of a labor movement that faced fierce political opposition, a dreadful economy, and a skeptical public?

THIRTY-EIGHT

TECHNOLOGY TAKES ITS TOLL

Wimpy's high speed tour of America at the wheel of his sleek black Trans Am came to an abrupt halt in Missouri, where the State Police arrested him for speeding and changing lanes improperly. He took great exception to the charges in a letter to the court, while pleading guilty, "reluctantly (very reluctantly)...the conduct cited by the arresting officer is no different than what is done as a matter of daily course and survival on the extremely crowded highways which I constantly use in my home locale," he wrote.

"The absence of damage to my automobile and the absence of traffic accidents on my record are mute but ample testimony to the fact that the manner in which I drive is not beyond my capabilities. It seems ludicrous that the State Police Officers in Missouri find unlawful the driving methods which are a daily occurrence where I live."[1]

Wimpy's arrest, and the fact that he would soon trade his beloved Trans Am for a more sedate Buick Skylark, seem fitting analogies for the difficult times that were falling on him and his union. Ronald Reagan's economy, which stressed unfettered defense spending, tax cuts for the wealthy, and the evisceration of social programs made IAM members long for the good old days of Jimmy Carter's incompetence. Unemployment shot up to nearly ten percent. Inflation raged on at more than six percent a year, and interest rates climbed weekly, with the Prime Interest Rate touching seventeen percent by the end of 1982.

Reagan successfully broke the PATCO strike, pushing labor into a period of significant retrenchment. Manufacturing plants, jobs, and capital fled the country at an alarming rate. The IAM and other unions began to see the most precipitous declines in membership since the end of World War I.

The nature of the workplace was changing fundamentally as well. Robots were replacing workers on assembly lines and factory floors. Electronic word processors and "video data terminals" were making their debut on desktops in offices across the land. Skilled factory machinists and aircraft and automotive mechanics were being retrained to use high technology machines in order to do jobs they had learned to do through years of apprenticeship and training. These faster more accurate machines required fewer and fewer skilled machinists to accomplish the same workload.

The political and class warfare that had characterized labor's struggles in past generations was still apparent, but this change was different. It proved to be more fundamental than a mere ideological battle. Wimpy was quick to recognize this phenomenon, and did his best to avoid the worst effects of the tsunami. He rallied the troops, telling the beleaguered members of the United Auto Workers:

> We're all, each and every one of us, victims of a barrage of bum raps these days. We're told our work is sloppy and of poor quality. We're told we're a bunch of lazy loafers looking for a soft touch and a fat paycheck. We're told we're corrupt, power hungry and violent—and we've got to be put in our place. We're blamed for everything from last week's blizzard to putting Reagan in the White House—from loose dentures to hemorrhoids. In the Machinists Union, we're damned sick and tired of this blatantly biased and cardboard caricature of the American worker and the trade union member in particular.[2]

The plight of the Auto Workers was emblematic of what was going on in American manufacturing in general. In August 1982, *Automotive News* reported that there were 21,124 domestic car dealerships in the United States, a decrease of 556 since the beginning of the year. In New Jersey alone, the number of dealerships dropped from 820 to 710 between 1980 and 1982.[3] As they disappeared, so too did the IAM mechanics jobs, like the one at which Wimpy had gotten his start in Cleveland at Lake Buick. Wimpy was angry and eloquent when *Fortune* Magazine asked for his response to reports that General Motors and other employers were replacing workers with robots at a rate of one robot per 1.7 workers in assembly plants and one per 2.7 workers in manufacturing facilities: "There is no consolation or satisfaction for the $250 to $300 per week auto mechanic working at a minimum wage in a McDonald's stand," he said in the June 1982 issue.[4]

By the time the IAM Executive Council met at Placid Harbor on April 4, 1982, it was becoming apparent that the loss of members was draining the union of its financial power. Gene Glover, the General Secretary Treasurer, had to deliver the first of many bad news reports. The continuing loss of members meant there would have to be layoffs of union staff and major cut-backs in spending. This was anathema to Wimpy who only had one gear—full speed ahead—but his fellow Council members helped him make the necessary adjustments.

Gene Glover:

> *Wimpy was such a good leader. You've got to understand, when you sit on that council you get a good reading of each other. You talk to each other, and there was no question when we were talking there was only one leader, which made it nice. Nobody else was pushing Wimpy, so that made it easier for him to express himself. Nobody thought they were*

smarter than Wimpy. Most of the guys were happy
to have him around because of the good programs.

We all agreed we ought to organize. Wimpy
was one hundred percent for that. For a number
of the vice presidents that was the big thing in the
organization, so he had their support. They might not
have agreed with him on other things, but this guy's
going on the right track, they thought.[5]

Organizing might help slow the bleeding, but the drop in membership was catastrophic. In September 1981, internal IAM documents showed that there were 731,958 dues paying members. A year later, that figure had fallen fifteen percent to 627,094. More than 100,000 IAM members were out of work. For the most part, these weren't layoffs: their jobs were gone.

Wimpy began speaking of four "profound movements" that he predicted would fundamentally change the workplace and the labor movement "well into the next century."

He prophesized—with deadly accuracy—that the introduction of new technology into the workplace, the decline of "liberal capitalism" around the globe, the unrestrained mobility of US capital, and what he termed the "sovereignty" of multi-national corporations, would bring about a new dynamic which would forever alter how workers related to their jobs and their union. Speaking at Florida International University in March 1982, Wimpy outlined what he saw happening with the influx of technology.

No one escapes. Microprocessors and video data
terminals take over offices, banks and insurance
companies. Skilled workers are de-skilled and
interfaced with computerized machines. College
graduates are trained to do skilled crafts work,

*and the semi-skilled and unskilled are displaced...
creativity and improvisation are straight jacketed
to programmed tapes, decision making is remote
and highly centralized, and personal communication
between workers and management is blocked or
stultified. A new breed of cat makes up the majority
of the workforce: mellow, laid-back, emotionless,
homogeneous, docile.[6]*

He predicted that these changes would lead to familiar problems: insecurity, stress and strain, alienation, frustration, and unemployment. Unions, he said, would have to adapt to this new environment, and these "new characters with non-traditional traits, habits and values."

In an age and time when many executives his age relegated computers and new technologies to back room staff, Wimpy, the old auto mechanic, rolled up his sleeves and got right under the hood. He was one of the first civilians to get a look at the Internet, then a pie in the sky application of the ten-year old Defense Advanced Research Projects Agency (DARPA), an arm of the Pentagon.

Tom Buffenbarger:

*Wimpy was invited by the Pentagon to take some
classes. It was mostly executives of big companies,
Wimp was the only labor guy. Whoever was doing
it for the Pentagon knew that Wimp was a real
gadget whiz. He was given a computer, and it was
almost the size of a small suitcase. I think it may
have been an Epson. The keyboard came down, it
had a small screen, floppy disc ports and all of that.
He took seven or eight classes, about an hour each,
where they were given instruction on this new thing*

called the Internet [the Pentagon referred to it at the time as "ARPANET"], developed by the Pentagon. They would get an hour of class instruction and then the next two hours were spent discussing potential applications for this, and how could it carry over into the commercial world?, That's where Wimp got his appetite well whetted about technology and how the union could use it.[7]

Wimpy quickly saw the power computer technology had to offer and began considering ways it might revolutionize his own operations. Don Wharton:

Wimpy was on that [Pentagon] panel, and they gave them all laptops. They call them laptops now, but these were really portable computers that were barely luggable. Wimpy got on that and he would communicate with different people in that group, and they would communicate with him. I was his executive assistant, and he said to me, "I think that our people in this building could use computers to help them do their jobs better."[8]

It wasn't long before Wimpy recruited Tom Buffenbarger and other young IAM staffers to form a committee to bring the newest technology to the union. Tom Buffenbarger:

He said, "I'm going to be calling a group to Washington to talk about modern technologies, and we'll tell your boss to send you in." We went to the old headquarters and met in the council room. There was a representative from each territory, plus Howie Dowd, our information systems guy, and Gene Glover, Donnie Wharton and Dave Hamilton. We read a raft of computer material Howie Dowd had sent us—it was all Greek to me—and we talked. But you could see the potential. It was that evident. And shortly thereafter two computers showed up in every regional office for the secretaries. And God, they were like tabernacles! Only certain people could touch them and there was a complete mystique about them.[9]

Labor was now confronting technology and its implications across a wide spectrum, not just in offices and on factory floors. The National Football League Players Association, the group Wimpy had nurtured from its infancy, and which still called the Machinists Building home, decided to strike the NFL ownership at the beginning of the 1982 football season. It was the first in-season strike in the history of the NFL and most of the news media characterized it as simply a fight over the portion of revenues available for player compensation. Many labor leaders and academics saw it differently. They claimed it was a fight about new technology and power in the workplace. *New York Times* business reporter William Serrin looked beyond the dollars and cents and told readers about a changing dynamic in the workplace and for unions:

The strike, involving workers with professional status, not blue collar workers, is also the kind of confrontation that can be expected to occur increasingly in the future, experts say, as new technologies alter the workplace and transform the nation's economy.

"These are turning point strikes," Arthur Shostak, professor of sociology and a labor expert at Drexel University in Philadelphia, said of the football strike and other recent strikes in what are regarded as professional, technical or white collar fields.

The nation is developing and installing new, sophisticated workplace technologies such as cable and pay television, which are key issues in the football industry strike, Mr. Shostak noted. And he said workers such as the 1,500 professional football players, now on strike against the team owners are 'on the cutting edge' of these technologies.[10]

Serrin detailed the efforts of NFLPA Executive Director Ed Garvey, and noted, "In building the union, he received large assistance from the outspoken William W. Winpisinger, president of the Machinists union."[11]

The strike was finally settled on November 16, 1982, after fifty-seven days of intense negotiations and non-stop media attention. The players opted to settle for less than they had asked for but managed to increase their pay, a significant victory at a time when most unions engaged in concessionary bargaining. Wimpy was glad to be able to watch his beloved Redskins again on Sunday afternoons, but wished the players had shown as much toughness at the bargaining table as they did on the gridiron.

"I laud the attempt Garvey made, but I deplore the fact that his members showed enough weakness that the owners just decided to sit it out and win. I have a hunch that out of this the members may have learned that when you select goals, you certainly have to be willing to withstand whatever rigors are entailed in reaching them."[12]

Another group that fell short of reaching its goal that fall was the National Organization for Women. The Supreme Court ruled on October 4, 1982, in *State of Idaho, et al. v. Freeman, et al.* that time had run out for ratifying the Equal Rights Amendment. It had been passed by Congress in 1972, and required the concurrence of three quarters of the country's state legislatures to become a permanent part of the Constitution. In the early 1920's, proponents of women's suffrage, who had succeeded in amending the constitution to grant women the right to vote, remained concerned that US law still contained vestiges of legal discrimination against women. They drafted a measure called the "Equal Rights Amendment" and first submitted it to Congress in 1923. There it sat, for the next forty-nine years, until the House finally passed it in 1971, and the Senate in 1972, which set in motion a constitutionally mandated seven-year clock for ratification, which was extended to 1982 by a vote of Congress in 1978. As the 1982 deadline approached, only thirty-five of the required thirty-eight state legislatures had passed the amendment, and five of those subsequently rescinded it, due largely to concerns about abortion, same sex marriages, or the possibility that women could be required to register for the draft.

Wimpy supported the ERA, and made many public statements to that effect, the first in 1978:

> It has been six long years since the Equal Rights Amendment sailed through Congress toward ratification by the states. Now we find our vessel of justice run aground by an insidious tide of reaction and the bombastic winds of the Right Wing. Those forces that have buffeted the women's movement have also obstructed the trade union movement.[13]

Despite the Supreme Court setback in 1982, women continued to make great strides within Wimpy's IAM.

Barbara Shailor:

> The Machinists Union…was such a male union, whom Wimpy had hired to coordinate energy issues

for the union. "I think Wimpy saw that he could shake it up some. That it would be important to have women in high-level, visible roles. That was important for him to do. You know, there would be some that would accuse Wimpy of being a terrible chauvinist. But my own experience was—there just wasn't a hint of chauvinism. There was an old-fashioned kind of male locker room bawdiness to Wimpy that maybe in today's time of political correctness someone would say was obscene or something. The fact is you knew him so well, and it had no sexual overtones. So he was a love. He was just great.

I can remember him sending me to the Cincinnati Club, or the Cosmopolitan, one of those clubs where women couldn't go in through the front door. I'm representing—I'm talking about the Boeing contract, it's all aerospace executives. And they won't let me in the front door. Long before cell phones, I called him and said, "They won't let me in the front door."

"What do you mean they won't let you in the front door?" He was livid, and screamed, "Goddamn it!"..."Well then just make sure you get in the meeting. Go around to the side door."

So I go around to the side door. Walk in the side door, and this person says, "Why are you here?" and I go sit in the room. And I'm with supposedly sophisticated business aerospace executives who, of course, think I'm the secretary who's walked into the room, and ask me for paper, coffee or something. I said, "No, I'm here as William Winpisinger's representative, on behalf of the Machinists Union," which they took as shocking, just shocking. But that was who Wimpy was.[13]

The other major trend Wimpy had to deal with as Reagan's economy eviscerated his membership was a widespread perception that Japan was winning a war against American manufacturing. Article after article appeared, touting "the Japanese miracle," suggesting that their superior work ethic and dedication to quality and so-called "quality circles" were allowing them to capture a larger share of the American automobile market and virtually take over the consumer electronics industry. Most articles laid a significant share of the blame on American workers and their unions. Many advocated adopting quality of work circles in American factories. Wimpy was having none of it. In a speech to the Japan Society in New York City, Wimp was typically bold:

> It is my observation that the new technology is rendering obsolete the doctrine of comparative advantage, which is so rigidly fixed in the minds of pure free traders here in the United States…Japan has no advantages—except one—over the United States. There certainly is no Japanese advantage in terms of natural resources, population, education, wealth or political power. On the whole, and in a state of nature, the Japanese worker is neither more nor less skilled, more or less innately intelligent than US workers or workers found anywhere else in the industrialized world…What, then, is the one comparative advantage Japan has over the United States—the one advantage that shows up indelibly in its favorable trade balances with the US?…Superior management.[14]

After railing against the shortsightedness of American capitalists who let Japan develop big leads in robotics, electronics, and auto manufacturing, he pointed out, as he often did, that wage comparisons between Japanese and American workers were misleading because of the lifetime guarantee of a job and enhanced social benefits provided to Japanese workers. Then he introduced a novel idea—that never caught on: "If, however, US managers continue to insist on competing on the basis of comparative wage levels, then workers and their trade unions have a legitimate right to insist that US managers receive pay and compensation comparable to that received by Japanese executives. And that means they will take pay cuts too."[16]

Wimpy then announced that the IAM had developed a "Technology Bill of Rights," and that it would begin to deploy "Technology Stewards" throughout the country to monitor how new technology affected the status of IAM workers. The Bill of Rights proposed the following:

> *New technology must be used in a way that creates and maintains jobs and promotes full employment.*
>
> *New technology must be used to improve the conditions of work.*
>
> *New technology must be used to develop the industrial base.*
>
> *Workers and their trade unions must have a role in the decision-making process with respect to the design, deployment and use of new technology.*[17]

At the same time, Wimpy adamantly opposed the rush to institute quality circles or "quality of worklife" programs because he felt they would dilute the collective bargaining process. He still harbored a tremendous grudge against American industry for the way they had closed ranks to defeat Labor Law Reform, and vowed never to trust its representatives again. At one point, he accused advocates of quality circles of "practicing Hegelian

Dialects," and said, "We don't believe this thing called worker participation is in our interest."[18]

The exact origin of quality circles is debatable, but many trace the strain that swept across America in the early 1980's to Dr. Kaoru Ishikawa. As a forty-seven–year-old academic and President of the Musashi Institute of Technology in 1962, Ishikawa introduced a revolutionary way of doing things at the Nippon Telephone and Telegraph Company. Instead of a rigid top down management scheme, managers would meet with workers and *ask* them how their jobs ought to be performed. Then the manager and the workers would form a team to implement the suggestions and thus improve the quality of their product. This was no small departure from the way of doing things in the rigidly structured Japanese society. It is often credited with turning the image of their products from one of cheap wind-up toys to that of high-quality electronic goods. By the early 1980's, many American consumers interpreted "Japanese made" as "well made," and "reasonably priced," and "American made" as "overpriced junk," particularly cars. Pressure grew to adopt Ishikawa's methods in America's factories.

The IAM Research Department conducted a survey of local lodges and found that eighty-six had quality circle programs. Only twenty-six of them had been covered by the collective bargaining agreement. Wimpy railed against quality circles, claiming he resented the idea of cooperating with management on the shop floor when they would be happy to "mug us at the plant gate."

> *Quality of work-life—improving it—is what unions are all about. We'd welcome any bona fide management interest in improving that quality. But, we don't see any genuine commitment to that objective in all the pop psychology and jargon among the proposals that most American firms are advancing. Generally, what*

they're talking about is improving the quality of life
of corporate moguls at the expense of the quality of
worker's lives. As long as that's the motive, and there
is no mistake that it is, we can't be a party to it.[19]

So far, the 1980's were proving to be as wild a ride as Wimpy's high speed travels had been in his Trans Am.

THIRTY-NINE

A MESSAGE FROM
MR. ANDROPOV

The Reagan Administration irritated Wimpy just as much as Carter's had. He minced no words in a *New York Times* op-ed on December 5, 1982: "The tragic fact is that the advent of Labor Secretary Raymond Donovan has opened the department to severe charges of failing to serve the constituency its charter requires. And this neglectful isolation of labor by the invisible Secretary has prompted some labor leaders to demand Mr. Donovan's resignation."[1]

In the same piece, Wimp also chastised the Occupational Safety and Health Administration for abandoning its core functions, needlessly endangering the lives of millions of workers: "Never before has an Administration stacked a Labor Department so heavily against labor and so mightily in favor of management."[2]

Donovan shot back at Wimpy with a letter to the editor that only seemed to further prove Wimpy's point. Donovan painted a picture of a defanged and decimated Labor Department which, in his own words, had seen "a forty-five percent reduction in the department's FY 1982 budget...and savings of over $2 billion in regulatory costs."[3] Donovan's handpicked OSHA Assistant Secretary, in his own letter to the *Times,* touted their "voluntary protection program," and a totally new concept in protecting worker's health and safety: "a self inspection program."[4]

As 1983 dawned, Wimpy and the IAM were facing an economic crisis of unparalleled proportions. More than half a million workers across the country were being laid off or permanently terminated each week. The brunt of those losses occurred in four industries where the IAM was dominant: machinery, primary metals, fabricated metals, and transportation equipment. Plants moving to low wage countries and robots in those that remained in the US were wreaking havoc on the hard working brothers and sisters of the IAM.

In his January "State of the Union" message, Wimpy was characteristically blunt.

> *Every indicator that we see, every event that transpires, seems to dictate an endless stream of bad news. The membership of our organization has been slipping badly over the past eighteen months: we are losing members at the rate of about 10,000 a month. The (budget) deficit mounted and mounted and mounted until we closed out 1982 with a deficit in the neighborhood of $4 million. And, frankly, that is the maximum deficit—along with what we sustained in 1981—that we can stand and remain financially healthy in the IAM.[5]*

Wimpy also pointed out that 2,623 collective bargaining agreements with 3,620 firms, covering nearly half the remaining IAM membership, were up for negotiation in 1983. Most if not all employers would be looking for concessions. He concluded his remarks with the rhetoric of someone facing a major battle: "Hang tight, and hang tough."[6]

The January meeting of the IAM Executive Council, held at the Hyatt Hotel on Union Square in San Francisco, was long and contentious. Over the course of three days, Wimp and the council wrestled with how to come to grips with the soaring deficit.

Gene Glover reported that he had met with the IAM Representatives Association, the union that represented the union's Grand Lodge Representatives and Special Representatives, and asked them to voluntarily forego scheduled pay increases for 1983. The request was denied. Reluctantly, the council concluded that they would have to begin trimming staff. Because of the bargaining agreement they had in place, the layoffs would have to be done by seniority in each territory and would be effective April 1, 1983. The IAM was about to lose its youngest, hungriest organizers and advocates.

The council also took a fine tooth comb to the costs associated with Wimp's beloved affiliations and support for outside groups. The Citizen-Labor Energy Coalition, the NFLPA, and the other pet projects that Wimpy had accumulated at IAM headquarters over the years would have to begin paying their own freight.

By mid-March, when the council met again at headquarters in Washington, the news was even bleaker. Gene Glover reported that the deficit had ballooned to more than $6.5 million. The council decided that they would have to cut at least $5 million from the operating budget by July 1. The initial forecast of how many staff would have to be laid off was revised sharply upward, and each General Vice President was instructed to come to the next council meeting with recommendations for further cuts. All air travel would be in coach class. The staff that remained after the layoffs would be instructed to squeeze every nickel until the buffalo cried.

One of the first staffers laid off was the new director of services to older and retired members, Mike Winpisinger. "I got laid off by my own father," Mike Winpisinger recounted. "There must have been sixty or seventy people that got laid off. They went by seniority, and I was fairly low on the seniority list, and he wasn't going to cut any slack for his own family. It didn't bother me anywhere near as much as it bothered him."[7] Wimpy was distraught at having to lay off anyone.

Maria Cordone remembered that she "saw him upset, almost in tears, when we had the retrenchment program and he had to lay people off. He was so upset by that, because this is not what he had in mind, this was not what this was supposed to be about. And he was in his office—I'd come here and he was sitting at his desk, and I could see he was just full—his eyes were just full."[8]

Reagan, meanwhile, was ratcheting up his rhetoric about the Soviet Union as a means of justifying ever higher defense spending—which he falsely claimed would stimulate the economy. In a speech to the National Association of Evangelicals on March 8, 1983, in Orlando, Reagan first called the Soviets an Evil Empire: "There is evil in this world and we are enjoined by scripture and the Lord Jesus to oppose it with all our might." He said those who favor a mutual freeze on new nuclear weapons ignore "the aggressive instincts of an evil empire."[9]

Three weeks later, in a speech to the nation, he called for the development of a "missile defense shield," allegedly to protect the country against nuclear attack. In what became known as his "Star Wars" speech (after the science fiction movie released around that time), Reagan proposed spending billions on the space based system that would, in the way of a science fiction fantasy, incapacitate nuclear missiles once they had been launched.

The idea for the program had been given to him by Edward Teller, the "father of the hydrogen bomb." Teller related to Reagan the breakthrough work of a young scientist at the Lawrence Livermore National Laboratory by the name of Peter L. Hagelstein. Working as part of a team known as "The O Group," Hagelstein had come up with a new x-ray laser that could be used to incapacitate intercontinental ballistic missiles. His supervisor on the project was Lowell Wood, one of Teller's protégés. When Teller related the news to Reagan, the President wasted no time rolling out the new program, and essentially telling the public to let the cost be damned.

"Those loud voices that are occasionally heard charging that the Government is trying to solve a security problem by throwing money at it are nothing more than noise based on ignorance," Reagan said, dismissing his critics.[10]

Wimpy, of course, was one of those "loud voices." In a speech the following week in San Francisco, Wimp's voice was loud and clear:

> A week or so ago I imagine most of us were watching when Ronald Reagan went on the tube and made what has become known as his "Star Wars" speech. With his usual flair for corny Hollywood showmanship, he dramatically unveiled a bunch of fancy charts and graphs, along with some suddenly declassified photographs to prove "The Russians are coming, the Russians are coming."
>
> His performance reminded me of the way William Randolph Hearst is said to have dragged the United States into the Spanish-American War. According to historians, Hearst sent a famous photographer, named Frederick Remington, to Cuba to get pictures of battles between Cuban rebels and Spanish troops. When Remington cabled Hearst that he couldn't find any war, Hearst cabled back, "You furnish the pictures and I'll furnish the war." In this case the CIA furnished Reagan the pictures and I'm afraid that he may end up furnishing us with a war.[11]

Wimpy railed against Reagan's out of control defense spending, and he took exception to the President's notion, accepted by some of his own membership, that robust defense spending was good for the economy:

> *Unfortunately, some trade unionists don't seem to care if defense spending bankrupts the country as long as it provides them with well paying jobs. I've become accustomed to complaints from Machinists Union members because I don't view defense spending as a legitimate source of jobs. Just before I left to come out here, for example, I got an angry letter from a member of one of our biggest Machinists lodges at McDonnell Douglas in St. Louis. He said, and I quote, "As an endorser of SANE you do not speak for members who pay your salary. Without defense work we would not have jobs for our families." I wrote back and told him among other things that although I respect his right to his opinion, "the continuing buildup of more and more and ever more implements of mass destruction is suicidal and I intend to go on saying so."*
>
> *If any of you are laboring under a similar delusion that defense spending creates jobs, let me disabuse you. As I went on to tell this member from St. Louis, we have looked into this issue very carefully. We have studied and researched defense spending from top to bottom. And we can prove that military spending destroys more jobs than it creates. This is not really hard to understand. Since the time of Adam Smith, the father of classic economic theory, it has been a basic economic principle that if more capital and labor is put into guns, there will be less for butter. You can't have one without sacrificing the other. Moreover, today defense industries have become so highly labor intensive, it takes a billion dollars to*

*create 45,800 jobs. That same billion put into the
civilian sector will create 58,000 jobs in construction
and 98,000 in public service.*[12]

When Wimpy visited the Kremlin in August 1983, Yuri
Andropov, the Soviet Premier, used their meeting to respond
to Reagan's saber rattling. After canceling a trip in 1979 because
of heavy-handed KGB tactics against Russian trade unionists,
Wimpy ventured to the heart of what Reagan was now calling
an "Evil Empire," to get a firsthand look at how working people
and labor activists were treated in the Soviet Union. Stepan
Shalayev, President of the All-Union Central Council of Trade
Unions, arranged a meeting between Wimpy's delegation and
the Premier.

Andropov was an imposing figure with penetrating eyes
and the menacing demeanor of an agent of the KGB, which
he had headed before becoming Premier. It was Andropov
who had crushed the Prague uprising with tanks in 1968, and
he had also been the chief proponent of the Soviet invasion
of Afghanistan. He was known for being brutally harsh with
dissidents, and it was his KGB that had effected the arrests
that led Wimpy to cancel his 1979 trip.

Andropov's purpose now was to appear reasonable while
discounting Reagan's "Evil Empire" construct. Terming Reagan's
rhetoric, "irresponsible, aggressive political statements and
actions in the spirit of the notorious cold war,"[13] he went on
to offer an olive branch through his visitor from the IAM: "We
do not want the arms race either on earth or in space from
which mankind might be threatened with mortal danger if
militarism is given free reign."

"If a hand of friendship is extended to us, it will always be
given a sincere handshake by the Soviet people."[14]

He also addressed the latest peace talks in Geneva and
Reagan's stated plan to deploy 572 Pershing II cruise missiles in

West Germany, Great Britain and other locations throughout Europe while demanding that the Soviets reduce their stockpile of SS-20 and other land based missiles, claiming that Reagan was asking him to stand "unarmed in front of NATO's nuclear missiles."[15]

> Naturally, we will never agree to that. The USSR, however, will continue following a constructive and flexible line at the talks in Geneva in the hope that the US side will at last change its negative approach, show interest in an honest agreement. We shall be doing so until the US Government, by starting deploying new nuclear missiles close to us, on European territory, compels us to concentrate on defensive countermeasures to ensure the security of the Soviet people and its allies.[16]

Wimpy may have been a valuable messenger in the international tug of war over nuclear arms control, but closer to home he faced daunting challenges of his own. Reaganomics, globalization, and the technological transformation of the American economy were sending billions of dollars and the jobs they would create overseas. In a speech at Kalamazoo, Michigan, Wimpy cited the work of two economists, Robert Frank and Richard Freeman, who calculated that each billion dollars invested overseas eliminated 26,500 jobs in the United States. "At the end of 1981, U.S. direct foreign investment—not including loans—in third world countries stood at $94.5 billion. In other words, U.S. employers have already exported two and a half million jobs to the Third World."[17]

As the flight of capital from American shores accelerated, the Fighting Machinists took steps to help their own. Reacting to job losses that saw some local lodges, including Local Lodge

1811 of Superior, Arizona, loose one hundred percent of their membership, the union established "Operation Share." Members who still had jobs donated cash to buy food for members across the country, including lodges in Arizona, Pennsylvania, and Minnesota.

In Arizona, a truck loaded with more than 35,000 pounds of food purchased at a Safeway supermarket rolled to Superior, where out of work members from locals 1811, 1634, and 1132 and their families gratefully accepted the help. Once the truck was unloaded, it made another swing to Tempe, where 17,000 more pounds of food were loaded on and delivered to members of local 1357 in Ajo. Similar efforts were underway in Allentown, Pennsylvania, and Minneapolis and St. Paul, Minnesota.

A few truckloads of food wouldn't cure the harm caused by the fundamental changes to the economy, but they demonstrated to everyone in the IAM that they were all in this together.

The May meeting of the IAM Executive Council brought yet more bad news. Wimpy reported that he had met with Harold McClendon, the President of the Bargaining Unit for IAM representatives. McClendon had declined to re-open the agreement to look for possible cost savings. Wimpy said McClendon reluctantly agreed to let the International President review certain elements of the pact but any outright re-negotiation was off the table. Furthermore, the representative's association informed Wimp that they had filed a grievance against the council for its edict that they fly coach and submit all airline tickets for verification.

McClendon did float one proposal that had cost-saving potential. He proposed that the council come up with a package of inducements for early retirements. The council debated the matter for a while but ultimately decided that they were in no financial shape to provide large cash payouts today for cost savings down the road.

The council then spent more time refining the lay-off process. They reviewed "bumping" rights, which would entitle some representatives to return to positions they had held previously, thus dislodging the person who had taken their place. They decided that the cuts would have to go beyond Grand Lodge Representatives, Special Representative and Grand Lodge staff. Now the cuts would include Business Representatives, General Chairmen, and even staff from the Organizing Department. The outlook was bleak indeed.

Wimp was just about tearing out what remained of his hair, trying to keep the IAM afloat. On the one hand, he was looking to the IAM Representatives Association for wiggle room in their agreement, and on the other, he was expounding on the dangers of concessionary bargaining as he wrote in the foreword to a book that would soon be published, *Concessions and How to Beat Them*, by Jane Slaughter.

> *Underlying these objections to concessions bargaining and coziness with capital is another more fundamental one that trade unionists must come to grips with ethically and morally: by what writ and on whose authority do any contemporary trade union leaders or trade union memberships concede and give back gains and benefits that have been achieved and won by the blood, sweat, tears and ingenuity of trade unionists in the past?*
>
> We in the trade unions today do not have the right to give away gains and rights won yesterday. They are not ours to give away. They belong to our heritage and our progeny. Their preservation is progress in times like these.[18] *(Emphasis as written by Winpisinger)*

IAM headquarters in Washington began to look like a ghost town. Offices were shuttered, their contents boxed up, and furniture was beginning to collect dust as the staff joined millions of Americans in unemployment lines.

Wimpy still reported to his office every day that he was in Washington. He showed up between 7:30 and 8:00, he rolled up his sleeves, drank coffee and discussed strategy with George Kourpias, his administrative assistant. He'd usually have lunch at his desk—a hamburger with just mustard and a carton of milk—as he poured over membership numbers, budget items, and organizing reports. Membership was down more than twenty-two percent; 170,900 dues paying members had lost their jobs. Seventy-five percent of the remaining membership worked in manufacturing, where the unemployment rate was higher than in the economy as a whole. Fewer members meant less income, $20 million less per year. The IAM's net worth nosedived, from $29 million when Reagan was elected in 1980 to just under $17 million by the end of 1983.

More bad news reached his office in mid-August when one of the members of his Executive Council, General Vice President Sal Iaccio of New York, succumbed to cancer at the age of sixty-one. Iaccio, the son of an Italian immigrant father, had been the face of the IAM in New York for more than a decade, and had also served as Vice President of the New York State AFL-CIO, and as a delegate to the New York City Central Labor Council.

Wimpy turned to his most trusted aide, George Kourpias, then fifty-one years old, to take Iaccio's place on the Executive Council in those difficult times. He had attempted to elevate Kourpias to the council four years earlier when there had been an opening in the Great Lakes Territory, but couldn't muster the votes. Wimp's original thinking was that Kourpias would move to New York City and occupy the office that had been Iaccio's. He was happy to have his friend and confidant join him on the council, but he was sure going to miss his steady hand and constant companionship at headquarters. Several members of the council picked up on Wimpy's dilemma. They pulled him aside and suggested he send George Poulin, then the Resident Vice President in Washington, to New York and keep Kourpias at headquarters. Wimpy brightened at the idea and made the re-assignment. The union still faced incredibly tough times, but Wimpy would now have his biggest asset close at hand for the fight.

FORTY

LET'S REBUILD AMERICA

All eyes were on Wimpy as the 1984 presidential election year approached. Would he convince Ted Kennedy to make another run, or would he cast his lot with one of the eight other Democrats testing the waters? Kennedy was making no overt moves toward a candidacy and there was a growing sentiment among the members of the AFL-CIO Executive Council that labor would be best served by choosing a candidate early and throwing their combined weight behind him.

Walter "Fritz" Mondale, Jimmy Carter's Vice President and a former Minnesota Senator, was pulling together the most formidable campaign. Other Democrats publicly eyeing a run included Colorado Senator Gary Hart, who was making an appeal directly to the young and liberal elements of the party; Ohio Senator and former astronaut John Glenn, a genuine American hero; former South Dakota Senator and 1972 nominee George McGovern; civil rights activist the Reverend Jesse Jackson; former Florida Governor Ruben Askew; South Carolina Senator Ernest "Fritz" Hollings; and California Senator Alan Cranston.

New York Times political reporter Seth King caught up with Wimpy on the eve of the AFL-CIO Executive Committee's summer 1983 meeting and published their interview as a series of questions and answers on August 4, 1983.

Asked if he thought an early endorsement by the AFL-CIO would benefit a candidate or be "a kiss of death," Wimp was enthusiastic: "I think that potentially there's lots to gain and very little to lose. It's time the labor movement articulated the notion that too often in the past we've had to vote for the lesser of evil choices in a Presidential race. We should try to influence the choice of candidates to get the best possible one before the electorate."[1]

Wimp dodged questions about who that candidate was likely to be, insisting that it was up to the combined memberships of the constituent unions, and that they were being surveyed. When King persisted, Wimpy admitted there was a front-runner, Walter Mondale. King then probed deeper, wondering if Mondale would be liberal enough for Wimp's taste, or if he thought the candidate would have to tack too far to the right.

> I don't see any purpose in trying to out-right the Reaganites nor in moving toward the center. The voters need an alternative. The dangerous trend over the past couple of decades is the conscious effort to pre-empt the center. The Democrats should start thinking in terms of, say, Roosevelt versus Landon, so voters have some chance, when they cast their ballots, of knowing where the country is going in the next four years. I think the Democrat who does something dramatically different than what has been done in the past has a chance of being elected.[2]

King then succeeded in getting Wimp to rate the field in terms of their appeal to him as a dyed in the wool liberal:

> Mondale is probably further out in terms of a program than any of the others. Cranston has some proposals, particularly arms control. But I don't have a feeling about the others. John Glenn has produced very little to date. And he doesn't have a reputation or voting record in the Senate to inspire my confidence that he's willing to stride out on that side of the political spectrum where I think we ought to go. Senator Hart has certainly swerved right since he was George

McGovern's campaign manager. And I suspect that's why they're running well back in the polls.[3]

Wimpy and the IAM may not have firmly settled on a candidate yet, but they had a platform. It was called "Rebuilding America." The idea and term first surfaced at the IAM Legislative Conference in January 1981, and by 1984, it was fully formed and presented to the world as both a book (*Let's Rebuild America*), an eight-act legislative proposal and a "Technology Bill of Rights."

The legislative package included bills to define corporate responsibility, promote domestic investment and production planning, regulate foreign trade, reform pension systems, coordinate investment strategies, rebuild the country's infrastructure, particularly in the inner cities, refine labor laws, develop a rational energy policy, and revamp the tax system.

The massive project of pulling these comprehensive proposals together was coordinated by Dick Greenwood, Wimpy's Special Assistant, and resident intellectual. In addition to a phalanx of more than two dozen IAM staffers, Greenwood turned to many of the outside groups Wimpy had been courting for the past decade to help draft the program. Robert Brandon of the Citizens / Labor Energy Coalition contributed the gas and oil segments. Vic Reinemer of the American Public Power Association helped with the electric grid component. Bob McIntyre of Citizens for Tax Justice pitched in for the tax policy. Randy Barber of the Center for Economic Organizing helped with pension investment strategies.

Wimpy also brought in intellectual leaders John Kenneth Galbraith, Michael Harrington, and Robert Lekachman to form a sort of mini-think tank and coordinate the efforts of a broader group of public thinkers and policy makers. They included Marian Anderson, Ira Magaziner, Harley Shaiken, Lester Thurow, and Joel Yudkin.

The campaign to rebuild America was going to be Wimp's blueprint for how to fix a country he felt was almost beyond repair. As he had done in so many other endeavors, Wimpy would orchestrate a vast network of disparate interests. At a briefing for the IAM Executive Council, Greenwood rolled out the 236-page economic and political manifesto, which was a framework to restructure the nation's economy along social democratic lines.

Wimpy then took to the road, promoting *Let's Rebuild America* at every stop he made across the continent.

"First, we foresaw, correctly, that the advent of the Reagan Administration was going to mean economic and social disaster on a scale not seen since the Great Depression Era" he said in a cover letter introducing the package.

Speaking to the Industrial Union Department of the AFL-CIO's legislative conference, he expanded on that theme.

> *It's time to put the nation's welfare ahead of corporate profits. The only way we're going to restore the American Dream is to come up with a trade union economic alternative that our employers and our politicians can't ignore. They are restructuring our jobs, our workplaces and our lives. We want to construct the framework on which to build a political economy founded on the values of peace and prosperity, not war and poverty.*[4]

Meanwhile, the AFL-CIO endorsement process was moving forward. Gerald W. McEntee, the youthful President of the AFSCME, urged that affiliate unions swear off independent endorsements of candidates in favor of action by the federation. The executive council embraced McEntee's idea, but Glenn Watts, President of the Communications Workers of America, looking squarely at Wimpy, warned against "mustangs" who went their own way with candidate endorsements. There was a palpable tension in the room as members of the executive council waited to see how the often incendiary leader of the Machinists Union would respond. Wimpy simply grinned at Watts, promised to behave this time, and said he would toe the federation line. With that, everyone in the room, including the unions that had refused to endorse Carter, quickly committed to abide by the federations' decision.

Lane Kirkland, the AFL-CIO President, arranged a series of get to know the candidate meetings for the executive council. John Glenn and Gary Hart got polite but unenthusiastic receptions. Alan Cranston was unable to make his session because of a Senate scheduling conflict. Kirkland told the council they already knew all they needed to about Fritz Mondale, but announced he would welcome an appearance by any Republican willing to challenge Reagan for the party's nomination. None took him up on the offer.

By December 1983, the council made its decision. Mondale would be their horse for 1984, and he'd have their undivided support from the Iowa caucuses to the final day of the fall campaign.

The economy and economic opportunity would be a central theme for Mondale's campaign. Reagan was touting what he termed an economic "recovery" but the devastation of the manufacturing sector was so severe that it was hard for IAM members to believe things were improving. But in February 1984, General Secretary Treasurer Gene Glover was able to report that the union's financial picture was improving. Things had finally bottomed out. The combination of staff reductions and strategic reinvestment of the union's cash assets had brought spending into line with revenue for the first time in more than three years. Perhaps there was light at the end of the long dark tunnel.

Just as US membership figures started a gradual upswing, another crisis erupted that threatened to sink the union. Mike Rygus, the General Vice President for the Canadian Territory, informed the executive council that the Canadians wanted out. They wanted to form their own union independent of the IAM. Rygus' move followed a trend of other Canadian segments of large American unions bolting because they wanted autonomy. The moves were also fueled by the belief that they had a better chance for economic survival if they could uncouple their fortunes from those of their financially burdened brothers and sisters south of the border. Some of the other Canadian unions, including the United Auto Workers, had been successful in their succession. George Kourpias remembered that Mike Rygus came to the IAM Executive Council and said that things were not well in Canada and that the membership there wanted out of the IAM.

George Kourpias:

> He said we should consider just letting them go. Wimp said, "Nobody's leaving this union. If anybody in Canada wants to leave they can, but they've got to understand they're not going to get a portion of our strike fund to take with them."
>
> The strike fund was a big thing. If they're going to set up their own union in Canada, a national union, then we were not going to help them.
>
> That was an all afternoon discussion. We broke for dinner and Wimp met with Mike [Rygus] privately and told him it wasn't going to happen. Mike said, "I'm quitting. I'm resigning." So we finished dinner and came back. Wimp told the council that General Vice President Rygus has an announcement to make. Mike said, "I'm resigning. I believe the situation in

*Canada is not well. If this council does not want to
take the proper action, then I'm out."*

*Wimp accepted his resignation and said to him,
"Well, who do you recommend?" [for GVP] Rygus
said, "The only guy I can think of is Val Bourgeois." Val
was Mike's administrative assistant. So Wimp asked,
"Do you think he'd make a good vice president?" And
Mike said, "Yeah." Wimp said, "Let's go call him." The
council agreed, if Val would accept.*

*Val didn't know a damned thing. Val said, "Yes,"
shocked.*[5]

Suddenly, the fifty-two-year-old Bourgeois, a thirty-two-
year member of the IAM from Local Lodge 594 in Moncton,
New Brunswick, was thrust into the highest level of leadership
of the IAM. Bourgeois was a railroader by trade, who had
joined the union while employed on the Canadian National
Railroad. He was the father of six children and a music
devotee who played the euphonium in a marching band. The
skills he learned herding six rambunctious kids and keeping a
top flight marching band in tune would serve him well in his
new post.

Mondale became the instant front runner as the AFL-CIO's
candidate. One of his first stops on the campaign trail was a
meeting in St. Louis of the IAM's District 9, where he drew
rousing applause for his attacks on Reganomics and his pledge
to provide jobs for the millions currently out of work. Rallies
were quickly arranged with the help of the IAM and other
AFL-CIO unions in Boston, Des Moines, Miami, Chicago, New
York City, and Dallas.

In early 1984, Ohio Senator John Glenn appeared to be
running second to Mondale. Glenn was making an unabashed

pitch to centrist and right-leaning Democrats, trying to reclaim the "Reagan Democrats" who had bolted in 1980. Colorado Senator Gary Hart tried a different approach, reaching out to young, educated Democrats, pledging a "new way" for the party. Civil rights activist Jesse Jackson was galvanizing minority voters, particularly African Americans, and George McGovern, the old liberal war horse from South Dakota, was pulling at the heart strings of aging hippies and baby boomers who had fueled his 1972 run.

Mondale, from neighboring Minnesota, managed a commanding victory in the Iowa caucuses. Hart finished a surprisingly strong second, with McGovern tight on his heels. The big surprise was John Glenn's fourth place finish. He had not spent much time organizing in the Hawkeye State, relying instead on heavy spending on television advertisements and paid telephone banks. Quizzed in Boston about what the poor showing meant to his candidacy, Glenn said he looked forward to the more populous New Hampshire primary a week later, which he claimed would be free of "outside influences," a veiled condemnation of the strong labor support Mondale had enjoyed in Iowa.[6]

It was snowing and twenty-four degrees the following Tuesday as voters trudged to the polls in the nation's first primary. CBS News and The New York Times did exit polling, interviewing 1,278 voters as they left the booth. Their data and the final vote tally would reshape the rest of the 1984 race. Gary Hart pulled out a stunning upset, beating Mondale forty-one percent to twenty-nine percent. John Glenn, who had been crafting his message to attract independent voters, finished with only thirteen percent of the vote.

The cause of Mondale's defeat, as revealed in the exit polling, sent shockwaves through his campaign. Half the voters surveyed said Mondale was "too close to organized labor."

Only one out of three voters questioned did not fault him for what he had proudly thought was one of his biggest assets.

"The Mondale people did all they should have done," said Jeanne Shaheen, Hart's New Hampshire coordinator. "The problem he's got is the problem he's had all along. It's that people aren't excited about him. But Hart's crowds have been excited all week long. We've had him all over the state and he's been mobbed."[7]

Two weeks later, voters in five more primary states weighed in. Hart took Massachusetts, Rhode Island, and Florida, while Mondale pulled out victories in Alabama and Georgia, and Jesse Jackson, benefiting from a heavy turnout among African-Americans, ran much stronger than expected in both states. Disheartened with a third place finish in Massachusetts, one of the two districts he had carried in the 1972 general election, McGovern quit. John Glenn, whose campaign was more than $2 million in debt, kept finishing no better than third, prompting his campaign staff to begin publicly urging him to drop out.

When all the votes were tallied, Mondale led with of 292 delegates to Hart's 198. Jackson had thirty-five, Glenn thirty-four, McGovern twenty, and 133 were uncommitted. There was still a long way to go to get to the magic number of 1,967 delegates needed to clinch the nomination.

A week later in Illinois, benefiting from labor's loyalty and muscle, Mondale bounced back from a six point deficit in public opinion polls to beat Hart forty-one percent to thirty-six percent. Jackson pulled nineteen percent, almost all from predominantly African-American wards in Chicago. Hart stumbled by accusing Mondale of dirty campaigning for having run a television commercial calling his credibility into question regarding a change in his signature and date of birth on some official documents. The only problem was that no such television commercial had aired. Hart also looked weak and foolish when he pledged to take down one of his television commercials, attacking Mondale for being too close to Democratic Alderman Edward "Fast Eddie" Vrdolyak, only to have those commercials continue to air. Mondale whacked him for the miscue, saying that if he couldn't control the advertising in his own campaign he wasn't qualified to be President.

The campaign got personal, bitter, and biting. At a debate in Atlanta in March, Mondale mocked Hart's "New ideas for a new generation" theme by asking "Where's the beef?" mimicking a popular television commercial of the day. Hart chided Mondale at every turn for being beholden to old line "special interests," by which he meant organized labor. Hart managed a win in Connecticut the week after Illinois, setting up a major showdown for New York's April 3 primary. All week they traded blows like heavyweight fighters, and Mondale trounced Hart in New York forty-five percent to twenty-seven percent, with Jesse Jackson taking twenty-five percent. With strong labor support, Mondale captured 137 delegates to Hart's seventy-six, giving him 946 on his way to the nomination.

Pennsylvania, where unemployment stood at nine percent because of the loss of manufacturing jobs, was the next crucial test. The IAM and organized labor were geared up and itching for a fight. Mondale beat Hart forty-six percent to thirty-four percent, with Jackson again capturing the majority of the African American vote. Exit polls showed that Mondale got a full fifty percent of his vote from union households, higher than the forty-eight in New York or the forty-six percent in Illinois. Mondale headed into Ohio's May 8 primary with 1,321 delegates to Hart's 746.

Hart eked out a narrow victory in Ohio, helped by Glenn's supporters who cast aside their philosophical differences with the Colorado liberal to give a thumping to Mondale, whom they viewed as having beaten their guy for front-runner status. Exit polls showed that while Mondale still managed to carry union households, it was by a smaller margin than he had in

Pennsylvania, Illinois, or New York. Voters also told pollsters that they had misgivings about the power of organized labor.

Mondale managed to win in Maryland and North Carolina that same day, while Hart took Indiana and his home state. With three weeks remaining, all eyes were on June 5, when California, New Jersey, New Mexico, South Dakota, and West Virginia would vote. Mondale needed only 245.5 more delegates to close the deal. He won in New Jersey and West Virginia outright, and finished close enough elsewhere to put him over the top. Hart took California by a slim margin, where exit polls again showed voters harbored strong anti-union feelings.

Mondale emerged from the primaries with enough delegates for the nomination in no small part due to the strength of his union support, but the image of organized labor was so poor, even among Democrats, that his supporters knew it could be a real liability.

It was ironic, even tragic, that labor's tarnished image was largely the result of the Teamster's seedy reputation and they were not even part of the AFL-CIO federation at the time. Even more ironic is that the Teamster's, a fierce enemy of the IAM, had endorsed Reagan in 1980 and were set to do so again in 1984. Their already vile reputation suffered another blow the day after the California primary, when the *Los Angeles Times* reported that the union's $491,056 a year International President, Jackie Presser, was an FBI informant against the mob:

The *Times*:

> Teamsters union president Jackie Presser, the target of a federal corruption investigation in Cleveland, has been an informer for the FBI since the 1970's, according to current and former federal law enforcement officials. Presser's cooperation with the FBI, considered rare for a high ranking official

of the scandal-plagued union, is believed to have complicated a Justice Department decision on whether to seek his indictment by a grand jury. That decision was considered sensitive because Presser has been virtually alone among major labor leaders in his political support for President Reagan.[8]

There was an endless stream of coincidences. Presser and Wimpy both were from Cleveland, and ran two of the biggest labor unions in the country. Wimpy had gotten his first assignment working as the point man on a joint organizing campaign with the IBT until they had been bounced out of the AFL-CIO for corruption, in a effort spearheaded by Al Hayes, the President of the IAM. Now the IBT was the most persistent adversary of the IAM, attempting, almost always unsuccessfully, to raid its members in jurisdiction after jurisdiction. Now the kid from Cleveland's West Side, Winpisinger, was recognized far and wide as a straight shooter and an intellectual powerhouse, while Presser, the East Side kid, was exposed as a fat, corrupt, snitch.

Asked for a reaction to the *Times* story, Wimpy said, "He'll have to go to work in a bullet proof limousine. I don't know anyone who respects a stool pigeon, either in our out of the trade union movement."[9]

Wimpy, who was more acutely aware than anyone of how the media fed the public's distrust of the labor movement, could only shake his head in wonder at this latest turn of events.

FORTY-ONE

OFF TO THE RACES

The presidential election wasn't the only race the IAM was involved in that year. In 1984, the union's Championship Auto Racing Team's car finished tenth at the Indianapolis 500. The IAM team ended the year in thirteenth place in total points among race teams at that elite level. The program Wimpy started nine years earlier had blossomed into a full-fledged professional racing operation.

Wimpy had so much fun at the first Indy race he attended that he combined his passion for the sport with his never ending desire to make the Machinists Union better known. He convinced the IAM Executive Council to sponsor two cash awards to be given out starting with the 1977 race at the Brickyard. From then on, the top mechanic of the winning car received a large IAM trophy and a check for $5,000. The chief mechanic of the car winning the pole position was awarded $1,000. And the IAM also gave $5,000 and a large silver trophy to the team that amassed the most points throughout the season and won the United States Auto Club Championship. That trophy remained on permanent display at the Indianapolis Speedway's Hall of Fame Museum.

Wimpy wasn't satisfied with just recognizing the accomplishments of others. He talked the council into sponsoring a 150-mile race at the Trenton International Speedway, to be carried live on CBS-TV on September 24, 1977. The race, called the Machinists Union 150, had twenty-eight sleek Indy cars entered. Hundreds of IAM members and their families bought discounted tickets and crowded into the speedway to see the cars roar around the track at speeds approaching 200 miles per hour in the qualifying events. But the weather didn't cooperate and race day was marred by heavy rain and deep disappointment. A dismayed Wimpy and USAC officials called off the contest.

In 1977, the IAM gave out $15,000 in prize money in nine races and for the championship. Many of the cars on the USAC circuit began sporting the Machinists Union's red, white, and blue decal.

The next year, Mario Andretti won the 1978 Machinists 150 in front of 18,000 people and a national television audience. This was a dramatic way for Wimpy to call the sporting public's attention to the work of the 120,000 auto and truck mechanics represented by the IAM. In fact, he had racing fever. The cash awards and the race sponsorship got all sorts of public notice for the IAM. They also put the old Cleveland grease monkey in the pits, where he could hear the roar of the engines, smell the high octane racing fuel, and feel the adrenaline pumping. He began to dream again. As the number two spectator sport in the country, with the cars as stars, Wimpy wanted the IAM to have a car of its own.

It was a pivotal period in racing. Indy cars were still the biggest attraction to race fans, but the National Association for Stock Car Racing (NASCAR) was gaining more popularity every year. The NASCAR vehicles *looked* like the cars people drove on the street, something that could not be said for the open-wheeled, rocket-like Indy cars.

Phil Zannella, Jr. remembered sitting in his parent's living room around that time discussing racing with Wimpy, "Wimpy asked me, 'if you had to put our banner on racing, which would you pick, NACAR or Indy?' I said, 'well, Wimp, personally, the cars people can relate to are NASCAR.' He said, 'You know, I agree with that, but the problem is it's stuck in the mud of the Southeast United States.' He said he'd done some checking and the number one spectator sport at the time was horse racing. And he said, 'There's no god damn way I'm putting our logo on the ass of a horse!'"[1]

Don Wharton remembered how much Wimpy loved racing.

> Long before we had a car he'd go to the Indy races. He liked the Indy's better than he did NASCAR. He became friends with Roger Penske, who was big in the racing field. They got to be friends, first of all because we had his dad's dealerships in California organized, and Penske liked him. We would go to Indy every year and normally go out and have dinner with Penske early in the month of May when there were time trials. Finally he decided to see what we could do.[2]

The IAM's first foray onto the track came in 1978, when they sponsored a car driven by thirty-seven-year-old Jerry Karl of Manchester, Pennsylvania. Karl had driven in the Indianapolis 500 in 1973, 1974, and 1975, but hadn't qualified for the past two years. Bud Melvin's memories were that the IAM sponsored a car with Jerry Karl as the driver.

> That was our first year. The mechanic was a union member from United Airlines. We were doing the racing circuit, we went back to Indianapolis, and we qualified last or next to last [actually twenty-eighth out of thirty-two]. It was a real makeshift operation. This mechanic had the engines. The car we had wasn't fast enough. So Jerry Karl had a McLaren car and they put an engine that a Machinist union mechanic owned in that car and qualified it, which is quite a thing to do at Indianapolis, really, your first time out. But we qualified. We ran the car. It's an older car and its going slower and slower and slower. We finished fourteenth. We were the last car of the

ones that were still running, and we were twenty-four laps behind the winner. What had happened was the intake manifold—metal fatigue had taken over and it had cracked open. They put rubber hoses around it to keep it from leaking. When we got the car in, the oil cooler was hanging by the hoses, it had broken loose. If we'd have gone any faster, we'd have broken apart altogether. But anyhow, we finished.[3]

The IAM team took home $20,930 in prize money for the race, a far cry from winner Al Unser's $290,364, but not bad for a rookie operation. Wimp's first season on the Indy circuit was less than stellar, but it whetted his appetite for more. He decided the union should quit messing around with hand-me-down cars that were old, slow and broke down. They should build their own car.

The 1978 season was a turning point in Indy car racing. Upset with what was widely regarded as poor management of the United States Auto Club, driver Dan Gurney wrote what became known as "The Gurney White Paper," outlining a laundry list of complaints. He claimed the USAC did a lousy job of promotion, offered purses that were too small for what was at stake, and was inconsistent and arbitrary in its enforcement of the rules of competition. The USAC reviewed Gurney's report and told him to get lost. A majority of car owners and drivers agreed, however, with the points Gurney was making and by the beginning of the 1979 racing season, Gurney, Roger Penske and Pat Patrick, all owners of Indy cars, split from the USAC and formed a new sanctioning body known as Championship Auto Racing Teams, or CART. The IAM would follow Penske's lead and race in the new league.

Wimpy took his idea for an IAM-built race car to the Executive Council at their January 1979 meeting. After considerable cajoling, he convinced them to put up $30,000 to get the new car program going. He hired a group from Tucson called Arizona Racing Associates (ARA) to build it. The owners of the group were Phil Threshie, a twenty-six year old driver who had raced twice at Indianapolis, and Chuck Looper, an experienced chief mechanic who had run Dan Gurney's championship Can-Am team, as well as the Lindsay Hopkins and Russ Polak teams. ARA joined the union and all personnel working on the new race car were members.

Wimpy reported to the Executive Council at their September 1979, meeting that plans for the new race car were moving forward. He told them he was trying to get either Ford or Chevrolet to give them a deal on stock-block engines, which sold for about $10,000 each, a far cry from the $40,000 that teams were paying for the turbo-charged Cosworth engines that dominated the Indy circuit. Looper developed a blueprint for a car that he called "evolutionary rather than revolutionary." He explained that "Aerodynamics is the major concern in its design. Airflow will be utilized to induce downforce wherever possible. Removable side pods will carry the radiator's and exhaust air to a rear venturi area. Front suspension will be conventional but the car will be carried on A-arms to ease the ducting of air from under the chassis."[4]

Keith Randol, an IAM member who was a mechanic on United Airlines in Portland, Oregon, was charged with developing the motor, a stock block Chevrolet. Randol used Donovan aluminum blocks and Brodix aluminum cylinder heads to keep the power plant as light as possible, hoping to compete with the turbo-charged Cosworths. To hedge their bets, Looper and Randol designed the car to accept either the custom engine or the more conventional Cosworth.

By November 1979, the car was getting ready to roll. Wimp's goal was that it be ready in time to qualify for the 1980 race at Indianapolis. He wheedled another $150,000 out of the council at their November meeting, above the original $30,000 and another $70,000 spent since then.

As the 1980 racing season was about to kick off, Wimpy reported to the council that the buildup of horsepower for the new engine was "exceptional." Andy Kenopensky, the IAM Automotive Coordinator who had spent twenty-eight years as the Business Representative for one of the union's largest automotive lodges, was tapped to oversee the racing program. In addition to Looper and Threshie, the team included Threshie's wife, Leslie, mechanic Phil Weider, and machinist / mechanics Howard and Anita Millican. The IAM team was unusual in that all were union members and because Anita Millican was one of a very few female race mechanics in the history of the Indy racing circuit.

The IAM race team got off to a rough start that year. Scrambling to get the car ready to enter the Indianapolis 500 on May 24, the shipping company that was transporting the car's new transmission from Los Angeles to Indianapolis dropped the crate and damaged it beyond repair. Penske's team came to the rescue and loaned the IAM team a used transmission from one of its cars, but Threshie failed to qualify at the time trials.

They did manage to get the car on the track and qualified for races at Milwaukee for the Rex Mays 150 and at Long Pond, Pennsylvania, for the Pocono 500.

The crew from Arizona was dumped after a season that *The Machinist* described as "…an experimental season managed by Arizona Racing Associates that failed to produce tangible results in either racing car design or competitive ability."[5]

Howard Millican was promoted to chief mechanic, and Larry Dickson, a forty-three-year-old veteran driver from Marietta, Ohio, was put behind the wheel. Dickson had been racing at Indianapolis since 1966, and had managed a ninth place finish in 1969.

Wimpy informed the Council at their January 1981, meeting that the racing team had purchased a car from the Penske racing team. The deal included two engines and a parts package. The car was a sleek, gleaming Penske P-C-7, powered by a Cosworth / Ford racing engine that turned 10,200 rpm's and delivered 700 horsepower. Unlike the car the union had raced the year before, the new model was capable of reaching an eye popping top speed of 230 miles per hour.

The team also purchased a Kenworth tractor and a Budd trailer to haul the race car around the country. "Machinists Union Racing Team" was stenciled on its side in 10-foot high letters. The IAM Communications Department produced a film about the racing program called *The Underdog*, and showed it at the IAM Automotive Conference. But had the IAM waited another year, the producers might have given the film another name. In 1981, for the first time, the IAM was moving up from the back of the Indy circuit pack to run with the big boys.

The race car program proved controversial with some members who thought it an extravagant waste of dues dollars. Others found it exhilarating. Voluntary contributions to the program flowed in from lodges around the country. Members bought IAM Race Team jackets, hats, t-shirts, and patches. Whenever the car made appearances at big races, the team would take it first to the nearest local lodge and put it on display. In the fall of 1981, the car was in California to race in the *Los Angeles Times* California 500. The race team showed up a few days early and displayed the sleek red, white and blue "Machinists Union Special" at Local 1980's headquarters in Pomona. Despite a heat wave that drove temperatures above 100 degrees, more than 1,000 members and their families got a close look at the car and met the crew. By race day, the stands were filled with members of Local 1980 and Districts 720 and 120, who took over a section of the raceway and erected a huge banner saying: "Go! Go! Go! Machinists Union Racing Team."

Dickson qualified the car at Indianapolis, starting nineteenth in the field of thirty-three cars. He managed to complete only 165 laps, finishing eighteenth, before a thrown piston forced him out of the race. The team was disappointed at being knocked out of the race but pocketed $30,652 in winnings.

In its first full year running the Penske car, the IAM race team finished fourteenth out of sixty-four CART teams, a very impressive showing. The team won a total of $87,613 in prize money, not nearly enough to break even, but helpful in keeping the program afloat. Wimpy was bursting with pride. "Our car, the only one owned by a union," he said, "symbolizes the skills of IAM members. Just as corporations demonstrate their products through auto racing, we are demonstrating our skills, and the skills of all American workers."[6]

The success the team had enjoyed in 1981 spurred them to try harder in 1982. Dickson was replaced as lead driver by thirty-five-year-old Roger Mears of Wichita, Kansas, older brother of Indy winner Rick Mears. The Mears family was well known throughout the world of auto racing and the tall, handsome new driver was a big attraction for the media. He immediately did his part to promote the IAM. "I'm proud to represent IAM members," he said. "I hope through my racing to deliver IAM's message to many people. Skills like those practiced by IAM members went into building the car I drive."[7]

For the 1982 season, a Penske PC9-B, was purchased that produced 700 horsepower at 10,000 rpm's. Phil Zannella, Jr. proudly displayed the car to millions of people at the Cleveland Auto Show, the Cleveland Autorama, and the city's Home and Flower Show.

Roger Mears qualified the car nineteenth for the Indy 500, a race in which his brother started in the pole position. He got tangled up in a horrible crash at the start of the race, and got knocked out without even completing a lap. Nonetheless, the team pocketed $41,719 for its efforts. Racing analysts began to take notice. The Indianapolis 500 Yearbook proclaimed, "We think the IAM car will have to be reckoned with as a front runner in the very near future."[8] By the end of the 1982 season, that prediction seemed prophetic. Mears and the IAM race team finished in the top ten in seven races and won $184,000. Mears was voted "Most Improved Driver of 1982." His chief mechanic, Dennis McCormack, was voted "Most Improved Chief Mechanic." IAM members were encouraged to purchase seventeen-inch replicas of the race car for $10.00 to show their support for the team.

Wimpy was thrilled by the success of the team and even involved members of his family. Ken Winpisinger remembered: "I was with the team for the better part of a year, maybe a little longer than that. I went with the team to all the races. My father would make most of them, I'd say, it was rare that he didn't show up."[9]

"I went to the Pocono's and I went to the Indy 500," daughter Linda Winpisinger recalled.

> But even after he retired, I remember they used to go to races in the RV and stay in the middle of the pit. My mom enjoyed going to the races-she loved the people, but she hated staying in the pit because there were no plumbing hook-ups. The other thing was that it was fun, too. A lot of times Paul Newman would be at the races, and he actually grew up not far from my dad.[10]

Ken Winpisinger remembered that his parents often went to dinner with Paul Newman "because he was very sympathetic toward a lot of the causes my father was involved with. He was pretty active in different political movements."[11]

Tom Buffenbarger recalled the camaraderie:

We'd take over a whole motel. We'd take over the whole property with all the Machinists folks traveling on busses out from DC. Gary, from Gary's Restaurant, one of Wimp's favorite haunts, did all the cooking for everybody. He'd set up the grills and bring special cuts of meat and everything. It was a lot of fun. One time we were at a race on Sunday morning and the race was going to be run on Monday because it was wet, so the race was postponed. I get a call in my room and it's Wimp. He says, "Want to go get some breakfast?" because we could walk to a Bob Evans restaurant, which was his favorite. Mine too. So I said, "Yeah, let's go over to Bob Evans." So we go over, we have a nice breakfast, chit-chat. We walk back, and there's Phil Zannella in the little common area, kind of like the late for dinner mother, arms folded across his chest, foot tapping. He looked at us and said, "Where the hell have you been?" and Wimp says, "Tommy and I went down to Bob Evans and had breakfast." Phil says, "I told you I was going to go out and get doughnuts for breakfast this morning!" And Wimp says, "What can I say, Phil, I forgot." And Phil says, "That's the problem with you, Wimp, you're *igorant!*" Wimpy said "I'm what?" "*Igorant!*" Phil screamed. Wimpy started laughing so hard I thought he was going to asphyxiate. Those were fun days.[12]

As the race team traveled to events in Milwaukee, Cleveland, Detroit, and a host of other cities, they were met by IAM hospitality tents at each track. Members and their guests were taken on guided tours through the garages and the pit areas and posed for pictures with the drivers.

Mears was joined for the 1983 season by twenty-one-year-old Josele Garza, from Mexico City. Garza had begun racing two years before. He was the 1981 Indy 500 Rookie of The Year, and the youngest driver ever to start at Indy. By May, he supplanted Mears as the top driver and qualified the IAM car eighteenth for the big race. He got knocked out by a nasty oil leak on the sixty-fourth lap, but the payday for their efforts amounted to $59,898.

The purses at Indy kept going up every year, and so did the cost of racing. In 1983, the IAM race team won $268,204 in prize money but fell about $350,000 short of breaking even. Wimpy decided that the IAM would have to find co-sponsors to keep the car on the track. He approached Stroh's Brewery, one of the companies the IAM had under agreement, and the company put up a sizeable amount of money in the name of their Schaefer Beer line. The car, number 55, would now be known as the "Schaefer—Machinists Union Race Car."

As a new car was purchased each season, the old ones were either kept as a back-up or put on display at exhibitions across the country. The IAM printed large color postcards with a picture of the race car on one side and a list of benefits of belonging to the IAM on the other and passed them out by the thousands at auto shows, parades and county fairs.

The 1984 season saw the IAM race team switch from the Penske chassis they had been racing to the British Formula Two March chassis. Garza qualified the car twenty-fourth for the 1984 Indy race, and finished tenth, seven laps behind winner Rick Mears. It was the best finish the team would ever achieve at Indianapolis. That day they won $66,910.

The IAM was racing two cars in most events by the start of the 1985 season. Johnny Parsons, the forty-one-year-old son of 1950 Indy 500 winner Johnnie Parsons, was brought in to drive the second car. Despite a disappointing thirty-first place finish at Indy because of a blown engine on the fifteenth lap, Garza and Parsons were getting closer to the checkered flag. Garza finished just one lap behind Mario Andretti at the Pocono 500, winning $21,523. In the best showing the team would ever post, he came in second to Johnny Rutherford at the Michigan 500, just 1.82 seconds off the pace.

Wimpy was ecstatic at the prospect of finally winning a race. "That's what we've been striving for," he said, "to be in a position to win at the end of a race. We were there, Josele gave it his best shot and we came up just a little short. But when you get to the point where you can win, you know your time is coming."13 Unfortunately, Garza made a near fatal mistake four weeks later at the Mid-Ohio Sports Car Course. He locked wheels with fellow racer Randy Lewis coming out of a turn, leading to a spectacular crash. The Schaefer/Machinists Union Special flew off the track, tore out more than forty feet of guard rail, bounced back onto the raceway, and started pin wheeling end over end down the track, slamming violently into the base of a bridge that crossed the track. The car was completely destroyed. Rescue crews rushing to the scene feared that Garza was dead. Fortunately, the stringent safety requirements of the CART circuit were enough to save his life. The wreck left the young driver with a fractured thigh bone and ended his season prematurely. The IAM team turned to a number of drivers to help finish the 1986 season.

Garza bounced back at the start of the 1987 season, racing the IAM's new March 87C. He finished fifth in the first race of the season, two laps behind winner Mario Andretti, and sixth the following week.

The cost of putting a competitive race car on the track continued to skyrocket. Wimpy had to scramble to find additional sponsors. He convinced the US Tobacco Company to put up a half million dollars to promote their Copenhagen brand. Hardee's restaurants sponsored the car driven by Parsons. The IAM team was costing the union nearly $2 million a year on top of what they brought in from prize money and co-sponsorships. But they were still at a competitive disadvantage to the teams led by Mario Andretti, who was sponsored by Budweiser, or Tom Sneva, who drove for Texaco. Those front running teams were spent upwards of $8 million a year.

The total purse for the Indianapolis 500 in 1978, the first year the Machinists qualified a car, was $1,139,684, with the winner taking home $290,364. By 1990, the final year the IAM had a car in the race (co-sponsored by Hardee's and driven by Pancho Carter, the half-brother of Johnny Parsons), the purse was $6,319,803, and winner Arie Luyendyk took home $1,090,940.

Wimpy pleaded his case time after time that race car program provided the Machinists Union with valuable exposure they couldn't afford to purchase through advertising. By the time he neared retirement age the spiraling costs were making it almost impossible for anyone other than a multi-national corporation to field a successful team.

"That race car was deep in his mind for many years," George Kourpias remembered.

> *Just stop and think: you win a race and you're in there for life. And guess what? People around the country are going to be saying "That's the union for auto mechanics." Our break just didn't come. We came in second. Had the break come, we would be racing today.*
>
> *When Wimp's term was about over and we were spending $2 million a year, and still losing a lot of members, he and I had several small discussions about the car. One day he came into my office and said, "George, I want you to do me a favor. Give me a memorandum that you want me to conduct a very thorough look at the race car and that you would like my opinion as to its cost and value." He was trying to take the burden of canceling the program off my shoulders. So I gave him a very thorough memorandum stating that we needed to assess what we'd accomplished, and what it had cost. He*

responded with his own memorandum stating that in his opinion, the cost was beyond us being able to continue racing. It was his recommendation that we get out. That's the type of man he was, I could have taken over as president and killed the program and it would have come down hard on me, because as the years went on, the union loved it. Monday mornings they would look to see what standing we were in. The race car was a great source of pride for our union.[14]

FORTY-TWO

DEFENDING PROGRESS

The cost of the racing program wasn't the only controversy facing Wimpy as the union met in Seattle for the 1984 convention. Delegates were grumbling about the cost of the Lear Jet and the new Placid Harbor training center. Another move was afoot to gain greater autonomy for the Canadian membership by changing the IAM constitution so that there would be a Canadian General Vice President elected solely by the Canadian members. The always volatile question of the per capita tax would also get a thorough airing.

The convention theme was "The Voice That Counts." Wimpy wasted no time using his voice to get out in front on the hot button issues. He began his opening speech by imploring members to remain united across the US - Canada border:

> *Right up front, let it be understood that within the IAM, Canada and the United States are indivisible. The interrelationship of our economies transcends narrow nationalism. When the one may sneeze, the other is sure to catch a cold, and no boundary can protect one from the other, nor must it ever be permitted to divide our strength or fracture our unity. We must ensure that no cunning employer or callous government can pit us against ourselves and thereby break the bonds of brotherhood and sisterhood, of camaraderie and trust, or of international solidarity.*[1]

Wimpy didn't shy away from any of the controversies on the agenda. He knew as well as any of the delegates that times had been tough. It was disconcerting to see money spent on anything but the barest of necessities as members lost their jobs. He truly believed, though, that his program was putting the IAM on the map and that he could sell that notion to a skeptical convention. After reviewing the trials and tribulations of the past few years—and laying most of the blame at Reagan's feet—he said that even though there had had to be some cuts, he would be, "damned if we were going to go out of business, even in part. We decided against going into a coward's crouch at either Grand Lodge or in the territorial offices, and scrap a solid program designed to prepare us for the rest of this decade and the next century."[2]

He let it be known that he felt their pain:

> We agonized, empathized and sympathized with those who have suffered the hardships and borne the brunt of the sacrifices made necessary by Mr. Reagan's economic war on families and workers.
>
> We know the anguish of powerlessness, the paralysis of frustration and the anger that arises out of fear. Each of us on the Executive Council has, at one time or another, ranted, raved and scapegoated.
>
> Given my volatile nature, I probably indulged in that behavior more than anyone else. Venting spleen and scapegoating are quite human reactions, after all. Facing unemployment and the perils of economic decline is a little like facing death. First, there's denial, then anger, then bargaining, and finally, acceptance. We've had to accept the harsh fact that we are not the relatively plush organization we once were.[3]

He spoke directly about his coveted programs:

Placid Harbor must become the brain cell and skill center where we can provide our staff, business representatives, financial secretaries, stewards and organizers with the mental and manual tools they need to survive and prevail in this so-called new international economic order.

Corporate employers have fleets of jets and the President of the United States has Air Force One. The best way I can compete for our member's attention and respect is through personal contact, and you can't get that with me sitting on my duff in Washington.

As anyone who has flown in it or seen it knows, it's not a luxury liner, and any time we have two or more seats occupied, which is regularly, we are breaking even in costs versus regular commercial air travel.

This brings us to the last object of some dissent and ire—the IAM race team program. The race team is a traveling billboard and skill exhibition all wrapped into one. Sure, we had to subsidize it to get it going and to move up in Indy car class and stay there. But in four short years we've made our mark on the circuit and we've done well enough in the standings these past three years…to gain the prestige needed to attract high-priced advertisers and sponsors, and to get some our employers to contribute to its cost and operation. Volunteer contributions from our members are picking up each year, too."

Put these three programs together, our Placid Harbor Education Center, the Lear jet and the race team, and we have the basic tools required to penetrate the shroud of ignorance and prejudice that pervades contemporary public opinion, with respect to the purposes, missions and visions of the trade union movement. Combined, these three programs permit us to attack anti-unionism on a broad front.

And we can do it with mobility, speed and substance.

Strip this organization of that arsenal of communication tools and it will be consigned to a relic of the past. We will go the way of the Coopers Union, the Horseshoe and the Shoemakers. At best, it would be like matching corporate America's vast tool crib with dime store tools. At worst, it would be competing for survival and growth in our supersonic and microelectronic world with a telephone, a handcar and the United States Postal Service.[4]

Wimpy knew he had a fight on his hands to preserve those communications tools. He pulled out all the stops to win. The second afternoon of the convention, Tuesday, September 18, he opened with a video featuring actor Ed Asner extolling his leadership and explaining the purposes and uses of the race car program and the Lear Jet. As the film concluded and the lights were still off, Asner began a long walk up the main isle from the back of the hall to the stage, bathed in the soft glow of a spotlight. The applause for the popular figure grew louder and louder as he shook hands and exchanged high five's with delegates on his way to the podium where he wrapped Wimpy in a big bear hug.

After an emotional personal appeal by Asner, Wimpy had another film to show, this one featuring actor Cliff Robertson, entitled: "The Voice That Counts." It outlined the many benefits the IAM's new Placid Harbor Education Center.

Once the lights were back up and the celebrities had cleared the building, the Law Committee put forth the first resolution of the convention. Resolution number 21, sponsored by Local Lodge 1786 of Webster, Texas, called for the abolition of the race car program, the sale of the jet and Placid Harbor, and a reduction in salary for all officers of the union. The resolution called the jet "a prestigious extravagance." The race car was "a liability to the majority of members and a waste of money." It claimed that Placid Harbor "fails to benefit the majority of IAM members whose dues paid for it."

Not surprisingly, the Law Committee recommended non-concurrence with the resolution. A parade of speakers made their way to the microphones to defend Wimpy's programs. Delegates acknowledged that times had been tough. But speaker after speaker talked of the union's pride and how the race car, airplane and training center were integral to that. After about a half hour of speechmaking, delegate D. R. Meinell of Local Lodge 777 moved the question. Wimpy stood at the podium, looked out at the crowd and called for a voice vote. An overwhelming roar went up in favor of the Law Committee's recommendation. That was followed by a scattering of "nay" votes. Wimpy declared the matter settled. He had won this battle. The next major one took place the following afternoon. Proposition 3 called for: "Eight American Vice Presidents nominated and elected by the membership they represent and one Canadian Vice President nominated and elected by the Canadian members."

The Law Committee recommended non-concurrence—a "no" vote, really - and the debate was on. Delegate C. Peretti of Local Lodge 2323 in Ontario pulled out a sheaf of papers he claimed were from the *Collier Encyclopedia* and read the definition of "territory," as "a term applied in the United States of America to an area similar to a State of the Union but not having the independent position of one." He then pointed out that Canada was a free country, not at all a subsidiary jurisdiction of the USA.

Delegate Dave Ritchie of Local Lodge 1755, Toronto, the main proponent of the proposition, spoke next and made clear that this proposal was not an attempt to secede from the IAM. "We are not for a separation of this great organization, the greatest organization in the world," he said, "because we are proud to be members of the International Association of Machinists and Aerospace Workers. However, what we are asking for is the right to elect the only member of the Executive Council which we as Canadians can have on that Board of General Vice Presidents."[5]

After more than two hours of debate, Wimpy called for a show of hands. The room seemed almost evenly divided. "The chair is very much in doubt," he conceded. Wimpy called for a "division of the house" or a standing vote. The Law Committee's recommendation against the motion carried 878 to 795. Delegate Szabo of Local Lodge 962 asked for a roll call. Wimpy asked for a show of hands in favor of a roll call vote, and 591 hands shot up, more than enough to set the vote in motion. General Secretary Treasurer Glover then proceed to call the roll. After more than an hour of voting and tabulating, the results were finally in hand.

Dave Ritchie rose, asked to be recognized for a point of personal privilege, and spoke briefly:

> *Brothers and sisters, we have not heard the results of this vote but in fact you have seen democracy in action. We have all had the opportunity to exercise our rights, whichever way this goes and I have a good feeling, even though it may not go the way I want. However, whatever way it goes, that is what this union and democracy are all about.[6]*

Wimpy answered, "This has been a long and hotly debated and emotional issue and I compliment you, my brothers and sisters from Canada on the way that you have conducted yourselves here this afternoon."[7]

The Law Committee's recommendation to deny the motion to change the IAM constitution for the specific election of a Canadian General Vice President was affirmed by a vote of 3,467 to 2,677.

With the two biggest bones of contention settled, the tensions in the atmosphere eased considerably. Fritz Mondale's appearance the following morning did little to disrupt the tranquility. The Democratic Presidential nominee was a lackluster orator with a flat Minnesota accent and a stolid style of delivery. Wimpy did his usual job of whipping the crowd into a near frenzy with his introduction, and the delegates did their best with loud whistles, a screaming siren and the tolling of the convention bell. The tall lean former Vice President just could not light up the room. His speech was a statistics-laden attack on Reagan for having no plan to move America forward. Playing off his successful gambit against Gary Hart in the primaries, where he asked, "Where's the beef?" this IAM convention speech was a call and response of "Where's the plan?"

He did score some points and tug at a few heart strings with his closing remarks, when he told a story Reagan had used at a dinner the two had attended the previous week. The President spoke of an immigrant Italian family who had arrived in America penniless, worked hard and sent their son to college and medical school. That son of immigrants had saved his life in the operating room when he was shot by John W. Hinckley, Jr..

It turns out that very same son of immigrants, Dr. Giordono, had written an op-ed piece in the *Los Angeles Times* saying that the cuts in social programs Reagan was making will make it impossible for future generations of immigrants to hope for such social progress.

> I tell that story because Mr. Reagan will never understand what Dr. Giordano is saying. There will never be policies under that Administration that understand what the life is like of decent, hard working, self respecting Americans who are doing everything they can to care for themselves and their families, but despite that most Americans every once in a while need a little help. They need a little help.
>
> This election comes down to what kind of people are we? Who are we, the Americans?[8]

The convention voted a unanimous endorsement of Mondale and his running mate forty-eight-year old Geraldine Ferraro, the first woman ever nominated on a major party ticket. Neither Wimpy nor the other political movers and shakers of the IAM invested nearly as much in his campaign as they had for Ted Kennedy in 1980. In fact, Wimpy didn't even take to the stump in the final days of the campaign as he had for Jimmy Carter in 1976.

On Election Day, Mondale took a thumping of McGovern-like proportion. Reagan polled 54,281,858 popular votes to Mondale's 37,457,215, and routed him 525-13 in electoral votes. Mondale took only the District of Columbia and his home state of Minnesota.

Wimpy, while disappointed, was hardly surprised. Speaking at a New Hampshire event two weeks later, he offered his analysis.

> An immensely successful senior citizen resides again in the White House.

Mr. Reagan's triumph was a personal one. He recreated old notions of limited and decentralized government, of genuine competition, of economic opportunity and free enterprise.

Since we, the people, have found it more comfortable to see where we have been than to think of where we are going, our state of mind has increasingly become that of the spectator—the TV viewer. There have been a lot of bad shows since Vietnam, Watergate and the first energy crunch. There's a keen sense of insecurity in the land. If the future seems dark, the past, by contrast, looks rosy.

...Vietnam and Watergate shattered our faith in established academic, business, governmental, media, religious and even trade union institutions.

So Mr. Reagan's trip to the past is right on schedule. History tells us, though, the tragedy is there's going to be many more losers than winners at the end of his voyage, just as there have already been more losers than winners in the first phase of his right wing revolution.[9]

Speaking to Americans for Democratic Action in St. Louis two weeks later, he leveled most of his criticism at Mondale.

The Mondale defeat reflected the failure of his campaign strategy, not rejection of the Democratic Party or its traditional activist role of promoting the interests of working and middle class Americans, and protecting the interests of society's disenfranchised.

In January, the Gallup Poll showed Mondale running even with Reagan. In July, Mondale was running two points ahead of Reagan. Then came the

> *Democratic Convention, and Mr. Mondale decided*
> *to reduce the deficit, balance the budget and raise*
> *taxes.We may have admired his courage and honesty,*
> *but God pity his judgment. It was all down hill from*
> *thereon.*[10]

Wimpy, frustrated by his party's inability to elect a President, was fated to serve the remainder of his term with Republicans controlling the White House.

FORTY-THREE

THE FINAL TERM

Wimpy's electoral success on his own behalf was much better than that of the Democratic presidential candidates he backed. He was re-elected International President of the IAM in 1985, for a term that would bring him to the union's mandatory retirement age of sixty-five. He was nominated by 674 of the 681 local lodges casting votes. His only opposition came from a token candidate from Local Lodge 709 in Marietta, Georgia, who received five nominations, and another from Local Lodge 1114 in Waukegan, Illinois, who managed only two.

With politics in the United States firmly in the grip of the Reagan Administration, Wimpy started paying more attention to the remarkable political transformations that were taking place outside the US. Political actions with significant union backing were bringing about massive changes in Poland, South Africa, Nicaragua, and El Salvador.

In Poland, Lech Walesa, who had led successful strikes against government controlled industries five years earlier, received the 1983 Nobel Peace Prize. His Solidarity Movement now numbered nearly ten million and was publishing approximately 600 weekly union newsletters, widely distributed throughout the country. The IAM had helped supply the presses used to print those newsletters through the International Metalworkers Federation.

Walesa was grateful for the international support: "Years ago it was sufficient for one single enterprise to defend itself. Now, even one country is not able to defend itself. So the solidarity of world labor is even more useful and necessary than ever."[1]

Solidarity and the IAM's help in supplying printing presses through the International Metalworkers Federation were but two of the topics raised in September 1985 when Wimpy led a small delegation to a private meeting with Pope John Paul II. Wimpy was in Europe to address the International Aerospace Conference in Toulouse. Weldon Granger, a young Houston attorney who represented District 19 in legal matters, convinced Wimpy to fly to Italy to present the Pontiff with a specially commissioned bronze sculpture of a dove, celebrating the cooperative relationship between American and Italian labor organizations.

"He knew it was important to me," Weldon Granger remembered. "I said I'd like to commission work from artists, young artists, some of whom are sculptors. I told Wimpy that I'd have a nice piece sculpted and we'd present it to the Pope on behalf of American and Italian labor. It was the Secretary of Labor for Italy who actually helped arrange this audience."[2]

The Pope, born Karol Jozef Wojtyla in Wadowice, Poland, was sixty-five at the time. He had served as Archbishop of Krakow under the Communist régime and was an active supporter of the Solidarity trade movement, which he viewed as a critical step in winning freedom for his native land.

The audience took place at Castel Gandolfo, the Pope's 17th century summer residence located about twenty miles south of Rome in the Alban hills overlooking Lake Albano. Although he had been raised as a Roman Catholic, Wimpy was not a religious man.

"As I remember it, Wimpy started out as a Catholic and became a nothing," George Kourpias recalled. "He always said to me he was probably the only atheist around. For some reason in his life he just had a bad feeling about organized religion."[3]

But despite his reluctance to engage in religious observance, Wimpy expressed great admiration for the leader of the Roman Catholic Church. John Paul II was a man who spoke ten languages fluently and had used the power and prestige of his position to aid the trade unionists in Poland.

Weldon Granger remembered:

> *There were six of us in a side room where we had probably a longer than usual visit. This was considered a private audience when you're not with 10,000 or 100,000 people. We had six people there and the Vatican photographers. I believe we ended up on Rome television news that night. He met us out in an area where this little presenter man in tails comes out and the Pope comes in. Part of the tradition when you go there is that you make an offering. The art work that I had had made for the Pope was a very nice gift, probably worth several thousand dollars, but this little man in tails asked for a contribution. Well, fortunately, I had some cash on me. The Pope, who had worked with labor people in Poland, appreciated Wimpy's position and what he did for working people. He expressed to Wimpy that he was thankful for the gift and mentioned that he was a man who had worked with his hands for years at shipyards in Poland. It was a nice experience. And of course Wimpy, who I would say never favored any particular religion, very graciously accepted nice prayer beads, as we all did, from the Pope. I think he mentioned that he would give them to his mother.[4]*

The struggle in Poland wasn't the only place where people were fighting for freedom and the right to belong to trade unions. In South Africa, the white-minority apartheid government still ruled. Nelson Mandela continued to serve a lengthy prison term. And yet, there were stirrings that would lead to the eventual establishment of a black-majority government with Mandela at its helm. Nearly 1,000,000 black South Africans had joined trade unions. Collective bargaining agreements were popping up in the automotive, light engineering, chemical, transport, and service industries. The government reported that there was an average of one strike a day in South Africa during the first half of the 1980's. This increasingly coordinated ability to bring the South African economy to its knees would ultimately play a pivotal role in reforming the country.

The most volatile situation, however, was in the Central American countries of Nicaragua and El Salvador where there were violent conflicts between local elements of the two sides of the Cold War. Many United States-based multi-national corporations had subsidiaries in the two Latin American countries. They feared leftists would nationalize their operations and seize their assets. They were pressuring the Reagan Administration to provide military and economic support to the right-wing Junta ruling El Salvador and to the rebels fighting the leftist government of Nicaragua as a means of protecting their investments.

In Nicaragua, the brutal right-wing dictatorship of Anastasio Somoza DeBayle had been overthrown in July 1979. It was replaced by a five-member left-wing "Junta of National Reconstruction," headed by thirty-four year old Daniel Ortega. Somoza's much feared National Guard fled the capital and led attacks under the banner of "Contras" against the new leftist régime. "Contras" was short for counterrevolutionaries.

The group, funded in large part by the US CIA, tried to destabilize what they termed "the Marxist government in Managua" by attacking infrastructure targets and by raping, torturing, and killing civilian populations sympathetic to the left-leaning government.

In El Salvador, three months after the Nicaragua coup, a right-wing junta overthrew leader Carlos Humberto Romero in a *coup de etat* that was supported by members of Somoza's National Guard.

The new regime used death squads, rape, torture, and kidnappings to tamp down opposition. The Roman Catholic Archbishop of El Salvador, Oscar Romero, who publicly urged the United States not to provide economic or military aid to the rouge regime, was gunned down while celebrating mass on March 24, 1980. Government-supported death squads then turned on mourners at his funeral, killing forty-two more people. That December, four American nuns in El Salvador were raped and murdered by government supported thugs.

The Contra's murderous activities became too much to bear. The United States Congress passed the Boland Amendment by a vote of 411-0 in December 1982. It prohibited the use of US funds to overthrow the government of Nicaragua. Although Reagan signed the bill, his operatives quietly argued that the measure applied only to *appropriated* funds. Money spent by the National Security Council or other sources would still be secretly used to overthrow the left-wing government.

Still, brutality in El Salvador and Nicaragua continued unabated. By 1985, Reagan, influenced by the corporations and their deliberate distortions, viewed the conflicts in the two countries as direct competition between communism and capitalism. He used every avenue available to him—even some that would prove to be of highly dubious legality—to fund and encourage the Contras.

Once the Boland Amendment passed, the AFL-CIO got dragged into the battle, which exposed a long-standing rift between the conservative and liberal unions of the federation. Naturally, Wimpy was a leader of the left-wing faction. He helped establish the "National Labor Committee in Support of Democracy and Human Rights in El Salvador." Known as the "NLC," it opposed aid to the Contras and urged the federation to adopt a resolution calling for a halt to all efforts to bring down the Nicaraguan government. The presidents of twenty-two other labor unions joined Wimpy, including

Gerald McEntee of AFSCME, Owen Bieber of the UAW, Henry Nicholas of the National Union of Hospital and Health Care Employees, Murray Finlay of the Amalgamated Clothing and Textile Workers Union, and Keith Johnson of the International Woodworkers of America.

Some staunchly anti-communist unions formed their own group to support Reagan's efforts to arm the Contras, called "Friends of the Democratic Center in Central America," known as "Prodemca." That group fell under the AFL-CIO's American Institute for Free Labor Development. Partially funded by per capita dues contributions from AFL-CIO members, AFID received substantial additional funding, estimated at up to ninety-five percent of its total budget - from the US government through the Agency for International Development and the National Endowment for Democracy.[5] Members of Prodemca included Jack Joyce of the Bricklayers Union, William C. Doherty of the AFIC staff, Penn Kemble, Chairman of the Coalition for a Democratic Majority, and Bayard Rustin, President of the A. Philip Randolph Institute.

The two labor groups went head-to-head at the 1985 AFL-CIO convention in Anaheim, California. They finally settled on a compromise resolution that said, "A negotiated settlement, rather than a military victory, holds the best hope" for achieving peace and democracy in Nicaragua and El Salvador.[6] In mid-November, Wimpy toured the two countries with five other labor leaders. He spoke with members of the Sandinista movement and got a first-hand look at the situation on the ground. He was not encouraged by what he saw.

Shortly before he left for Central America Wimpy had hosted a gathering of more than 150 leaders of progressive political groups at Placid Harbor. His aim was to establish a grassroots political network that could rival what he saw as a coordinated right-wing cabal.

He still had a copy of Fred Cook's 1962 article, "The Ultras: Aims, Affiliations and Finances of the Radical Right" in his desk drawer. He had recently read a book that confirmed his belief in the reality of the right-wing conspiracy. John S. Saloma III's *Ominous Politics: The New Conservative Labyrinth,* had so inspired him that he devoted an entire speech to Americans for Democratic Action to it: "Here, in 150 pages, is the most damning evidence of the new right's scheme to overturn America that I have ever read. [It] reveals almost everything I have always believed and sometimes observed about the right wing, but never had the time to research and document."[7]

In his work, Republican Saloma outlined eleven elements of the burgeoning right-wing infrastructure: think tanks and academics and journalists, foundations, political action committees, religious organizations, corporations, conservatives in Congress, the Republican Party, conservatives in the media, purportedly "public interest" law firms, conservative Democrats and libertarians, and black Republicans as the constituent parts of the grand scheme.

Wimpy now had a book, written by a *Republican,* which underscored the beliefs he had held since first reading the Cook article some twenty-three years earlier. He decided it was time for the Left to finally get its act together. He invited a vast array of leaders for a weekend session at the union's Placid Harbor campus on the Maryland shore in October 1985. The group included members of the Senate and House of Representatives, state and local elected officials, executives and staff of the many social action groups with which he was affiliated, political professionals, academics, fellow labor leaders, and public opinion pollsters.

He asked Heather Booth of the Midwest Institute, who had helped him found the Citizen Labor Energy Coalition, to serve as convener. "As you know, we come here for two purposes," Booth said in her opening remarks. "First is to focus our efforts and generate resources to support the building of grass roots organizations that can raise issues and provide political machinery to help elect progressive candidates, especially in 1986, when so many Senate seats and governorships and other offices are at stake. Second, we need to take some steps toward developing a set of progressive messages that we can convey across campaigns, across organizations and across other division lines to give a sense of positive progressive presence in motion. We hope to take some steps across deep divisions which have prevented joint action, across lines by constituency or candidate or political concern. It's certainly true that what unites us is greater than what divides us."[8]

In the audience were Illinois Senator Paul Simon, Iowa Senator Tom Harkin, Maryland Representative Barbara Mikulski, Michigan Representative John Conyers, Texas Representative Mickey Leland, and California Representative Esteban Torres. The group also contained theorist Michael Harrington, Senior Citizen advocate Bill Hutton, California activist Tom Hayden, Georgetown professor Norman Birnbaum, Americans for Democratic Action Executive Director Ann Lewis, and Donna Brazille from the Black Women's Congress.

In his opening remarks, Wimpy laid out the agenda:

> Our assembly this weekend neither represents nor anticipates an overnight political success...Among many things we've each learned...is at least an understanding that nothing is so common in our time as unsuccessful people with talent...So ours is an attempt to bring those talented people together and make talented people successful...We are fused, not so much by pecuniary interest as by political and social ideal. Our quest is not so much to fulfill a desire for dialogue as to make a commitment to action in the cause of reclaiming America for the nobler purposes

of government and life in a civilized society...We seek to ground our national security in the people's economic and social security; to define our national interest in terms of global realities; to propagate and practice the ways of peace, not war...Democratic progressivism is our only partisanship.And that is our bond. So let us begin.[9]

The group broke into nine workshops, dealing with a united liberal message on such issues as tax reform, toxic waste cleanups, health care, trade policy, affirmative action and human rights. Wimpy bounced from group to group, challenging them to take their action to the streets. "We need to develop a grassroots political voice in this country," he said, "just as our philosophical enemies did on the ashes of Barry Goldwater's defeat in 1964. That means ringing doorbells and putting together the machinery at the grassroots level."[10]

Wimpy had given up his notion of starting a third political party. He decided that he would once again try to steer his Democratic Party away from the center and leftward toward the issues he cared about so deeply.

Noting that although some groups shared common goals, there were intense rivalries, Michigan Congressman John Conyers remarked, "This is an ideal meeting. This is one of the ones that only Bill Winpisinger could put together to bring us here under these kinds of circumstances."[11]

Wimpy, who had been defeated repeatedly in trying to install a liberal Democrat in the White House, used the meeting to plant seeds that would take years to mature. He was still willing to fight the good fight in the short term, but realized his best bet was building a structure that could endure for years and keep the flame of liberalism alive.

FORTY-FOUR

TROUBLE AT EASTERN AIRLINES

Early 1986 saw two major mechanical disasters, one here and one abroad, and a major business reorganization that would profoundly affect the IAM.

The first occurred on a cold Tuesday morning, in January 1986, the day President Reagan was scheduled to deliver his State of the Union address. After two days of delays because of weather and minor mechanical issues, the space shuttle *Challenger*, the workhorse of NASA's fleet, lifted off from the Kennedy Space Center's launch pad 39-B. The flight, with the first civilian in space, thirty-seven-year-old Christa McAuliffe, was supposed to launch two satellites. As thousands of spectators watched from the jam-packed official viewing area, including McAuliffe's family and her students from Concord High School in New Hampshire, the temperature hovered close to the thirty-one degree minimum for a launch. McAuliffe's presence on the flight had turned the take-off into an international spectacle, with TV cameras trained on the spaceship and millions of viewers glued to their sets. Finally, after a two-hour delay because of the malfunction of a fire prevention device and because of ice on the vehicle's ground support structure, the Challenger blasted skyward with a thundering roar. One minute into its assent, mission control officer James D. Wetherbee radioed to flight commander Francis R. (Dick) Scobee, "Challenger, go with throttles up." Scobee immediately replied, "Roger, go with throttles up."

A few seconds later, a spectacular burst of white and orange smoke filled the sky, baffling millions of spectators around the world. No one would know for quite some time what had happened. NASA investigators would eventually determine that the shuttle's 500,000 gallons of liquid hydrogen mixed with oxygen from its other tank, causing the vehicle to disintegrate instantaneously. Rubber O-rings designed to keep the volatile fuels separate failed and led to one of the most widely viewed disasters in American history.

Disbelieving spectators on the ground at Cape Canaveral and those watching on television gasped in horror as the *Challenger* rained down into the Atlantic in a million pieces. Debris from the explosion continued to fall for nearly an hour, causing NASA to close access roads, trapping the stunned onlookers at the site of the launch. All seven astronauts aboard, including McAuliffe, were killed. NASA's space program was immediately placed on an indefinite hold.

A business maneuver a month later in Miami, while far less dramatic, would nonetheless have disastrous consequences for the IAM. Eastern Airlines, the nation's third largest carrier, was in dire financial trouble. In addition to suffering a New Year's Day crash that had killed all twenty-nine people aboard a flight in La Paz, Bolivia, the company was running into serious labor trouble. Negotiations between Eastern and its unions had deadlocked in January, and a thirty-day cooling off period imposed by the National Mediation Board under the Railway Labor Act, was set to expire.

The IAM, the largest of the unions representing Eastern's employees, refused to accept an offer by Eastern chairman Frank Borman of a twenty-percent cut in wages, a reduction in health care benefits, and drastic changes in their work rules. Borman then threatened to sell the airline or take it into bankruptcy, thus abrogating the IAM contract. Charlie Bryan, the General Chairman of IAM District 100, was fed up with Eastern and Borman. The local had already granted more than

$800,000 in wage concessions to the company by accepting a twenty-two percent pay cut in 1984 in exchange for an equity stake in the company and a seat on the board of directors. Those concessions had allowed Eastern to turn a profit of $6.3 million in 1985, its first since 1979. Now Borman wanted the IAM to cut back an additional twenty-percent to meet a deadline imposed by Eastern's creditors, who held more than $2.5 billion of the company's debt.

Wimpy, Transportation Vice President John Peterpaul, and Charlie Bryan were in Miami trying to hammer out an agreement. Wimpy and Borman had developed something of a friendship over the years, and Borman was a regular part of Wimpy's annual jaunt to Indianapolis for the big race.

Borman, fifty-eight years old at the time, and a former astronaut, had commanded the *Gemini 7* and *Apollo 8* missions. He had led Eastern for the past ten years, and had clashed with the hardboiled fifty-two year old Bryan. In the cutthroat world of deregulated airlines, Eastern was facing tough competition from low cost carriers like Frank Lorenzo's Continental Airlines. Lorenzo, it was rumored, would make a play for Eastern if Borman couldn't come to terms with the Machinists. As both sides met on Friday, January 21, Borman discounted that threat. He told Wimpy he found Lorenzo so despicable that he would send the airline into Chapter 11 bankruptcy before he would sell it to him.

Borman came to terms with the carrier's other unions. Local 553 of the Transport Workers Union, representing 7,000 Eastern flight attendants, agreed to a massive pay cut and saw 1,010 of its members furloughed. The Airline Pilots Association, with 4,600 members, reluctantly agreed to the airline's terms after Henry Duffy, their International President, bargained directly with Borman. Now it came down to the Machinists.

Wimpy and Peterpaul sensed that Borman and Duffy were trying to cut Bryan out of the loop. They told Borman they would do everything they could to help save the carrier but that Bryan spoke for his members. To reinforce their point they left Miami and returned to Washington. Bryan then delivered a counter offer: the members would take a fifteen-percent wage cut, but Borman had to step down as chairman. Naturally, Borman refused.

Sunday afternoon, January 23, with time running out to reach an agreement, Eastern's board met to try one last time. At Borman's request Bryan met separately with two of his fellow board members, Harry Hood Bassett and Peter O. Crisp, who tried in vain to get Bryan to agree to the twenty-percent pay cut. Borman was in a panic. While Bryan was meeting with Bassett and Crisp he tried desperately to reach Wimpy on the telephone. When he couldn't, he called Maria Cordone, Wimp's secretary, at home and pleaded with her to somehow track him down. Wimpy called back a few minutes later and agreed to speak with Bryan. Borman barged into the meeting. "I've got Wimpy on the phone, he wants to talk to you," he said to the Machinists leader.[1]

In his book, *Grounded: Frank Lorenzo and the Destruction of Eastern Airlines*, author Aaron Bernstein describes what happened next:

> The two walked back to Borman's office. Bryan went in and got on the phone as Borman paced the hall outside. Bryan told Winpisinger about his talks with the two directors. He said the board was split and didn't necessarily back Borman. When Borman came back, Winpisinger told him there was nothing he could do. Borman knew it was over. Charlie wasn't going to give in. And no one could make him.[2]

Frank Lorenzo made his bid for the airline. When the board realized that Charlie Bryan and the Machinists were not going to back down, they began discussing whether to accept Lorenzo's offer or file for bankruptcy. After a long, contentious meeting that lasted until 3:00 AM the following morning, the board voted 15-4 to sell to Lorenzo for the bargain basement price of $600 million, more than $300 million of which would be in debt issued by the company. Bryan voted against the sale.

Forty-six-year-old Francisco A. Lorenzo, one of the most controversial figures in the history of commercial aviation, now owned the country's third largest airline.

Two months later, a mechanical failure of catastrophic proportions was visited upon the world when an inexperienced night shift crew caused Reactor Number Four at the Chernobyl Nuclear Power Plant to explode. The RMBK-style reactor, located about thirty miles north of the Ukrainian city of Kiev, was scheduled to be shut down for routine maintenance. Operators of the power plant planned to use the shutdown process to experiment with use of the back-up turbine generators to see if they could provide sufficient coolant to the three-year-old reactor. As they reduced the level of power to approximately half capacity on their way to a full shut-down, another unrelated regional power station experienced an unexpected problem and went off line. The director of the Kiev electrical grid immediately called the operators at Chernobyl and asked that they postpone the shutdown until the other plant resumed operation. Chernobyl complied. Reactor Number Four continued to generate half its normal power.

At approximately 11:00 PM, the grid coordinator signaled to Chernobyl that they could conclude their shutdown. Unfortunately, an inexperienced nighttime crew, few of whom had any experience working with nuclear reactors, had taken over operation of the plant. They either didn't know or didn't realize the consequences of the delay in the shutdown. As if nothing had happened, they removed the system's control rods and shut down the reactor much too fast for safety. When they didn't get the reaction they expected, they reinserted the control rods and caused the system to crash. A massive amount of steam erupted and graphite fires ignited. The horrified operators issued the SCRAM order, an industry-wide protocol for an emergency shutdown of a nuclear reactor. It was too late.

At 1:23 AM, the reactor blew up. A massive cloud of radioactive steam began escaping, contaminating a wide swath of land downwind. Before the disaster could be contained, 336,000 people had to be relocated and forty-seven of the workers sent to quell the fire lost their lives. Nuclear contamination spread throughout Belarus and as far away as Scandinavia.

In a speech to students from Indiana and Purdue universities in May, Wimpy offered his reaction to this series of disasters and the Delta Airlines crash.

> *Given catastrophic events of the first four months of this year, all else in the discussion about ending the arms race and the nuclear arms race in the first instance—all else seems superfluous.*
>
> *If the Challenger and Delta crashes and the Chernobyl catastrophe prove nothing else, they do prove that technology is not neutral nor fail safe— that rocketry and nuclear technology do kill—and kill indiscriminately.*
>
> *The odds that we mortals cannot control them, are based on the mathematical probability of chance; it's*

always a 50/50 proposition that accident, mistake or malfunction is going to turn that technology against its users. And if it is nuclear loaded, that means it is turned against humankind and life itself.[3]

Non-nuclear technological changes continued to have a profound impact on IAM members. More and more robots replaced production workers. New composite materials were introduced into the metal working industry changing the very essence of the trade machinists had practiced for a century.

Wimpy turned to a veteran IAM member from Cincinnati, sixty-year-old Robert K. Buffenbarger, to look after member's interests. He appointed him to the advisory panel for the Congressional Office of Technology Assessment. Buffenbarger, an experienced negotiator, had served on the bargaining committee with General Electric's aircraft engine division and had long had an interest in how new technology influenced the workplace. In his new capacity, Bob Buffenbarger would be the sole trade union representative advising members of Congress and their staffs about the potential impact of advanced ceramics and composite materials on American manufacturing.

"The ceramics technology exists here but I'm not sure we can hold our lead," Bob Buffenbarger said in an interview with *The Machinist.*

While we're still doing basic research, the Japanese are building product—fish hooks, scissors, and other small consumer items—while they learn.

They're far ahead of us in developing ceramic engine blocks. Ceramic blocks are much, much lighter, withstand intense heat which means they don't need cooling systems and will be much more fuel efficient than anything we're building today."

> *These materials will affect workers. At General*
> *Electric, we're using ceramic inserts instead of carbide.*
> *They're cheap. They're throw-aways. They're no good*
> *for precision cuts, but boy can they hog metal.[4]*

Wimpy continued to nudge the Democratic Party back to the left. He followed his summit meeting at Placid Harbor with a number of appearances in 1986 in which he decried the effort of some Democrats to move to the center. Instead, he called for his party to reach out to the disaffected.

Speaking before the Democratic committee in his adopted home of Montgomery County, Maryland, Wimpy blasted the shift to a service economy and the Democrats who were promoting it.

> *It takes two people to provide the necessities of life*
> *that one breadwinner could provide in 1973. The*
> *service economy is a low wage economy. There is a*
> *permanent standing army of 10 million unemployed*
> *to keep it that way. Forty years after passage of*
> *the Full Employment Act, the workers of this nation*
> *still do not know the security and stability of full*
> *employment.*
>
> *Too many Democrats in positions of influence*
> *and power are trying to be more Republican than*
> *the Republicans; more right than the right wingers.*
>
> *The Democratic party can only grow and prosper*
> *if it maintains its traditional populist and progressive*
> *principles and sells itself through the dialogue of the*
> *populist idiom and progressive ideals.*
>
> *Since 1976, the Democratic Party has already*
> *alienated nearly half of its constituency—those*
> *dwelling on the lower rungs and margins of the*

economic, educational and social order. They don't vote because no one articulates their concerns or interests.

A neo-liberal, pro-business tack by the Democratic Party now and in 1988, will assuredly see the alienation of those middle class voters who are still its backbone and mainstay, but who are on the slippery slopes of economic decadence and declining living standards.

The time is ripe for the Democratic Party to reassert its traditional values, regroup its coalition and reassert its traditional populism and progressivism.[5]

In April, the Reverend Jesse Jackson prevailed upon Wimpy to be one of the key players at the founding convention of his National Rainbow Coalition. Jackson hoped to build on his surprisingly strong finish in the 1984 Presidential race. He wanted to be the alternative the Left craved as an answer to the Right-Wing machine. Wimpy issued a statement at the beginning of the three-day meeting, saying the IAM had "sound and fundamental reasons for working with the Rainbow Coalition."[6]

Playing on the theme he established at his own summit at Placid Harbor, Wimpy encouraged Jackson to focus on some of the nuts and bolts mechanics necessary for political success. Wimpy opened the IAM purse strings and helped fund workshops on how to manage campaigns, deal with the media, raise and manage money, and organize local grass roots chapters of the Rainbow Coalition.

The highlight came at the conclusion of the convention when Wimpy was called upon to introduce Jackson for his keynote address. Waxing eloquent, Wimpy began with, "Two months to the day after Jesse Jackson drew first breath and saw his first South Carolina light in this world…" and continued on for five pages. It was a rousing if somewhat longwinded introduction—and the crowd loved it. As Jackson stood next to Wimpy at the podium, acknowledging the standing ovation, he leaned over, covered the microphone with his hand and said, "Thanks Wimpy. I thought *I* was the one who was supposed to deliver the speech tonight!"

Wimpy made it as clear as possible that while he wholeheartedly supported the efforts of the Rainbow Coalition, he was not endorsing Jackson for President—yet.

The following month Wimpy was back on stage at a 1,000 person gathering dubbed a conference on "New Directions." Organized by his friend and intellectual mentor Michael Harrington, the conference brought together Jesse Jackson, Ann Lewis of Americans for Democratic Action, and labor leaders, academics, social activists, minority leaders, feminists, and peace activists who were hoping to stem what they termed the "highjacking of the Democratic Party" by centrists and conservatives. Wimpy delivered a speech entitled "America and the World":

> The question of economic change in America is no longer whether we will have socialism, but rather whose socialism we will have and whom it will serve. Currently private and public wealth is being redistributed by government away from the working class majority to the most powerful corporations and the wealthiest one-half percent of income receivers. We have socialism of no taxes for the most profitable corporations, which translates out to zero effective tax rate for thousands of the wealthiest individuals.[7]

Wimpy kept pushing the party leftward. He knew that his best bet to achieve that was by developing a counterbalancing force to the Right-Wing conspiracy. He had been down the road of challenging Democratic orthodoxy once before with his promotion of Ted Kennedy in 1980. It was beginning to look like he just might do it again with Jesse Jackson.

FORTY-FIVE

ONE MORE TRY TO ELECT A DEMOCRAT

Wimpy never missed a chance to return home. He loved the city on the shore of Lake Erie and made a point of accepting any invitation to a speaking engagement with a Cleveland postmark no matter how esoteric the group.

He also cleared his schedule whenever District 54 hosted a golf tournament and was often found on the links, smoking a big long cigar, trying to keep from laughing as his buddy Phil Zannella flailed away with vigorous but largely unsuccessful swipes at the little white ball. Wimp, the old athlete, had a powerful, graceful swing and could really move the ball. Phil was built like a fireplug and opted for brute strength and vile language, trying to intimidate the ball to follow his will.

Edith Winpisinger, Wimpy's mother, still lived in the city and he visited her faithfully each time he was in town. Even in her late 70's, Edith was still full of life and was unmoved by Wimp's status as a nationally known powerful union president. As she always had, she offered him copious advice about how to behave.

After taking care of whatever business brought him to town, Wimpy would unwind with the boys down at District 54 headquarters on Euclid Avenue, sitting in Phil Zannella's office with a cigar in one hand and a Courvoisier in the other.

Phil Zannella, Jr. remembered:

They'd keep about a half dozen shot glasses and a towel in the top desk drawer and a bottle of Courvoisier in the credenza. Wimpy loved that stuff. He'd come and visit after a lot of the state council meetings. He always came back for our golf tournaments. He was competitive as hell and could really whack the ball. Wimpy enjoyed golf and Wimpy enjoyed a cigar. He got my father out golfing with him, got him a big bag with his name on it and everything, but my father was not a sports person. He didn't like sports, didn't play sports, except when Wimpy dragged him out on the golf course.[1]

Wimpy would also use his trips to Cleveland to replenish his supply of local delicacies. "Every time he'd come to town we'd load up his plane," Phil Zannella, Jr. recalled.

My father would bring platters and platters of Italian meats and we'd pack them onto the plane for him to take back to Washington. Another thing he just loved was Dan-Dee potato chips. He couldn't get them in DC, so every time he came here we had to round up boxes and boxes of the damn things. I remember one time I went into a store and asked the guy if he had any Dan-Dee potato chips. He said, "Sure, how many do you want?" I said, "A couple hundred bags." He looked at me like I was crazy![2]

Back in Washington, Wimpy was trying to position the union to play an influential role in the 1988 Presidential Election. The bubble of Reagan's popularity had finally burst. *Ash-Shiraa*, a Lebanese news magazine, broke an incredible story on November 3, 1986. The United States government was secretly selling arms to Iran. This shocking news not only proved true, but American investigative reporters soon uncovered an even deeper plot. A little known aide to the National Security Council, Lieutenant Colonel Oliver North, had cooked up a scheme to mark up the price of the weapons by $15 million in order to send the extra money to aid the Nicaraguan Contras. Not only was the Reagan Administration sending thousands of BGM-71 anti-tank TOW missiles to its avowed enemy, they were using the proceeds to blatantly sidestep the Boland Amendment, which prohibited the Administration from trying to overthrow Nicaragua's democratically elected government.

The deal was complicated and secretive. Its disclosure was severely damaging to the Administration. Under intense media and congressional pressure, the President appointed a special commission, headed by former Republican Senator John Tower, to investigate. Unlike most such commissions, which whitewash the situation, the Tower Commission let Reagan have it with both barrels in its final report: "The President clearly didn't understand the nature of this operation, who was involved and what was happening," Tower said in a news conference as the report was released.[3]

New York Times writer R.W. Apple, Jr., in a piece titled "The White House in Crisis: The Presidency; At a Crossroads," wrote of Reagan's eroding capacity to lead. Citing what foreign policy analysts had termed his "ill prepared" and "badly executed" performance at the recently concluded Reykjavik summit with Russian Premier Mikhail Gorbachev, Apple paraphrased the Tower Commission findings saying they "came close to picturing him as a man who sometimes inhabited a fantasy land."[4]

Wimpy reacted with scorn in a speech he gave soon after to a Central Labor Council in Chicopee, Massachusetts:

> The question may not be: what does he know and when did he know it?
> The question may be: does he know he knew it?
> What this president has created is more than a White House mess and more than an international scandal. He has created a free market in global

terrorism! The highest ransom is paid to the lowliest pirate. But no one knows where the cash has gone.

If the President's mistakes were, indeed, the result of a "mental dysfunction," then we better be prepared to experience a constitutional crisis in this country—not unlike the Watergate crisis—before the next two years are out.

Whenever I hear some politician invoke the name of God, wrap himself in the flag, invoke motherhood and all manner of personal morality, then launch a fanatical crusade against communism, that's when I figure we've got a crook and a liar on our hands. Put those damned pinch-mouthed conservatives and right wing zealots in power and they do it every time. Wage war on liberals, trade unions, women and minorities and try to create a panic the Russians are coming.

Show me a reactionary zealot who is raising hell about foreign policy, morality and patriotism, and I'll show you a crook damned near every time.[5]

Public reaction to the revelations was equally harsh. A *New York Times / CBS News* poll taken in early March found Reagan's approval rating at a four year low and dropping. The President had lost twenty-one percent of his support from the previous November when the Iran-Contra scandal first surfaced. Now he had lost an additional ten percent. Only forty-two percent of Americans approved of the job he was doing while forty-six percent disapproved. Asked whom they thought was in charge at the White House, only twenty-four percent said Reagan while two-thirds said someone else was running the government. The poll also showed a big drop in support for Vice President George H.W. Bush, who lost a theoretical match up with former Colorado Senator Gary Hart forty-seven percent to thirty-four percent.[6]

The Democrats sensed a chance to finally recapture the White House. Gary Hart announced his candidacy April 3, and was immediately installed as the front-runner. Those running against him included Tennessee Senator Albert Gore, Jr., Missouri Congressman Richard Gephardt, Delaware Senator Joseph Biden, Illinois Senator Paul Simon, former Arizona Governor Bruce Babbitt, Massachusetts Governor Michael Dukakis, and Wimpy's personal favorite, the Reverend Jesse Jackson.

Within days of the start of his campaign, rumors started circulating that Hart was a womanizer. Responding to the question in a *New York Times* Sunday Magazine profile, Hart denied the charges and told political correspondent E.J. Dionne, Jr., "Follow me around, I don't care. I'm serious. If anybody wants to put a tail on me, go ahead. They'd be very bored."[7]

The *Miami Herald* did just that. In a story published the very next day, it alleged that an attractive young blonde had spent the night at Hart's Washington, DC, townhouse. Hart denied the charges. Soon a photograph him holding a comely blonde named Donna Rice in his lap, aboard the aptly named yacht *Monkey Business*, sunk his candidacy once and for all.

With Hart out, Michael Dukakis shot to a lead in New Hampshire polls. Wimpy very much wanted to support Jesse Jackson and to put on the kind of effort he had for Ted Kennedy in 1980. Yet, he was becoming far more pragmatic with age. He realized that the bulk of his membership would not support Jackson. He also assessed that Dukakis just might have the horsepower to win the nomination and possibly the Presidency.

The MNPL conducted its quadrennial cattle call for Presidential Candidates in late May. All of the remaining Democrats showed up, and six of the seven Republicans did as well, with only former Nevada Senator Paul Laxalt refusing to participate. Bush was being challenged for the nomination by Kansas Senator Robert Dole, former Delaware Governor Pierre "Pete" DuPont, former Secretary of State Alexander Haig, New York Congressman Jack Kemp, and televangelist Marion "Pat" Robertson.

Wimpy was clear that he liked Jackson, but was equally adamant that it was his personal preference and not necessarily that of the IAM as an institution. He didn't object, however, when the union's monthly newspaper, The Machinist, said of Jackson: "Jackson's ideas on fair trade, on jobs, on worker protections and living at peace with our neighbors appear to be closer to the IAM's views for a truly democratic society than are those of any other candidate of either party at this writing."[8]

The Presidential race wasn't the only battle Wimpy was following closely. Things at Eastern Airlines had turned from bad to worse since Lorenzo had taken over.

General Vice President John Peterpaul reported to the IAM Executive Council at their November 1986 meeting in Hollywood, Florida, that more than one thousand IAM members had been laid off since Lorenzo acquired Eastern in February of that year. Lorenzo was effectively trying to merge the unionized Eastern with his non-union Continental. The horrible consequences Wimpy had forecast when Congress passed the Airline Deregulation Act in 1978, when he said the impact on workers would be "cruel, predatory, dehumanizing and demoralizing," were coming to pass. IAM members at Eastern owned twenty-percent of the company's stock, yet they were still being asked to contribute an unreasonable forty-seven percent cut in their wages. Meanwhile, grievances against the company were up more than 300%. More than 300 employees had been fired in a Machiavellian attempt to thin the ranks of unionized workers.

At a Washington, DC, conference on Air Transport Labor Relations in July 1987, even the chairman of a competing airline agreed that the situations at Eastern and elsewhere were dreadful. Robert Crandall, Chairman of American Airlines, told attendees: "Deregulation has proved to be far more anti-labor, anti-people to be more precise, than anyone dreamed. A disturbing trade-off occurred. Passengers won low fares, but part of their gain came at the expense of the people who provide airline service."[9]

Wimpy, speaking at the same conference, picked up on Crandall's theme:

> Some 27,000 IAM members have had their lives and jobs disrupted by mergers, acquisitions, route transfers, bankruptcies, and cost cutting drives. We still have some 8,000 airline employees on the street.
>
> Mr. Lorenzo is pitting his substandard and subscale Continental employees against our unionized Eastern members to force down Eastern members' wage, hour and work standards.
>
> In this struggle with Texas Air Corporation our heads may become bloodied, but we will not bow.[10]

Wimpy was gearing up for another fight, and it would be a big one.

FORTY-SIX

WIMPY PLANS FOR THE FUTURE

The chain of events that led to Wimpy's presidency of the IAM can be traced to a meeting at the Marcal Restaurant in Cleveland in 1966. It was there that two titans of the union, Matt DeMore and Ernie White, both sixty-three years old, decided the fate of the union for the next quarter century. They agreed that the IAM's mandatory retirement age of sixty-five should not be changed, thus frustrating Roy Siemiller's attempt to remain in office. They also decided upon a line of succession that would see Red Smith elected for two terms to be followed by Wimpy for three.

As 1988 dawned, Wimpy had just turned sixty-four and would be forced to retire when his term expired the following July. Gene Glover, who held the union's second most powerful position as General Secretary Treasurer, had reached age sixty-five in December 1987 and had retired. Glover's post was filled by Tom Ducy, the dean of the Executive Council, who moved from Chicago, where he was General Vice President of the Midwest Region. The fifty-eight-year-old Ducy was another in a long line of IAM leaders who had roots in the Cleveland office—he had begun his climb up the leadership ladder as Red Smith's Administrative Assistant when Smith was Vice President of the Great Lakes Region.

Wimpy recognized the need to do some succession planning of his own to assure that the IAM would carry on his tradition when he was gone. He appointed his Administrative Assistant, Don Wharton, to fill the vacancy on the executive council created by Glover's retirement, and sent Wharton to Cleveland to be General Vice President for the Great Lakes

Region. Wharton was a fellow Ohioan and a loyal supporter. He had distinguished himself locally long ago having been elected President of the influential Ohio State Council of Machinists before going on the International Staff in 1968. In 1981, Wimpy brought Wharton to headquarters and assigned him a number of important jobs, culminating in Administrative Assistant to the International President, in 1983.

Putting the forty-nine year old Wharton on the council not only gave Wimpy a reliable vote, it also put Wharton in a position where over time he would rise to be the General Secretary Treasurer. Wimpy then reached back to Ohio to fill the vacancy on his own staff created by Wharton's elevation to the council. He chose thirty-seven-year-old Robert Thomas Buffenbarger, known as Tom, who had spent the last two years at headquarters working in the Organizing Department, to be his Administrative Assistant. Tom Buffenbarger was a second generation IAM member and the son of Robert Buffenbarger, whom Wimpy had appointed the previous year to the influential Congressional Office of Technology Assessment Advisory Panel.

Tom had been an IAM member since 1970, when he immediately distinguished himself as shop steward for his apprentice class at General Electric in Cincinnati. He moved up quickly through the ranks, getting elected District 34 Representative in 1977, and being appointed to the International Staff in 1980. Buffenbarger, like so many of the rising stars of the IAM before him, spent time in the Cleveland office of the Great Lakes Territory, where he was Administrative Assistant to General Vice President Merle Pryor. Wimpy had tremendous affection for the young Buffenbarger and brought him to headquarters in 1986.

Tom Buffenbarger recalled, "When Wimpy told me I was coming to Washington to work in the Organizing Department, he said 'Don't get too comfortable in that department.' I took that as a sign that he had bigger things in mind for me, and it turns out he did." In addition to his primary job, Buffenbarger took on an active role with the MNPL, rising to the position of Co-Chairman.

Wimpy now had his ducks lined up. With his friend George Kourpias serving as Resident Vice President and Chief of Staff of the union, Wharton on the Executive Council and Buffenbarger at headquarters as his Administrative Assistant, Winpisinger, like Matt DeMore and Ernie White before him, had established a line of succession that would serve the IAM for the next quarter century.

Thinking long term was important in a union that was about to celebrate its one hundredth birthday. For its 1988 Grand Lodge Convention the IAM chose to return to Atlanta, where Tom Talbot and eighteen intrepid machinists had banded together to start the organization. The convention was to be Wimpy's last as International President, and it was a bittersweet affair for him. He had first come to the attention of many of the members of the IAM when his cool presence saved the 1972 convention from descending into complete chaos. He had been called upon to do the same in 1976 when President Red Smith was again in danger of losing control. Wimpy's first two conventions as International President had been orderly and well run because of his skill at keeping discussions about serious and contentious issues on an even keel.

The 1988 convention was moved up to late April so the delegates could complete their work and be present in Atlanta for the May 5 birthday celebration. Remarkably, there were no roll call votes during the ten days of proceedings. The most controversial matter, changing the constitution to allow the Canadian members to elect their own General Vice President, was accomplished on a voice vote. By 1988, it was clear that the Canadians were not planning to bolt from the IAM to form an independent union. With that fear off the table, the Law Committee recommended approval of the change. Five Canadian members rose to speak in favor. Not a single delegate spoke against it.

Toronto Delegate Bill Shipman from Local Lodge 2323 summed up his remarks with, "Brothers and sisters, keep our lifeline to the future strong in Canada for the strength of our internationality, for the strength of this great union, and to keep the IAMAW the best and strongest union representing Canadians in Canada."[2]

Wimpy called for a voice vote on the motion and it passed overwhelmingly. The delegates rose and delivered a rousing and sustained ovation to their Canadian brothers and sisters. Wimpy commented from the podium:

> I wanted to interject just very briefly and quickly into the committee's report and thank this delegation for the showing that you just made for our brothers and sisters in Canada and to compliment them. I know this is highly unusual, but I want them to know how much we all appreciate the manner in which they have pursued their objectives in an orderly and proper way over the past several years. We're indebted to you.[3]

The field of Democratic presidential candidates had been winnowed by the early primaries, and only two candidates remained, front running Michael Dukakis and Wimp's emotional favorite, Jesse Jackson.

Dukakis was unable to attend the convention but he sent his state Secretary of Labor, Paul Eustace, who was a member of IAM Lodge 1726, to speak on his behalf. Wimpy offered Eustace a brief and polite introduction, calling him "a long-time friend and acquaintance of mine."

He was much more effusive in introducing Jesse Jackson:

> ...I know we've all watched over the past many months, if you are like me, with a near sense of awe as Jesse Jackson has campaigned the length and breadth of this country for the Democratic nomination for the Presidency of the United States, and that makes it doubly important that we acknowledge how extremely pleased we are that he could take time away from that noble and strength-sapping endeavor to join with us today.
>
> He has made our fight his fight. And he's walked the picket lines with us until we achieved the ends of justice that we sought. You have seen him in many of those appearances, and I know that you certainly must feel the same sort of elation and gratitude that I feel as I present to you the Reverend Jesse Jackson![4]

Jackson was equally effusive acknowledging Wimpy's introduction: "So today I want to express my thanks to a friend, plain talking, no-nonsense, hard-nosed leader that can be counted on at the point of challenge. He deserves a very special, a very special round of applause, for in him there is work. In him there is continuity. In him there is lots of love."[5]

Jackson then used a bit of humor to diffuse the race issue:

> This is a rather historic moment, the 100th anniversary of this tremendous movement. Nineteen railroad workers started this organization one hundred years ago, and you can be assured of the fact that they were hoping you would be here, but they did not expect I would be here, but we're here.

> *They didn't expect me to be up here in the cab of this train. They had a caboose program one hundred years ago. But nonetheless, we are on the same track now.*[6]

Jackson gave his usual stem winding speech, and was warmly cheered by the delegates. Wimpy had decided that there was no way Jackson would overtake Dukakis in the remaining primaries. Despite his personal affection for the fiery preacher, no motion was made to endorse his candidacy.

May 5, 1988, the centennial birthday of the IAM, was a warm clear spring day in Atlanta. The thermometer touched seventy degrees as delegates crowded into the Georgia World Congress Center for the final day of the convention.

After dispensing with the formalities, an emotional William W. Winpisinger mounted the podium for his final address to an IAM convention. He used the metaphor of a rocket ship hurtling through time as the framework of his speech, drawing together memories of past struggles with hope for the future.

> *...the quest for knowledge of our past and those dedicated mechanics who rebelled in that roundhouse pit here in Atlanta 100 years ago is not an idle luxury or an insignificant pursuit. Our existence as family, a union, demands it.*
>
> *And while things may be different from those of our founders era, our values remain the same; our objectives remain essentially the same; and I suspect, the institutional, economic and political and social problems of the past, present and future will ever be basically the same.*
>
> *On a personal note, this phase of the journey began for me at a headquarters staff meeting*

convened at 12:01 AM on July 1, 1977, a meeting at which I began the process of attempting to lead this great organization in some new directions. Throughout my tenure as your International President, I have consciously, consistently and—I hope—conscientiously, pursued that goal.

I will continue to lead in those same directions, as well as any new ones ordained by this convention, for the next year and two months—right up until another fateful midnight signals the end of my tenure as your International President.

And be assured, your unswerving loyalty and support have made my job an easy one, and I will leave it a proud, happy, contented man, albeit still a little frustrated. Frustrated because I have always wished that we could do more and move faster. But I'll be satisfied, and be satisfied in a way that most people in a position like mine never experience or even know. I'll be satisfied that I did the very best I could for every day that I served.[7]

FORTY-SEVEN

GEORGE KOURPIAS GETS THE NOD

It was much hotter in July, nearly ninety degrees and humid, when Wimpy returned to Atlanta for the Democratic National Convention. Dukakis had the nomination sewn up with 2,876 delegates to Jackson's 1,218, but both candidates would have their name placed in nomination.

One of the two nominating speakers was precise, eloquent and to the point. The other decided to use his moment in the national spotlight for all it was worth and droned on for a full thirty-five minutes.

For once, Wimpy was not the one guilty of prolixity. He put Jesse Jackson's name before the convention with a flowing, poetic speech:

> [Jackson is a man] who has shown us the way to thaw the ice of indifference, smug self-satisfaction and meanness that too long has masked the heartbeat of America.
>
> Who has ignited the passionate fires of justice in our souls as no other contemporary has.
>
> The man who has dared sound our call to greatness.
>
> He has brought us together here in the phoenix of Atlanta—amid the smoldering ruins of nearly two decades of defeat—challenging the Democratic Party to reclaim its heritage and rainbow identity.[1]

The speaker who nominated Dukakis spoke of his integrity, competence, compassion, his history of fighting for social justice, and just about every other trait possible to attribute to a human being. By the time he was twenty minutes into his speech, the delegates were restless. Some fidgeted in their chairs, others got up and walked around. At the thirty minute mark, there were derisive cat calls from the audience. And when, thirty-five minutes into his speech, Arkansas Governor Bill Clinton said, "And in conclusion," he got the biggest cheer of the evening.

A month following his convention speech, Wimpy was in Kona, Hawaii, for the IAM Western States Staff conference. He knew the executive council would vote to choose his replacement as International President at their next session, which would be held in Florida two days after the national election, and he decided it was time to pass the torch. His natural choice was George Kourpias, his loyal friend and confidante of many years. Two other general Vice Presidents, George Poulin, in charge of the Northeast Territory, and John Peterpaul, who handled the union's Transportation division, were also interested in seeking the post. Both Poulin and Peterpaul had lobbied Wimpy personally, but in each case, he told them he didn't intend to push any particular candidate. Now Wimpy decided it was time to light a fire under Kourpias.

George Kourpias remembered their conversation in Hawaii:

> One afternoon Wimp came over to my room and said we needed to talk. We sat out on the balcony of my room overlooking the Pacific. I told him when he made me a vice president that I had no intention of wanting to be considered for his job. Now he was making it clear to me that he wanted me to run. He said, "Well, are you thinking of going?" and I told him I was. He said, "Well, how many people have

you talked to?" I told him I'd talked to everyone [on the executive council] but Poulin and Peterpaul, and the only vote I'd lost was Tom Ducy. He just beamed at me with a big smile and said, "Well, that's pretty damn good isn't it?" And I said, "Yeah."[2]

Poulin and Peterpaul continued to lobby Wimpy, hoping that perhaps he'd relent and exert his considerable influence with the council to back one of them as his replacement. Peterpaul, whose public profile was growing daily because of the ongoing strife at Eastern Airlines, was particularly persistent. Wimpy eventually told him to stop pestering him and get on the phone and call his comrades on the council and see what they had to say.

Wimpy and the IAM endorsed Mike Dukakis after the convention. The AFL-CIO added its endorsement, and Wimpy spent a fair amount of time campaigning on behalf of the Democratic ticket from Labor Day to Election Day. He may not have been wildly in love with Dukakis' relatively centrist politics, but he loathed the idea of another Republican president, particularly George H.W. Bush.

Dukakis, for his part, ran a horrible campaign. He roared out of Atlanta with a double digit lead in the polls and immediately went on vacation. Meanwhile, Bush and his Republican spin machine went into overdrive. They produced one negative television ad after another, attacking all of the Dukakis attributes Clinton had listed in his nominating speech. One ad in particular cut deep into the Democrat's support. Called "Weekend Passes," it told the story of Willie Horton, a former Massachusetts prison inmate who had been granted weekend furloughs under a program the state correctional system ran. After starting the ad by saying Bush supported the death penalty while Dukakis opposed it, a fast paced narrator went on to belittle the furlough program and the felons who participated: "One was Willie Horton, who murdered a boy in a robbery attempt, stabbing him nineteen times. Despite a life sentence, Horton received ten weekend passes from prison. Horton fled, kidnapped a young couple, stabbing the man and repeatedly raping his girlfriend. Weekend passes: Dukakis on crime."[3]

The Horton ad was racially charged and controversial. The Bush campaign took it off the air after just a couple of days, but the damage was done. Bush then put up an ad called "Revolving Door," which showed menacing looking prison inmates, many of whom were black, being released to do harm to an innocent public. Wimpy watched in horror as yet another Democratic presidential candidate self destructed. A week before the election, with Dukakis trailing badly in the polls but starting to mount a faint comeback, he offered his assessment of the campaign to IAM members at the Canadian Staff Conference:

> He [Dukakis] tried to run his campaign by remote. He figured Jackson, the Rainbow Coalition and trade unions would do his hard work for him, because they always do and have no other choice, while he tried to win some big money support.
>
> Of course it all backfired and for the past few weeks now, Dukakis has taken off his suit coat, and started shirt sleeving his way through plant gate crowds, farm meetings, and Jobs with Justice rallies in major cities. He seems to be closing on Bush, who has been content with Dukakis' own shortcomings as a campaigner, and has sat back and let negative TV ads do his job. The bitter irony of this campaign may be that a mad negro criminal may have more to say about who the next President is than the US citizenry.

> *So it is the same old story of the Democratic*
> *candidate having to learn the hard way that*
> *conservatives and Republicans always will take*
> *whatever Democrats will give them, but the more*
> *Democrats move to the right, the more conservatives*
> *and Republicans will demand they move further. And*
> *they will never, never come over to the Democratic*
> *side or candidate.*[4]

Dukakis' campaign failed to respond effectively to the Bush attack ads. His lead in the polls melted away. By Election Day, he was trailing Bush and hoping for an improbable come from behind victory. It didn't happen. Bush defeated Dukakis 48,886,597 to 41,809,476, taking 426 electoral votes to Dukakis' 112.

Two days later, the IAM Executive Council met in Fort Lauderdale, Florida, to select their next International President. Wimpy convened the session and gave a brief speech thanking the council for their support throughout his presidency. He then turned to the task of shepherding Kourpias into the presidency.

George Kourpias remembered it this way:

> *We went down to Miami and stayed at the Embassy*
> *Suites in Fort Lauderdale. I was pretty nervous as were*
> *John [Peterpaul] and George [Poulin]. He opened up*
> *the meeting, and said, "From what I understand, we*
> *have three candidates. I would consider the fact that*
> *each of them, right now, has one vote. We should*
> *dismiss them from this meeting, but before we do*
> *that, I want each of them to tell the council why they*
> *should be the International President." And we did.*
> *Then the three of us went outside. You know how*

those railings are, we leaned over them, not saying a
god damned word to each other. Waiting, waiting and
waiting. It was probably a half hour, but it seemed
like five hours.[5]

Wimpy called the candidates back in, announced that
George Kourpias would be the next International President,
and enveloped him in a bear hug.

George Kourpias recalled that: "Wimpy told me later: 'You
had the votes, George, but I wanted John and George to get
a good feeling that we didn't do it so quick.' I would say that
he was happy that I succeeded him. I think he was very, very
happy."[6]

FORTY-EIGHT

GROUNDED

A new Executive Council, with George Kourpias as International President-elect, had been decided upon, but Wimpy had a few more fish to fry before his term ended.

The situation at Eastern Airlines was bad and getting worse by the day. After stealing Eastern for a paltry $300 million in 1986, Frank Lorenzo began stripping away its assets. He formed a holding company, Texas Air Corporation, and placed Eastern and Continental in it along with four other airlines he owned that were in bankruptcy, People's Express, Frontier, New York Air, and Texas International. He then set up a double-breasted operation, transferring Eastern's assets to Continental, whose unions he had already broken. He sold Eastern's computerized reservation system, System One Direct Access, with a value estimated at up to $450 million, to Texas Air for $100 million, then charged the airline nearly $10 million a month to use it. He created another company, Protective Services Corporation, and tried to ship the jobs of fifty security guards who were IAM members to that non-union subsidiary. Two months later he went after the baggage handlers, forming yet another non-union shell called Airport Ground Services Corporation, and trying to ship the bulk of the 6,000 IAM baggage jobs there. The IAM went to federal court and secured a restraining order to stop Lorenzo from devastating the Eastern workforce.

Undaunted, Lorenzo kept up with the fire sale. He created new shell companies to split off fuel services (Texas Air Fuel Management) and even the airport club lounges (Ionosphere Clubs, Incorporated). Six Airbus 300 jets were sold to Continental for $162 million, $67 million of which was in promissory notes, and Continental immediately unloaded the planes to a new buyer for a tidy $169 million in cash. Airport gates across the country were sold to Continental at bargain basement prices, and bad debt from other non-performing Lorenzo airlines found its way onto Eastern's books. By mid-1988, Eastern was emaciated and in constant need of cash to keep planes flying. The IAM contract was up, and Lorenzo was seeking another $159 million in concessions from IAM members, including pay cuts of up to fifty-percent.

Lorenzo and his minions terrorized the workers at Eastern, resorting to tactics that Wimpy likened to being treated like common criminals. "He starts off by refusing to talk to anybody from any union," Wimpy explained in an interview.

> *Tries to implement his plans. And he told us very promptly he was going to cut our wages in half. And he had it all his own way, firing people left and right. Jesus, we had a wave of firings that transcended many times over anything we had ever experienced before. They'd come down and take you right out of the jet shop, they'd come with two security guards, grab you, march you out of the goddamn place. Like a common criminal. Everything to put the pressure on.[1]*

The battle between Lorenzo and the IAM was immediately viewed by the AFL-CIO and the entire labor movement for what it was: a new attempt to drive trade unions out of business. The PATCO strike in 1981 had initiated a new era of adversarial relations between labor and management, with employers emboldened to take tough stands. If Lorenzo managed to break the union and keep Eastern flying, it would signal a whole new chapter in that relationship, and not a good one for labor.

In "*Grounded: Frank Lorenzo and the Destruction of Eastern Airlines*," Aaron Bernstein wrote:

Many in corporate America agreed that the battle was a watershed. To them, Lorenzo represented a new breed of managers with the strength to break unions and restore America to its rightful prominence. Some executives were torn between this view and the new alternatives of cooperative management that had begun to spread across US industry. A Lorenzo victory would go a long way toward validating the confrontational wisdom that had served the US so well for so many decades. "This struggle is greater than just Eastern," said [Frank] Borman. "Labor is trying to reassert the momentum it lost under Reagan."[2]

When Lorenzo refused to negotiate with the IAM, the case was sent to the National Mediation Board. Wimpy sent a letter to the board on January 5, 1989, asserting that if Lorenzo failed to reach an agreement with the IAM, the union would strike not only Eastern Airlines, but also its other air carriers and rail lines as well. The threat of a secondary boycott—legal only for airline and railway unions under the terms of the National Railway Labor Act of 1926—raised the stakes tremendously. The AFL-CIO Executive Council met and agreed to back the IAM to the fullest extent possible. Lane Kirkland personally assured the IAM leadership that if a strike occurred, the other unions at airlines and railroads would walk off the job in solidarity.

Wimpy appealed to President Bush to declare an emergency and appoint a Presidential Emergency Board to settle the dispute. "I think President Bush, if he's going to be even-handed, would declare that a state of transportation emergency does exist," Wimpy said.[3]

Bush called a half-hour meeting of his advisors in the Oval Office on Friday afternoon, March 3rd, the last day before the strike was scheduled to begin, and made his final decision: the IAM could drop dead.

At the stroke of midnight, March 4, 1989, the IAM walked off the job at Eastern Airlines and set up picket lines. The pilots, flight attendants, and other airline unions agreed to honor the lines and Eastern was effectively grounded. Two hundred of the airline's thirty-seven hundred pilots, mostly management, crossed but the airline was able to get only sixty-six of its 1,040 flights off the ground.

The coalitions that Wimpy had built with organizations outside the labor movement sprung into action in support of the strike. Members of the Rainbow Coalition, the National Council of Senior Citizens, the Gray Panthers, and the National Organization of Women attended rallies, walked picket lines and contributed money to the strike fund. The executive board of the International Transportation Workers Federation voted unanimously in Paris to call on its 6.5 million members world-wide to refuse to service Eastern or Continental airplanes. The International Metalworkers Federation fired off a telegram to President Bush urging him to relent and appoint a Presidential Emergency Board. Wimpy was heartened by the outpouring of support, but was angry and frustrated that the situation had been allowed to deteriorate so badly.

"Frank Lorenzo epitomizes all the reasons I became active in the labor movement more than forty years ago," Wimpy told *The Machinist*.

> He and his ilk would put workers' rights back to the 19th century. Their selfish, ruthless greed knows no bounds.
>
> My first thought when I awake each morning is "What can I do today to hurt Lorenzo?" I could

never do enough to make up for the way he has bashed his employees.[4]

The day-to-day operations of the strike were in the hands of Charlie Bryan, the General Chairman of District 100, and General Vice President for Transportation John Peterpaul. Wimpy monitored the situation closely, getting reports at least three times a day, but beyond rallying support and an aggressive media campaign, where he appeared on nearly a dozen television news programs, there wasn't much more he could do.

He had scheduled his third and final trip to the Soviet Union for April, with Jack Sheinkman, President of the Amalgamated Clothing and Textile Workers Union, and the two had arranged for a private meeting with Soviet President Mikhail Gorbachev. Wimpy was prepared to call the trip off to stay on top of the Eastern situation, but Kourpias and Peterpaul finally convinced him they had matters in hand and that he should go to Russia.

Wimpy made his first trip to Russia in 1983, after calling off a visit in 1979 because of KGB harassment of trade unionists. On that trip, he met with the stiff, formal Yuri Andropov, General Secretary of the Communist Party, and was made an honorary cosmonaut. He visited again in 1986, when fifty-five-year-old Mikhail Gorbachev was in the first year of his term and had just rolled out the revolutionary programs "*Perestroika*" (reconstruction) and "*Glasnost*" (openness or liberalization). Now those programs were in full swing, and Wimpy was anxious to get a first-hand look. "I wanted to see what it meant to the average Soviet citizen—to the man or woman that does the work."[5]

A man whom Wimpy had snubbed in 1979, Nicolai Zonoviev, president of the Heavy Engineering Workers Union, was his host. Zonoviev arranged for Wimpy and Sheinkman to visit a factory in Kiev that had been converted from military production to producing men's suits. Sheinkman was impressed with the quality of the machinery and the product they were producing, telling Wimpy the suits could command top dollar in the US market. Wimp acknowledged that one factory did not necessarily constitute a full economic re-conversion but gave them credit.

"If one is a cynic, which I am not, one might say that it was the only plant they've converted," Wimpy told a reporter for *Labor Today*. "But I'll tell you something: I saw that factory and those who would detract from my judgment have never seen it. Even if it is the only one that's been converted, it's one more than has been converted over here." [in the US][6]

After the factory tour, Wimpy and Sheinkman met with 200 full time officers and staff from Zinovyev's union. "I was never one to turn down an opportunity to talk to anyone," he said in the same interview.

> *I made a very perfunctory speech, actually. I told them it was impossible to understand each other unless we establish some kind of ongoing exchange where you can tell me your problems and why you feel that way, and I can tell you mine and why I feel that way. I made the pitch about how we both inhabit this spaceship we call Earth and how, if we blow the whole thing up, we really aren't accomplishing anything.[7]*

Wimpy then took questions from his audience. But, he noted, "Not a damn one dealt with anything I'd said. They took all that as a given."[8] Instead, the questions for the American labor leaders were more procedural. 'How do you run your union?' 'How many departments do you have?' 'What do they do?' 'How do you translate that to problems on the shop floor?' 'How do you handle grievances?'"[9] Wimpy was delighted at the exchange. "You could just see the light go on. And I said to myself, 'What an opportunity to come in here and try to help them find their own way and explore new ideas in terms of representing workers.'"[10]

The Kremlin meeting was an intimate affair, with just Wimpy, Sheinkman, Gorbachev, Stepan Shalayev, Chairman of the Central Council of Trade Unions, and their interpreters. Wimpy was much more taken by Gorbachev than he had been by Andropov, describing him as "an amazing man—more than amazing. He has charisma, imagination, a willingness to stake something in the crap game out of the certain knowledge that if you don't risk something, you don't get anything."[11]

As Andropov had done, Gorbachev used the meeting with Wimpy to send a message to the Bush Administration about issues beyond the scope of labor relations. "Experience shows that we can discuss everything with American leaders to get to know each other's positions better, and, when there is an opportunity, to find a way to settle problems, in any case to continue the dialogue," Gorbachev told his guests.

> This is a sign of relations of a new type. We proceed from the premise that Soviet leaders and the US Administration understand that the capital accumulated in establishing these relations should be treasured and developed, not wasted. And we shall be persistent in opposing everything that might disrupt this process.
>
> In relations between the USSR and the USA, just as in relations with all countries, we proceed at every level from the principle of new thinking, which presupposes respect for the choice made by the people itself. If such an approach is established in international practice, this will make it possible to advance more successfully to a better world. Meanwhile the differences—I won't tire of saying so—are not at all a tragedy, but a stimulus for the

> *exchange of experience, for borrowing what is useful*
> *and acceptable, for cooperation.*[12]

Gorbachev then turned to a theme Wimpy had been championing for more than a decade—disarmament and the conversion of military manufacturing capacity to peace time endeavors. He said:

> *We have embarked on real disarmament, and,*
> *naturally, the problem of conversion becomes ever*
> *more topical and is discussed in both the USSR and*
> *the United States. I am not inclined to underestimate*
> *the problem. It has very serious social aspects.*
> *And political demagogy on this theme is out of*
> *place because the destinies of very many people*
> *are affected. Nevertheless, it is very important to*
> *visualize the goal and not to lose sight of it in heated*
> *debates.*
>
> *If we are for disarmament, for reducing*
> *armaments and armed forces to the amounts*
> *sufficient for defense—in other words, if we are for*
> *consolidation of real security, which is a vital necessity*
> *now—it is time to think about reduction of the war*
> *industry, about converting military plants to civilian*
> *production.*[13]

Gorbachev brought the meeting to a close by explaining that things were changing fast in the Soviet Union:

> *You have visited our country at a time of great*
> *changes. There is much tension here. Transformations*
> *affect all areas of life, all sections of the population.*
> *Every effort is exerted in the perestroika drive. And*

this has turned out to be most difficult. There are achievements, and there are also losses. It is not easy to overcome what everyone is used to. But we are confident that without undue haste, and at the same time firmly pursuing the course, we will solve the tasks of the present very important stage.

Blunders and miscalculations are, perhaps, unavoidable because of the great scope of the tasks, but disorganization in society, in production, in state management are not to be permitted. Attention is concentrated on this.[14]

A head of state was finally saying what Wimpy had longed to hear about an end to the insane arms race and a conversion to a peace-time manufacturing economy. Unfortunately, they were being said by the Soviet leader, not the President of the United States. Nonetheless, Wimp was very impressed with Gorbachev and told the *Labor Today* reporter:

When you sit down with a person one-on-one or two-on-two and talk about problems, as we did with President Gorbachev, it either meshes or it doesn't. Given the fact that we could end up by blowing the world to hell, it behooves us to make things mesh.

They don't want to continue the level of nuclear terror that has existed in the world for a long period of time... They have no aversion to backing away from the nuclear precipice... They are sincerely trying to create an atmosphere in which competition can take place for better or worse in order to make the lot of the average Soviet citizen better than it is now... I believe all of that.

He impresses me as a man who is absolutely committed to confronting the problems they face. He's prepared to risk his whole political future and his not insignificant position in the world on his success or failure. That's pretty high-powered stuff where I come from.[15]

Back home, Wimpy was in the final days of his presidency. He had situated his protégés, Kourpias, Wharton, and Buffenbarger, so that they would be in positions of leadership of the IAM for the next quarter century. He was immensely pleased with that but saw one last opportunity to break with tradition and free the union of the last vestiges of its hidebound past.

Joe Manners, Chief Legal Counsel for the IAM, was a couple of months older than Wimpy and had reached the mandatory retirement age. He was given the traditional gold watch and a hearty send-off to a retirement in his native Florida. There were three lawyers working under Manners in the counsel's office and it was likely that one of them would be promoted to the top spot. The youngest, at thirty-eight, was Allison Beck, a feisty and tireless attorney who had handled some of the union's most delicate cases. Odds were stacked against her though: no union the size of the IAM had ever appointed a woman as Chief Counsel.

Allison Beck remembered:

About a year before Joe retired, I knew they were beginning to think about a successor, and I really hadn't thought about putting myself out because I didn't think it was doable. I had a lot of young children at that point and was not willing to make the compromise. Joe and I had a conversation and he said, "Allison, I really like you, you're really competent, but you're not going to be general counsel, and it's not so much that you're a woman—you're a Jewish woman."[16]

What Manners didn't take into account in his assessment was that Wimpy was never afraid to buck convention if it meant doing something that would help the IAM in the long run. There may have been those who would look askance at the appointment of a young female general counsel, and there may even have been some fading anti-Semitism from the union's Masonic past, but Wimpy didn't give a damn. He'd worked closely with Beck and knew she had the skills to do the job. A month before his term expired Wimpy decided to act. Beck was out on maternity leave, but she had been working on a complex sexual harassment case and there was a possibility of a settlement. Wimpy had Maria Cordone call Beck at home to ask her to come to the office to discuss the case.

"It was ten days after my son was born and we were in the middle of a very ugly sexual harassment case that I was basically handling," Beck recalled.

> *We were in settlement discussions, and Wimp called me in. I just struggled to find something to put on to come in. We talked about the case, and then as we were getting up and walking out of the room, he said: "You interested in being general counsel of this union?" I said, "Yeah, yeah." And he said, "Fine, the job's yours." And I said, "Hold on here, wait a minute." He said, "The job's yours." I said, "Hmm, oh my God! Thank you!" He said, "Don't thank me, you earned it" and basically walked me out the door.[17]*

FORTY-NINE

WIMPY REFLECTS

As the clock ticked off the final few days of Wimpy's presidency, the hard-charging auto mechanic - who had been so eager to change things that he began his term with a midnight staff meeting - turned philosophical.

He published a number of retrospective pieces, compiled a book, and made some bold predictions of what he thought the future would hold for his union and his country. He was remarkably accurate. In a speech to the British Columbia Labor Federation, he foretold a world consisting of three mega-economic blocs:

> One will consist of China, Japan and the Asian Rim countries, after Hong Kong is returned to the Chinese in 1994.
>
> The second mega economy will be on the European continent after the European community unites in 1992. Increased European Community trade and economic ties with the Soviet Union and Eastern Bloc nations will dwarf the home markets of Japan and the US.
>
> The third mega economic bloc will be the North American one, consisting of Canada, the US and Mexico.
>
> This in a nutshell is what the "modern" capitalism is up to: restructuring the global economy into three mega economies.
>
> Private capital is super mobile and, therefore, super sovereign. Multinational corporate enterprise

is shedding all pretense of economic nationalism, or economic patriotism, if you will. Japanese, German, French, Swedish, and Italian firms are buying into the North American economy to secure and develop their markets here. Canadian and US firms that have not already gained a foothold in the European mega economy are moving to do so. Ditto the Asian mega economy. And Japanese, Australian and Chinese are buying into the North American bloc too.

We in the trade unions are locked out of the loop. So what does it mean to us? It means the corporate state political agenda, of course![1]

His book, *Reclaiming our Future, An Agenda for American Labor*, edited by John Logue, with a foreword by Senator Ted Kennedy, was a 260-page distillation of the speeches he had given during his tenure as International President. It covered his many familiar themes: the creeping influence of Corporate America, transitioning from a war-based economy to a peace-based economy, the role of science and technology in the workplace, and the future of the labor movement.

In his introduction to the work, Logue describes Wimpy:

"Poetic, prophetic, and occasionally profane, William W. Winpisinger has been the most outspoken and most quotable American labor leader of this generation. He has variously been described in the press as everything from "a loudmouth auto mechanic," and "labor's last angry man," to merely being "brash" and "skilled at capturing the spotlight." No one has ever described him as mincing his words or pulling his punches.[2]

He was typically straightforward in his parting shot to the membership, published on the front page of the June 1989, issue of *The Machinist*, under the headline: "See you on the Battle Lines."

Before I leave office, I owe you a final accounting of where we as a union stand, and what I feel we've accomplished.

The Placid Harbor Education Center ranks as one of our proudest achievements. Information is power. There is no hope for the worker's movement in this or any country, unless members and leaders alike understand and are prepared to tackle the challenges at hand.

At Placid Harbor thousands of us gather each year to learn the truth about ourselves and our history, to share experiences and to receive professional training in everything from collective bargaining to micro-computers.

We've launched the electronic newsletter, the first regular video production by any US union. We've trained hundreds of newsletter editors. We've taught scores of leaders how to use TV, radio and the press to the union's benefit, instead of being afraid of the media or being slandered by it.

When I became International President the American labor movement was like a big snapping turtle, plodding along, all alone. When anyone tried to get near, we'd pull into our shell, snap at them and call them nasty names—kooks, weirdoes.

In 1977, we began to rebuild coalitions with the very groups that lent strength and vitality to so many historic labor battles—students and community groups, people who believed, as we do, that you can have good jobs and a healthy environment, peace and prosperity, justice and security.

Never in my darkest nightmares did I see an America that would throw people out of mental hospitals, raise interest rates, slash support for low-cost housing—and then mock the homeless and people on our streets.

Never did I dream that this government would openly conspire to destroy our nation's industrial base—sell our technological secrets to the highest foreign bidder, and ship millions of good paying jobs overseas."

So I am filled with mixed emotions as I leave office. I am greatly heartened by a revitalized, rejuvenated worker's movement, brimming with new ideas and a new willingness to innovate and engage the enemy.

I am also profoundly troubled—afraid, in fact— for the future of my country and this planet. Opposing multi-national giants will require a higher degree of global cooperation between people, governments and unions than has ever been achieved.

Each of us, brothers and sisters, bears a solemn obligation. Each of us is the guardian of the dreams and aspirations of working men and women engaged in the worldwide battle for social and economic democracy.

I am retiring as your International President, but I most certainly am not retiring from that fight. I look forward to seeing you on the battle lines in the months and years to come.[3]

It was raining and hot on June 23, 1989, as Wimpy walked into the Machinist Building on Connecticut Avenue for the last time as International President. Headquarters was busting with activity, unusual for a summer Friday, but this was no ordinary day. The Executive Council was seated in the conference room next to his office when he walked in at ten o'clock sharp with George Kourpias at his side. Wimpy took his customary seat at the head of the table and called the meeting to order.

John Peterpaul provided an update on the strike at Eastern Airlines. Tom Ducy reported on the operating costs for Placid Harbor. The cost of telephone lines for computer communications was discussed and the council decided that local lodges would be asked to pick up the tab starting in January.

Kourpias presented a special resolution to abandon plans to build the new headquarters building on Route 29 in Maryland, and instead to purchase a tract of land at 8800 Presidential Avenue in Upper Marlboro, Maryland, and build the new facility there. After a brief discussion, the resolution was passed by a unanimous vote.

Wimpy thanked the council, cleared his throat, picked up the telephone and asked Maria Cordone to send in the photographer.

The council stood and lined up against the wall, with Kourpias at the head of the line, Ducy next to him and the remaining members staged in order of seniority, Edgar House, the newest member, at the very back. Wimpy picked up a leather-bound copy of the IAM constitution and asked them to raise their right hands. Slowly, deliberately, and with perfect diction, Wimpy read the oath of office, pausing after each phrase so the council members could repeat his words. It was just after 10:30 when he finished. Wimpy shook hands with George Kourpias, the new International President, wished him well, and adjourned the meeting.

That evening, Kourpias presided over Wimp's retirement dinner at the Washington Hilton. The gathering included a number of surprise guests—Ed Asner, Studs Terkel, and Edith Winpisinger, Wimpy's eighty-seven-year-old mother. Tom Buffenbarger had been dispatched to Cleveland on the IAM jet to fetch her for what would be her first ride on an airplane. He was afraid she was going to be terrified to fly, but, he said, "She bolted up the stairs to the plane. She was a great sport about it."[4]

Fifteen hundred well wishers crammed into the International Ballroom to hear Tom Donahue, the Secretary Treasurer of the AFL-CIO, deliver a brief farewell speech, followed by a gift presentation from Tom Ducy. The speech making was kept to a minimum to allow time for three video tributes, including one starring Edith Winpisinger, in which she recounted the story of getting Wimpy fired from his first job as a paperboy.

As Wimpy took the microphone to thank everyone, the crowd was hushed, even tearful. He was solemn and gracious, saying that he accepted the tribute paid to him not on his own behalf, but on that of the members of the IAM whom he loved and had served faithfully. With his voice cracking and tears welling up in his eyes Wimpy brought his remarks to a close:

> God speed. Stay in the fight. And for those in this audience from the IAM, may I simply say to you: Love this union. Don't just love it, clutch it to your breast. Nurture and protect it. And every once in a while, sacrifice a little for it—because sacrifices will

have to be made. And always remember when you do it, that this institution is more important than any single component of it. And it's by getting together and giving it that kind of respect that we can preserve it.[5]

* * *

EPILOGUE

Wimpy left a long and enduring legacy in the IAM and the American labor movement. George Kourpias served as International President from 1989 to 1997. He was succeeded by Tom Buffenbarger who, as of this writing, has served more than a decade in that post. Don Wharton was elected General Secretary Treasurer of the IAM in 1993, and served in that capacity until his retirement in 2002. Allison Beck has served as General Counsel for the IAM for nearly two decades. Heather Booth and Barbara Shailor both have had long and successful careers in senior executive positions for the AFL-CIO, and Maria Cordone has continued to serve the IAM as Director of the Community Services and Retirees Department.

Countless other activists who got their start with Wimpy, both labor union members and individuals working for the social justice organizations he championed, are today providing leadership and inspiration to another generation of progressives.

The training center Wimpy founded is now called the William W. Winpisinger Education and Training Center at Placid Harbor. Guide Dogs of America's major fundraising efforts each year, the William W. Winpisinger Charity Banquet and the William W. Winpisinger Charity Golf Tournament, have raised millions of dollars to support that institution.

To the surprise of many, when Wimpy retired, he actually *retired*. He and Tom Ducy each bought large recreational vehicles and traveled the country together with their wives enjoying the nomadic lifestyle. Wimpy and Pearl often stopped in Cleveland and picked up Phil and Ruth Zannella to join them.

He also devoted more time to his children and grandchildren than his work in the union had ever allowed. Daughter Vickie Winpisinger recalled, "After my dad retired, he was able to attend many of my son Chris's baseball and football games. He really enjoyed these and I think he regretted not being around more when we were younger." His son Ken Winpisinger remembered, "It seemed like he had put aside the things he was interested in and started acting like he was more interested in the things I was doing. I actually got him to go to motorcycle races, and I never thought that would happen. He used to call me a lot too, and ask me questions about mechanics and stuff on his motor home, almost once a day. Then at one point I realized he was calling not so much because he's concerned about a mechanical problem, but because he just wanted to talk to me." Vickie Winpisinger related, "He tried very hard to learn how to use the computer, and he would call me, just about every day. 'How do you do labels? How do you do labels?' and I'd walk him through it. After he died, I went back to clean out his office and he had boxes and boxes of labels with his return address on them. Just boxes!"

Maria Cordone recalled that Wimpy like to shop at the Sears store in Silver Spring, and that he spent so much time browsing in their tool department that a new employee there actually made the mistake of assuming he was a fellow sales clerk.

Daughter Linda Winpisinger remembers him menacing the neighborhood at the wheel of a tractor the IAM had given him as a convention gift. "He always prided himself of being such a good driver," Linda recalled with a laugh, "he had this huge riding mower, actually, it was a John Deere tractor. He hit a neighbor's car with it, he hit a tree with it and he hit my car with it. Then he yelled at me because my car was parked in the driveway!"

Wimpy continued to champion liberal political causes and attended meetings of the Democratic National Committee, Americans for Democratic Action, or the Democratic Socialist Organizing Committee whenever his travel schedule permitted.

He was appointed to the Board of Directors of Trans World Airlines, and was a forceful advocate for the carrier's workers until his health declined and he was diagnosed with cancer in 1997.

George Kourpias recalls visiting Wimpy at Johns Hopkins Hospital in Columbia, Maryland, shortly before he succumbed to the disease. "He was a strong man," Kourpias recalled fondly, "He didn't have a fright. On his death bed he said, 'You know, I told my brother that maybe he would never see me again. But I told him not to be upset, I didn't need that. I don't want that. I've lived a good life, and I'm not afraid of death because I've seen it.' He had the strength that it takes to do it, and he never made you feel that you ought to be suffering too. He was willing to face it. He was a strong guy."

William Wayne Winpisinger died on December 11, 1997, the day after his seventy-third birthday.

WIMPY—FOOTNOTES

Chapter One

1. *Reclaiming Our Future,* William W. Winpisinger, (Westview,1989) p 1
2. Ibid, p 18

Chapter Two

1. *Cleveland Free Press* 8/14/78 by Mike Feinsilber, UPI
2. *Reclaiming Our Future,* William W. Winpisinger, (Westview, 1989) p 4
3. *"We Aim to Please",* 1934
4. *Reclaiming our Future,* William W. Winpisinger, (Westview, 1989) p 5

Chapter Three

1. World War Two Timeline, University of San Diego
2. *Cleveland Press,* 10/16/42
3. *Invasion,* John J. Spano, p 15
4. Ibid, p 16
5. Ibid, p 19
6. Ibid, p 20
7. Ibid, p 21
8. Ibid, p 29
9. Ibid, p 31
10. *D-Day,* Stephen E. Ambrose, (Touchstone, 1995) p 320–321
11. "Fires of France Dim Golden Moon", by Gene Currivan, *The New York Times,* 6/7/44
12. *Invasion,* John J. Spano, p 46
13. *Reclaiming Our Future,* William W. Winpisinger, (Westview, 1989) p 5

Chapter Four

1. *Reclaiming Our Future*, William W. Winpisinger, (Westview, 1989) p 6
2. Tom Buffenbarger interview, Dorothy Fennell, September 16, 2003
3. Winston Churchill speech at Westminster College, Fulton, Missouri, March 5, 1946

Chapter Five

1. *The Fighting Machinists*, Robert G. Rodden, Kelly Press, p 6
2. *The Machinists, A New Study in American Trade Unionism*, Mark Perlman, (Harvard University Press, 1962) p 6
3. Secret Societies and the Labour Movement, Dr. Bob James, Australian Society for the Study of Labour History, 1999
4. Order of United Machinists and Mechanical Engineers of America circular, T.W. Talbot, September 10, 1888
5. Ibid
6. International Association of Machinists Journal, October, 1892, p 260
7. Memories of the Past, by P. J. Conlon, International Association of Machinists Journal, May, 1922, p 308

Chapter Six

1. Report of Vice President Conlon, International Association of Machinists Journal, November, 1915, p 998
2. Report of Vice President Conlon, International Association of Machinists Journal, December, 1915, p 1116–1117

3. *John L. Lewis, Labor Leader*, Robert H. Ziegler (G.K. Hall & Company, 1988) p 81

4. *John L. Lewis, A Biography*, Melvyn Dubofsky and Warren Van Tine (University of Illinois Press, 1986) p 161

5. *The Machinists, A New Study in American Trade Unionism*, Mark Perlman, (Harvard University Press, 1962) p 84

6. *The Fighting Machinists*, Robert G. Rodden, Kelly Press, p 111

7. International Association of Machinists Journal, March, 1944, p 111

Chapter Seven

1. Reclaiming our Future, William W. Winpisinger, (Westview, 1989) p 7

2. Scrappy Machinists Leader Pushes Labor to the Left, by Daniel D. Cook, *Industry Week*, April 2, 1979, p 33

3. Tom Buffenbarger interview, Dorothy Fennell, September 16, 2003

4. The Machinist, April 24, 1947 p 3

5. Ibid

6. The Machinist, June 26, 1947 p 1

7. *The Fighting Machinists*, Robert G. Rodden, Kelly Press, p 152

8. Truman Wins with 304 Electoral Votes, by Arthur Krock, *The New York Times*, November 4, 1948, p 1

Chapter Eight

1. *The Fighting Machinists*, Robert G. Rodden, Kelly Press, p 116

2. *The Machinists, A New Study in American Trade Unionism*, Mark Perlman, (Harvard University Press, 1962) p127

3. George Kourpias interview, Patrick S. Halley, August 2, 2006

4. *The Fighting Machinists*, Robert G. Rodden, Kelly Press, p 212

5. George Kourpias interview, Patrick S. Halley, August 2, 2006

6. *The Machinist*, May 26, 1949 p 1

7. *The Machinist*, August 11, 1949 p 8

8. The *New York Times*, September 25, 1949

9. *The Machinist*, September 29, 1949 p8

10. *The Machinist*, November 17, 1949 p1

Chapter Nine

1. Tom Buffenbarger interview, Dorothy Fennell, September 16, 2003

2. The Cleveland *Plain Dealer*, September 29, 1950

3. *Reclaiming Our Future*, William W. Winpisinger, (Westview, 1989) p 8

Chapter Ten

1. Don Wharton interview, Patrick S. Halley, June 15, 2006

2. Ibid

3. *Reclaiming Our Future*, William W. Winpisinger, (Westview, 1989) p 8

4. Ken Winpisinger interview, Patrick S. Halley, August 3, 2006

5. Mike Winpisinger interview, Dorothy Fennell, October 7, 2003

6. Ken Winpisinger interview, Dorothy Fennell, October 7, 2003

7. Mike Winpisinger interview, Dorothy Fennell, October 7, 2003

8. Ken Winpisinger interview, Patrick S. Halley, August 3, 2006

9. George Kourpias interview, Dorothy Fennell, September 16, 2003

10. *Reclaiming Our Future*, William W. Winpisinger, (Westview, 1989) p 8

11. Don Wharton interview, Patrick S. Halley, June 15, 2006

12. *Reclaiming Our Future*, William W. Winpisinger, (Westview, 1989) p 8

13. *Reclaiming Our Future*, William W. Winpisinger, (Westview, 1989) p 7

14. The Machinist, March 10, 1955, p 1

Chapter Eleven

1. The Machinist, September 29, 1949, p 1

2. *Mobbed Up*, James Neff, (Atlantic Monthly Press, 1989) p 63

3. Ibid, p 57

4. Tom Buffenbarger interview, Patrick S. Halley, August 2, 2006

5. The Machinist, July 27, 1950, p 1

6. *The Fighting Machinists*, Robert G. Rodden, Kelly Press, p 173

7. The Machinist, September 27, 1956, p 2

8. The Machinist, February 17, 1955, p 2

9. Ibid

10. George Kourpias interview, Dorothy Fennell, September 16, 2003

Chapter Twelve

1. The Machinist, April 11, 1957, p 8

2. Ibid

3. *The Enemy Within*, Robert F. Kennedy, (Harper Collins, 1960) p 6

4. Ibid, p 3

5. The Machinist, February 7, 1957, p 1

6. "The Rise and Fall of Labor Giant Dave Beck," by Dan Raley, *Seattle Post Intelligencer*, December 3, 1999

7. Corruption and Reform in the Teamsters Union, David Witwer, (University of Illinois Press, 2003) p 133

8. The Machinist, May 16, 1957, p 4

9. The Machinist, May 30, 1957, p 3

10. *The Enemy Within*, Robert F. Kennedy, (Harper Collins, 1960) p 75

11. *George Meany and His Times*, Archie Robinson, (Simon and Schuster, 1981), p 196

Chapter Thirteen

1. Mike Winpisinger interview, Dorothy Fennell, October 7, 2003

2. Ken Winpisinger interview, Patrick S. Halley, August 3, 2006

3. The Machinist, August 28, 1958, p 3

4. Mike Winpisinger interview, Dorothy Fennell, October 7, 2003

5. Ken Winpisinger interview, Patrick S. Halley, August 3, 2006

6. Mike Winpisinger interview, Dorothy Fennell, October 7, 2003

7. The Machinist, January 31, 1957, p 12

8. The Machinist, April 3, 1958, p 8

9. The Machinist, March 6, 1958, p 8

Chapter Fourteen

1. "NAM Historical Highlights," National Association of Manufacturers website, (nam.org)

2. The Machinist, September 3, 1959, p 3
3. The Machinist, November 5, 1959, P 8
4. The Machinist, September 22, 1960, p 3
5. Ibid
6. The Fighting Machinists, Robert G. Rodden, Kelly Press, p 218

Chapter Fifteen

1. Website of The Nation, (thenation.com)
2. Ralph Nader, The Nation, May 5, 2003
3. The Ultras, by Fred J. Cook, The Nation, June 30, 1962, p 565
4. Ibid, p 567
5. Ibid, p 569
6. Ibid
7. Ibid, p 590
8. Ibid, p 591
9. Ibid, p 592

Chapter Sixteen

1. The Kennedy Tapes, edited by Ernest R. May & Philip D. Zelikow, (Harvard University Press, 1997) p 46
2. Ibid, p 276-277
3. The Boston Globe, October 23, 1962
4. The Cleveland Plain Dealer, October 23, 1962
5. The Machinist, November 1, 1962 p 1
6. Vickie Winpisinger interview, Dorothy Fennell, October 7, 2003
7. Ken Winpisinger interview, Dorothy Fennell, October 7, 2003
8. Letter from Birmingham Jail, by Dr. Martin Luther King, Jr., April 16, 1963

9. Remarks of Dr. Martin Luther King, Jr., Washington, DC, August 28, 1963

10. Remarks of President John F. Kennedy, East Berlin, Germany, June 26, 1963

Chapter Seventeen

1. George Kourpias interview, Patrick S. Halley, August 2, 2006
2. Ibid
3. George Kourpias interview, Patrick S. Halley, October 18, 2005
4. *The Machinist*, September 24, 1964 p 2
5. Ibid
6. *The Machinist*, January 30, 1964 p 1
7. George Kourpias interview, Patrick S. Halley, October 18, 2005

Chapter Eighteen

1. *The Machinist*, March 18, 1965 p 1
2. *The Machinist*, July 8, 1965 p 1
3. *The Fighting Machinists*, Robert G. Rodden, Kelly Press, p 239
4. *The Machinist*, June 24, 1965 p 5
5. George Kourpias interview, Patrick S. Halley, August 2, 2006
6. *The Machinist*, March 11, 1965 p 3
7. *The Machinist*, June 17, 1965 p 3
8. *The Machinist*, June 24, 1965 p 8
9. *The Machinist*, September 2, 1965

Chapter Twenty

1. George Kourpias interview, Patrick S. Halley, October 18, 2005
2. George Kourpias interviews, Patrick S. Halley, October 18, 2005 and August 2, 2006
3. "Strike Bill Vowed" by David R. Jones, *The New York Times*, July 17, 1967, p 19
4. Ibid, p 1
5. *The Machinist*, September 7, 1967, p 1
6. *The Machinist*, August 17, 1967, p 1
7. Ken Winpisinger interview, Patrick S. Halley, August 3, 2006
8. *The Machinist*, August 3, 1967, p 3
9. *The Machinist*, August 10, 1967, p 12
10. *The Machinist*, August 17, 1967, p 10
11. *The Machinist*, November 17, 1968, p 8

Chapter Twenty-one

1. *CBS Evening News*, February 27, 1968
2. *The Machinist*, February 1, 1968, p 1
3. "Johnson and Nixon Given Big New Hampshire Edge, by Warren Weaver, Jr., *The New York Times*, March 10, 1968, p 1
4. Ibid
5. "McCarthy Rides on 'Student Power'", *The New York Times*, March 10, 1968, p E-1
6. *The New York Times*, March 17, 1968, p 1
7. "Johnson Says He Won't Run" by Tom Wicker, *The New York Times*, April 1, 1968, p 1
8. "Kennedy Appeals for Non-violence" by R.W. Apple, Jr., *The New York Times*, April 5, 1968, p 33
9. "Guard Troops into Capital" by Ben A. Franklin, *The New York Times*, April 6, 1968, p 1

10. "Statement by President on Rights Bill," The New York Times, April 12, 1968, p 19

11. "The Death of Bobby Kennedy," by Ivor Davis, *The Ventura County Reporter*, December 7, 2006, p 1

12. "World Morality Crisis," by James Reston, The New York Times, June 6, 1968, p 20

13. "Dementia in the Second City," *Time Magazine*, September 6, 1968

14. "Daley Defends his Police," by R. W. Apple, Jr., *The New York Times*, August 30, 1968, p1

15. Ibid

16. *The Machinist*, September 12, 1968, p 3

17. Ibid

Chapter Twenty-two

1. *The Machinist*, September 19, 1968, p 2

2. *The Machinist*, June 11, 1970, p 1

3. *The Machinist*, June 24, 1970, p 5

4. *The Machinist*, July 31, 1969, p 6

5. "Astronauts Land on Plain; Collect Rocks, Plant Flag," by John Noble Wilford, *The New York Times*, July 21, 1969, p 1

6. *The Machinist*, February 6, 1969, p 1

7. *The Machinist*, September 25, 1969, p 9

8. *The Machinist*, June 19, 1969, p 5

9. *The Machinist*, June 11, 1970, p 8

10. Ibid

Chapter Twenty-three

1. *The Machinist*, September 14, 1972, p 2

2. Ibid, p 8

3. Don Wharton interview, Patrick S. Halley, June 15, 2006

4. Paul Eustace interview, Patrick S. Halley, November 30, 2006

5. George Kourpias interview, Patrick S. Halley, August 2, 2006

6. Ibid

7. Proceedings of Convention, 1972, p 181

8. Ibid, p 182

9. George Kourpias interview, Patrick S. Halley, August 2, 2006

10. The Machinist, September 21, 1972, p 2

Chapter Twenty-four

1. George Kourpias interview, Patrick S. Halley, November 10, 2006

2. George Kourpias interview, Patrick S. Halley, August 2, 2006

3. Ibid

4. William W. Winpisinger, speech to the Great Lakes Territory staff conference, Cincinnati, Ohio, March 30, 1974

5. Ibid

6. William W. Winpisinger, speech at Carnegie-Mellon Institute, Pittsburgh, Pennsylvania, October 28, 1976

7. William W. Winpisinger, notes for remarks, Arden House, June 17, 1976

Chapter Twenty-five

1. William W. Winpisinger, notes for remarks, Illinois Council of Machinists, February 7, 1976

2. Ibid

3. Ibid

4. *The Machinist*, February, 1976, p 5

5. Phil Zannella, Jr. interview, Patrick S. Halley, March 28, 2006

6. Bud Melvin interview, Dorothy Fennell, November 11, 2003

7. Ibid

Chapter Twenty-six

1. William W. Winpisinger, notes for remarks, Fort Wayne, Indiana, October 29, 1976

2. William W. Winpisinger, remarks to the American Arbitration Association, New York, New York, April 19, 1977

3. William W. Winpisinger, speech at ADA Dinner, Baltimore, Maryland, May 1, 1977

4. Ibid

5. Ibid

6. William W. Winpisinger, notes for remarks, A. Philip Randolph Institute, Cherry Hill, New Jersey, June 4, 1977

7. Ibid

8. Ibid

9. Ibid

10. William W. Winpisinger, remarks to the NAACP, St. Louis, Missouri, June 28, 1977

Chapter Twenty-seven

1. George Kourpias interview, Patrick S. Halley, August 2, 2006

2. "Reclaiming Our Future" by William W. Winpisinger, (Westview, 1989) p 18

3. "Drive to Isolate J. P. Stevens is Renewed" by Michael C. Jensen, *The New York Times*, March 17, 1978, p D-3

4. President Jimmy Carter's message to Congress on Labor Reform Legislation, as quoted in *The Machinist*, August, 1977

5. William W. Winpisinger, remarks to The Industrial Relations Research Association, San Diego, California, September 21, 1977

6. *The Machinist*, August, 1977, p 1

7. *The Machinist*, September, 1977, p 5

8. William W. Winpisinger, Notes for Remarks at ADA Meeting, Washington, D.C., September 17 and 18, 1977

9. William W. Winpisinger, remarks to The Industrial Research Association, San Diego, California, September 21, 1977

10. Ibid

11. *The Machinist*, October, 1977, p 3

12. "Unions Win a Victory on Labor Legislation," by Philip Shabecoff, *The New York Times*, October 5, 1977, p 19

13. *The Machinist*, November, 1977, p 1

14. "House Passes Bill Aiding Union Drives," by Philip Shabecoff, *The New York Times*, October 7, 1977, p 6

15. Ibid

16. William W. Winpisinger, Notes for Remarks to Third Annual Convention, Citizen's Action Coalition of Indiana, Indianapolis, Indiana, November 5, 1977

17. George Kourpias interview, Patrick S. Halley, October 18, 2005

18. Maria Cordone interview, Patrick S. Halley, November 10, 2006

19. George Kourpias interview, Patrick S. Halley, October 18, 2005

Chapter Twenty-eight

1. William W. Winpisinger, remarks to General Electric Components Management Meeting, Sarasota, Florida, January 9, 1978

2. William W. Winpisinger, remarks to MNPL Planning Committee meeting, Washington, DC, January 23, 1978

3. "Senate is Deluged by Lobbyists As It Studies Labor Law Change," by Philip Shabecoff, *The New York Times*, January 27, 1978, p 1

4. Ibid

5. *The Machinist*, March, 1978, p 1

6. "The President's Proposed Energy Policy", speech by President Carter, April 18, 1977

7. "CIA Sees Oil Price Increase Unless Conservation Cuts Demand," by Edward Cowan, *The New York Times*, April 19, 1977, p 24

8. William W. Winpisinger, remarks to Massachusetts Americans for Democratic Action, Boston, Massachusetts, March 12, 1978

9. George Kourpias interview, Patrick S. Halley, November 10, 2006

10. Heather Booth interview, Dorothy Fennell, October 7, 2003

11. William W. Winpisinger, remarks to Energy Coalition Luncheon, Washington, DC, March 16, 1978

12. Heather Booth interview, Dorothy Fennell, October 7, 2003

13. Ibid

14. Ibid

15. The Machinist, May, 1978, p 3

16. Ibid

17. Barbara Shailor interview, Dorothy Fennell, October 6, 2003

18. William W. Winpisinger, Remarks to Debs-Thomas Awards Dinner, Chicago, Illinois, May 7, 1978

19. "Big Labor's Bogeyman," by A. H. Raskin, *Fortune Magazine*, June 5, 1978, p 150

20. William W. Winpisinger, remarks to Industrial Relations Association of St. Louis, St. Louis, MO, April 19, 1978

21."Momentum Is Seen Shifting to Labor Bill Opponents, by Philip Shabecoff, *The New York Times*, June 18, 1978, p 35

Chapter Twenty-nine

1.Maria Cordone interview, Patrick S. Halley, November 10, 2006

2.George Kourpias interview, Patrick S. Halley, October 18, 2005

3.The Machinist, September, 1978, p 3

4.William W. Winpisinger, remarks to IAM Staff Conference, Cincinnati, Ohio, September 6, 1978

5. Ibid

6. Ibid

7. Ibid

8. Ibid

9. Ibid

10. Ibid

11. Ibid

12. Ibid

13. Ibid

14. Ibid

15. Ibid

16. Ibid

17. William W. Winpisinger, remarks to IAM Staff Conference, Cincinnati, Ohio, September 8, 1978

18. Ibid
19. Ibid
20. Ibid
21. Ibid
22. Ibid
23. Ibid
24. Ibid
25. Ibid
26. Ibid
27. Ibid
28. Ibid
29. Ibid

Chapter Thirty

1. William W. Winpisinger, letter to the President of the United States, September 25, 1978
2. Ibid
3. *The Machinist*, January, 1979, p 3
4. "Mayor's Group Vows to Oppose Cuts in Urban and Social Funds," by Robert Reinhold, *The New York Times*, January 25, 1979 p B 13
5. Ibid
6. William W. Winpisinger, remarks at Press Conference on Budget Priorities, Washington, DC, January 25, 1979
7. George Kourpias interview, Patrick S. Halley, November 10, 2006
8. *The Machinist*, February, 1979, p 6
9. Ibid
10. William W. Winpisinger, remarks to Consumer Federation of America Assembly, Washington, DC, February 8, 1979
11. "Carter Doubts that US Could Eliminate OPEC," *The New York Times*, February 11, 1979 p D 1

12. William W. Winpisinger, remarks to Energy Coalition Rally, Washington, DC, May 6, 1979

13. "The Moral Equivalent of the Gas Line," *New York Times* editorial, June 24, 1979, p E 20

14. "OPEC Pricing: An Antitrust Question," by Philip Taubman, *The New York Times*, June 25, 1979

15. "Split Price on Oil Expected By OPEC, Saudis Seek $18 Top," by Youssef M. Ibrahim, *The New York Times*, June 28, 1979, p A 1

16. *The Machinist*, June, 1979, p 16

17. William W. Winpisinger, remarks accepting the Israeli Prime Minister's Award, Washington, DC, 1979

18. William W. Winpisinger, remarks to Rural America Conference, Washington, DC, June 26, 1979

19. "Poll Shows Carter is Trailing in South", by Wayne King, *The New York Times*, July 8, 1979, p 13

20. President Carter's Address to the Nation, July 15, 1979

21. Ibid

22. Ibid

23. "William Winpisinger: A leader of the Dump-Carter Movement," by Michael Kernan, the *Washington Post*, July 7, 1979, p B 1

24. Ibid

25. Ibid

26. Ibid

27. "OPEC Is Dismissed From Suit," by Pamela G. Hollie, *The New York Times*, August 21, 1979, p D 1

28. "US Accused on OPEC." Associated Press, *The New York Times*, August 23, 1979, p D 1

29. Ibid

30. "Judge Backs OPEC in Antitrust Suit," by Pamela G. Hollie, *The New York Times*, August 24, 1979 p D 1

31. "Judge Rejects Suing of OPEC," Associated Press, *The New York Times*, October 17, 1979 p D 1

32. *George Meany and His Times*, by Archie Robinson, (Simon and Schuster, 1981) p 391

Chapter Thirty-one

1. *The Machinist*, August, 1979, p 6
2. *The Machinist*, August, 1979, p 6
3. Ibid
4. William W. Winpisinger, remarks to The Liberal Party of The Yale Political Union, New Haven, Connecticut, September 13, 1979
5. William W. Winpisinger, letter to Nikolai Zinovyev, August 30, 1979
6. Lane Kirkland, Champion of American Labor, by Arch Puddington, (Wiley, 2005) p 91
7. *Sixty Minutes*, CBS News, October 14, 1979
8. Ibid
9. Ibid
10. "Teheran Students Seize US Embassy And Hold Hostages," by Reuters, *The New York Times*, November 5, 1979, p 1
11. "Kennedy Declares His Candidacy, Vowing New Leadership of Nation," by Hedrick Smith, *The New York Times*, November 8, 1979, p 1

Chapter Thirty-two

1. "Carter Calls Soviet Actions A 'Threat'," by Bernard Gwertzman, *The New York Times*, December 28, 1979, p 1
2. Personal observation by the author
3. Ibid
4. "Kennedy Is Confident on Iowa Despite Poll," by B. Drummond Ayres, Jr., *The New York Times*, January 13, 1980, p A 22

5. George Kourpias interview, Patrick S. Halley, October 18, 2005

6. "Carter Wins Strong Victory in Iowa As Bush Takes Lead Over Reagan," by Adam Clymer, *The New York Times*, January 22, 1980, p A1

7. Winpisinger Profile, by Alan Thompson, the *Cleveland Plain Dealer*, March 21, 1980, p B1

8. Ibid

9. Ibid

10. Ibid

11. Ibid

12. Ibid

13. George Kourpias interview, Patrick S. Halley, November 10, 2006

14. Edward M. Kennedy speech at Georgetown University, January 28, 1980

15. "Kennedy Is Said to Stem New Hampshire Decline," by Hedrick Smith, *The New York Times*, February 1, 1980, p A 13

16. "Khomeini Statement Jolts U.S. Officials," by Bernard Gwertzman, *The New York Times*, February 24, 1980, p 11

17. William W. Winpisinger, Remarks to IAM Aerospace Conference, April 9, 1980, San Diego, California

18. "Kennedy Stepping Up Pace as Prospects Grow Dimmer," by Drummond Ayers, Jr., *The New York Times*, May 25, 1980, p 1

19. "Last Primaries Held," by Adam Clymer, *The New York Times*, June 4, 1980, p A1

Chapter Thirty-three

1. George Kourpias interview, Patrick S. Halley, November 10, 2006

2. William W. Winpisinger, remarks to the NFL Players Association, Las Vegas, Nevada, January 6, 1977

3. The Machinist, December, 1978 p 6

4. George Kourpias interview, Dorothy Fennell, September 16, 2003

5. Ibid

6. *The Machinist*, July, 1980, p 15

7. William W. Winpisinger, remarks to IAM District 98 Annual Meeting, Harrisburg, Pennsylvania, May 10, 1980

8. "I wish I Had...," by George Lardner, Jr., *The Washington Post*, July 19, 1980, p 1

9. "Koch Calls Carter Weak in New York," by Irvin Molotsky, *The New York Times*, August 1, 1980, p A1

10. "Carter Aides Yield On TV Debate Time And Win Unity Vow," by Hedrick Smith, *The New York Times*, August 6, 1980, p A1

11. William W. Winpisinger, Remarks to the Democratic National Convention, New York, New York, August 12, 1980

12. "A Bid To 'Keep Faith,'" by Hedrick Smith, *The New York Times*, August 13, 1980, p A1

13. Paul Eustace interview, Patrick S. Halley, November 30, 2006

14. Ibid

15. Maria Cordone interview, Patrick S. Halley, October 17, 2005

Chapter Thirty-four

1. Minutes of the AFL-CIO Executive Committee meeting, August 20—21, 1980, Chicago, Illinois

2. *The Machinist*, September, 1980, p 1

3. Bob Kalaski interview, Patrick S. Halley, April 16, 2007

4. Proceedings of the 30th IAM Grand Lodge Convention, p 9

5. Ibid, p 9
6. Ibid, p 10
7. Ibid, p 12
8. Ibid, p 12
9. Ibid, p 14
10. Ibid, p 29
11. Ibid, p 30
12. Ibid, p 61
13. Ibid
14. Ibid
15. Ibid, p 64
16. Ibid
17. Ibid, p 66
18. Tom Buffenbarger interview, Patrick S. Halley, August 2, 2006
19. Proceedings of the 30th IAM Grand Lodge Convention, p 313
20. Tom Buffenbarger interview, Patrick S. Halley, August 2, 2006

Chapter Thirty-five

1. Bob Kalaski interview, Patrick S. Halley, April 16, 2007
2. The Machinist, May, 1980, p 16
3. Ibid
4. Bob Kalaski interview, Patrick S. Halley, April 16, 2007
5. Proceedings of the 30th IAM Grand Lodge Convention, p158
6. Bob Kalaski interview, Patrick S. Halley, April 16, 2007
7. Ibid
8. The Machinist, October, 1979, p 3
9. William W. Winpisinger, Remarks to the Western Labor Press Association, Los Angeles, California, June 13, 1980

Chapter Thirty-six

1. "Biting the Bullet," by David Courtright and William Winpisinger, *The New York Times*, October 26, 1980, p E 19

2. "Carter and Reagan Dispute Views on Arms Policy, Economy and Iran in Broad Debate Before Nation," by Adam Clymer, *The New York Times*, October 29, 1980, p 1

3. William W. Winpisinger, Politics Today and Alternative Political Parties, University of Massachusetts, Amherst, Massachusetts, October 15, 1980

4. Ibid

5. Ibid

6. Ibid

7. William W. Winpisinger, Remarks to Iowa Fourth Congressional District Democrats, Des Moines, Iowa, May 2, 1981

8. George Kourpias interview, Patrick S. Halley, November 10, 2006

9. William W. Winpisinger, "The Pentagon Five Year Plan, A Major Threat to Peace and Security," remarks at Florida State University, Tallahassee, Florida, November 13, 1980

10. The Machinist, January, 1981, p 6

11. Ibid

12. Tom Buffenbarger interview, Patrick S. Halley, August 2, 2006

13. William W. Winpisinger, Keynote Address to the New Democratic Party of Canada, Vancouver, British Columbia, July 2, 1981

14. Ibid

15. Bob Kalaski interview, Patrick S. Halley, April 16, 2007

16. "US Rules Out Rehiring Striking Air Controllers," by Warren Brown, *The Washington Post*, August 7, 1981, p A1

17. Ibid

Chapter Thirty-eight

1. William W. Winpisinger letter to Traffic Violations Bureau, Warrenton, Missouri, October 20, 1981

2. William W. Winpisinger remarks to UAW/CAP Dinner, Sheboygan Labor Council, Sheboygan, Wisconsin, January 23, 1982

3. "New Car Dealers Dwindling As Industry's Troubles Grow," by Fran J. Prial, The New York Times, August 28, 1982, p b1

4. "Work Won't Be the Same Again," by Jeremy Main, *Fortune* Magazine, June 28, 1982, p 58

5. Gene Glover interview, Dorothy Fennell, September 17, 2003

6. William W. Winpisinger, remarks at Florida International University, Miami, Florida, March 31, 1982

7. Tom Buffenbarger interview, Patrick S. Halley, August 2, 2006

8. Don Wharton interview, Patrick S. Halley, June 15, 2006

9. Tom Buffenbarger interview, Patrick S. Halley, August 2, 2006

10. "Behind the Football Strike: New Questions for Labor," by William Serrin, *The New York Times*, October 17, 1982, p B1

11. "In a Year of Concessions, This Union Made Gains," by A.H. Raskin, *The New York Times*, November 21, 1982

12. "Message for ERA," by William W. Winpisinger, July 9, 1978

13. Barbara Shailor interview, Dorothy Fennell, October 6, 2003

14. "America Mismanaged," remarks of William W. Winpisinger to the Japan Society, New York, New York, April 23, 1982

15. Ibid

16. Ibid

17. William W. Winpisinger, remarks to UCLEA Professional Council Conference, St. Louis, Missouri, December 2, 1982

18. The Machinist, June, 1982, p 7

Chapter Thirty-nine

1. "Abandoning Its Original Mandate," by William W. Winpisinger, *The New York Times*, December 5, 1982

2. Ibid

3. Letter to the Editor, by Raymond J. Donovan, Secretary of Labor, *The New York Times*, December 19, 1982

4. Letter to the Editor, by Thorne G. Auchter, Assistant Secretary of Occupational Safety and Health Administration, *The New York Times*, December 19, 1982

5. "State of the Union, January, 1983," The Machinist, January, 1983, p 3

6. Ibid

7. Mike Winpisinger interview, Dorothy Fennell, October 7, 2003

8. Maria Cordone interview, Patrick S. Halley, October 17, 2005

9. "Excerpts From President's Speech to National Association of Evangelicals," *The New York Times*, March 9, 1983

10. "President's Speech on Military Spending and a New Defense," *The New York Times*, March 24, 1983

11. "Effect of US Foreign Policy on American Workers," speech by William W. Winpisinger, San Francisco, California, April 9, 1983.

12. Ibid

13. "Andropov Promises Flexibility At Arms Talks," *The New York Times*, August 18, 1983 (Foreign Desk)

14. Ibid

15. Ibid

16. Ibid

17. "Robots and New Technology," speech by William W. Winpisinger, Kalamazoo, Michigan. April 4, 1983

18. "*Concessions and How to Beat Them*," by Jane Slaughter (Labor Education and Research Project, 1983), Foreword by William W. Winpisinger, p 2

Chapter Forty

1. "A Liberal Union Chief On The Politics Of 1984," by Seth S. King, *The New York Times*, August 4, 1983

2. Ibid

3. Ibid

4. "AFL-CIO industrial unions call for rebuilding America," *The Machinist*, June, 1983, p 4

5. George Kourpias interview, Patrick S. Halley, November 10, 2006

6. "Mondale Wins Handily In Iowa," by Howell Raines, *The New York Times*, February 21, 1984

7. "The Campaign Reshaped," by Hedrick Smith, *The New York Times*, February 29, 1984

8. "Mobbed Up," by James Neff (The Atlantic Monthly Press, 1989) p 389–390

9. Ibid, p 391

Chapter Forty-one

1. Phil Zannella, Jr. interview, Patrick S. Halley, March 28, 2006
2. Don Wharton interview, Patrick S. Halley, June 15, 2006
3. Bud Melvin interview, Dorothy Fennell, November 11, 2003
4. *The Machinist,* June, 1980, p 10
5. *The Machinist,* May, 1981, p 8
6. *The Machinist,* December, 1981, p 4
7. *The Machinist,* March, 1982, p 13
8. Ibid
9. Ken Winpisinger interview, Patrick S. Halley, August 3, 2006
10. Linda Winpisinger interview, Patrick S. Halley, August 3, 2006
11. Ken Winpisinger interview, Patrick S. Halley, August 3, 2006
12. Tom Buffenbarger interview, Patrick S. Halley, August 2, 2006
13. *The Machinist,* December, 1986, p 9
14. George Kourpias interview, Patrick S. Halley, August 2, 2006

Chapter Forty-two

1. William W. Winpisinger, Opening Remarks to the 1984 Grand Lodge Convention, Seattle, Washington, September 17, 1984
2. Ibid
3. Ibid
4. Ibid
5. Proceedings of the IAM 1984 Grand Lodge Convention, p 126

6. Ibid, p 134
7. Ibid
8. Ibid, p 140
9. William W. Winpisinger, remarks at dinner honoring Earl Bourden, New Hampshire, November 16, 1984
10. William W. Winpisinger, remarks to Americans for Democratic Action, St. Louis, Missouri, December 1, 1984

Chapter Forty-three

1. *The Machinist*, May, 1984, p 8
2. Weldon Granger interview, Patrick S. Halley, November 28, 2006
3. George Kourpias interview, Dorothy Fennell, September 16, 2003
4. Weldon Granger interview, Patrick S. Halley, November 28, 2006
5. "A Look at Machinist President William W. Winpisinger and His Work With the National Committee for the Support of Democracy and Human Rights in El Salvador," by Carla Winkler, May 1, 2006, p 20
6. "Labor Resolution Criticizes US Role in Central America," by William Serrin, *The New York Times*, October 30, 1985
7. William W. Winpisinger, remarks to American for Democratic Action, St. Louis, Missouri, December 1, 1984
8. *The Machinist*, November, 1985, p 2
9. William W. Winpisinger, remarks at Public Interest Network Seminar, Hollywood, Maryland, October 4, 1985
10. *The Machinist*, November, 1985, p 2
11. Ibid

Chapter Forty-four

1. *"Grounded: Frank Lorenzo and the Destruction of Eastern Airlines"* (Beard Books, 1999), by Aaron Bernstein, p 46
2. Ibid
3. William W. Winpisinger, remarks at Indiana University—Purdue University, Indianapolis, Indiana, May 19, 1986
4. The Machinist, January, 1986, p 3
5. William W. Winpisinger, remarks to Montgomery County Democrats, Washington, DC, January 13, 1986
6. William W. Winpisinger, statement endorsing the National Rainbow Coalition, Washington, DC, April 17, 1986
7. William W. Winpisinger, remarks at New Directions Conference, Washington, DC, May 3, 1986

Chapter Forty-five

1. Philip Zannella, Jr. interview, Patrick S. Halley, March 28, 2006
2. Ibid
3. "The White House in Crisis: The Tower Report Inquiry Finds Reagan and Chief Advisors Responsible for Chaos in Iran Arms Deal," by Steven V. Roberts, *The New York Times*, February 27, 1987 p1
4. "The White House in Crisis: The Presidency; At a Crossroads," by R. W. Apple, Jr., *The New York Times*, February 27, 1987
5. William W. Winpisinger, remarks at Pioneer Valley Central Labor Council, Chicopee, Massachusetts, March 7, 1987
6. "Poll Show Reagan Approval Rating at 4-Year Low," by E.J. Dionne, Jr., *The New York Times*, March 3, 1987

7. "Gary Hart The Elusive Front Runner," by E.J. Dionne, Jr., *The New York Times*, May 3, 1987, Sunday Magazine
8. *The Machinist*, June, 1987, p 7
9. *The Machinist*, August, 1987, p 4
10. Ibid

Chapter Forty-six

1. Tom Buffenbarger interview, Patrick S. Halley, August 2, 2006
2. Proceedings of the 1988 Grand Lodge Convention, p 209
3. Ibid, p 211
4. Ibid, p 274
5. Ibid, p 274-275
6. Ibid, p 275
7. Ibid, p 372-373

Chapter Forty-seven

1. William W. Winpisinger, remarks to the Democratic National Convention nominating Jesse Jackson for President, Atlanta Georgia, July 20, 1988
2. George Kourpias interview, Patrick S. Halley, November 10, 2006
3. Transcript of "Weekend Pass" Americans for Bush, September, 1988
4. William W. Winpisinger, remarks to Canadian Staff Conference, November 2, 1988
5. George Kourpias interview, Patrick S. Halley, November 10, 2006
6. Ibid

Chapter Forty-eight

1. "Winpisinger Speaks Out," interview in Multinational Monitor, Marcj, 1989
2. *"Grounded: Frank Lorenzo and the Destruction of Eastern Airlines"* (Beard Books, 1999), by Aaron Bernstein, p 153
3. "Gambles for Eastern," by William Stockton, *The New York Times*, March 13, 1989
4. *The Machinist*, May, 1989 p 2
5. "William Winpisinger: Positive Changes going on in the USSR," by Fred Gaboury, *Labor Today*, June 22, 1989
6. Ibid
7. Ibid
8. Ibid
9. Ibid
10. Ibid
11. Ibid
12. "Gorbachev Meets With Winpisinger and Sheinkman," Soviet Embassy Information Department, April 21, 1989
13. Ibid
14. Ibid
15. "William Winpisinger: Positive Changes going on in the USSR," by Fred Gaboury, *Labor Today*, June 22, 1989
16. Allison Beck interview, Patrick S. Halley, October 19, 2005
17. Ibid

Chapter Forty-nine

1. William W. Winpisinger, "Creeping International Fascism," remarks to the British Columbia Labor

Federation Convention, Vancouver, Canada, November 30, 1988

2. "Reclaiming our Future," by William W. Winpisinger, (Westview, 1989) p 1

3. *The Machinist*, June, 1989, p 1

4. Tom Buffenbarger interview, Patrick S. Halley, August 2, 2006

5. *The Machinist*, July, 1989

INDEX